The Longest Four Years of My Life

A View from the Field by a Black Fed in the Trump Administration

Deric A. Gilliard

A Gilliard Communications Publication

Copyright © 2025 by Deric A. Gilliard

All rights reserved.

No portion of this book may be reproduced in any form without written permission from the publisher or author except as permitted by U.S. copyright law.

Library of Congress Control Number: 2024909986

ISBN (Paperback): 979-8-9906200-9-4

ISBN (Ebook): 979-8-9906200-7-0

Endorsements for The Longest Four Years of My Life

The creator of the 1960s comic strip Pogo, Walt Kelly, coined the phrase, "We have met the enemy, and he is us." It seems this is apropos of the current state of affairs for our nation. We truly hope that the uniquely American attributes of civility, unity, and compromise that have been coursing through our collective vein over the past 200+ years will lead us out of this dark chapter. The world surely needs us now, more so than ever before. Gilliard adeptly addresses this and more during his time working in the Trump administration and its chaos and divisiveness from the perspective of race, faith, and justice.

Baoky Vu, *former Dekalb County (GA) Board of Elections Vice-Chairman*

Every American should buy at least two copies of this book.

David Nolan, *St. Augustine historian*

The Trump administration recruited and hired some of America's brightest minds – men and women who could make America great. These men and women were denied the opportunity to showcase their talents and patriotic zeal. Donald Trump didn't allow them to shine. His ego and limited knowledge prevented his administration from greater success. Gilliard's detailed assessment of Trump's handling of COVID, his attacks on the Affordable Care Act, and his attitudes toward people of color shed important light on a presidential term that failed to live up to its enormous potential.

Charles Person, *an original member of the 1961 Freedom Riders*

We're demanding that we have voting rights passed. Gilliard, a son of the civil rights movement, understands this challenge and shares his justice journey during his time in the Trump administration, through Trump's dismissal of the dangers of COVID, his attempts at voter suppression, the Republicans' attacks on the ACA, and the justice marches against over-policing of Black people. This is the most important election in our lifetime. We are all-hands-on-deck to elect this nation's first female president and preserve democracy!

LaTosha Brown, *Co-Founder, Black Voters Matter*

Also by Deric A. Gilliard

Living in the Shadows of a Legend: Unsung Heroes and Sheroes Who Marched with Dr. Martin Luther King, Jr.

Dedication

I dedicate this book, first and foremost, to my Lord, Savior, and Redeemer, Jesus Christ. Though I've strayed from His protective shadow more times than I care to admit, He has never once abandoned me.

I also honor my amazing nuclear family and my children, each of whom is a dynamic leader. They are each hard-working, confident, resilient, well-centered people, largely because of the influence of their mother, the love of my life. Each of my children is the product of outstanding lineage, including a maternal grandmother who ensured that literally hundreds of inner-city Chicago kids received exposure to a bigger world and earned college degrees that created new vistas and launched them into the middle class and beyond. She also raised four trailblazers in their respective careers and exerted her agency to brave the racism of a segregated, all-white neighborhood that fought tooth-and-nail to keep her family out. She adopted me as her own and, in her unique way, showed me a mother's love, much as my Aunt Mamie Lee Dabney, Ida Bell, and Beatrice Hennings did. On my children's paternal side, my father and his family were worthy heroes who modeled for me manhood, perseverance, love, and resiliency in a world that callously rejected their humanity. Six brothers, each of whom served in the military for a nation that relentlessly demeaned them as second-class citizens, and five sisters, many of whose children's children rose from a rural, segregated agrarian society that saw them as little more than tools, to overcome the odds and make meaningful marks, coast to coast. I also dedicate this work to my father-in-law who accepted me and supported his daughter and me unconditionally, and my mother, who was haunted by her own demons and whom, tragically, I never really knew.

I also dedicate this work to people I've loved and lost: my parents, my fraternity brothers Tom Vaughn and Eddie Williams III, my dear friend Kelly Draheim, my maternal first cousins, my shipmates and brothers beloved, as well as all those who stuck with me through the toughest of times.

I readily admit I anguished over the writing of this book, largely because of the volatile nature of the country and world at a precipitous moment when history's most hallowed, continuous democratic republic stands on the brink of crashing and burning. To *not* write what I know, what I believe, what I have seen and experienced, would require me to turn my back on all who have nurtured me and all who have modeled courage and valor in the face of insurmountable odds, even though they knew that they themselves would not benefit from their sacrifices. I write this work in the spirit of Lula Joe Williams, Dolores Huerta, Sojourner Truth, Alice Tregay, Angela Davis, Ella Baker, Charles and Shirley Sherrod, Heather Heyer, Anne and Carl Braden, Rev. Willie Bolden, Rev. R.B. Cottonreader, Rev. Frederick Douglass Taylor, Brenda Davenport, Willy Seigel Leventhal, Evelyn and Joseph Echols Lowery, Medgar and Myrlie Evers, James Baldwin, Kwame Ture, Roxanne Gregory, J.T. Johnson, Albert Turner, Bayard Rustin, Roy Wilkins, Maynard Jackson, Ambassador Andrew Young, Freedom Riders Charles Person, Hank Thomas, Joan Trumpauer Mulholland, Rev. James Orange, Fred Bennett, Lou Gossett, Jr., Paul Robeson, Muhammad Ali, Rev. Hosea Williams, Rev. C.T. Vivian, Dr. W.E.B. DuBois, Dana Swan, Kat and Henry Twine, and legions more. I dedicate this work to the brave and underappreciated members and supporters of the Southern Christian Leadership Conference "ground crew" and all they did, non-violently, in their quest to "Redeem the Soul of America."

"The proof that one truly believes is in action."
Bayard Rustin

"Hear me clearly: The battle for the soul of America is not over."

President Joe Biden spoke at a Voting Rights event at Atlanta University Center, the world's biggest consortium of Black higher education in the country, on January 11, 2022.

"It has to be crystal clear that is not patriotism; it is not standing up for America to stand up for one man (Donald Trump), who knows full well that he lost. What happened on January 6th, and the effort to keep that spirit alive, is the utter antithesis of what America stands for. It is the pure embodiment of tyranny and authoritarianism."

U.S. District Court, District of Columbia, Amy Berman Jackson ruling on 7-year sentence of Iowan Kyle Young, September 27, 2022.

"… Similar things with other countries, like the European Union," said President Donald J. Trump, touting a need to assess China's tariff on all imported goods. "They're [China] a big abuser. But it's all working out. And just remember: what you're reading and what you're seeing is not what's happening," said Trump, addressing the VFW in Kansas City, Missouri. "And I'll tell you, I have so many people that are so in favor – because we have to make our country truly great again."

C-Span, President Trump at VFW convention, July 24, 2018 {Accessed: February 27, 2023}, https://www.cspan.org/video/?448868-1/president-trump-urges-supporters-stick-vfw-speech

"Hold fast to your dreams, for without them, life is a broken-winged bird that cannot fly."

Langston Hughes, "Montage of a Dream Deferred," 1951

Table of Contents

Dedication iii
Introduction 2
Chapter 1: The Great White Way 14
Chapter 2: Appropriation 28
Chapter 3: The Patient Protection and Affordable Care Act 36
Chapter 4: Clueless 48
Chapter 5: The Reckoning 52
Chapter 6: The Chosen One 66
Chapter 7: On the Road Again: ACA Revisited/Albany, GA 68
Chapter 8: Trump's Regional Directors 72
Chapter 9: Unequal Injustice 78
Chapter 10: Voter Suppression 88
Chapter 11: The Donald Disconnect: Don't Piss on Me and Tell Me It's Raining 96
Chapter 12: UACs 106
Chapter 13: Dawn of a New Day 112
Chapter 14: The Grand Princess Cruise Ship 118
Chapter 15: Day to Day Operations 122
Chapter 16: Be Careful What You Ask For 132
Chapter 17: An Unspeakable Cruelty to At-Risk Communities of Color 144
Chapter 18: Hydroxychloroquine or Kool-Aid 154

Chapter 19: Being Black or Brown in America Should Not Be a Death Sentence..162

Chapter 20: White Pomposity...172

Chapter 21: You Say You Want a Revolution........................180

Chapter 22: Trump's Twisted Juneteenth...............................190

Chapter 23: So I Said to My People, Slow the Testing Down.196

Chapter 24: MIA..208

Chapter 25: For the Love of Money..212

Chapter 26: McCarthy, Wallace and Donald J. Trump: Race Baiting...218

Chapter 27: The "Resistance" Strikes Back............................228

Chapter 28: Protecting our Mental Health In the height of COVID 242

Chapter 29: Don't Make Us Write Obituaries........................260

Chapter 30: America's Biggest Terroristic Threat: Young Angry White Men 276

Chapter 31: Denier-in-Chief...286

Chapter 32: Despicable Disparities..292

Chapter 33: 80,000 New COVID Cases a Day: A New U.S. Record..298

Chapter 34: Covid: Is There an End in Sight?.......................304

Chapter 35: The Highly Effective Vaccines Produced by Operation Warp Speed..316

Chapter 36: Repudiation...324

Chapter 37: Life in the Real World Working for the Trump Administration 338

Chapter 38: An American January for the Ages 358

Epilogue 396

Acknowledgments 404

Notes 406

Index 495

About the Author 512

Introduction

If you're looking for an account that strictly focuses on politics – all I've seen, all I've participated in, all I've been subject to – put this book down. It's *not* for you. Indeed, you will get that from me, as someone who has served political appointees for the past five presidents, from Clinton to Biden. I will examine the politics and policies, but you'll also get the unabashed perspective of a Black man in America, one who, as Charles Dickens famously said, has seen "... the best of times and the worst of times."[1] Yes, Black people, in fact, people of color, by and large, see the world differently than most Caucasians because, frankly, they *must*. If, indeed, they don't, they are living in what my old boss and civil rights lion, Dr. Joseph Echols Lowery, longtime president of the Southern Christian Leadership Conference (SCLC), called "the 51st state of denial." Seeing life through realistic, yet hopeful, eyes is part and parcel of a successful blueprint for living in a country that often sees Black people as inferior or a threat. Yeah, I said it.

So, this is *my* story, told as honestly as possible, but from the perspective of someone who almost exclusively has worked with Anglo leaders at the very top, most of whom I've respected and personally liked, even when I adamantly disagreed with them. Much has changed since I left Dr. King's organization, the Southern Christian Leadership Conference, and went to work for the government in 1998. Back then, I was confident about who Republicans were and what they stood for, whether I agreed or not. Today, it's a sad situation when I can trust and have more confidence in Afghani nationalists – whom, by the way, we left to fend for themselves against the ruthless, sexist Taliban – than in some of my Republican brothers and sisters who have become mesmerized and cultish to the point where they are beyond recognition.

Let's face it. By 2016, after eight years of a Black president who politely challenged America and pushed it to face its ugly racial bias and privilege – and dared say, "Trayvon could have been my son" – much of conservative white America was looking for a hero.[2] Yes, they were looking for the next John Wayne, who, for those under 50, was the swashbuckling, gun-toting, hard-drinking, tall, handsome badass who took no shit off anyone. Yes, Wayne was also paternalistic and racist, though Black folk – including me – were conditioned to love him as the quintessential American hero, but that's a discussion for another time.[3] Leading up to and during the election cycle of 2016, conservative, *change-is-happening-too-fast* white America thought they had found their John Wayne in Donald John Trump, whom many progressive/liberal Americans dis-affectionately call "45," or, as Bill Maher named him, the "Orange Orangutan."

Trump surely had his triumphs and was right about certain things. Trump oversaw a soaring economy and stock market, though it can be argued that he built on what Obama had created. Trump sweet-talked another hot-blooded, button-pushing, threatening leader, North Korean President Kim Jong Un, and passed the long-awaited Republican dream, a major tax cut that benefits his people, the richest of Americans. His administration negotiated the release of prisoners from North Korea and Venezuela, both lorded over by strong-arm dictators. He also tried to bring about a new standard for drug and medical procedure price transparency, although the impact has been marginal, at best.

His administration also focused on blunting the HIV crisis in America, targeting the 20 most impacted counties, many of which are minority-dominated. Trump's administration also tried to slow the burgeoning opioid epidemic, which was fueled by the massive flow of fentanyl and impure drugs. A focus on faith-based institutions that served foster care children was another important priority. HHS Secretary Alex Azar, whom I worked for until the end of the Trump administration, had a strong commitment to stemming the Ebola virus that was ravaging African nations, including the Democratic Republic of the Congo, which I once visited on a short-term mission trip that changed my life. Trump also employed some talented, quality leaders at HHS, including FDA Director Scott Gottlieb, COVID czar Dr. Anthony Fauci, and the Black lone stranger, U.S. Surgeon General Dr. Jerome Adams, all of whom sought to bring scientific balance to a band of all-too-often political zealots who lacked training or talent that matched their positions.

But then, there were the obvious, glaring contradictions. We care about HIV and opioids while taking every measure to starve the Patient Protection and Affordable Care Act, even though it was – and still is – the law of the land. We defunded Meals on Wheels, which is a lifeline for the elderly, many of whom have worked for 40-plus years. We also reduced Aid to Families with Dependent Children (AFDC)[4] while stripping its Office of Family Planning, which gave women choices, one of which was abortion and contraceptive services, which a Trump-appointed Supreme Court struck down through the Dobbs decision.[5] Though I think the Trump administration did admirable work to address human trafficking and support its victims, bolster adoption, and prioritize fighting the opioid crisis,[6] where was everybody when crack cocaine was ravaging Black and brown communities?[7] This, of course, was not under Trump's watch. But based on his disdain for Black, brown, and East Asian people, I can't help but doubt he would have focused so much time, money, or energy seeking treatment and solutions if opioids and fentanyl primarily impacted BIPOC (Black, Indigenous, People of Color) communities. Under the Trump administration, our office also spent a great deal of time focused on assessing and hearing from health executives on the shortage of nurses and its impact on providing quality care, broadband issues, and gaps in OBGYN rural health care.

However, for most in the middle class, those living on the margins, far too many people of color, and even poor and working-class whites who voted against their own best interests in support of Trump, the "booming" economy and soaring stock market have meant little.[8] The median African American income in 2017, when Trump took office, was $40,258, $50,486 for Hispanics, $68,145 for whites, and $81,331 for Asians. Only 29.2% of U.S. households earned more than $100,000 in 2017.[9] His tax cuts for his buddies came at the expense of the middle class and working poor, who suddenly saw their deductions for key expenses like student loans and property tax gutted.[10] From my perspective, it was like the super-rich were getting richer while the working poor and middle class were being asked, much like Black Americans during Reconstruction and the Israelites under the pharaoh, to make bricks without straw.[11]

I worked with many mid-level and upper-mid-level income earners. Several physicians of color – including my own doctor and dentist – have told me Trump had been wonderful for them, as their portfolios doubled in value, and one was able to sell property that sat useless during the Obama administration. I respect that, and I was happy to hear that *someone* who looked like me had benefited from Trump's tax cuts and economic strategy. However, most working poor and middle-class Americans simply aren't in the stock market because the bulk of their net worth is tied up in their houses, if they are fortunate enough to "own" one, which most Black and brown people don't. And yes, there are jobs aplenty, but far too many of them won't earn you a living wage that affords you housing, transportation, food, and even a modicum of leftovers to enjoy life. Quite honestly, while I live in the suburbs of a big city, I would ascertain that relatively few people of color, or even those struggling to earn a living wage, reveled in the rewards of the vaunted Trump tax cut of 2018, which allowed the nation's 400 wealthiest people to pay the nation's lowest tax rate.[12]

Yes, Trump served his base in a relentless quest to "*M*ake *A*merica *G*reat *A*gain." He tried valiantly – but unsuccessfully – to build a wall and keep out those dangerous brown people from south of the border. He had, in many instances, crippled the agricultural backbone of our nation, the Midwestern farmers who grow and export much of our crops, through his punitive export taxes on China, even though his premise that they steal our technology ("weather balloons") and take advantage of us is basically correct, as was his insistence that we are far too dependent on foreign products and services, like microchips.[13]

So, unlike former secretary of State Al Haig, who infamously declared "I'm in charge," after President Reagan[14] was shot in a failed assassination attempt, Trump made sure everybody knew that he was in charge from the "get-go" and that he and he alone could fix it, whatever "it" is.[15] But at what cost? I have to ask. … Ripping innocent children from the breasts of their mothers and fathers, many of whom dared to risk a torturous, hot, 2,000-mile trek from dangerous countries like Haiti, and the northern Central American countries of Guatemala, Nicaragua, Honduras, and El Salvador, in hopes of better opportunities and safety? Tragically, at the start of 2019, HHS still had over 1,600 unaccompanied minors in its custody.[16]

Several of my co-workers, in fact, were drafted to serve as public information officers in those camps in Texas and Oklahoma. It was one of the few times I was truly ashamed of the work I was doing and the department I represented, the Office of the Secretary for the U.S. Department of Health & Human Services. Using these, the most vulnerable people to grace our shores – since the first importation of African slaves in 1619[17] – as bargaining chips to "build that wall?"[18] Railing against the southern border immigrants, Trump unashamedly also proclaimed that what America **really** needs is more immigrants from Nordic (yes, *white!*) countries like Norway instead of those "shithole" African nations.[19] Chumming up with North Korean dictator Kim Jong Un, perhaps the most ruthless dictator in the world at the time? Looking the other way, as Saudi Arabia, which spends billions in trade with the U.S., slaughtered journalist Jamal Khashoggi in their embassy? (Trump's successor, Joe Biden, would later lower himself by looking the other way and fist-bumping Saudi leader Prince Mohammed bin Salman in an attempt to increase oil production.) Telling The Squad, the four female freshman congresswomen, that they were "incapable of loving our country" because they had the audacity to criticize him and his policies? Days earlier, in fact, Trump said Congresswomen Rashida Tlaib, Ayanna Pressley, Alexandria Ocasio-Cortez, and Ilhan Omar, three of whom were born in the U.S. – the fourth escaped war-torn Somalia and is now a naturalized citizen – should "go back and help fix the totally broken and crime-infested places from which they came."[20]

Less than a month later, I might add, my wife and I went to Baltimore – one of those cities Trump criticized – for our anniversary and had a splendid time. I'm so thankful we didn't listen to *our* president, who, in theory, is the leader of the free world. We thought about Frederick Douglass, who was born in Talbot County, only 65 miles from Baltimore, and how Trump didn't know that this great Black freedom fighter and abolitionist, formerly a slave, had been deceased for over 120 years when he spoke about him like he was a current Black leader growing in notoriety.[21] While in beautiful Baltimore, headquarters of the NAACP and the city represented by Black freedom fighter and then-Congressman Elijah Cummings, we toured the museum honoring the great Reginald Lewis and the brilliant CEO of

Beatriz Foods and visited the phenomenal Black wax museum.

Trump's verbal castigations of Latino immigrants, Asians, Black folk and their homelands, people with special needs, and women in general, were all deeply troubling episodes, to be sure. But beyond that, Trump – who I had naively hoped would focus on the economy instead of his Twitter thumb – continually expressed deep disdain for the press, people of color, the "have-nots," and anyone who didn't fit his version of the American Dream. That included his viral critique of NFL players, who, along with the NBA, were some of the few professions that included influencers who could boast the financial independence to openly defy him.[22] They even dared to challenge American hegemony by protesting an unjust criminal justice system by taking a knee or refusing to salute the flag. His response? "Fire those sons of bitches!"[23]

Then there was his assault on Critical Race Theory (CRT), an academic, legal, and societal look back at America's treatment of people of color, particularly Black people.[24]

Clearly the most megalomaniacal president of my adult lifetime, Trump never accepted blame but always claimed credit, even when it wasn't his. "Sometimes, you have to toot your own horn because nobody else is going to do it," he explained once.[25]

As I watched President Donald Trump stand at the microphone at his various – yet precious few – press conferences, I saw behind him a sea of old white men, virtually without fail. I remember early in his administration when HHS sent out its first photo showing the HHS leadership team before the August 2018 confirmation of Surgeon General Jerome Adams. The painful "joke" at HHS, certainly in the Atlanta regional office, where much of the leadership was Black, was the hashtag #HHSsowhite, due to the cringe-worthy lack of diversity at headquarters.

My first boss in the Trump administration, former North Carolina Congresswoman Renee Ellmers, a political appointee who swept into office as part of the stunning Trump victory, constantly said, "elections have consequences," which I fully agree with. What I couldn't reconcile, however, is because this administration had very few women, fewer people of color, and only two Black men of significance – one of whom is Dr. Ben Carson, who seemed all but invisible and totally out of his element and depth – how was I supposed to feel about how my community and I were being represented? The answer? I wasn't, because my community and I – Black folk – along with Asians, Native Americans, Latinos, immigrants, the LGBTQ+ community, young people, and even white progressives who didn't agree with Trump, were, in his eyes, irrelevant people who weren't truly the fabric of this great republic we call the United States of America. In fact, Ellmers was initially the only female regional director in the Trump administration, despite the four previous administrations having females dominate in this position.

The Trump administration, more than any other during my adult lifetime, embraced white identity politics. If you were Caucasian and believed that white people were *unfairly* losing ground to an emerging melting pot that portends that people of color will be the majority in the U.S. in the mid-2040s, and you feared losing control of a society you have dominated for 400 years, Trump was your guy because he had fed the flames and said "hell no" to the inevitable darkening of America. Period.

Consequently, Trump surrounded himself with a cadre of young people who had been groomed to believe POCs (people of color), especially Blacks, were a threat to "their country." They were joined by even more dangerous, seasoned political zealots who believed it was their duty to protect certain Christian tenets. These included protecting unborn children, traditional marriage, narratives that told only of American greatness, U.S. borders, and the right to determine who can vote, all in the name of Christianity. There were some whom I didn't work with, including Jon B. Perdue, a special assistant at the Department of Labor, who allegedly accused the Dems of "ethnic cleansing," and an attempt to "liquidate" the white working class.[26] Another, Housing Secretary Dr. Ben Carson – in his very first address as HUD secretary – famously declared slaves to be one of the earliest versions of "immigrants," who, by the way, happened to arrive in the belly of slave ships. Even as slaves, he posited, "… they, too, had a dream that one day their sons, daughters, grandsons, granddaughters, great-grandsons, great-granddaughters might pursue prosperity and happiness in this land."[27] Others, part of the so-called Trump "beachhead" team, included nearly 40 lobbyists, whom candidate Trump vowed not to hire, and predictably, at least eight people from the ultra-conservative Heritage Foundation and various conspiracy theorists.

Then there were the HHS officials that I did have to interact with or follow the directives of, including Darcie Johnston, a former Trump Vermont campaign director, who was drawn to Trump due to his promise that "on day one of the Trump administration, we will ask Congress to immediately deliver a full repeal of ObamaCare." Johnston, according to HHS career officials who worked at HHS headquarters through a variety of administrations, both Republican and Democrat, was not hesitant to announce that she was at HQ to serve as a "watchdog" for the administration. In March of 2017, Johnston was appointed HHS director of Intergovernmental and External Affairs.[28] Another was Shannon Royce, an ardent pro-life, anti-LGBTQ+ attorney, whom Secretary Alex Azar appointed to head the Center for Faith-Based and Neighborhood

Partnerships. Royce, sporting a reddish-brown bob, was clear about her focus on engaging with and enlarging the Evangelical Christian relationship with the administration, but often at the expense of other faith groups. AL.com, Alabama's statewide news network, captured her presenting "herself [at a meeting] not as an official receptive to Christian involvement, but rather as a Christian actively working within government to promote church-based engagement in public issues."[29]

I would actually spend much of two days with Royce during one of the administration's first faith-based outreach visits, which I largely orchestrated for her and our regional director in Atlanta in 2018.[30] My issue with Royce, a former COO for the Family Research Council, was that, at the time, she wanted to work *only* with conservative Christians while excluding other faiths. Another was Laura Trueman, a former congressional staffer who worked for Reagan on his Adolescent Family Planning Program, an abstinence-based, anti-abortion initiative that opposed Title X. Also a lobbyist, she staffed for then-majority whip Steve Scalise. Trueman served Trump as both deputy and IGA director.

*

On the evening of November 8, 2016, political newcomer Donald John Trump was elected the 45th president of the United States in a major political victory that *The New York Times* called a "stunning repudiation of the establishment."

"Now it's time for us to bind the wounds of division and come together as one people," announced Trump during his acceptance speech after fielding a concession call from Democrat nominee Hillary Clinton.

As I sat watching the proceedings and culmination of a hard-fought, in many ways surprising result, my thoughts quickly turned to "what does this mean for me, work-wise?"

Of course, I had already worked for one Republican president (George W. Bush) and two Democrats (Clinton and Obama), so switching gears had become a part of the process, regardless of my political views. I was only one of the millions of career feds who had sworn allegiance to the United States government.

However, in my capacity in the Office of the Secretary of HHS, regardless of the administration, I *always* worked for a political appointee who managed the eight southeastern states for the HHS secretary, meaning I was expected and directed to carry out initiatives and missions that were highly political, while at the same time being responsive to all communities, whether they were Democrats, Republicans, independents or non-voters. So, I could handle anything Trump would bring on, right? And besides, he would focus on beefing up American business and industry, his so-called area of expertise, right?

Little did I know that inconceivable challenges I could not have dreamed of lay ahead.

Chapter 1: The Great White Way

"It was designed that way from the beginning. We weren't supposed to be here. Reservations were supposed to be temporary. We were supposed to learn how to be white and live in cities. Then, this land could be sold, too. But we didn't learn to be white. And now, here we are. And the government won't help because it doesn't want to. It wants us to die; it wants us gone because it wants the land. That's all it ever wanted." Chairman Tom Rainwater, Confederate Tribe of Broken Rock Reservation.

Yellowstone, season six, episode two.

The landscape after Obama – who was criticized roundly by a section of the Black population who expected him to "do more" for Black America – became as hostile and volatile for Black Americans as it had been since the 1960s. In fact, the hostility didn't even wait until Obama's second term ended in 2016, but, in many ways, existed throughout much of his presidency, from 2008 until he left office. However, the anti-Black, anti-Latino, anti-Asian, anti-female, and anti-immigrant rhetoric – often spearheaded by Trump – ramped up considerably beginning in 2014, when the campaign to replace the nation's first Black president took center stage. Along with it came the largest increase in the purchase of firearms by individuals in U.S. history.[31] White Americans overwhelmingly purchased the weapons. Besides the surge in firearms, assassination threats also mushroomed.[32] Predictably, it was not unexpected, considering America had elected its first African American president who even had a Muslim name, a monumental accomplishment I never expected to live to see.

"'The threats have leveled off in recent months,' officials said, 'and Mr. Obama now receives about the same as his two most recent predecessors.' But several officials said they took no solace in the fact that the volume of reports had receded because it was the nature of the threats that concern them and because the factors behind the increase remain – Mr. Obama's race prime among them."[33]

One such threat was concocted by 20-year-old Kody Brittingham, a Marine lance corporal. His "letter of intent," discovered at Camp LeJeune, detailed his desire to eliminate "domestic threat" President Barack Obama.

Let's face it: if a certain segment of white America needed a reason, or excuse, to assault, demean, denigrate, or even kill innocent Black folk – and I'm not even talking about the predatory criminal element among Blacks that breaks into homes, hijacks cars, victimizes their own communities through gang violence, or peddles drugs – Donald Trump gave it to them. Why? Because he sees America as "the great white way," a country built *for* and *by* white folk. That doesn't even address the fact that white Europeans, employing the Doctrine of Discovery, invaded the Americas (and much of the rest of the world) with sophisticated weaponry and alien diseases and wiped out, or subjugated, entire indigenous populations, especially the Native Americans, often in the name of Christianity and Manifest Destiny. If you were Latino or Asian and came here seeking a better life, or you were an African American, you were ridiculed and disdained, never mind that many Blacks serve as mayors, police chiefs, and other key influencers in America's major cities, such as Chicago, Detroit, Atlanta, San Francisco, Houston, or Baltimore.

His divisive rhetoric, from proclaiming inner cities "slums only fit for rats," Mexican immigrants, "robbers and thieves," African countries, "shithole" nations, while calling for more immigrants from Norway, "stoked the flames for those who felt they were being replaced, or displaced."[34]

Frankly, it didn't much matter whether you were a highly respected Black attorney and stalwart like Maryland Congressman Elijah Cummings, Georgia's "living saint" Congressman John Lewis, or Chicago Mayor Lori Lightfoot, the 45th president raked you and your hometowns over the coals.

This marginalization and demonization of minorities from the world's most powerful leader empowered legions of his supporters and people who believed what he brazenly said to act out their fears and anxieties in thousands of filmed or documented "incidents" that traumatized, demeaned, and marginalized people of color during his four years in office.

Even when African Americans and other minority communities are being enterprising, productive, and striving for our part of the American Dream; our motives, intentions, and, especially, our right to exist are routinely questioned.

In one instance, Lolade Siyonbola, a Black graduate student at Yale – incidentally, home of one of the first Black studies departments in the country – fell asleep in her dormitory's common room, a normal occurrence for college students burning the candle at both ends. To her surprise, a white woman, another student, came in, turned on the lights, and accused her of being there illegally. The white girl called the police, who demanded Siyonbola "prove she belonged." The police, who later insisted they did nothing wrong, asked her for her ID. "I'm not going to justify my existence here," she said before she relented, showing her ID and using her key to enter her apartment.[35] Ironically, *living while Black* has always been a painful challenge in the land of the free and the home of the brave.

In another assault, Jordan Rogers, a Black girl, was selling water in front of her California home, which would have been seen as cute and industrious had she been white. However, in this instance, the result was that the white neighbor woman, Alison Ettel, called the police on the eight-year-old Black girl trying to raise funds for a trip to Disney for selling without a license.[36]

In yet another story, a woman took her son to a pool in an upscale subdivision when the chair of the homeowner's association pool asked her, but not others, for identification. Adam Bloom, "chair" of the Glenridge Homeowners' Association in Winston-Salem, North Carolina, called the cops on her after she accused him of racially profiling. Bloom told officers that swimmers were required to carry their ID in their swimwear, though that decree was posted nowhere. "Nobody else was asked for their ID. I feel this is racial profiling," mom Jasmine Abhulimen, who is Black, said in the video. "I am the only black person here with my son in the pool."[37]

Oregon Rep. Janelle Bynum, canvassing door-to-door, armed only with a cell phone, had to explain herself to a cop when a "neighbor" called 911 on her.[38] Thinking fast, as Black people must do in this all-too-common situation, Bynum, who had canvassed 70,000 homes without incident, realized that not only her political future, but likely her sense of safety in the neighborhood depended on it. She said, "I knew my interaction with him was going to determine a few things. Whether I was going to be able to continue to campaign, whether I was able to go home feeling safe at night. At the end of the day, I want to know my kids can walk down the street without fear."[39]

For white Americans, feeling safe is a given, a situation demanded and often taken for granted. Why, in the Black community, does our society create a climate that requires us to pray over and fear for the safety of our children every time they leave home?

Another woman intent on teaching her 11-year-old son, Uriah, the benefits of demanding work and reward, had her plan shattered when a neighbor called the police officers on the boy. "I was confused," she said. Stopped by police on his first day of delivering papers in Columbus, Ohio, Uriah was working within the ordinance that papers had to be delivered on the porch. He, initially, mistakenly delivered the paper to two houses that were not on the list. Uriah's mom, Brandie Sharp, said she wasn't mad at the woman who called cops on him, but said she wished she would have done things differently.[40]

Why are people of color, especially Black and brown people, so often put in the position of *needing to prove* we belong? Why do we always have to be so understanding of jerks and people who assume we are "out of place," though we are simply living our lives?[41]

New Jersey referee Alan Mahoney, who had a history of racial insensitivity, gave Black wrestler Andrew Johnson of Buena Regional High School two options when he showed up for his match: 1) forfeit the match, or 2) cut his dreadlocks. Johnson, faced with an untenable situation, cut his locks, then won the match in overtime. "This is not a feel-good story," a reader tweeted. "This is an athlete being penalized before a match because his blackness was penalized."[42]

Laquan McDonald, an unarmed Chicago teen, was shot 16 times by a policeman while walking *away* from the officer. Botham Jean, a youth pastor in Dallas, was home, minding his own business – in fact, eating ice cream in his apartment – when a white police officer, Amber Guyger, entered. Later, insisting that she thought it was her apartment, which was one floor above, Guyger shot him twice, killing him.[43] Even white Evangelicals, whom I have a great deal of respect for and listen to regularly, are often racially tone-deaf. Dr. David Jeremiah of Shadow Mountain Community Church in El Cajon, California, a tremendous storyteller, shared the tragic confrontation on one of his shows. Jeremiah pointed out that Jean's younger brother, Brandt, forgave Guyger for shooting and killing his older brother because of his belief as a Christian. He applauded Jean's near saintly resolution but, at the same time, told his listening audience that Guyger, an attractive blond, clearly a broken woman after taking an innocent life, had certainly entered the apartment one floor below by accident. Perhaps. Indeed, the explanation is plausible. But why does the blond, white woman always get the benefit of the doubt, and why was her first response to shoot an unarmed man sitting on a couch that clearly wasn't hers? Why do others most routinely get the benefit of the doubt, while Black people forgive?

In Westport, a suburb of Kansas City, Missouri, Michael Dargy, Jr., an off-duty public safety officer, stopped by the Buzzard Beach Bar. Dargy, a former Olathe police officer, asked the Black bartender, Alobar Bandaloop, to make him a "Trayvon Martini," while allegedly telling Bandaloop to add one shot of vodka "… because it only takes one shot to put him down.[44]

"Who can trust this man in any interaction with an African American?" asked Bandaloop, referring to the killing of unarmed teen Trayvon Martin by neighborhood watchman George Zimmerman in a tragedy that galvanized hundreds of thousands of people of all races to march in protest in 2012. Thankfully, Dargy was fired quickly by

Chelsey Brown International, which insisted it has "no tolerance for hate."[45]

Deandre Somerville, the young Black man convicted of oversleeping and missing his commitment to jury duty, was originally sentenced to 10 days in jail, a year of probation, and 150 hours of community service. Somerville, 21, spent his time in jail, then returned to the court to ask the sentencing judge for leniency. The judge, Palm Beach County Circuit Judge John S. Kastrenakes, said Somerville's absence delayed the civil court case for 45 minutes as the magistrate talked to jurors about the importance of their roles. Somerville expressed deep regret and remorse and said the experience was a strong lesson learned.[46] The young man had no previous record.

So, do I defend Somerville's 2019 juvenile decision to blow off jury duty? Hell no, especially based on the number of times I have had to serve and the long, sordid history of Blacks being excluded from serving on juries. It is critical that people of color serve on juries so that their communities and perspectives are factored in, making it less likely that people of color will be railroaded.

However, once again, I must ask, would little white Jenny or Johnny get the same sentence as Somerville, given the same circumstances? My assessment, by and large, is a resounding "NO!" Instead, we have the Genny Thomases of the world ... well, yes, there is only one wife of a Black U.S. Supreme Court justice ... call elected officials and *openly* lobby people in power to overturn the 2020 election results and advocate submitting fake lists of electors in a shameless attempt to maintain power illegally and immorally for a corrupt presidency.

Before the January 6th committee, which consisted of a bipartisan group of congressional, Thomas, as late as September 2022, continued to insist the election was stolen.

That, my friends, is both delusional and dangerous. Thomas and millions of other Americans continue to live in Lowery's "51st state of denial."

I cannot help but contrast the harsh judicial treatment of many Black people with the cases of young white men, such as Brock Turner and Dylann Roof, just two of many I can cite. Turner, an elite swimmer at Stanford, was convicted in 2016 of sexually assaulting an unconscious woman next to a dumpster. His sentence? Six months, though the prosecutor pushed for six years. Turner, white and privileged, served only three months due to the Criminal Justice Realignment Act of 2011.[47] Where his attitude came from became clear – from his wealthy father, Dan Turner, who insisted his son's life would never be the one that he "dreamed about and worked so hard to achieve," and that his sentence was "a steep price to pay for 20 minutes of *action* [emphasis added] out of his 20-plus years of life."[48] No mention of or concern for the unconscious woman Brock attempted to rape while she was unable to object or defend herself in any manner.

Dylann Roof committed an even more heinous act. After a trial run from his hometown, Roof calculatingly and deceitfully entered a historic Black church in Charleston, South Carolina, Mother Emanuel, on June 17, 2015, on the pretense of attending Bible study.

Roof was welcomed with open arms, which is the tradition in the Black church, even when people are different. In the end, it was all a tragic, savage ruse, as the neo-Nazi Roof calmly executed nine parishioners, including Pastor Clementa C. Pinckney, an elected official. When police arrested him the next day, they asked the 21-year-old if he was hungry and bought him Burger King on the way to jail for his booking. Inconceivably, he wasn't even handcuffed![49] When do you think the last time that happened to a Black man? How about the mass shooters who killed eight in Boulder, Colorado, 22 in El Paso, Texas, and the gunman who murdered eight at two Asian spas in Georgia? All were white men, and all lived to tell their story. Yes, all claimed mental problems. Who the hell doesn't have mental problems when they kill multiple people in anything less than the defense of their life, or those of loved ones? And where does all this young, white rage and hatred waged on innocent Jewish, Palestinian, Black, brown, LGBTQ+, and Asian communities come from? Much of the blame lies at the feet of Donald J. Trump.

I cite these incidents, which became anathema during the years of 2016-2021, because Trump undoubtedly fanned the fires of white nationalism, elitism, classism, and, if not outright racism, at the very least, prejudicial rhetoric. His hate speech was not only deeply divisive, but also prompted and emboldened his supporters (and those who already believed that minority advancement had come too far) to strike out at innocent people because they were Asian, Latino, Jewish, Muslim, Black, or from the LGBTQ+ community. Horrific assaults were occurring somewhere in the nation, seemingly each week.

From his response to the "Jews will not replace us"[50] march and assaults in Charlottesville, Virginia, his call for more Norwegian immigrants,[51] his criticism of "shithole" (African) nations,[52] his characterization of COVID-19 as the "China virus," calling Latino immigrants "rapists and thieves," his attempt to desecrate the memory of the Tulsa massacre by holding a rally there on the anniversary, or his call to zealots to mount an insurrection at the U.S. Capitol on January 6th, Trump lit the fuse, tossed the bomb, and unashamedly justified his every position.

Trump continued to become increasingly agitated as more cities voted or moved to take down now-controversial symbols of the Confederacy that honored slaveholders, or those who upheld the dehumanizing practice. In New

Orleans, for example, the Liberty Place monument, a celebration of the white supremacists who plotted to overthrow a biracial Reconstruction government, was quietly removed at night under the threat of death. Two other statues of Confederate Generals Robert E. Lee and P.G.T. Beauregard, along with the president of the Confederacy, Jefferson Davis, who many say launched the Civil War by attacking Fort Sumter on April 12, 1861, were next, in the spring of 2017.

"We will no longer allow the Confederacy to literally be put on a pedestal in the heart of our city," said white New Orleans Mayor Mitch Landrieu, whose city is predominantly Black.[53] Surely, Trump realized he presided over the nation that *actually won* the Civil War, not those he had defiantly defended for insisting on continuing to glorify 150-year-old statues of generals who fought to preserve slavery, who often enslaved people personally, and who tried to overthrow our government? Certainly, he knew. He served as a firefly on a moonless night, giving comfort and courage to legions of disaffected Americans who believed the vitriol he routinely spewed.

*

Yes, it's true. I could have worked for EPA and experienced Trump gutting the agency's leadership and desecrating First Nation land and water sources, building whenever and wherever they wanted to in favor of the almighty dollar. Or I could have worked for the Department of Education, where I would have shuddered at his mischaracterization of the 1619 Project and its work, to tell the truth about America's brutal and racist treatment of Black and Native residents in a twisted assault on Critical Race Theory (CRT) and DEI (Diversity, Equity, and Inclusion). Or I could have had to amplify the message, shuffle, grin, and wave, as Trump erroneously claimed to have created so many jobs for Black Americans while uplifting the race. Or I could have worked for U.S. Immigration and Customs Enforcement (ICE), where I would have to defend the practice of separating parents from their children at the border, or a policy that discourages people of color from immigrating while insisting we need more people from Europe. (A year later, to be sure, the Biden administration was embarrassed as Federal Border Patrol, on horseback, herded Haitian refugees like cattle. Black Americans looked on with disgust and horror; the only thing Border Patrol lacked – they had whips – were cattle prods.)

In my case, I worked for the U.S. Department of Health & Human Services. More specifically, in fact, for the Office of the Secretary, which meant I reported to a political appointee. This meant that during the Trump administration, all the unprecedented work and policy created and fought for under Obama – the implementation of the Affordable Care Act (ACA) and its expansion of health insurance for 12 million Americans, humane treatment of immigrants, and an embrace of Americans from all corners of the globe, religions, and sexual orientations, were under intense attack. On top of that, Trump thumbed his nose at the Obama administration-developed pandemic playbook, left as a guide for his successor, then denied the danger of COVID for months, before reluctantly ramping up research and funding for a vaccine.[54]

For me personally (as someone who worked directly for three Trump presidential appointees who, even if they personally didn't adhere to his divisive doctrine, were sworn to support his positions), the five years beginning with Trump's nomination were fraught with trepidation, tension, conflicts of interest, and fear of reprisal. Having worked directly for presidential appointees in five administrations – Clinton, Bush, Obama, Trump, and, finally, Biden – I can make earnest comparisons, certainly from the perspective of someone who works to carry out the mission in the regions where we deal with *everyday* people with ongoing kitchen table issues, not the rich and privileged who reside inside the beltway, but *real* America that represents the heart and soul of the republic.

Though the Trump administration was chock full of millionaires and billionaires who were out of touch with the American working class, there were some principled exceptions, including Trump Secretary of State Rex Tillerson, who condemned hate speech and bigotry as "un-American," and resigned because of it, saying, "Racism is evil. It is antithetical to American values and the American ideal." Unable to stomach Trump's alt-right America, he joined the short line of those who resigned.[55] Big ups to Tillerson, sadly and disgustingly one of the seemingly rare high-profile Republicans whose principle and commitment to the lofty ideals of the nation were more important than ambition and fealty to a man who would set aside the hallowed constitution to stay in power.[56]

Yes, racism and implicit bias are real. As a 67-year-old Black man, I had certainly experienced it in numerous situations. But so have many other people who are Muslim, women, Black, Latino, trans, Jewish, immigrants, Asian, Native Americans, and the working poor. To allow racism, sexism, or even classism to define us would be giving in to the evil those practices present, and are fueled by – and racism and prejudice are not simply a southern or rural thing.

For instance, as recently as September of 2022, I was in Northbrook, Illinois, with a mostly white Christian group checking into a highbrow hotel. As my wife approached the registration desk, she was told there was no room available for early check-in, even though others in the same group, most of whom were Anglos, were given rooms, all of which had been secured under the same block.

On the other hand, some 30 years earlier, I also gratefully remember an occasion when a young white police officer showed me unmerited favor and kindness, something several others certainly had not. When the officer stopped me for driving without an updated license plate – with my two young sons in the back seat apprehensively looking on as we were driving to their school – I feared I might be arrested. However, when the police officer pulled up my record and read that I had no warrants or tickets, he wrote me a note saying I would not be going to jail that day. The encounter allowed me to see his humanity, as he recognized mine.

We were living hand to mouth, my wife and I, both with professional degrees and relatively low-paying jobs. She worked for an air purification company, and I was a starving journalist seeking to make it as a public relations practitioner. We had our kids in a private Christian school in an effort to get them the best education we could(n't) afford, all the while deciding from week to week – or day to day – which bills to pay while leaving the rest in the hat for their next opportunity.

I've also had several instances where honorable, equity-seeking white men and women have taken extra time and attention to fortify and enhance my opportunities for success.

I am convinced such encounters with people who are civil and respectful to police are the rule, and not the exception; at the same time, fearful, racist, and bigoted police who have been taught to expect that Black men are dangerous, are far more common than respectful society would choose to believe.

Chapter 2: Appropriation

ap·pro·pri·a·tion: the action of taking something for one's own use, typically without the owner's permission.

Jason Kessler, the head of Unite the Right, said that he's not a racist but instead compares his activism to the Civil Rights Movement. He, along with Ben Carson, Omarosa, and Trump, who should have been the protector of the nation and leader of the free world, were all imposters, appropriating titles and positions they did not deserve.

Like the Freedom Riders who journeyed to the South to challenge segregated bus routes in 1961, and faced white supremacists and intransigents who attacked them when they got off the bus, Kessler said his group prepares for the same level of resistance. White rights are under intense attack, he contends, invoking the name of Martin Luther King, Jr., and the movement he spearheaded. To compare the two ... what an *abomination!* Sounds a lot like Trump's demagogue and elitist policy czar, Stephen Miller, the architect of some of Trump's most racist policies, who also started an organization to protect the rights of white men.[57] Cry me a frickin' river.

King and the SCLC lived out their motto, "To Redeem the Soul of America," in hundreds of direct action, civil disobedience campaigns rooted and grounded in the principles of non-violence.[58] Their fight was for equality under the law, *not* white supremacy, which is a desperate attempt to maintain vise-like control over a country that is becoming increasingly multi-cultural. To the best of my knowledge, no white segregationists or white power racists were ever killed in a King-led peaceful protest, though numerous white justice advocates, including Rev. James

Reeb, Rev. Jonathan Daniels, Viola Liuzzo, Rev. Elijah Lovejoy, William Lewis Moore, Rev. Bruce Klunder, Andrew Goodman, and Michael Schwerner, who stood with Black non-violent protesters, paid the ultimate sacrifice for their courage and conviction.[59] And yes, Kanye and Kyrie, while you're both brilliant at your crafts, keep in mind that many Jews, including Mickey Schwerner and Andrew Goodman, died for your right to vote at the hands of white racists who hated that voting rights would move the nation toward seeing Black folk as equal and fully human.

That list does not include those like Heather Heyer and several other unarmed 21st-century white activists killed during marches and rallies against white power advocates and police who kill unarmed Black and brown men and women. King's ground crew was committed to the principle of non-violence and determined to "turn the other cheek," as Jesus modeled for His followers, and Gandhi showed the world how to live out in India. Kessler and his band of zealots, who felt threatened by the growth of populations of color in this nation, frequently targeted Jews as their biggest threat to maintaining a vise-like grip on the direction and imaging of America. However, the "melting pot" that is this nation cannot be restrained or deterred. Most of today's immigrants did it the hard way, not through theft, privilege, power, or appropriation. As the old saying goes, "they [Anglos] want our rhythm, but not our blues."[60]

Some were willing to challenge Trump and the atmosphere he, acolytes Steve Bannon, Michael Flynn, Mike Pompeo, and others consistently created that encouraged tragedies like Charlottesville, where white radicals chanted "Blood and Soil" and "Jews will not replace us," while waging war in the streets.

"I blame the Trump administration and the GOP that preceded him and that are governing with him for the nature of violence in this country right now," said Rev. Traci

Blackmon, executive minister of Justice and Witness Ministries of the United Methodist Church. "They made it a safe place to hate here. It didn't start with Donald Trump. It started with the eight years that preceded him when the GOP made a pact to disrespect the first Black president publicly and openly. Not just his [Obama's] policies, but they made a pact before he made policies that they would support nothing that he did. That made room for a Donald Trump, who ran on a platform of hatred."[61]

Following the tragedy of Charlottesville, Arizona Senator John McCain tweeted, "There's no moral equivalency between racists and Americans standing up to defy hate and bigotry. ... The president of the United States should say so."[62, 63] One year after Charlottesville, 65% of Americans polled thought that race relations had worsened under Trump, 16% thought they had improved, and 18% thought they were the same.[64]

Joe Biden, commemorating 2021, the four-year anniversary of the Charlottesville carnage said, "We must acknowledge what America's intelligence community has already confirmed, and what Charlottesville and so many other communities know all too well: The most lethal terrorist threat to our homeland in recent years has been domestic terrorism rooted in white supremacy. We cannot ignore it. We must confront the spread of hate-fueled violence in every form."[65]

Finally, long after the fact, Black reality star Omarosa, who exemplified much of the White House inner circle – unqualified for their positions, far out of their experiential depth, and there due only to their politically right leanings or allegiance to Trump – had acknowledged that she was part of the problem.

"I was complicit in this White House deceiving the nation," said former *Apprentice* star Omarosa Manigault Newman.[66]

The Nadir

The Nadir began roughly 100 years before I graduated from college, in 1877 – the end of Reconstruction – until the start of the 21st century, according to historian Rayford Logan. Other historians, including John Hope Franklin, insisted that it continued until around 1923. What was the Nadir, you ask? It was perhaps the darkest time in American history for Black folk. It was the period, as much as any since slavery, that drove Black folk to their knees, seeking solace and relief from a God they knew as their Redeemer, their deliverer, from the gnawing and oppressive weight of racism and Jim Crow. The era of Trump certainly isn't the Nadir, but he threatens to drag Black people, immigrants, and women back to the era of terror with his autocratic leanings, framing those who oppose him as "vermin" while saying immigrants are "poisoning the blood of our nation" and promising his loyalists that if he returns to the Oval Office, he will be their "retribution."

The history of Black folk in America has long been one step forward, two steps back. You fight to be recognized as human instead of three-fifths of a "man." Nearly 200 years later, having fought and died in unprecedented percentages in World War I and World War II, Black soldiers returned home to be treated worse than they had been overseas. Black soldiers, in fact, returning from World War II, were denied the right to buy FHA houses in New York because federal laws prevented them while allowing white soldiers who had taken the same or lesser risks to build generational wealth.[67] These warriors – true patriots – rejected by the country they fought for, were much more worthy of the title of Americans than Trump, the draft dodger elected president in 2016.

There were 700,000 new African American jobs under Trump, while only 195,000 under Obama, according to then-Trump press secretary Sarah Sanders. Yeah, yeah, yeah. Are those statistics true, I wondered? Good question. I'd heard them disputed by Obama senior staffers. Turns out that this statement – like so many more that came out of this administration – was another blatant lie, this time to lure gullible Black folk into his lair.[68]

Frankly, I didn't give a damn how many jobs Trump created for Black people. His ugly and divisive rhetoric, his race-baiting, xenophobic, misogynistic treatment of women and anyone who wasn't a white man turned my stomach, elevated my blood pressure, and created in me a disdain for an American leader like none I could have ever before imagined.

Had someone had the guts to control his Twitter finger and put tape over his mouth, he could have gone down in history as an effective president, even though most of his accomplishments benefited the rich and the white, despite his insistence otherwise. Yes, I'm Black, underpaid, yet privileged. However, it wouldn't matter how much I was paid. I could not sell my soul to the devil and buy the drivel Trump was selling (and still is!) about how good he was for the country in general and Black folk in particular. While I did my job well, many days it was like drinking castor oil or having an enema. Afterward, I frequently felt rotten to my core.

Some social justice advocates asked me whether I felt like a "sellout" because I stayed in the administration despite sharing information about positions I felt were morally wrong. These included separating children from their parents at the border, directing my office to vet cities and communities for friendly sites to house those children, justifying taking away people's health insurance and reducing benefits like Meals on Wheels for seniors, and aid to families and children. Yes, I felt bad sending the Trump administration's often poorly written and slanted news releases and advisories to seasoned media, some of whom derisively wrote back that there was "no way" they were going to print that garbage.

But I knew that as distasteful as some of what I had to do was, there were still subtle ways I could help those out there trying to preserve the (still lawful) Affordable Care Act and assist those who needed to navigate and acquire health insurance, even as Trump and HHS sought to kill it and bad-mouthed it at every opportunity. Besides, I knew there were people out in the field, trying to help the vulnerable, who realized what a complicated and morally reprehensible position my officemates and I were in. And while I am not a hero, and never saw myself as one, I was, in a sense, a part of the remnant: one of those chosen to fight the good fight from within, hopefully without compromising my commitment to the people I served, while at the same time exerting all my talents and abilities to make my regional directors look good and fulfill their commitments to the leadership in Washington. I usually felt like one of my son's Subversive Witnesses.[69] And yes, often, more so than working for Bush, Clinton, Obama, or Biden, it was excruciating.

Why was working for Trump so difficult? As his top spy, former CIA Director John Brennan, put it, "He is, I think, the most divisive president in American history." Consequently, Brennan's security clearance was revoked on August 15, 2018, in a virtually unprecedented move by a U.S. president.[70]

Another veteran, a government official in intelligence, Frank Figliuzzi, had pointed out the danger of Trump's complicity and coziness with Russia that tainted the 2016 election. "This strikes at the heart of free speech," Figliuzzi said of Trump's revocation of Brennan's clearance.

"He [Brennan] knows the case. He's been briefed on the Russian involvement. That's why every American should be concerned about this action today."[71]

So yes, I'd worked for presidents I'd disagreed with – hell, all of them, at one time or another. But never, ever did I work for one accused and suspected of being un-American, complicit with seeking to undermine his own country's democratic process, and at odds with *his own* FBI, Homeland Security, and CIA leaders – and certainly not one who called for the violent overthrow of his own government, the one he was sworn to protect.

Chapter 3: The Patient Protection and Affordable Care Act

"Of all the forms of discrimination and inequalities, injustice in health is the most shocking and inhuman."

Martin Luther King, speaking to the Medical Committee for Human Rights, March 25, 1966, in Chicago.

How We Got Here

In 2008, the Office of the Regional Director Office of the Secretary for the U.S. Department of Health & Human Services, where I had worked since 1998, was excited. This was the third president I had worked for, beginning at the tail end of the Clinton administration, then working for eight years for George W. Bush. As part of that outreach and messaging, I treasure the night I met the great Amelia Boynton following a presentation I made in Tuskegee, Alabama, about the ACA. I have some great memories of that time.

Following the euphoria of watching television on election night in November of 2008, when the world's most powerful nation elected a Black man as the leader of the free world, our all-Black career staff was excited about a new, unprecedented reality. We also wondered what it would mean for us.

When administrations change, it usually takes a while before the new leadership is in place in the regions. It is not as "sudden" as it might appear to some. First, the new president must select and swear in their new cabinet, which, in our case, was HHS Secretary Kathleen Sebelius. Following that decision, the HHS Secretary must select their leadership team, including the Surgeon General and the directors of the CDC, FDA, NIH (National Institutes of Health), and others. After that, the ten regional directors, who represent the secretary in the fifty states across the country as their political point persons, are selected.

The landmark Patient Protection and Affordable Care Act, usually shortened to the ACA, was passed in March 2010. As a result, we soon went into planning mode to determine how we would educate the public and potential partners about what the passage of the ACA would mean to them and their communities.

I still remember when, in May of 2010, we were informed that South Carolina State Representative Anton Gunn would be appointed to serve as the regional director for the eight southeastern states and our new boss. Gunn would become the first appointed Black HHS regional director since Republican Sam Williams directed Region IV during the first Bush administration in the 1980s. His boss, Dr. Louis Sullivan, was the nation's first and *only* Black HHS Secretary.

I'll give you some perspective here. The federal government and politicians, more specifically, can be fickle and strange creatures. After having worked in five administrations, I have noticed some interesting comparisons. Granted, I was trying to figure out which way was up when I went to work for the Clinton administration in the summer of 1998. When George W. Bush was elected, by the thinnest of hanging chads, as we know, they went about their business of appointing and selecting leaders quickly, probably with the tutelage of Bush's father, George Herbert Walker Bush.

During this administration, I remember very little distrust as the new regional director, Constantinos Miskis, who came from the state government in Florida, arrived. In fact, during Bush's eight years, we had more autonomy and authority as a representative of the secretary than in any other, with the possible exception of Obama's. Some of those aspects included the publishing of a monthly newsletter for the eight southeastern states, which was a carryover from the Clinton administration, as well as an expectation that we would communicate and work with regional congressmen and women, as well as governors. Eight years later, none of that was allowed under the Trump administration.

Bush, a Republican who came from a privileged family and had made his own share of missteps with alcohol and drugs, put forward an agenda that included what he termed compassionate capitalism. While he received his share of justifiable criticism around the federal response to Hurricane Katrina in New Orleans in 2005, as well as the trumped-up invasion and overthrow of Iraq's Saddam Hussein, he did implement initiatives that addressed the least of these, including a fatherhood initiative, a healthy marriage initiative, and programs that focused on supporting the families, especially the children, of the incarcerated.

From my lens, as the person responsible for media relations and gaining what is termed "earned media," or non-paid media exposure, we had a long leash to do what we needed to promote our message and our programs. Part of that included "living" on the bus during the rollout of Medicare Part D, which meant going from community to community and explaining to constituents what the new benefits of turning 65 meant for their insurance coverage, which included a prescription drug benefit, beginning in 2006.

I remember being on a bus with then-CMS Administrator Mark McClellan as we traveled through Tennessee, North Carolina, and South Carolina, meeting with a governor, a host of constituents, and key organizations. It was, in many ways, a precursor to what my professional life would be like five years later when I spent a great deal of time on the road promoting and educating citizens and partners about the benefits and timelines around the ACA, or ObamaCare. And while there is certainly room for criticizing Bush, there was also a certain sensitivity to those on the margins I never saw during the Trump administration.

Under Bush, we were very focused on a Fatherhood Initiative designed to model fatherhood in communities where fathers were often missing from homes. Levitt, under Bush, also oversaw the Healthy Marriage Initiative of the ACF, or The Administration for Children and Families, which was another staple example often missing in some at-risk communities, including the Black community. They also empowered and authored a Grandparents Raising Grandchildren initiative,[72] particularly critical in poorer communities and families where the heads of household were oftentimes incarcerated. Trump, on the other hand, did have a focus on addressing the foster care and adoption systems, especially in conservative lanes, but from my perspective, not much else. Negatively, he instituted tax laws that fattened the coffers of his billionaire buddies while removing women's rights by choking federal family planning avenues for birth control and abortion[73] and cutting funds for the community development block grants that support the 5,000 Meals on Wheels programs across the country,[74] a critical safety net for many of America's elderly and afflicted, including veterans.

I would come to understand that Obama was, early on, like Trump in some ways. He was a novice in such rarefied air and bore the weight of the world on his shoulders as the first African American president of the greatest country in the world. Though he was bold and decisive in some areas (bailing out the auto and banking industries and pushing for the passage of the Affordable Care Act), in other ways, he was reluctant to make a *big mistake*. But after all, I reasoned, he was not only trying to navigate the well-being and economic security of the most powerful nation in the world, but also the legacy of America's first Black president. In many ways, he was the hope and glory for his race all over the world. He was also the opposite of Trump in his preparation. He was known as a voracious reader and inquirer regarding the hundreds of pages of critical briefing documents presidents are confronted with regarding the economy, foreign affairs, and any number of other pressing issues each week. Trump, on the other hand, was notorious for his refusal (or inability) to read or absorb them.

When the health insurance marketplace opened on October 1, 2013, with great fanfare and extreme controversy, ironically, a federal shutdown occurred on the very same day. The Republican-led House and Senate, many of whom vowed, like Senate Majority Leader Mitch McConnell, to be a thorn in 44's side and make Obama a one-term president, were committed to shutting the government down.

On the first day of the shutdown, Obama said, "At midnight last night, for the first time in 17 years, Republicans in Congress chose to shut down the federal government. Let me be more specific. One faction of one party in one house of Congress in one branch of government shut down major parts of the government all because they didn't like one law."[75] Just damn, I mumbled to myself, as I grappled with the ramifications.

We had planned and planned for the opening of the marketplace, meeting weekly to strategize and examine the strengths and weaknesses of each market. In fact, for the months preceding the launch, we visited all our key cities, which for me were Jackson, Mississippi; Columbia and Greenville, South Carolina; and Birmingham and the Gulf Coast, Alabama. We also worked vigorously in metro Atlanta, Middle Georgia, and Savannah. Our process was to meet with willing partners, explain what was about to happen, and assist in building coalitions that could carry out the work. My colleague, April Washington, worked the major cities in Florida, Tennessee, and North Carolina as Kentucky became the only state in Region IV that chose to expand Medicaid, while the other seven refused, requiring us to set up FFMs, Federally Facilitated Marketplaces.

A big part of that was the federally funded health insurance navigators, which included at least one well-funded group in each state charged with leading the effort to educate and enroll those who needed help, weren't computer literate, or may have been a little less trusting of government. Other key components of the coalition of enrollers were the federally qualified health centers – That includes over 1,200 centers across the nation, which are funded by HRSA (the Health Resources Services Administration), which is part of HHS.[76] For nearly 50 years, HRSA has provided health care for the uninsured and the underinsured on a sliding fee scale, meaning the less you make, the less you pay for primary care services. In fact, the FQHCs, established under President Lyndon Johnson in 1965 as part of his War on Poverty, provides roughly 40% of the health care in the U.S. on a free or sliding fee scale, which is a well-kept secret.[77]

At the launch of the HIM (Health Insurance Marketplace), however, these centers were now staffed with additional personnel who were specifically charged with educating and enrolling the uninsured and the underinsured who qualified for the ACA, popularly known as ObamaCare. The truth is, in some places, especially in our region, where there was deep resistance to a Democrat – much less the nation's first Black president – though FQHCs were funded to do outreach and enrollment, many did only the very least they could get away with.

In some of our states, I had excellent relationships with the leaders of the primary care associations, which headed the FQHCs, like South Carolina's Crystal Evans, Barry Knighton, and Lathran Woodard; Mississippi's Maria Morris; and Georgia's Duane Kavka and Cathy Bowden. Roz Goodwin of the South Carolina Hospital Association was another invaluable partner. Other key players in the coalition of enrollers were the insurance agents and brokers, who, quite naturally, were frequently the most learned and adept at knowing which were the most appropriate of what were often dozens of choices for the uninsured – and we mean strictly those who weren't covered by their jobs and companies – to choose from. Then, there were churches, denominations, and faith leaders, like the National Baptist Convention and the African Methodist Episcopal (AME), and several prominent mosques, which were diligent in their effort to educate and enroll citizens, many of whom had never been insured before.

Other affinity groups, including the NAACP, the Latin American Association, the Black Chamber of Commerce, The Children's Defense Fund, My Brother's Keeper, several Black fraternities and sororities, including Omega Psi Phi, Delta Sigma Theta, Alpha Kappa Alpha, Alpha Phi Alpha, and Kappa Alpha Psi, many colleges and universities, mayors, county commissioners, and others, were all willing participants in closing the gap between the haves and the have-nots, the insured and the uninsured.

We also worked with people like Sarah Brechin and Marianne Chung of the Center for Pan Asian Communities (CPAC), and Brigid Scarbrough and Alejandro Lopez of the Health Initiative, an LGBTQ+-focused organization, each in Atlanta, along with Hosea's Feed the Hungry, Lisa Flagg, the executive director of the Fulton-Dekalb Hospital Authority in Georgia, and countless others. Extraordinary partners who coordinated assister groups included Jim Carnes of Alabama Arise, Stephanie Priester of New Horizon Family Health Services of Greenville, South Carolina, who coordinated enrollment efforts in the Upstate assisters, Dwight Hanna, director of Human Services for Richland County, who opened doors in deeply rural South Carolina, and Carrie Sinkler-Parker, a former classmate of Congressman Jim Clyburn, who drove many miles each week to spread the word about the ACA to dozens of Black, rural South Carolinians. Chris Moseley and Emmett Turner of Birmingham Healthcare, Shaftel Benson of Quality-of-Life Health Services, Sonja Smith of AIDS Alabama and statewide coordinator Jim Carnes of Alabama Arise, along with Dr. Michael and Lottie Minor of Get Covered Mississippi, and the Boat People of coastal Mississippi, were tremendous partners. The amazing Huxie Wilkins, SEEDCO's lead navigator, was phenomenal, as were Florida's Jodi Ray and South Carolina's Shelli Quenga, each highly organized, creative, and dogged in their pursuit of health equity.

As critical as any of those groups, however, was Enroll America, an organization that didn't enroll anyone but coordinated, promoted, and carried out local, state, and national campaigns and initiatives aimed at increasing education and enrollment into the ACA.

Four years after the launch of Healthcare.gov and the Affordable Care Act's health insurance marketplace, the initiative's impact was significant, especially for Mississippi. A report from HHS showed that 81% of the state's marketplace consumers could get a plan with a premium of less than $75 per month, while 85% could get plans with premiums below $100 per month. In addition, approximately 22,000 Mississippians who were paying full price for plans outside of the ACA marketplace could also qualify to save money.[78] Perhaps most importantly, in one of the poorest states in the nation – and lest we forget, the Blackest state and the one with the most descendants of slaves – Mississippi's uninsured rates had plummeted from 30% in 2010 to 12.7% in 2016, thanks to the ACA.

Furthermore, 90 percent of 2016 Mississippi marketplace consumers qualified for tax credits that would reduce premiums, as well as 85% of marketplace-eligible uninsured Americans.[79] In the end, 104,538 Mississippians were covered, and 93% of them received tax credits for 2015 that averaged $353 per month. That shot in the arm, in one of the poorest states in the nation, where 56% of the marketplace enrollees were new to Healthcare.gov, many of them receiving insurance for the first time, was monumental.[80]

Another critical state where amazing progress was made was Florida, which housed the nation's largest group of navigators, the federally funded entities that were designed and established to help educate and enroll citizens who needed help with the process of choosing the best and most affordable insurance for themselves and their families. Jodi Ray, based in Tampa, directed Florida Covering Kids and Families. In September of 2016, two months before Trump was elected, the Census Bureau reported that, following year three of the ACA, Florida's uninsured rate had dropped from 21.3% in 2010, when the law was passed, to 13.3% in 2015. Also, during the first quarter of 2016, that rate fell to a record low of 8.6%. The result: by February, 1.6 million Floridians had enrolled to receive health coverage in 2015.[81] The results for higher quality showed that hospital readmissions for Medicare beneficiaries dropped by 2.7% between 2010 and 2015, meaning 3,161 fewer beneficiaries had to return to the hospital due to stronger laws ensuring quality care.

"Affordability, access and quality are how we measure success in the health care system," HHS Secretary Sylvia Burwell said following the report. "This week's data shows Florida is making progress on all three under the Affordable Care Act."[82] Nationally, between 2010 and 2016, the rate of "patient harms" fell by 17%, which translates into fewer infections, medication errors, etc., for 2.1 million patients, meaning 87,000 avoided deaths and an estimated $20 billion in savings.[83] Though the ACA was handicapped by what we call narrow insurance networks, which is essentially giving citizens in a state only two or three plan options instead of the five or seven they had before Trump came into office, and though six of our eight Republican governors did nothing to support the ACA, the ACA's legacy remained one of survival and success.

Eight years after Obama was elected, in 2016, when Trump entered the scene, the mistrust shown by the incoming administration of career government officials was probably more distinct than at any time in my career. Why do I say that? When Regional Director Renee Ellmers, a former Congresswoman from North Carolina and one of the first to endorse Trump, was appointed as the regional director for the eight southeast states, they didn't even trust her, nor many of her colleagues. Ellmers, the only former member of Congress, as well as the only woman, chosen to head one of the 10 HHS regional offices early in the Trump administration, was a vehement anti-ObamaCare attack dog. Confident, poised, and seasoned before the camera, she would have played well in the deep South, the Trump stronghold, articulating the administration's rationale as to why the ACA was a failure, why no one should be required to buy health insurance, and why it should be replaced and repealed.[84]

However, not only did the administration apparently not trust us, the career staffers, but they also refused to allow her to do what she did best. The few times they allowed her to do interviews and public speaking, she was passionate, convincing, and well-prepared. Instead, they chose to listen to a cadre of right-wing, radical anti-abortionists who, at least in several instances, had little or no formal background in journalism or public affairs, yet were staunch Trump loyalists. Highly paid talking heads like Charmaine Yost sent to the regional offices highly biased "news releases" that much more closely resembled partisan editorials and perspective pieces. When they did that, of course, the expectation was that we would disseminate them and, ultimately, they would be picked up in the newspapers and published. Conversely, however, on several occasions, my colleagues and I would get snarky replies from editors we had, in many instances, worked with through multiple administrations, deriding the idea that anyone in Washington – or us, for that matter – possibly hoped that they would print the slanted, though backed with little or no facts or evidence, drivel the administration called news releases. In many ways, frankly, they were as empty as Trump's feckless, fact-less claims that COVID would "disappear ... into thin air," the 2020 election was "stolen," and that the FBI had planted evidence of missing files during their 2022 raid on Mar-a-Lago to retrieve the classified documents he had ferreted away from Washington after his 2020 defeat.

As should be clear by this point, each day of Trump's presidency was a thrust deeper into chaos.

Chapter 4: Clueless

"Daily, the Negro is coming more and more to look upon law and justice, not as protecting safeguards, but as sources of humiliation and oppression. The laws are made by men who have little interest in him; they are executed by men who have absolutely no motive for treating black people with courtesy or consideration; and, finally, the accused law-breaker is tried, not by his peers, but too often by men who would rather punish ten innocent Negroes than let one guilty one escape."

W.E.B. DuBois, The Souls of Black Folk, 1903

Throughout his administration as president (and even before and after it), Trump's insensitivity stuck out like a sore thumb. So, how clueless has Donald Trump been when it comes to race and ethnicity? I'll start with a story. Kaepernick, the former NFL star who led the San Francisco 49ers to one step from a world championship in 2012, said, "Believe in something. Even if it means sacrificing everything."[85] That quote seems totally appropriate for a former star drummed out of the league after electrifying the nation by beginning to kneel during the national anthem in 2015, stoking heated passions on both sides. *To this day*, Trump and his minions still don't understand – or refuse to acknowledge – that the protest was about criminal and social injustice, about far too many cases of police and private citizens gunning down unarmed men, and most often, men of color, Black and brown, during either police stops or no-knock raids.

When Nike came out with its signature commercial featuring freedom fighter Colin Kaepernick to protest the rash of documented police shootings of unarmed Black motorists, the Twitter-trigger president rushed to weigh in: "Just like the NFL, whose ratings have gone WAY DOWN, Nike is getting absolutely killed with anger and boycotts. I wonder if they had any idea that it would be this way? As far as the NFL is concerned, I just find it hard to watch, and always will, until they stand for the FLAG!"[86]

I remember a Thursday in late September of 2019 when the residents of South and North Carolina were struggling to recover from the onslaught of Hurricane Florence, which a week earlier had begun to batter the 300-mile area with several feet of what proved to be continual rain and flooding that cost over 30 lives. That same day, September 20th, I and my nine regional public information colleagues across the nation were charged with disseminating a news release from the White House entitled "President Donald J. Trump's Administration Has Helped Lead A Historic Recovery Effort In Puerto Rico." The subtitle of the release, again, just more than a year after Hurricane Maria devastated Puerto Rico, taking nearly 3,000 lives and leaving the island ravaged and largely dysfunctional a year later, said, "… And we stand with Puerto Rico, and we are helping them to rebuild stronger and better than ever before." Hmm …

Let's keep in mind that President Trump – the same one that flipped rolls of paper towels to media and attendees at his Puerto Rico press conference – had insisted that Maria simply didn't compare to a "real" hurricane disaster like Katrina.[87] While bringing a tremendous amount of rain and destruction to the Houston area, Florence, seemingly well managed, resulted in the loss of 63 lives, but far fewer than Maria's nearly 3,000.[88] As a result, for those of us who served as "messengers" who were not drinking the Kool-Aid, this was just another inane lie uttered by this president and administration.

One member of the media, *Atlanta Inquirer* editor David Stokes, upon receiving my email, which included the news release, called me and said, "DT administration has not helped lead a historic recovery effort in Puerto Rico. They just proved that not to be true this week, alone. It's very interesting that you all chose to put this out today. Again, it's not true. Also, it is crazy, and [number] three, it's nothing but politics, anyway. And what do you want me to do with this? I know not to print this in the Black press."[89]

This statement, unfortunately, was only one example of the media's disgust with the Trump administration's press office in the first two years of the administration.

Another editor, Elaine Owen, who lived and worked in mostly white Fannin County in North Georgia, was similarly disgusted by a news release I was directed to send, which came from headquarters, entitled "President Trump is Making Progress on the Opioid Crisis in Georgia." The October 7th, 2019, op/ed elicited this response from Owen:

"I am a reporter/editor, and I keep up with the news," she said. "I am also a Republican. What you [HHS] have written about what our president has done/will do is baseless and unfounded – and I am sure that you know that. I WILL NOT print anything you write in this vein. FACT CHECK is something I teach my reporters – and (obviously), you did NOT do that.

"Thank you – but DO NOT send me any more of this crap," editor Owen continued. "This president has done more harm in the short time he has been president than most of our presidents do in four years. Don't send anything else to this email, or it will be marked 'SPAM.'"[90]

Though I didn't have the clearance to say so, I was encouraged by her response. Owen reminded me that there are still *traditional* Republicans, people I could understand and identify with, as opposed to MAGA "Republicans."

Sadly, this sort of response from credible, earnest journalists was not uncommon during the Trump administration and was something I never recalled having received during the Clinton, Bush, Obama, and Biden terms, even though many disagreed with their politics and priorities. I'm convinced there were others who thought the same but decided it wasn't worth saying or accurately assessing the nature of the beast. Either way, several of my more seasoned counterparts in the other nine regions would, like me, literally cringe when we disseminated some of the drivel we were told by Washington to send out.

Chapter 5: The Reckoning

"At the same time, Trump and HHS Secretary Price repeatedly called for allowing the ObamaCare marketplace to collapse. I didn't call it sabotage. But that's what it is."

Roy Mitchell, director of Mississippi Health Advocacy Program

It began quietly enough. Three days earlier, the regional offices had finally been told during a national internal call, which we had regularly, that for the first time since the inception of the Affordable Care Act, the regional directors and their staffs would not be actively supporting education and enrollment efforts in their respective regions. We had been waiting for weeks for an official decision, and while, frankly, I'd hoped we'd get the green light to travel and work with state and city coalitions, as we had done the first four years of the ACA, the determination to shut down that work did not come as a surprise. After all, both Secretary Tom Price, a former Georgia Congressman, and Trump, dogged and denigrated the ACA at every opportunity, even though it was still federal law.

My first reaction, as all 10 regional offices listened via Zoom to the news our IGA director shared with us, was to continue looking into the screen, stone-faced, determined to show no emotion. No one of the regional career staff reacted, as we all expected the decision. I'm sure some agreed with the decision, but for most of us, we'd spent the previous six years laying the groundwork for the Affordable Care Act and knew that our work would be drastically altered. I thought about the key communities and partners in the field that would see this as abandonment and, in some cases, even an act of betrayal. Others, fortified by foundations and well-heeled community partners and with strong leadership and support systems, would find a way to maintain strong enrollment numbers, even considering Republican attacks against a program that had driven uninsured rates to all-time lows.

Immediately following the meeting, I huddled with our regional director, Renee Ellmers, regarding our next steps. She quickly agreed that I would need to notify MHAP (Mississippi Health Advocacy Program) and the Mississippi Primary Care Association that I would not be joining them for our annual, pre-planned tour of the state, which was scheduled to take place in less than two weeks. The event generally began in Hernando, just outside Memphis, then moved to a city in the Delta, maybe Tunica or Clarksdale, on to metropolitan Jackson, the state's capital, then Hattiesburg and south to the Gulf Coast, usually Biloxi or Gulfport. The trip, which included driving along the Mississippi Blues trail was, admittedly, one of the highlights of my year. That's because despite the widespread poverty, illiteracy, lack of broadband, and stark health disparities in the state, as well as an acknowledgment that they were at a disadvantage, the people of Mississippi consistently showed a fierce pride and determination to survive, move forward, and improve their life chances.

Praying over my message, the following day, I showed her my proposed email, which she approved, and then sent it off to the tour planning team, which included MHAP, Dr. Michael Minor of Get Covered Mississippi, and Maria Morris of the Mississippi Primary Health Care Association.

"Dear friends," I wrote, "We have been informed that the HHS regional office will not be supporting marketplace efforts by being out in the region this year. I will certainly miss the interaction and the opportunity to share departmental updates and positions, even though they have changed drastically. My apologies for taking so long to provide a definitive answer. If someone would like to discuss further, please feel free to call me. All the best in your endeavors."[91]

Shortly after sending it, I received a response from MHAP Keri Abernathy, asking me to clarify my message. With a knot in my stomach, I reiterated that I would not be able to join them on the tour and that the support we had provided their assister community and the other six in our eight-state region (Kentucky was the only state in the deep South that had expanded Medicaid), would not be part of our mission, going forward.

Within days, I received my regular copy of the Mississippi Health Advocacy Program's (MHAP) newsletter, which directly pointed out, in a headline, that HHS had left them high and dry as they were attempting to jumpstart the annual health insurance marketplace open enrollment.

Immediately after receiving the newsletter, I alerted RD Ellmers that it was coming. I also forwarded the newsletter to my principal contact at Intergovernmental Affairs, Greg Hunt, our HHS leadership for the regional office, as I braced for the pushback. Shortly thereafter, Ellmers and I received a call from the IGA Director Laura Trueman and Personnel Director Nikki Bratcher-Bowman. Almost right off the bat, Bratcher-Bowman asked me, "Why did you feel the need to send the email saying you would not be coming to be part of their tour and HHS's regional office would not be providing on-the-ground support for marketplace enrollment in 2017?"

Amid all my own angst, I felt a cringe of sorrow for the woman leading the conversation, IEA's Nikki Bratcher-Bowman, whom I had known – though not well – and worked with for over a decade and the only Black person in senior leadership at Intergovernmental and External Affairs. I imagined she likely felt like I did when I had to send out bogus news releases and advisories. I don't think she wanted to ask the question, or even challenge the fact that I reached out to the Mississippi leaders to say that I would not be coming. She and I never talked about the conversation, but I'm confident she was aware enough to know that Mississippi is one of our most at-risk states, with extensive poverty, sky-high co-morbidities, health disparities, low public education rates, and significant racial distrust. More importantly, however, I knew that she, though at a much higher level and pay grade, was seeking to survive in an administration that cared very little about the working poor, minorities, and access to healthcare for those who couldn't pay for it. Conversely, I felt little remorse for the MAGA leadership team that was happy to rake us over the coals, though I sometimes wondered if they really bought into the Trump hype as things began to spiral out of control during COVID, and we received increased criticism about our care for families separated at the border.

"What did you want me to do?" I asked her as calmly and respectfully as I knew how. "Would it have been better if I simply didn't show up?"

I had, after all – though in a very different administration – been going to Mississippi for the past four years to be part of their kick-off events to educate and motivate citizens about the changes and opportunities for the new open enrollment season, and they counted on us. After a few more minutes of conversation, we left the meeting with Bratcher-Bowman directing me to send an apology to the Mississippi stakeholders that our HHS ASPA (Assistant Secretary for Public Affairs) would write. In addition, Trueman directed me to write an explanation of why I thought it was important to support the Mississippi stakeholders in their ACA work. It was at that exact moment, however, that my Region IV colleagues and I realized that the next three years would be fraught with peril, and we would exist in a fishbowl under a giant magnifying glass.

On that September 2017 evening, I wrote an extensive history of our work in establishing or, as we called it, "standing up," the health insurance marketplaces in our seven states and sent it to HHS IGA External Affairs Director Kyle McGowan and copied Trueman, Bratcher-Bowman, Ellmers, and others. It included our painstaking efforts to identify and cultivate relationships with affinity groups like the Children's Defense Fund and My Brother's Keeper, community-based organizations (CBOs), health advocacy groups, colleges and universities, elected officials, and others. I also went on to explain why certain groups, those who had systemically lagged behind more progressive and leadership-inclusive states for decades, demanded (needed) more help. As I always tried to do, I penned this missive very carefully, respectfully, and with much prayer. Ultimately, I knew in my spirit that whatever I said wasn't going to change a damn thing about IEA/HHS/POTUS's approach to the ACA, or our non-engagement in supporting those stakeholders, even though the ACA was still the law of the land. McGowan, who was thirty-something, was previously deputy chief-of-staff to then-Georgia Congressman Tom Price, Trump's first HHS Secretary and, thus, my boss. McGowan, who stayed at IEA for 14 months before leaving to become chief-of-staff at the CDC, predictably thanked me for the background piece and, as expected, that was the end of it. I was, essentially, doing damage control and covering my ass, albeit with a face towel, not a bath towel. My boss, on the other hand, Regional Director Renee Ellmers, the former North Carolina congresswoman who had been one of the first to endorse Trump, was openly furious, a privilege that I, as a Black mid-level employee, never felt the freedom to be. I, too, was boiling, but much more adept at what W.E.B. DuBois labeled performing "double consciousness," today called code-switching.[92] Still an ardent supporter of Trump, she had little respect for the mostly political zealot, far right-wing, anti-abortion group running the show at IEA. That crew was led by Charmaine Yost, HHS/IEA's Assistant Secretary of Public Affairs, who stayed at HHS for only ten months before leaving for the Office of National Drug Control Policy. They were well-placed anti-abortion advocates, yet narrowly focused and ill-equipped to manage the other important aspects of HHS, the world's most comprehensive agency, one that addresses health and social services of Americans from the cradle to the grave.

"They had four years to come up with a health care plan and repeal and replace ACA, and didn't do it," said Ellmers, noting that her party had to own up to its own failure. Though not a fan of ObamaCare, as a public servant, she felt responsible for serving the needs of the eight southeastern states until Trump passed another plan to replace the ACA and said, "We need to be serving the needs of the people." For that stance alone, I deeply respected her. She stormed out of the office that day, upset like the rest of us, saying, "If I don't come back next week, it's been good working with you all."

As far as the "apology" ASPA was writing for me to send, six years later, I'm still waiting on it. My belief is that it was never sent to me because it would provide written proof that HHS and the Trump administration were deliberately and systematically sabotaging the ACA.

Within 48 hours, the floodgates had opened wide. I began getting calls from major market media outlets, such as CNN's Jeremy Diamond, *The New York Times*, and Politico, asking for confirmation that HHS was not going to be supporting assisters during open enrollment. Of course, in no instance was I going to provide an answer to the people calling. Instead, I asked that they put their questions in writing and said I would forward them to the appropriate people who would, or could provide answers.

Here is an example of a written message I received from the press. "Hi Deric," wrote Dylan Scott of VOX in an email.

"I have already reached out to the Washington office but wanted to reach out to you as well. I am writing about the decision not to take part in marketplace events this year.

"If you ha[ve] any more light to shed, I would really welcome it. The group I have spoken with in Mississippi seemed very caught off guard by the announcement this week, and I really thought these events brought a lot of value.[93]

Thank ya."

-**Dylan Scott**

Policy Reporter

I forwarded his email to the appropriate people, knowing that any response from me wouldn't help and, in fact, might only make matters worse. Instead, it was much better to see HHS squirm, laying its cards on the table, instead of covertly, calculatingly, deconstructing the ACA, brick by brick.

As more calls came in to not just our regional office in Atlanta, but others across the country, it became clear to the media and those who closely followed the battle over whether ACA lived or died, that the attempt to kill the ACA involved a muffling of the process, not just in the Southeast, but also in the other nine regions across the country. The challenge, however, was that the South traditionally included more minorities, more poverty, and a higher incidence of diabetes, heart disease, and cancer, coupled with lower health literacy and all the predictable social determinants of health. South Carolina, Georgia, Mississippi, Alabama, Louisiana, and Texas, comprised not only the Bible Belt, but also the stroke belt.[94]

MHAP's Roy Mitchell, who I'm sure was bombarded by reporters seeking answers far more than I was as it became clear that my regional contacts were forwarding queries to headquarters, instead of stepping into a boatload of even more controversy, understandably played the situation for all it was worth. "HHS's destructive actions will ultimately reduce enrollment, increase costs, and drive up the uninsured rate in Mississippi," he assessed.[95]

"In the absence of any kind of federal marketing, we're working on a plan to go directly to consumers, rather than trying to work with the navigators," said Mitchell, pointing out that the Mississippi assisters canceled their tour when HHS declined to participate. "At the same time, Trump and HHS Secretary Price repeatedly called for allowing the ObamaCare marketplace to collapse. I didn't call it sabotage," added Mitchell. "But that's what it is."[96]

In all honesty, I couldn't argue with Roy Mitchell, Shelli Quenga, or Jodi Ray, the brilliant and highly-effective navigator leads I worked with in South Carolina and Florida, respectively, who I knew felt deeply abandoned and betrayed by their government and who publicly lambasted the decision. I, of course, felt the same way, though I never could say it publicly. It absolutely *was* sabotage, and the real problem I had with it was that the Trump administration didn't have the guts to say that was what they were doing.

The following day, September 28, 2017, Mitchell, the head of MHAP and someone I had a lot of respect for, showed up on MSNBC to be interviewed on *The Beat*, Ari Melber's show. The subject was, of course, HHS's nonsupport of the federal program implemented by Obama, the Patient Protection and Affordable Care Act. In his segment, Mitchell detailed why HHS's support was important to Mississippi, a Medicaid non-expansion state, meaning the state refused to set up a marketplace so that citizens could enroll in a healthcare program, leaving it to The Feds to do so. As part of his explanation, Melber put my email up on the screen, detailing the message I sent informing them I would not be part of their annual rollout. "Time for our special report," said Melber. "While Republicans failed to repeal ObamaCare this week, they have done something else that might be very important. We've obtained new evidence on efforts to undermine ObamaCare from within Trump's HHS Department. We learned about this on *THE BEAT* from Roy Mitchell, who runs a health care program in Mississippi that works with people to get them enrolled in the ACA."[97]

"Shit!" I mumbled to myself, knowing full well that after this interview and the inevitable heat on me that would come along with it, all hell was going to break loose.

"Mitchell is now blowing the lid off this, releasing this email and saying it shows an effort to sabotage ObamaCare in the field after Republicans failed to repeal it in D.C.," said Melber, using my email as evidence. "And there's evidence for that. The administration has already slashed advertising by 90 percent, cut funding for the people who guide consumers to these plans, and cut the time available for Americans to choose plans in open enrollment by 50 percent."[98]

"This was essentially the most minimal effort they could make in Mississippi," explained Mitchell, pointing to our office's supporting the ACA educational tour. "Attending meetings convened by nonprofits to get the word out about the ACA enrollment period. As you know, the enrollment period has been cut in half. The funding for advertising is cut by 90 percent. Navigators are real. Their budget has been cut by approximately 60 percent. So this was the least they could do, is go out with us throughout the various regions of Mississippi and explain what ACA enrollment was going to look like this year."[99]

Initially, I was, as my daughter likes to say, "in my feelings." I felt somewhat hurt that Mitchell, a colleague in the struggle to serve the least of these, blindsided me by not alerting me that he was going public with the news that HHS had pulled out of the tour and stopped supporting marketplace enrollment. A few days later, however, I realized he was doing exactly what he needed to do for the survival of his organization and to shine the light on the insensitivity and callous disregard the administration had for the law, the underinsured, and the working poor. Through dumb luck, he had been hand-delivered a gift by an administration that could no longer toss Molotov cocktails from the shadows and continue to deny their complicity in undermining the law of the land, the ACA.[100] Mitchell had, in effect, done what I could not do – expose the fact that Emperor Trump and his minions had no clothes, as well as the thuggery of the administration's attack on the ACA.

While I stopped hosting stakeholder calls for Georgia assisters and participating in calls with South Carolina, Mississippi, Alabama, Tennessee, North Carolina, and Florida assisters, I did continue to disseminate CMS (Centers for Medicare and Medicaid Services) weekly stakeholder updates to keep the navigators, certified application counselors (CACs), and FQHC enrollers, abreast of changes and enrollment themes. At least one of my colleagues at CMS, however, would not continue to do these things. "I have two girls at home, and they like to eat," my colleague said. True dat.

I experienced many sleepless nights over the next several weeks and months, dreading what the next shoe to drop might be.

Mitchell, a leader in the fight for health equity in the nation's poorest, Blackest state for two decades, was someone I deeply respected and admired. Years later, when we finally met again, face-to-face, during the Biden administration; Mitchell shared with me that "on at least one occasion" during the Trump administration, two attorneys from the U.S. Justice Department showed up at his office using a threatening tone and pushing him to disclose where his non-profit's funding came from, in what Mitchell perceived as a "shakedown."[101]

Ultimately, the Mississippi grit and winning spirit would win out, however, as it did in many other places across the country. In 2018, while national signup was down 5%, Mississippi was one of five states that *increased* total marketplace enrollment over 2017, despite the insurance marketplace networks narrowing to the point that Mississippi only had Ambetter Insurance as an enrollment option.[102] Though flawed and controversial, ObamaCare steadily increased in popularity as the Trump administration tried time and time again to destroy it, despite never coming up with a plan to replace it. Generally, it's difficult to take something away from people once they get used to it. Still, despite the fierce determination to access never-before available healthcare insurance in the state with the highest percentage of African Americans in the U.S., Mississippi remained next to last among the 50 states, with nearly 12% of its citizens without insurance. "The Affordable Care Act gave states the ability, using mostly federal funds, to cover a large segment of their poor adult populations with Medicaid," said Mitchell, lamenting the fact that Mississippi, along with virtually every Republican-controlled southern state, refused to expand Medicaid. "We've foregone a huge opportunity to get preventive care to a lot of working Mississippians."[103] Yep, the poorer and worse off states were, the more determined their governors were to resist giving their constituents the very health care *they* themselves possessed. What's that all about?

Try as they might, Trump simply could not kill ACA, despite a promise to "let ObamaCare implode" on its own. The assault became so blatant and intense, however, that four cities, Baltimore, Chicago, Cincinnati, and Columbus, Ohio, filed suit in federal court claiming Trump has "waged a relentless effort to use executive action alone to undermine and ultimately, eliminate the law." Indeed, Trump's executive orders increased health coverage costs by shrinking enrollment and narrowing insurance networks by discouraging companies from entering the market because of increased instability. "I have just about ended ObamaCare," proclaimed Trump. "We have great healthcare. We have a lot of great things happening right now. New programs are coming out."[104] In reality, however, four years later, right up until the 2020 elections, Trump was still promising that he was coming out with a plan to replace the ACA, despite having every chance to do so during his term since the House and the Senate were both majority Republican. By then, however, Trump had a new nemesis, patriot John McCain, someone he despised nearly as much as the first Black man in the White House. Though McCain had not supported the ACA, he voted against its repeal in July 2017.

While Trump hadn't killed the ACA, he was certainly chipping away at its viability. By 2017, premiums in the marketplace had risen 37%, with three million fewer people insured than in 2016, Obama's last year in office.

"We had repeal and replace done (and the saving to our country of one trillion dollars)," proclaimed Trump, "except for one person [McCain], but it is getting done anyway. The individual mandate is gone, and great, less expensive plans will be announced this month. Drug prices are coming down right in time!"[105]

Two years later, the Trump administration had deliberately and calculatingly moved to reduce the effectiveness of the health insurance marketplace by withholding advertising and introducing "junk plans" that provide bare-bones hospital coverage. The administration also stripped away the mandate that all policies include the ten essential health benefits, and struck down the mandate that anyone who can afford insurance, but chooses not to obtain it, be assessed a penalty, known as the individual mandate.

Chapter 6: The Chosen One

"Nobody knows the system better than me, which is why I alone can fix it."
President Donald Trump[106]

Trump, rebuffed by Denmark Prime Minister Mette Frederiksen following his open and casual announcement that he had an interest in the United States purchasing Greenland, called her "... nasty. I thought the prime minister's statement that it was 'absurd' was nasty. All she had to do was say she was not interested," Trump said while announcing he was canceling a planned visit to the country, one of the U.S.'s allies.

Frederiksen's "nasty" comment? She said, "The time when you buy and sell other countries and populations is over."[107] The prime minister joined a long list of prominent women he called "nasty," including Hillary Clinton, then-Senators Elizabeth Warren and Kamala Harris, Michigan Governor Gretchen Whitmer, Speaker Nancy Pelosi, and Meghan Markle, the Duchess of Windsor.

In another instance, the all-knowing Trump pronounced, "In my opinion, if you vote for a Democrat, you're being very disloyal to Jewish people and very disloyal to Israel. Only weak people would say anything other than that."

Responding quickly, Anti-Defamation League Director Jonathan Greenblatt lashed back: "I will be exactly clear on what that was: antisemitism. The charge of disloyalty, or dual loyalty, has been used against Jews for thousands of years."[108]

"One thing I had to do economically is take on China because China has been ripping us off for many years. Somebody had to do it," he [Trump] said, looking skyward. "I am the chosen one."[109] Yes, I respect him for facing down China and its economic tactics that worked against the U.S. Fair enough. In many ways, we are still suffering today from our inability or unwillingness to address China's harmful trade policies and intellectual property theft.

But "The Chosen One"? Wow! And I recall how often the far-right columnists Charles Krauthammer, Sean Hannity, Rush Limbaugh, George Will, and former British Prime Minister David Cameron all expressed that position.[110] Well, if the far-right thought Obama was a narcissist, what descriptor can we use to describe Trump? Disrupter-in-chief? Divider-in-chief? He relishes separating children from their families at the border. Woman hater? Supporter of "white-males-only" immigration? Slanderer-in-chief of major American cities, or simply, THE CHOSEN ONE? Sadly, the disdainful choices are endless.

Chapter 7: On the Road Again: ACA Revisited/Albany, GA

"The COVID-19 crisis in the Albany metro area is one of the worst in the United States."

Johns Hopkins University, April 6, 2020

I first got the message Sunday night, late November 2018. Yes, I did say Sunday night. My boss, Renee Ellmers, a very decent, personable, and transparent Republican, emailed to give me the heads up that starting Monday, we would suddenly be promoting the health insurance marketplace, the signature program of Trump's predecessor, Barack Hussein Obama, for the first time during the Trump administration. The reason? An SEP, or special enrollment period, was being enacted due to the impact of Hurricane Michael, a category 5 storm that wreaked havoc on the Gulf Coast states in September.

Remember, this was the same administration that, in 2017, ordered us off the road and told us to stop organizing and supporting coalitions and federally paid navigators in promoting and messaging around the ACA. It was also the same administration that called ACA everything but the devil's spawn and called both Ellmers and me on the carpet for daring to send a message to the Mississippi organizers saying we would not be coming to support their annual signature, kick-off tour, as we had the previous four years, and telling me I must write a letter of apology for communicating with them. Shaking my head in wonder, I blinked a few times, reached for my spectacles, and reread the message in disbelief.

Excited, I reached out to our Georgia navigator, Dr. Kathleen Conners, to alert her to the fact that I had indeed been approved to help with promotion efforts around the health insurance marketplace in South Georgia during the SEP or special enrollment period. Hurricane Michael had ravaged the area, bringing severe flooding and damage to an area of the state already plagued by poverty, illiteracy, and a scarcity of hospitals. FEMA had designated 69 counties as disaster areas, triggering the SEP announced by CMS. The area was also largely Black and rural, a place where deep racial divides still existed.

Conners wrote to RD Ellmers: "To maximize impact, we request your support through the assistance of Mr. Deric Gilliard. Gilliard was the Regional Office of the Secretary's lead for Affordable Care for the initial four years of the program. We first met him in that capacity and greatly benefitted from his support. In addition, Gilliard has a long and strong background in understanding the needs of Georgia's minorities and how to effectively work through community organizations and infrastructure, both formal and informal."[111]

Conners was being far too kind. My best asset was that I could convey to people that I truly cared about improving their situations, and I usually knew how to connect with community leaders, or someone who could introduce me to them.

Leaning into my background as a civil rights activist, I reached out to the Albany Civil Rights Museum, where I connected with executive director Frank Wilson. Wilson, my Omega Psi Phi fraternity brother, had previously hosted me as a speaker at his center, where I talked about my first book and the contributions of the "unsung heroes and sheroes" of

Dr. King's movement. A member of Albany's first Black church and a pillar of the community, Wilson was eager to help.

Given that the ACA was still federal law, Ellmers was happy to allow me to participate in the SEP, which had previously been expected to be in effect only until December 15, but was extended to February 20, 2019, due to the challenges brought about by Hurricane Michael in a deeply rural, relatively impoverished area that included 45% of the state's counties.

For me, this was perhaps the best and most important and rewarding part of the job – getting out into communities, building on existing partnerships, and forging new ones, all in a collaborative mission to improve the lives of our constituents, especially the poor, BIPOC (Black, Indigenous, People of Color) communities, the elderly, and others at high risk. My success in this area had little to do with talent, or a silver tongue, but much more with having a genuine interest in maximizing the options for the health and wellness of the working poor and middle class and, at key points, being committed to pushing forward toward health equity and justice. As someone who had lost family members due to a lack of health access and witnessed firsthand its impact on communities and groups who lived on the margins, with limited access, for generations, I understood the need for at-risk communities to be at the table when decisions about their very existence were being made.

Chapter 8: Trump's Regional Directors

Republican Party

political party, United States [1854-present]

"The term Republican was adopted in 1792 by supporters of Thomas Jefferson, who favored a decentralized government with limited powers. Although Jefferson's political philosophy is consistent with the outlook of the modern Republican Party, his faction, which soon became known as the Democratic-Republican Party, ironically evolved by the 1830s into the Democratic Party, the modern Republican Party's chief rival."[112]

I honestly believe that each of the three Republican appointees I worked for under Trump, Renee Ellmers, a former North Carolina congresswoman; John McGough, former chief-of-staff for Maine Governor Paul LePage; and April Weaver, a former state senator from Alabama, were compassionate people. Except for one, all the regional directors I've worked for during my 25 years have had an obvious area of passion and focus.

For Ellmers, a nurse, it was telehealth. Ellmers, who told her staff she pushed for a focus on telehealth at every opportunity with IEA leadership and in meetings with her RD colleagues, all men, was frustrated and marginalized in her position. Her fight for a focus on telehealth made real sense due to the dozens of states that were primarily rural and losing hospitals each year, including six of the eight in our region.[113] Had her suggestions been heeded, HHS and the nation would have been much more prepared to treat the poor, elderly, fragile, and those in rural areas with limited transportation when COVID-19 emerged.

McGough's focus was opioids and other substance use disorders (SUDs), along with programs that empowered at-risk families. The most prolific and driven RD I ever worked for, McGough prided himself on being in his home region of New Hampshire, Vermont, Connecticut, and Massachusetts, and then in our massive eight-state region when he took over as acting RD. He always wanted to be, and was, first in the nation in building out and orchestrating the substantial meetings that the Trump administration wanted to hear were taking place in the regions.

For my colleagues, Natalia, who ran the office as our executive officer, and Karen, who managed the calendar, it was a hell of a lot of work; but we always wanted to show anyone we worked for that we could produce an excellent product and meet their standard, however high it was. For McGough, we met with every major city health director, all the state pharmacy association executive directors, and Dr. Penny Shelton, executive director of the North Carolina Association of Pharmacists. We also visited and conferred with dozens of the top organizations that focused on SUD treatment, as well as hundreds of other key organizations in the HHS focus areas. When we spoke to the pharmacists, we used the Trump talking points, including one that said that for the first time in 40 years, the retail price of prescription drugs fell in 2018 and that average Medicare Part D basic premiums had decreased for the last three years by 13.5%.

April Weaver, who focused on the health of mothers and the unborn, as well as youth and drugs, alcohol, and tobacco, was nearly as driven to make her mark as McGough. Weaver, like Ellmers, was an attractive blonde whom we worked with for an entire year, yet I never met her in person, due to COVID. A typical week working with her, as well as for the other regional directors, consisted of setting up interviews with subject matter experts (SMEs) who focused on HHS priority areas. For instance, during the week of August 10, 2020, our weekly report included a Zoom meeting with Dr. Veda Johnson, director of the Partners for Equity in Child and Adolescent Health, Dept. of Pediatrics, for the Emory University School of Medicine. This meeting focused on their efforts around outreach, innovations, pilot waivers, and flexibilities. Another August 18, 2020, meeting with DePriest Waddy, CEO of the Community Foundation for Northeast Georgia, and Julio Carrillo, chief of staff, and Paula Moody, senior director of Families First, was held to share news of Trump's executive order designed to strengthen America's outcome for children and families in the foster care and adoption systems. Waddy and staff shared how community partners were doing strong work in the areas of child welfare, foster care, adoption, and residential care, which IEA needed to share on a broader scale. Another meeting I set up for the following day was with Meredith Peffley, executive director of CrossRoads, a sexual assault response and resource center in Burlington, North Carolina. Peffley shared her CBO's (Community-Based Organization) efforts to combat human trafficking in the southeast. CrossRoads has served child and adult survivors of sexual assault, abuse, and human trafficking through confidential counseling, advocacy, child medical treatment, education, and community awareness since 1976.

  The following day, we met with Glen Cassel, president and CEO of Florida's Embrace Families, again to share news about Trump's executive order with dozens of entities, though they were overwhelmingly conservative. Embrace Families, based in Orange County, Florida, is the region's largest non-profit organization serving children and families in Orange, Osceola, and Seminole counties. My regular work largely focused on outreach, vetting, and setting up these meetings on a weekly basis, as well as monitoring what governors and mayors had to say about the federal responsiveness to COVID-19, including testing, vaccine availability, supply chain issues, etc. Cultural competence, and where testing and vaccination sites were located, were also a high priority in assessments. I also monitored and reported media response, HHS's role in caring for children at UAC centers, as well as general inquiries from consumers, the media, and federal (senators, congressional), state (governors), and local (county commissioners, mayors, state reps, and senators). On July 20, I scheduled a meeting for RD Weaver and our staff with Larry Lehman, president and CEO, and Joey Helton, COO of Positive Impact Health Centers based in Atlanta. We shared the secretary's priorities, especially as they pertained to HIV/AIDs, telehealth, and mental health issues, while hearing from them about emerging trends, challenges, and best practices. Dr. Sharon Weissman, a clinical professor of internal medicine and the chief of Infectious Diseases at the University of South Carolina School of Medicine in Columbia, was our featured guest on July 20th. She shared information about their efforts to fight HIV/AIDS.

Laurie Stern, ED of Bethany Christian Services in Florida, was our briefing guest on July 31, 2020, followed by Lindsey Simmons, ED of Mississippians Against Human Trafficking. Simmons shared with Weaver and her team how 90% of trafficking cases begin on the internet with children in poverty, foster care, and the homeless as prime targets for sex traffickers. The following day, August 4, we also met with Pam Strickland, founder of NC Stop Human Trafficking, to learn more about the strategies for fighting the horrible crime against humanity in the Southeast. We also met with Amna Osman, CEO of Nashville Cares, the city's largest safety net for a broad range of CBOs or Community-Based Organizations.

Ellmers, who was appointed by her former colleague, then-Secretary Tom Price, was an ardent and vocal supporter of Trump, as well as a staunch anti-ACA critic. Meanwhile, McGough, whom I traveled with on occasion to Tennessee and Alabama, was a firm believer in Republican principles, yet, said very little about Trump, leaving me to believe he was not a big supporter of the man. My opinion was the same regarding Weaver, who, like McGough, was a demanding, effective leader who knew her job and was outstanding at it. Ellmers, on the other hand, was probably the best communicator and most seasoned media spokesperson of all the first RD's appointed by Trump. She was hired in May of 2017, but being the lone HHS female RD, was routinely dismissed by the good ole boy club. Quickly tiring of the circus that was being orchestrated by HHS leadership and not being allowed to do what she did best, while her prophetic pleas to ramp up telehealth were pushed to the side, she left HHS at the end of 2019.

The Special Enrollment Period (SEP) was hugely important to the 69 counties assigned as disaster areas in October 2020. Due to the widespread destruction and deep disruption of the ACA consumers' ability to access services and see and meet with enrollment assisters (navigators and certified application counselors), CMS had extended the health marketplace insurance place enrollment period an additional 60 days through February 20, 2019. During that period, Kathleen Conners of Georgia Health and Refugee Mental Health made numerous trips to South Georgia, organizing community partners and staging enrollment and educational events.

My forte was tapping into existing partners and striving to create new ones, largely in minority and at-risk communities, which could open doors, host events, or connect us to people who could. Most of my success was attributed to valuing and cultivating those treasured relationships, and certainly not my extraordinary abilities. On this particular trip, I reached out to Frank Wilson, then the interim executive director of the Albany Civil Rights Institute, which told the powerful story of the Albany Movement, which was fueled by students, SNCC, and directed by SNCC's Charles Sherrod, Cordell Reagon, local NAACP leader Dr. William Anderson and others. In Albany, a federal courthouse was named after the unrelenting leader, C.B. King. Albany, Georgia, was ultimately the first city where the tried-and-true methods of utilizing non-violent civil disobedience to fill the jails and frustrate racist southern sheriffs by provoking them to perform "un-American" acts against innocent, unarmed Black citizens, had a minimal effect. That's because Sheriff Laurie Pritchett had an effective plan to both arrest and house the dissidents, while keeping southern de facto Jim Crow justice more humane than in Birmingham, Selma, St. Augustine, and elsewhere.

Thanks to Wilson, the marvelous connections provided by his pastor, and other key leaders who continued to point us toward other key Black leaders who understood the importance of health equity and justice, the campaign turned out to be tremendously successful. It was yet another example of why it is critically important in my business, which is largely media, community, and governmental relations, to connect with the right people with a posture of humility and a purity of purpose to achieve a common goal.

Chapter 9: Unequal Injustice

"I saw a black person standing at my door. I screamed at him and asked him what he was doing there. He told me he was going to school."

Trump had vowed during his presidential campaign to appoint conservative judges, and he did. As the controversy raged over Supreme Court nominee Brett Kavanaugh's rowdy, youthful past, Trump spoke of the trepidation of being a young man in America, though most of us believed he meant a young white man.

"I think it is a very scary time for young men in America when you may be guilty of something that you may not be guilty of," said Trump, three days before the projected vote on the Kavanaugh investigation.[114] Limbaugh, Donald Trump, Jr., Laura Ingraham, Tucker Carlson, and Sean Hannity agreed, apparently, as they ardently defended Kavanaugh, at that point, a potential swing vote on the U.S. Supreme Court. The president said he hoped for a "positive" vote in the Senate that week for Kavanaugh, as he sought to fulfill his promise of putting conservative judges on the Supreme Court, but it will "be dependent on what comes back for the FBI."

Where the hell was all this Trump outrage when Black men were being gunned down at police stops, choked out while selling singles, playing their music at gas stations, defending themselves from overzealous community watchmen, or shot three times by a cop while minding his own business in his own apartment? Deathly silent, that's what he was. Yet in 1989, when five Black and Latino youth were rounded up and charged with the brutal assault of a white female jogger in Central Park, Trump quickly called for the death penalty. If a privileged, highly educated, and cavalier attorney like Kavanaugh, accused of sexual assault by a well-respected white woman, Professor Christine Blasey Ford, should see the world as "scary," what could be the hope of young Black and brown men, already viewed and treated with suspicion, as they lived their everyday lives?

Raymond Santana, one of the five Black boys arrested for a brutal rape they didn't commit in Central Park, reflected on his pain. "When I saw what he [Trump] said – the first thing that came to my mind was he didn't have that same energy for us," Santana told the *Atlanta Journal-Constitution*. "We didn't get that type of benefit. We were fourteen, fifteen-year-old kids, and you calling for the death penalty? We have been telling you that this dude is full of [expletive]. Now people seeing it."[115]

Clearly, I was in a deep funk of my own, asleep at the wheel at this time to not realize or remember the wretched, racist attack Trump's ad used to condemn those boys.[116]

Dana Barrett, a radio host on WSB in Atlanta, said she was "embarrassed" that Donald Trump was her president after his comments that this is now a "dangerous time in this nation for young men," following Dr. Christine Blasey Ford's charges that a drunk Judge Brett Kavanaugh assaulted her when they were teens.

"Give me a fricking break," groaned Barrett, commenting on Trump's "scary time for men [meaning white men] in America" statement.

I guarantee you that not once – not a single time – did Trump's father, or Trump and the mother of sons Eric and Don Jr., or Trump and Melania *ever* have to warn their sons as they headed out the door about how to act when a policeman pulled them over for anything. Never did they have to caution their sons to be polite, calm, respectful, and even subservient when stopped by cops for questionable reasons, or none at all. No, the danger was and is not for young white men in America, but it continues to be for Black men in America. Just ask the families of Philando Castile, Botham Jean, Ronald Greene, Elijah McClain, Terence Crutcher, Daunte Wright, George Floyd, Ahmaud Arbery, and hundreds of others, and some Black women, including Breonna Taylor and Sandra Bland. Did their parents have the same talks we had with our sons as they reached their teen years? Perhaps a better question is, why do Black and brown families have to add such cautionary layers to the protection of their children and loved ones as they try to stay alive in an imbalanced society where code-switching and navigating an often-hostile environment outside the dominant culture already is fraught with a multitude of inherent risks? So no, Donald Trump, we don't feel sorry for young white men. You, sir, were simply stoking more fear because a society that has ruled for 400 years was grudgingly coming to grips with the fact that power and influence must be shared in a society that was becoming more multicultural by the year. Instead, feel compassion for the families of the more than 150 unarmed Black people killed by police since 2015.[117]

*

    In Marietta, Georgia, a white woman noticed a Black man in a car with two white children sitting in the back. The "graciously" unidentified white woman called the police so they could check on the kids by asking the ten-year-old white girl if she really knew the Black man driving her and the other child around. She asked the dispatcher, after the police came, whether she should follow the car with the Black man.

It turned out that the Black man, named Corey Lewis, ran an afterschool program and served as a mentor to the two white kids, as well as others. The woman followed Lewis's car, despite the fact that the children were clearly laughing and relaxed as they left a Subway and then stopped at a gas station. Corey Lewis later said he had "a funny feeling" as she followed him home.[118] Though advised by the police dispatcher not to follow him, she did anyway, ala George Zimmerman, the slayer of Trayvon Martin. "This is 2018, and this is what I have to deal with. I cannot go out with two kids who do not look like me without something being weird," said Lewis, 27, so frustrated he started taping the "engagement" for Facebook and drove to his nearby mother's house with the children out of a sense of self-protection.[119]

Once contacted, the white father, David Parker, told the embarrassed officer, "We think the world of [Lewis]; we are so comfortable with him. Part of his mission is to have a diverse class. That helps kids grow up and not see that division."[120]

So, as a Black parent, I can't teach my child to ask for directions or help when lost or confused, right?

That's the case of a 14-year-old in Michigan, Brennan Walker, who, when lost, went to a stranger's door in Rochester Hills, Michigan, carrying only a book bag. The homeowner, a white man shirtless, came to the door with a shotgun, and the terrified boy took off running for his life as the white man took aim and fired. His wife said she shouted in alarm to her husband because "I saw a black person standing at my door. I screamed at him and asked him what he was doing there. He told me he was going to school."[121]

Ziegler, the homeowner, said he tripped, making the weapon fire, but was called a liar by the local sheriff, who said Ziegler clearly aimed his shotgun at the terrified, fleeing teen. The surveillance video at Jeffrey Ziegler's house proved he was lying.

"That's simply unacceptable on any level," said Oakland County Sheriff Mike Bouchard. Thank God, both for authorities who seek to do the right thing, and for video cameras.

As edgy comedian Chris Rock famously said, these racist assaults didn't just begin or amp up. They're just being filmed now. Ziegler, a retired firefighter, is being charged with intent to murder.[122] If we pay attention, we can find dozens of racist incidents of what I call white pomposity perpetrated on the Black community daily.

Hilary Brooke Mueller, who stalked a Black resident because she didn't believe he really lived in the same upscale St. Louis apartment as she did, blocked business owner D'Arreion Toles's entrance into the inner sanctum of the building, despite the fact that he showed her his key. After respectfully speaking to her for a few minutes (while videotaping), he pushed his way past. Undeterred, she and her dog followed him into the elevator all the way to his apartment. Finally, after he again showed her his key and entered the apartment, she proceeded to call the police. After reviewing the video, her employer, Tribeca STL, ironically a minority-owned firm, fired Mueller, saying: "The Tribeca-St. Louis firm is a minority-led company that consists of employees and residents from many racial backgrounds. We are proud of this fact and do not and never will stand for racism, or racial profiling at our company." To Toles's credit, he did not gloat, telling media sources he hopes Mueller is left alone and not harassed.[123]

A few days later, a Black father – apparently yelling instructions to his son during a soccer game outside of Tampa – was sent packing from the park by a monitor who thought he was yelling at a ref and "behaving badly." When other parents backed the Black dad, and insisted he was shouting to his child – not criticizing the refs – they, too, were kicked out of the park by the lady labeled "Golf Cart Gail."[124]

"This man was simply trying to watch his son's soccer game and cheer for him from the sides," Ginger Williams, who is also white, wrote in a Facebook post. "He yelled 'The ref is right!' when he saw his kid out there getting frustrated after a call."

When I hear these stories – and this is just a small sample – on a weekly, if not more often, basis, what am I to tell my children and grandchildren? How can I put a positive light on how you are judged or assessed – regardless of your education, level of success, aptitude, or attitude, or what kind of situation you emerged from while growing up Black in America?

Is there any wonder that there is such a high incidence of high blood pressure, mental illness, domestic violence, drug and alcohol abuse, violence, and predatory behavior, when a significant percentage of the broader society sees you as lesser than the "Other," and by default, less than human? Should I go on? Please don't make me. Trump certainly didn't personally execute any of these grievous assaults on the dignity and humanity of Black people. He did, however, absolutely fan the flames of white racial supremacy that empowered dozens of white and would-be white Americans to demonstrate and perpetrate white pomposity toward people of color with little concern for accountability, or retribution.

Republicans were once the party of both Lincoln and the emerging African American population in the United

States. This was during the era of the Dixiecrats, the ardent Southern groundswell of white segregationists who strained to hold fast to an iron domination of the Jim Crow South. Founded in 1948, Richard Russell of Georgia, Jim Eastman of Mississippi, and Strom Thurmond of South Carolina were all key segregationist leaders of the Dixiecrats.[125] And while the right-wing Democrat splinter group is officially gone, Alabama Governor Kay Wallace, Georgia Governor Brian Kemp, Arkansas Governor Sarah Sanders, Mississippi Governor Trent Lott, Florida Governor Ron DeSantis, South Carolina Governor Henry McMaster, Tennessee Governor Bill Lee, and Texas Governor Greg Abbott all exemplify tenets of states' rights/Dixiecrat tradition, stifling the life chances of Black and brown people with restrictive voting laws, harsh immigration policies, or refusing to expand Medicaid to provide healthcare for the working poor. These positions and policies were all encouraged and personified, if not spearheaded, by Commander-in-Chief Trump.[126] Many of these states, including the governors and mostly allied state legislatures we worked with, were largely in lockstep with the administration on policy and purpose.

Megyn Kelly is attractive and well-spoken, but she also reeks of white privilege and is too stupid to know when she's shoved her foot halfway down her throat. Why do I say that? Once AGAIN, in the fall of 2018, she was tightly wrapped in a controversy of her own making. This time, she asked, "What's wrong with blackface? I did it all the time when I was a kid," much to the horror of the on-air guests she was interviewing.[127] If this was a single faux pas, it might possibly be dismissed or explained away. However, this is the same Megyn Kelly who famously proclaimed that beyond any shadow of a doubt, "Santa is white," and "Jesus is white."[128] Such viewpoints are important because they are patently racist and another classic example of white pomposity, casually promoted by a national media personality. No longer on highly conservative, largely white-viewed FOX, Kelly got a fresh start on NBC, which sports a highly-diverse audience and the only Black evening news anchor, Lester Holt, of the "big three" (ABC, CBS, NBC). If I, or my child or grandchild, happen to hear Kelly insist that Santa, or even more critically, Jesus, whose doctrine says "God is no respecter of persons," is white … if everyone or everything considered wholesome or "American" is white … what am I or people who look like me supposed to feel about our worth or value? In other words, what is Black America to think if you consistently proclaim that defaming and denigrating people of color is okay if done in jest, and it's perfectly fine for a national media figure to proclaim that the fat dude who brings good tide at Christmas and the man whose life we celebrate on that same day, the Savior of the world, HAVE to BE WHITE? Kelly did apologize, and it sounded legit. What wasn't was her fawning audience giving her a standing ovation for her disgusting display of hoof-and-mouth disease.

"She owes a bigger apology to folks of color around the country," said co-worker and veteran Black weatherman Al Roker. "Because this is a history, going back to the 1830s, minstrel shows, that denigrates a people."[129] Damn skippy, Al. And many of us appreciate your calling out a longtime colleague who should know better than to promote racist tropes.

Iowa Congressman Steve King says he sees nothing wrong with white nationalism, even though he lives in one of the most diverse nations on the planet. King also proclaims that if there is a culture war, the "red states have eight billion bullets, while people in the blue states will be trying to figure out where the bathroom is."[130] Though terrifyingly sad, his statement has, time and time again, rung true.

I'm a man of faith, though deeply flawed. But how in God's name does Trump, who says he goes to church once a year, have his Secretary of State, Mike Pompeo, who rarely ever holds a press conference, call one, and restrict participants, *exclusively,* to those who represent faith publications and outlets? Whatever happened to of the people, by the people, and for the people? Or separation of church and state? A good friend of mine, Tony Renfrow, always says, "Who does that make sense to?" If every president who ever had a beef with the press determined who could attend press events based on whether POTUS was on good terms with them, or feuding, the long-held amendment of freedom of the press would be irrelevant.

Clearly, without question, those of the Jewish faith are also under attack, statistically, even more than African Americans and other people of color. If anyone ever fails to remember that, they need only turn to the horrors of October 27, 2018, when James Borders barged into the Tree of Life in Squirrel Hill, a quaint Pittsburgh neighborhood. Armed with an assault weapon and three Glocks; the crazed, 46-year-old white terrorist, shouting "Kill all Jews," slaughtered 11 worshippers. The victims, ages 56-97, never knew what hit them. Along the way, four police responders were also wounded. This terroristic assault – yes, undeniably a terroristic assault – was once again carried out by a white man, much like the hate-filled young man Dylann Roof, who casually entered a Bible study at historic Mother Emanuel Baptist Church in Charleston and gunned down nine.[131] "I wish with a passion that n_____s were treated terribly throughout history by Whites, that every White person had an ancestor who owned slaves," Roof wrote on his website, TheLastRhodesian.com. Devin Kelley, only 26, gunned down 26 worshippers on a fall Sunday morning in the First Baptist Church in Sutherland Springs, deep in the heart of Texas. Victims, including eight in one family, ranged in age from 18 months to 77 years.[132] The carnage at a Walmart on the U.S.-Mexican border in El Paso, Texas – one of three mass shootings in this country in a span of days – was directly aimed at Latinos and fanned by the racist rhetoric of Trump. The challenge, to me, is that all of these were carried out by white men. Hell, we need to worry a lot less about the Abdullahs and Jamals of this world than the homegrown terrorists we are raising in white America. As a friend of mine from Colorado often says, half-jokingly, we need to place a chip in the head of every white boy born so we know where they are and what they are doing.

Chapter 10: Voter Suppression

"We want a change in this society in America because, you see, we can no longer ignore the facts."
Fannie Lou Hamer

In case anyone may be unaware, voter suppression in the United States of America is nothing new. In fact, it is as old and "American" as mom, the flag, and apple pie. This is why, as we moved toward the 2022 mid-terms, all Americans should have been mortified that over 50 Republican electors – including at least 10 that attended the January 6th insurrection speeches – were being supported by Trump.

Black people reached their numerical zenith in the late 1700s when 20 percent of the population was African American, principally, of course, slaves. That was consistent from about 1760 through 1790.[133] The three-fifths compromise of 1783 allowed southern states with robust populations to count every three of five slaves in order to have more "people" and thus garner more seats in Congress, even though those "people," then called Negroes, did not have the right to vote. So, how hypocritical is that? They used Black people to inflate their numbers, but gave them no voice or vote; in fact, they used the slaves to boost their profits and build their fortunes. That's because Black folk, who far outnumbered the white southerners who owned them, were considered property.[134]

Later, during the period following the Civil War known as Reconstruction, Blacks were elected to roughly

2,000 positions, including the U.S. Senate. Unhappy with the progress of Black people recently freed from slavery following the Civil War, President Andrew Johnson imposed the restrictive "black codes," which stifled Black progress and looked the other way while states sought to clamp down on recently earned gains.[135] Emoting shades of Donald Trump, Andrew Johnson took America to a new low just a few years after its fresh start dictated by the Emancipation Proclamation in 1863 and the dawning of a new society.[136] Disdained even by his own party for the regressive and repugnant acts he perpetrated – *publicly* starkly different from Trump – Johnson was impeached in 1868 for "high crimes and misdemeanors."[137]

Fast forward to the 1920s. This period was known as the previously mentioned Nadir, which meant the dark ages in Black American history.

In the early 1960s, just after the March on Washington, desperate to get Black people who had been disenfranchised for two centuries registered to vote and take another step forward toward full citizenship, Freedom Summer, an expansive, dangerous, unprecedented campaign, was launched in June of 1964 to register as many Blacks as possible in Mississippi, perhaps the most racially oppressed state in the deep South. Aaron Henry, Lawrence Guyot, and Amzie Moore were among the local leaders who had lived through a lifetime of Jim Crow reality, while knowing their forefathers and mothers had been oppressed for generations untold. A meteor in her life's witness, a consummate organizer and sharecropper, Fannie Lou Hamer served as co-founder of the Mississippi Freedom Party. Hamer, a robust Black woman, was beaten with a blackjack by police while jailed and also given a hysterectomy without her permission by a white doctor in 1961, a routine atrocity commonly referred to as a "Mississippi appendectomy."[138] When first trying to vote in 1964 after being threatened and then fired for standing in line to register, Ms. Hamer eventually passed the literacy test after three tries, and 16 bullets were shot into her home to deter her from voting.[139] The two coordinating organizations of Freedom Summer, COFO (Council of Federated Organizations), and SNCC (Student Nonviolent Coordinating Committee), were largely led by Bob Moses, Hollis Watkins, and SNCC Project Director Unita Blackwell. Moses, who had earned a master's degree from Harvard in 1956, served as field secretary of SNCC. Born in Harlem, New York, Bob Moses would later found the Algebra Project. Blackwell, who lived on a plantation in Lula, Mississippi, in her early years, would become the first Black female mayor in Mississippi when she was elected to lead Meyersville in 1976.

Fast forward again, this time to 2018, two years after the election of Trump. In Dodge City, Kansas, which is not a big town, but one with a significant Latino population, the polling place for most of the Latino voters was suddenly moved several miles outside of town. Who was the secretary of state for Kansas? None other than Chris Kobach, who led Trump's ill-fated effort to declare, then prove, that millions of Americans had voted illegally during the 2016 election, which he actually won, though not, I must point out, without the help of Russian interference via social media, WikiLeaks, stolen polling data from the Clinton campaign, and God only knows what else.

In Georgia, my home state, just like in neighboring Florida, 2016 provided many with the hope that America would elect its first African American governor during what would prove to be a stinging referendum on Trump, who had restructured the American landscape in ways few could have imagined in less than two, helter-skelter, roller coaster years. One of the most egregious images was of Governor Kemp and an inner circle of all (but one) white legislators standing in front of a photo of a plantation, right after they passed more repressive voting laws, after barring a Black legislator from entering the room.[140] Georgia State Rep. Park Cannon, a Black Democrat, was arrested the same day, seeking access to the room to find out what was going on.

Along with Andrew Gillum, the charismatic mayor of Tallahassee whose campaign was later sunk due to personal credibility issues, Stacey Abrams, the leader of the Georgia House of Representatives for six years, was the Democrat standard-bearer in the 2016 election. I didn't know Abrams personally, but I had worked extensively with her staff for the first three years of the ACA or ObamaCare. My job, as the point person for Mississippi, Alabama, South Carolina and, in this case, Georgia, was to help secure presenters who could explain the who, what, when, where, and why of the health insurance marketplace, including who was eligible and what enrolling should cost them. Abrams's office, because of its penetration into the state's deep pockets of unregistered voters, was consistently reaching out to obtain speakers. Working with Dante McKay and his outstanding team at Enroll America, conducting phone banks, scheduling speakers, promoting campaigns and events, and scheduling one-on-one enrollment appointments for navigators and CACs, helped keep us jumping and busy. Weekly, during our enrollment assister calls, we would share needs for presenters in cities like Augusta, Columbus, Riverdale, Marietta, Snellville, Decatur, or Conyers.

Abrams, a respected leader, attorney, author, and visionary, had experienced some personal tax issues, yet voiced a clarion call for expanding Medicaid and the need for access to healthcare for all Georgians. Speaking in a clear, defiant voice, Abrams drew a "line in the sand" distinction between herself and opponent Brian Kemp. Like Kobach of Kansas, Kemp had refused to resign his office as Secretary of State before running for governor. Abrams made it clear that she opposed arduous and discriminatory immigration policies, voter suppression, and the state's steadfast refusal to expand Medicaid to its working disabled and working poor who made less than $11,800 per individual.

Trump, in many ways the least equipped to determine who was qualified and credible than any president, at least in modern U.S. history, couldn't help but jump in to influence what was shaping up to be razor-thin elections in Florida and Georgia.

Trump on Abrams: "She's not qualified to be the governor of Georgia," said Trump, who frequently repeated himself. "She's not qualified," he proclaimed of the successful businesswoman, minority leader for six years, and tax attorney with a Yale education.[141]

Her opponent, Brian Kemp, was elected governor in a highly contested election where thousands of votes were disallowed, and Kemp, who refused to step down as attorney general, the office that oversees voting, won in the closest gubernatorial election in Georgia history. In the two years leading up to the 2018 election, Kemp oversaw the removal of nearly 800,000 Georgians from the voting rolls because they had moved, or not voted in years. That's 11 percent of the state, ranking as the eighth biggest percent in the nation. At the same time, a robust 900,000 new Georgian registrations were recorded, marking a 14 percent increase over 2016.[142] The judicial system expressed concern over Kemp's oversight of the process. In fact, "two federal judges found him derelict in his duties and forced him to allow absentee ballots to be counted and those who are captured by the exact match system to be allowed to vote," said Abrams.[143]

Alas, unfortunately, it is indeed as Lenin proclaimed: It's not who votes that counts, it's who counts the votes."[144]

Later, Joy Reid of MSNBC's AM Joy called Kemp the man who "virtually pickpocketed 'Jim Crow.'"

So, for me as an African American, joined by hundreds of thousands of Anglos, Latinos, Asians, and white progressives, we had no choice but to feel cheated out of the opportunity to elect Georgia's first minority governor, one who wasn't promoting rounding up all the "illegal aliens" from Mexico and who wanted to expand Medicaid for the 300,000 Georgians who would become eligible with the simple stroke of a pen. Yes, expanding Medicaid – again, exactly what Obama envisioned when he fought for and signed the ACA into existence – would cost the state $300 million dollars over ten years. But that's a far cry from the $1.75 billion a year the state spends on uncompensated care when the uninsured show up at the emergency room because they have no access to preventative care and frequently wait until their situation is dire before going to see a doctor. The argument for expansion doesn't even include the thousands of jobs that would be created by the expansion of Medicaid, which would certainly fortify the state's coffers. The same argument could be made for Florida, North Carolina, South Carolina, Mississippi, Tennessee, and Alabama, all of which refused to expand Medicaid, yet struggled mightily to care for their uninsured. I love and respect what Republican governor John Kasich, one of several who did expand Medicaid for the 800,000 uninsured in Ohio, said: Saint Peter is "probably not gonna ask you much about what you did about keeping government small, but he's going to ask you what you did for the poor."[145]

Obama, the most hated Black man in American history – likely followed by O.J. Simpson – wanted to expand Medicaid, which would have cost Georgia about $35 million per year to provide healthcare for 500,000 people. Georgia, it is worth noting, would have brought in $1.5

billion over the same decade in new revenue.[146] Not only was expanding Medicaid an economic win for the state, it would have generated thousands more jobs. Why not make a "no-brainer" decision? ... Because it would benefit Black, brown, and the working poor people. Plain and simple. It was all about politics, as it was in almost every state that refused to expand.

billion over the same decade in new revenue[?]... Not only was expanding A[merican] an economic win for the state, it would have generated thousands more jobs. Why not make the same decision? ... Because it would benefit Black brown and the working poor people. Plain and simple. It was all about politics ... it was the minority community that refused to expand.

Chapter 11: The Donald Disconnect: Don't Piss on Me and Tell Me It's Raining

"Who's going to pay for the wall? Mexico!"
President Donald Trump

This is where Donald Trump doesn't get it. As a particular type of Black man in America – and I'm sure this sentiment is shared by many Latinos, Native Americans, immigrants, women, the LGBTQ community, etc. – I don't give a damn how strong the economy is, what kind of deals you're creating, how much progress you're making in pushing China to stop stealing our intellectual secrets and manipulating the currency. Granted, those are important issues, but I've struggled for most of my life. What I *do* care about is who you are bullying, who you are castigating as the enemy and deeming less an American than you, and how you denigrate the office of the presidency and run roughshod over the emoluments clause. In fact, if you can't treat me with respect, speak of me, and see me as an equal, not the "Other" – I will forever find you and your regime vile, repugnant, white supremacist, and racist. You, Mr. President, epitomize white pomposity, but your devoted followers and some of their loved ones are not far behind.

Take, for example, the mother of Jacob Chansley, infamously known as the QAnon Shaman, who was sentenced to 41 months for his role in breaking into the U.S. Capitol on January 6th. Martha, Chansley's mother, said her son wouldn't eat in prison because he's "used to eating organic food."[147] Chansley, the bare-chested, horned man with the spear who left a threatening note for VP Pence and sat in the Speaker of the House's chair in the Congressional chambers, was soon moved to a prison that would honor his organic diet. If my ass – or anybody Black or brown – was in prison for my role in an insurrection, do you think I'd be given a special diet?

NO one who consistently insults the people who inspire me, the people who have risen to high levels of service and humanity, or even those who are just trying to make their way in the world is anyone I can possibly trust, partner with, or frankly, proudly follow.

I'll admit it – something I'm doing quite a bit of during this treatise – I never, in my wildest nightmares, believed that America could regress to where it has under Donald J. Trump. I knew it could – and was part of a cadre of folk crying in the wilderness, warning that failure to move forward, inevitably, meant moving backward; yet, I believed that we were beyond this – that the 20th-century regressive politics of Strom Thurmond, Joe McCarthy, George Wallace, and David Duke were in our rearview mirror. Boy, was I ever wrong!

Trump is a fear-mongering opportunist. Does he believe the things he says? Probably not. Does he know that they are effective? Damn skippy, he does. All he has to do is draw on just enough of the hegemonic, white supremacist belief that – in this case – the immigrants, the Mexicans, and all those rapists and "very bad people" from Central America, including M-16 – are en route to America to do the sanctity of the white European race no good; in fact, to kill, rape and take, while earning citizenship illegally. Never mind that his own wife, Melania, is the benefactor of the very chain migration policy he sees as a destructive bane to America.[148] Or the fact that the father of his own son-in-law, Jared, was brought here to the U.S., sponsored and cared for by the very Jewish synagogue that saw 11 worshippers slaughtered by a white racist shooter encouraged by Trump's divisive words and dogma.[149] But hey, they're good white people, which makes it okay, right?

If – and that's a big caveat – America is who it proclaims itself to be, there's never a good or acceptable reason to deny, inhibit, intimidate, or impede eligible citizens the right to vote. ... Period. Non-negotiable.

Tell that to officials across the country, including in Fulton County, the home of Atlanta, the "city too busy to hate,"[150] and Dougherty County, where Dr. King's Albany movement was baffled by a shrewd sheriff and fifty-five years later, had to have a judge rule that it must count all of its citizens' votes.[151]

Racism is insidious in this country. Admittedly, it is so ingrained in the body politic that some white people – and those who see themselves as white, or who want to be – can casually and routinely do and say things that are racist, whether intentional or not. Take the promotion in Dorchester, a community in Boston that certainly has had a historically racist past. There, in 2018, the Dorchester Historical Society, of all organizations, produced a promo proclaiming, "we're wishing for a white Christmas." Keep in mind white Christmases in Massachusetts are about as common as hot Augusts in Alabama. You certainly don't need to wish for them. So, was the message a veiled exclusionary missive, or simply recklessly thoughtless?[152] In the era of Donald Trump, where whites are losing their centuries-old position as a racial majority, these issues and instances must be questioned. Conversely, simply existing and being respected as a human being on equal footing with everyone, is something far too many BIPOC people can't routinely expect, or experience.

AT&T, the nation's largest telephone company at the time, committed an equally egregious racist trope in 1993.

The company's internal magazine included people from every continent utilizing AT&T's superior services to communicate across the globe. The problem was that the "caller" representing the African continent, happened to be a gorilla, sparking a barrage of outrage over what the company ultimately called a "racist illustration."[153]

AT&T sent an apology for the racist depiction following a firestorm by numerous civil rights groups, including the one I worked for, Dr. King's SCLC, even though the cartoonist, who was later fired, said everything had been blown out of proportion, insisting he "didn't mean to hurt anyone." The company, in which 15% of its U.S. employees were Black, wrote this to its employees: "The editors of *Focus* magazine apologize to our readers and, in particular, to people of color, for an illustration that perpetuates racial stereotypes."[154] Sadly, almost 30 years later, little had changed in terms of corporate callousness, fueled by the racist rants of Commander-in-Chief Trump.

A young rising professional media man I had a lot of respect for, Royal Marshall, the producer for conservative WSB-radio juggernaut Neal Boortz, who I believe was grappling with his role and allegiances just before he unexpectedly died in 2011, used to say, when he had an epiphany, "Just damn!" As I continued to watch the unraveling of the Trump administration and the Mueller probe, the Saudi Arabia Jamal Khashoggi debacle, and Trump's continual affirmations of being a "tariff man" as the stock market careened up and down like a yo-yo, I said, "Just damn!" And still, "Teflon Don" once again slipped through the criminal nets, apparently because special prosecutor Mueller felt constrained by the FBI's guidance that sitting presidents should not be eligible for prosecution.

*

"Who's going to pay for the wall? Mexico!" shouted Trump, with a smug, gleeful shout, as his faithful revelers then yelled in jubilance. Yeah, right. The great Elton John sang, "I'm still standing, yeah, yeah, yeah." Well, I'm still waiting, yeah, yeah, yeah! Biden, nearly three years into his first term as President, had sworn there would be no wall erected on the southern border in his administration. To his credit, with an unsustainable influx of thousands of immigrants pouring in every day – and frequently being shipped to Northern sanctuary cities like New York, D.C., and Chicago – Biden had the common sense to reverse course, in effect, admit he had been wrong, and bypass over a dozen federal laws to begin erecting a wall to stop the bleeding. Trump, as far as I can tell, has never acknowledged he was wrong about anything.

Wow! What a cultural flip. MSNBC's Lawrence O'Donnell, cool as the other side of the pillow, reviewed an incredible day which saw former Trump personal attorney Michael Cohen remark that "the revolution will be televised."[155] (For Black folk from my era, Gil Scott-Heron's powerful message *"The Revolution will not be Televised"* was a call to action and consciousness.)[156] Cohen, of course, was guilty of doing the dirty work for Trump and, ultimately, sent to prison for it. Compelling evidence tells us once again that if you're powerful enough, you orchestrate the crimes and bury the evidence, leaving the more vulnerable as collateral damage to take the fall.

Despite all efforts to destroy and disable the ACA, 2018 drew to a close, nearly two years into the Trump presidency, with 4.3 million having selected ObamaCare plans by December 14, 2018, and 4.6 million enrolling in 2017, according to the CDC. Yep, it's mighty difficult to take away a benefit once it's granted. The ACA, much like Social Security and Medicare, had become a part of the

American fabric, much to the chagrin of Trump and Secretary Alex Azar.

Nearly at the same time, on Friday, December 15, 2018, the ever-Trumpers and conservatives won, at least a temporary victory, as a Texas judge, U.S. District Court Judge Reed O'Connor, ruled the individual mandate – hated by Republicans and Libertarians – of the Affordable Care Act unconstitutional, opening the floodgates for a brutal battle that would end with all roads headed to the Supreme Court. While focused on the individual mandate, the Texas ruling put into question the health care of 20 million Americans. Overturning the law meant no cap on out-of-pocket costs, no insistence on ten essential health benefits, and children couldn't stay on parents' policy until age 26; all of those landmark tenets would be null and void.

Occasionally, I agreed with President Trump. One example is Trump's apparent pardon of Major Golsteyn for killing a Taliban bombmaker. Good damn riddance! We should find a way to punish China for manipulating currency and stealing our intellectual property, though not at the expense of all the farmers who feed us and much of the world. The progress his administration made with the bipartisan crime bill is commendable. The economy, for those of us who are solidly in the stock market, has been wonderful, though it simply has not benefited – just like the tax cut – middle America, or the working poor. I wish the positive list was longer, and unfortunately, I could have another birthday chronicling the negative list, not to mention the dozen-plus communities he has derided and disdained, most notably Latinos, women, Black people, women of color, major American cities, and virtually anyone who isn't a white male.

On March 26th, only days after the long-awaited Mueller report found no cause to indict Trump on charges of colluding with the Russians over the 2016 elections and could neither implicate nor exonerate Trump from charges of obstructing justice in the investigation of his possible involvement with Russia, Trump once again loudly proclaimed his innocence, while characteristically mislabeling, or lying, about the findings. Fresh off the heels of his "I-told-you-so" parade, where he crowed about his being officially cleared to anyone who would listen; he immediately turned his attention, once again, to attacking ObamaCare. Unable to leave well enough alone, he proclaimed war on the Affordable Care Act, even though concern over the lack of health care (or the threat to take it away) was the number one issue that dogged the GOP as an unprecedented number of women – including Muslim, Native American, Lesbian, and African American – drove the blue wave that swept the Dems back into control of the House. Unwilling to "let well enough alone," Trump called for the complete repeal of the ACA, despite the fact that nearly 13 million Americans had gained health insurance through Medicaid expansion, 2.3 million were able to stay on their parents' health insurance until age 26, and 52 million Americans with pre-existing conditions were able to gain insurance that previously was unattainable. Unbelievably, Trump and his colleagues, who had lied through their teeth publicly about protecting those with pre-existing conditions, while voting against it every time, still had the unmitigated gall to say, "I will always fight for and always protect patients with pre-existing conditions. The Republican party will soon be known as the party of health care."[157] Well, if indeed he had been proven to be right, and I mean no disrespect to the Jewish community here – it would be like Hitler deciding to protect the Jews during the Holocaust. Or, as my dear, departed mother-in-law used to say, "Don't piss on me and tell me it's raining."[158]

In December 2019, the 5th U.S. Circuit ruled the ACA's individual mandate, which taxed people who refused to buy health insurance, invalid, while leaving the rest of the law intact. The 2-1 ruling upheld the 2018 ruling of Texas-based U.S. Judge Reed O'Connor, who ruled the "individual mandate" was unconstitutional. In a preemptive move in 2017, Congress had already reduced the tax on people without insurance to zero.[159] At the same time, Trump moved forward to allow states to import brand-name meds from Canada, while working through wholesalers and pharmacists. They would include narcotics, biologic drugs, and insulin. Step two of his plan, directed by my boss, Secretary Alex Azar, included allowing drug companies to import drugs from any country, which was ambitious and forward-thinking but, in the end, not effective.[160]

Consistently emboldening and encouraging young white racist zealots, Trump tried his best to explain away the violence of Charlottesville, where white nationalists, shouting "Jews will not replace us," and chanting "Blood and soil," clashed with those who rejected their presence, and a young white woman was killed as a young white man barreled through a crowd in the middle of a major street.

"I don't like the fact that my daughter was the sacrifice. But sadly, it took a white girl dying before anybody paid attention to civil rights around here," said Susan Bro, Heather Heyer's mother, following the conviction of James Alex Fields, 21. "The civil rights battle has gone on for the black community for 400 years now, and we didn't pay attention."[161] Fields was a self-pronounced neo-Nazi who attended the Defend the Right march and rally in Charlottesville, where he plowed his car through a street full of counter-protesters, injuring 12 and killing Heyer.[162] Fields called Bro, who graciously expressed that she did not want Fields to receive the death penalty, a "communist and an anti-white supremacist."

What does this have to do with Trump? Unwilling to point the finger at the white supremacists, Trump instead fanned the racial fires saying, "There's blame on both sides and good people on both sides."[163] Rarely, if ever, did he unequivocally condemn white racists, while full-throatedly condemning brown immigrants, women overall, Black athletes, women journalists, politicians of color, and Blacks from African nations that he called "shithole" countries.

It was abundantly clear to me that Trump, who could be the big bad wolf from behind the curtain, or in the other room, preferred to throw the rock and hide the hand, rather than call a spade a spade. Constantly declaring ObamaCare, or the Affordable Care Act, the worst thing since World War II, Trump, who clearly had a hard-on to destroy President Obama's legacy, did everything possible from the time he took office right up until November 1, 2017, launch of the health insurance marketplace, to ensure that enrollment numbers were dismal, advertising was minimal, private insurance companies were scared away because of unstable markets, and federal help and contractors who had been a critical part of the safety net factor, were suddenly muted and grounded.

Chapter 12: UACs

"Undocumented immigrants contribute billions of dollars to our Social Security system that they themselves will never be able to collect. They contribute with their spending, and they contribute with the sweat of their labor."

Dolores Huerta

The federal government's Unaccompanied Children (UAC) is a classification of children designated by the Homeland Security Act of 2002. It involves the care of children under 18 who enter the country without their parents, and is operated by the Office of Refugee Resettlement (ORR), an agency of the HHS Administration for Children and Families (ACF). The program has since been renamed the UC program.[164]

The first time my office was involved with outreach involving unaccompanied children (UACs) was in alerting elected officials in and around Homestead, Florida, a Miami suburb, in March of 2018. It would not be the last. This was during year two of the Trump administration. These children, ranging in age from about six to 17, had traveled in some instances thousands of miles, sometimes as far away as from the "northern Triangle" of Central America, which included Honduras, El Salvador, and Guatemala, as well as Mexico. For some, the arduous, dangerous trip, littered with bugs, searing heat, dire thirst, and hunger, as well as eluding capture and human predators, could be as long as 1,000 miles. No one, it seems to me, would take such a perilous, dangerous journey unless their life at home was without hope, or a future.[165]

These children, and the parents, guardians, or whomever they traveled with, if they were lucky enough to get to the border, often were arrested trying to slip into the country, usually in south Texas. If not, they were processed while the adults they traveled with applied for asylum. These children, and many more like them, were some of the many who ended up in Homestead, Florida, following their separation from the adults they traveled with, lacking virtually everything but the clothes on their backs, usually speaking no English.

My colleagues Natalia Cales, and Karen Jordan and I, were assigned to reach out to a bevy of local officials, community-based organizations like Catholic Charities, and other entities who might have concerns (or interest) that their community would become a temporary home for displaced children. The role of HHS, assisted by my agency, Intergovernmental and External Affairs, was to care for, protect, and fortify the lives of these children as well as possible, given the extraordinary circumstances. As we, each of us African Americans, watched, along with the rest of the nation, some of the gut-wrenching images of crying parents, horrified children who were being separated from their relatives, and even children washing up on the shore after drowning in a frantic, desperate quest to get to the U.S., I was deeply anguished each and every time I picked up the phone to make a call on behalf of the UAC initiative. After all, these children, brown and Black, could have been our children. And though more than 160 years had passed since slavery had been outlawed in the U.S., I couldn't help but imagine the horror felt by these children and families, even though their arduous voyage to the U.S. had been voluntary, while my ancestors were captured and sold, arriving after months-long voyages in the belly of slave ships. The consistency was that people of color, be they Black, brown, or yellow, had historically not been warmly welcomed to this nation, the home of the brave and the land of the free. Their arrival starkly contrasted with the words of *The New Colossus,* penned by Emma Lazarus in the late 1800s and posted on the Statue of Liberty at Ellis Island. One wonders if Ron DeSantis, Greg Abbott, Brian Kemp, or Donald Trump ever read them:

> *Give me your tired, your poor,*
>
> *Your huddled masses yearning to breathe free,*
>
> *The wretched refuse of your teeming shore.*
>
> *Send these, the homeless, tempest-tossed to me,*
>
> *I lift my lamp beside the golden door!*[166]

Two more times, we were directed to seek homes for the unaccompanied children who had been taken from their parents, many of whom had been sent back to their countries of origin. The second time, we were told to reach out to county commission chairs, mayors, and other elected leaders in communities within roughly one hour of Atlanta, asking them whether they would allow The Feds to set up a camp in a vacant, or "appropriate," part of town and serve as hosts for hundreds, or thousands of undocumented children. Atlanta was an ideal location in part because it was accessible, being home to the world's busiest airport.

The final time this happened was in June of 2019. This time, our external affairs director, Darcie Johnston, known to some as the "Undertaker's Daughter," was dispatched – or took it upon herself to go – to Fort Benning, Georgia, one of the nation's largest bases, located right outside Columbus.[167] Benning, one of ten Confederate generals for whom military bases were named, is known for its School of the Americas and is a training ground for special troops. Benning was renamed Fort Moore in 2023 as part of the Army's commitment to honor patriots, as opposed to those who sought to overthrow the United States of America.[168] As we conducted surveillance and gathered lists of key partners who needed to be alerted that Benning was being considered as a UAC site, Darcie Johnston, a Vermonter who likely had never been south, except perhaps to Florida, allegedly rolled into town like John Wayne and ruffled more than a few feathers. Fort Benning did not end up being a site for the UACs. Publicly, Columbus mayor Skip Henderson said all the right things.[169] Children were also relocated to Chattanooga, Tennessee, in 2021, roughly 90 miles from Atlanta, where the mayor publicly cited concerns over an information vacuum.

"The phones have rang [sic] quite a bit here wanting to know more information. It's kind of embarrassing that we don't have additional information," said Mayor Jim Coppinger, during a county commission meeting. "And I actually learned about what was going on through one of the local media outlets."[170]

I remember the day in 2019 when the three Black people in my office, Natalia, Karen, and I, saw an image of a 10-month-old baby washing up on the shore of the Rio Grande. We were incredibly quiet, jarred by a "zero tolerance" policy, a system that would allow it, a system we were by direct association a part of.[171] In another instance, a father and his two-year-old daughter, tethered together in his shirt, drowned together, desperately risking life for freedom.[172] The images and the recognition of man's inhumanity to man left me shaken, reeling from what I could not help but see as a shocking lack of sensitivity to the human condition.[173]

Mexican migrants come across northern borders in record numbers, 70,000, some freezing to death, as opposed to dying of heat stroke crossing the southern border. We know why people are so desperate to get into the U.S.; what is unclear is why we are so determined to keep them out.

Like a dangerous, wounded, cornered, dying animal, the GOP is running out of time and will soon be out of step with a growing cavalcade of millennials, women who have been dismissed and put down, and Black and brown people who have been told in no uncertain terms "you don't belong here," and go back to where you came from, and Trump realizes this. So, if you know that ten years from now, you have virtually no chance of retaining control of a country that is two decades away from becoming a minority-majority nation, what the hell do you have to lose, you ask? If I'm going down and about to become irrelevant, why not go down crying foul, bending the rules, restricting voting at every opportunity, focusing on waging culture wars, and demonizing "the Other"? The MAGA GOP, in particular, has chosen to flame out on its own terms, taking the gloves off and proclaiming that it runs this country and white is certainly going to be right, as long as they have anything to say about it.

Chapter 13: Dawn of a New Day

"I believe this nation's diversity is its promise, not its problem."

Maryland Congressman Elijah Cummings

I am a member of what I consider to be a very progressive, biblically-based, multi-cultural church situated in the heart of one of Atlanta's roughest and most under-resourced neighborhoods, yet one with a rich history and heritage. Over the past five years, our church, which has a senior white pastor, has gone from being majority white to majority Black, as many of the young Anglos in our congregation have drifted away, in large part tiring of the enduring focus on biblical justice and racial reconciliation. Even at our church, however, we've had instances of little white children in the nursery telling little Black children to go back to Africa. And while the white parents, who are indeed committed to social justice and reconciliation, insisted the child didn't know what he was saying – and I'm sure he didn't hear it at home – I believe the incident was a missed opportunity for teaching what is right and acceptable, and why such behavior is never acceptable. There is a litany of examples of "the Other," generally people who are not the ruling majority, being told to go back to where they came from.

President Abraham Lincoln, in fact, met with Black leaders in 1862, and suggested they all return to Africa, even though most had never been there before, and those who had – or their ancestors – were brought to America in chains to build the wealth of white people, who themselves had come here as invading foreigners (though most whites probably think of their ancestors as merely "white settlers," a more innocuous term). "You and we are different races,"[174] and it was "better for us both ... to be separated,"[175] President Lincoln told the five Black Washingtonian leaders during an 1862 meeting, a few months before he issued the Emancipation Proclamation.[176] Therefore, we as a country have a long and sordid history of telling people we think are not like us that they should "go back where they came from." Lincoln ultimately did the right thing, and I'm grateful for it, as it likely cost him his life.

We must note, however, that his priority was not freeing the slaves, but preserving the Union. Lincoln carefully noted his official position: "If I could save the Union without freeing *any* slave, I would do it, and if I could save it by freeing *all* the slaves, I would do it; and if I could save it by freeing some and leaving others alone, I would also do that."[177]

For that reason, it was not a new refrain to hear Trump shrill at freshman Congresswomen Ilhan Omar, Ayanna Pressley, Rashida Tlaib, and Alexandria Ocasio-Cortez, that "they go back and help fix the totally broken and crime-infested places from which they came," in another of his infamous tweets.[178]

While Patrick Henry was apparently part of a movement to end the importation of slaves to Virginia in 1778, when he died in 1799, he did own 67 slaves.[179] No small potato, he was one of the United States of America's founding fathers and the governor of Virginia. His owning slaves gives a twisted irony to his often-quoted and universally celebrated clarion call: "Give me liberty, or give me death!"

Rep. Elijah Cummings, a bright light in perhaps a lesser era than the heyday of Congressmen John Lewis and Andy Young, may have put it best: "I believe this nation's diversity is its promise, not its problem." When we finally get to the point and place where the overwhelming majority of Americans not only believe that, but are willing to make a stand to ensure that premise, we will continue to struggle and be stuck in a racial and cultural quagmire. According to many white Americans who reject being "woke" – though precious few can define it, and simply see it as a liberal boogeyman – "this is my house and you're just living in it."

January 20th, 2020, was in some ways, a rough day for me. I am always thankful for the fact that my country, the one in which I invested much, hoped for more, yet now believe in less, does officially honor one of its Black moral prophets, Dr. Martin Luther King, Jr. On the holiday, I love to watch the service honoring the man who gave his life for the least of these from his home church, Ebenezer Baptist, on historic Auburn Avenue in Atlanta, only two blocks from the office I worked in for four years, at Dr. King's beloved SCLC. On that day, though it was a holiday, I retweeted from the accounts of the senior officials I usually retweeted messages from my HHS account: Secretary Alex Azar, CMS Administrator Seema Verma, ASH Giroir, Deputy Secretary Eric Hargan, and Surgeon General Jerome Adams. My issue was that, in many ways, they parroted key King messages and paid homage to his greatness, while at the same time undermining the principles of equity, access to health care, housing, fair wages for the working poor, and redistribution of wealth, that King lived and died for.

Our secretary, whom I respected, despite his disdain for the Affordable Care Act, retweeted this from POTUS: "Today, we pause to honor the incredible life and accomplishments of Dr. King, who helped shape the Civil Rights Movement, gave hope to millions experiencing discrimination, and whose enduring memory inspires us to pursue a more just and equal society."[180]

Seema Verma, the CMS administrator, tweeted this: "Today, as we remember Martin Luther King Jr. - a man who stood for peace and equal justice - we must also remind ourselves to continue to fight for his dream by living and working every day with respect for every American."[181]

On King's actual birthday, however, Verma tweeted this: "Let's look at the Medicaid program. It was designed for our most vulnerable citizens ... The program has not been updated in the last 50 years, and this is the number one or two budget item for states, and states are having trouble paying for the program."[182]

On January 8, a week before, Verma tweeted: "CMS's primary goal has been to provide a seamless Open Enrollment experience for consumers who want to enroll in Health Insurance Exchange (HIM) coverage, & the data show we have been meeting this goal year after year."[183] The problem was that, under the Trump administration, the goal was lockstep with that of most conservative governors – to minimize Medicaid enrollment and make it as difficult as possible for people to select quality health care plans through the ACA, not to make things seamless.

HHS Deputy Secretary Eric Hargan retweeted this: "This Dr. Martin Luther King, Jr. Day, we take the time to ask ourselves 'What are you doing for others?' Today, take some time to reflect on how we can work together to advance health equity."[184] The tweet also included this visual, with the image of King: "life's most persistent and urgent question is, 'what are you doing for others?'"

Dr. Jerome Adams, the U.S. Surgeon General and one of the few senior Black officials in the Trump administration, actually went to the King memorial to take his photo and to tweet. In addition to retweeting King's "most persistent and urgent question," he shared his own heartfelt sentiments: "Today we honor not just the man, but the incredible legacy that is Dr. Martin Luther King, Jr."[185] Each of these tweets is in line with honoring an American hero, except for Verma's, which notes that the U.S. has continually improved the ACA enrollment marketplace experience, year after year. What she fails to mention, however, is the fact that the Trump administration did everything it could for four years to stifle and stunt the ACA, while introducing and allowing for "junk plans" that provided a minimal level of coverage for enrollees in states that refused to expand Medicaid. Verma's tweet and the administration's positions also directly contrast with King's, who said, "Of all the forms of inequality, injustice in health is the most shocking and inhuman."[186]

How racially blind and insensitive is this nation? Let me answer it this way: Somehow, someway, it took until the summer of 2010 for the U.S. Congress to erect commemorative plaques inside the U.S. Capitol to honor the fact that African American male slaves had labored without recompense through the blistering, sweltering summers and the unrelenting, brutal winters from 1793 until 1800, to construct the U.S. Capitol. Working six days a week, 12 hours per day, not being paid themselves, but earning their owners $5 per month, they worked not just building the marvelous structure, but also slaving in the rock quarries to acquire the materials for the building. Meanwhile, the slave women and their children were used to mold clay that went into the furnaces.[187]

It makes certain words from the lofty Declaration of Independence ring ghostly hollow, such as … we hold these truths to be self-evident, that all men (should have said "and women") are created equal, with certain inalienable rights, life, liberty, and the pursuit of happiness.

Yas. Massa. Dem slaves were mighty happily building the chambers of the legislative body of the most powerful nation in their world for even less than slave labor, no pun intended. It should come as no surprise, since Black slaves had built the wealth of this country since 1619, to the benefit of those who saw them as less than equal and mere beasts of burden to be used, abused, re-populated, and used again. So yes, nearly 135 years after the end of legal slavery and the Emancipation Proclamation,[188] and a full 35 years after the passage of the Voting Rights Act of 1965, Congress decided to finally honor the poor souls who built their magnificent cathedral of an office. How mighty damn white of them. Hey, who knows? Maybe by 2060, the U.S. government might finally believe it is time to formally apologize to Black Americans for inflicting nearly 250 years of chattel slavery and another 80 years of de facto slavery on them.[189] These daunting numbers don't even address the ten to $20 trillion in reparations owed Black folk and the descendants of slaves for the building of this nation, which I certainly don't anticipate ever seeing.[190]

Chapter 14: The Grand Princess Cruise Ship

"All of the 91 US cruises currently at sea have confirmed or suspected COVID-19 on board."[191]

On January 28, 2020, Acting White House Chief-of-Staff Mick Mulvaney proclaimed that the coronavirus was the latest ploy by the Dems and the media to take down Trump. Effectively, he was amplifying the message from on high by his boss, who insisted the virus was a hoax while urging people who were sick to simply go back to work because the burgeoning disease spread would soon die out.[192]

On the morning of March 9, 2020, I hurried into the room at the specified location at Dobbins Air Force Base, anxious to get a good seat. My mission, approved by IGA Director *Trueman*, IEA Principal Deputy Laura Rigas, and IEA External Affairs Director Darcie Johnston, was to document the conversation, identify concerns, and make sure I could spot the key elected officials and public health officials who were gathering in advance of the influx of the mostly elderly citizens being ferried to Marietta, Georgia, for treatment and quarantine following weeks on the Grand Princess cruise ship. The attendees consisted of the Cobb County Sheriff's office: Dr. Janet Memark, the Cobb County health director; Jennifer Davis of WellStar Systems; the chief of police; the fire chief; metro ambulance; EPR Director John Houser; state HPP (Hospital Preparedness Program) Director Kelly Nadeau; local government officials; and key staff led by Craig McPike, Vice

Commander, 22nd Air Force, Dobbins Air Reserve Base. The base commander led an organized, well-oiled staff, something I was used to seeing growing up on military bases. From our side of the house, Region 4 ASPR Director Tom Bowman, whom I had worked with for nearly 20 years, and his capable staff were to provide the briefings.

The Grand Princess cruise ship was supposed to dock at its home base in San Francisco, but it was initially refused entry. The vessel, carrying 3,500 passengers, had departed on February 21st for Hawaii. It eventually cut the 15-day cruise short and allowed the two passengers who contracted the disease on the ship's earlier trip to Mexico to disembark in Santa Rosa, under quarantine.[193] One elderly man from California died on the cruise, becoming the first known Californian to die of COVID. This time, beginning March 9, the sick were able to disembark first in Oakland, but with a list of over 3,000 passengers, only so many could be checked and reassigned to the four military bases that had been designated as quarantine sites. Twenty-one confirmed coronavirus victims were on the ship, including a good number of the crew.

The manifest included 34 Georgians, as well as more than 400 others, who were being shipped to Dobbins, an Air Force base just miles northwest of Atlanta. Dobbins had a history of serving unique and acute patients. In fact, in 2015, Ebola patients were flown into the base for quarantining, before ultimately being moved to Emory University for care. In 2018, ASPR and HHS cared for citizens from the Virgin Islands, Puerto Rico, and Dobbins, who needed acute care after being displaced by Hurricanes Irma and Maria in October of 2017.[194] Our office and I personally have been involved in each of these endeavors. Several of our staff who were people of color, including Edecia Richards, a United States Public Health Officer from the Virgin Islands, and another Black responder took exception to what they saw as disparate and culturally insensitive treatment of the Black and brown evacuees who were ultimately housed in metro Atlanta hotels for several months.

The very day that three more people died in Washington and another 97 succumbed overnight in Italy, Trump compared COVID-19 to the common flu. This was, however, the very early stages of the COVID pandemic in the U.S. It was so new, in fact, that Georgia had only reported five confirmed cases of the virus by March 8, 2020.

The following day, March 10, 2020, I was contacted by a producer for CNN out of Miami. He wanted answers to some questions regarding the incoming citizens from the Grand Princess who were to be quarantined at Dobbins. After returning his call, I asked him to send me an email with his specific request so that I could forward it to IEA, who would determine who in our media shop would respond. However, because I had put my name on a board at the briefing the day before – per the request of the base commander to all outside attendees – and the base PIO referred them to me – certain parties at IEA freaked out, thinking they would be deluged by calls.

As a longtime communicator and public affairs practitioner who has managed and initiated literally hundreds of press conferences, if there's one thing I do know, it is that you always want to control the message, if at all possible – especially in the midst of a crisis. So, while you would have thought IEA would have embraced the opportunity to craft for the media the message they thought was both accurate and important, they were running from responsibility while blaming me for putting them in that position. I knew enough to know that not I, but someone they would send down from headquarters, or a designee from the CDC, would ultimately be the HHS spokesperson.

Now, had I not gone out there, as directed, to meet political reps and gauge the level of anxiety in the local communities near where the patients would be quarantined, then alternative sources would have been granting interviews and providing messages counter to what headquarters wanted, and I would have been seen as the bad guy, or derelict of duty, for *not offering myself* as a contact, or, as my EO says, a media filter. Knowing that HHS would ultimately be responsible for the care of the evacuees, 1st Lt. Alan Abernathy, a spokesman for the 94th Airlift Wing Public Affairs at Dobbins, placed the responsibility squarely where it belonged. "As with previous efforts, DOD would provide housing, and HHS would be responsible for the aspects of the quarantine," Abernathy explained at a press conference.[195] It was the classic case of damned if you do and damned if you don't. Some of the dysfunction was due to the paranoia of the Trump administration, but part of it was also government dysfunction. All too often, those inside the beltway simply didn't know the quality or experience of the assets they had in the field and, thus, did not trust them to do their jobs. Furthermore, all too often, they were too thin to send someone they trusted to manage the process. Par for the course, unfortunately, in the alternative universe of Trump. One thing none of us can dispute, however, is that beyond anything else, the man in the White House understands the importance of controlling the message. Much of his senior leadership, however, were misplaced loyalists who froze when the bright lights were on instead of asserting HHS's natural leadership role in the crisis.

Chapter 15: Day-to-Day Operations

Opioids, Workforce Development, MAT, Rural Health, White Christian Evangelicals, and the "Family Glitch"

During the Trump administration, in 2019, our office held literally hundreds of high-level calls. Our second appointee, Acting Regional Director John McGough, prided himself on leading the pack of ten regional directors nationwide in booking and reporting both trends and actionable intel on those calls. Those included reportable calls with the South Carolina Hospital Association (August 16) and its seven counterparts, the Florida Primary Health Care Association and its seven counterparts, the top insurance companies in each state, including Anthem of Kentucky, South Carolina (August 16), and major cities and counties conducting methadone-assisted treatment (MAT), including Tennessee and Kentucky, our most impacted states. In the final analysis, he and his team, which included Cales, his Executive Officer Jordan, his admin, and me (his outreach and public and intergovernmental affairs lead), were exceedingly busy virtually every single day. We ran a similar schedule with his successor, RD April Weaver, generally conferring with two to three stakeholders per day from our eight southeastern states on issues ranging from child adoption, youth drug prevention, broadband access, workforce shortages, opioids and other SUDs (substance use disorders), and services for unwed mothers.

I'm not sure what happened with all the information we collected. I do know it looked good on the reports. In the Biden administration, however, under Director Marvin

Figueroa, I do know that real, tangible policy changes took place. One correction was to the long-despised Family Glitch, which penalized families by making them ineligible for ACA subsidies, even though they needed them. That statute was changed within the first two years of the administration.

During those conversations that also included big city and county medical directors, state medical directors, sheriffs, and organs that treated and managed substance-abuse patients, rural health associations, pharmacists, medical associations, centers that housed and supported human trafficking and other abuse victims, and adoption centers, we generally asked the same questions: What are your biggest needs and obstacles? How can we support you in your work? Where does the government get in your way? What keeps you up at night? What are you most proud of? What models have you utilized, and how have you been innovative or adaptive, especially during COVID-19?

In another instance, our region – again, with eight states, the largest in the nation, was – along with all the other nine regions, directed to do extensive inquiries of up to an hour with two key hospital CEOs from each state on a myriad of issues. Those events included vetting, soliciting, firming up the appointments, and then taking dictation that was reduced to reports culled from copious notes and recordings. This directive came at the end of November. Of course, when you talk about top hospital CEOs at level-one trauma hospitals in places like Miami, Atlanta, Memphis, and others, including safety net, private, and rural hospitals, many of the large hospital leaders had already left for the Riviera on their Christmas vacations. Nevertheless, as usual, in an all-hands-on-deck approach, Natalia, our executive officer, Karen Jordan, our executive assistant, and I, all worked the phones and emails fiercely, lining up hospitals in Miami, Nashville, coastal South Carolina, and elsewhere. In what we saw as a minor miracle, we scheduled and executed all 16 hospital CEO briefings, even with Laura Rigas, a fairly new HHS appointee, as the department's lead, instead of our acting Regional Director, McGough. One of those was Greg Strahan, President and CEO of Owensboro Health Regional Hospital, with whom we discussed the secretary's priorities, especially as they pertained to hospital outreach, HHS regulations, Medicare and Medicaid, rural health, workforce issues, telehealth, and trends, challenges, and success. Exhausted, yet proud that we had delivered again, we proved to ourselves and IEA that we were warriors. Ironically, for me personally, the fact that we accomplished the feat for and "under" someone who had disdain for us was bittersweet, at best. Some months earlier, new HHS IEA Principal Deputy Director Laura Rigas, a communications person like me, came to IEA to help with messaging and strategy. Rigas, who didn't know me and had only met me once, when McGough hosted the RDs a few months earlier, had told several of her colleagues at the HHS headquarters in D.C., the Humphrey Building, "I don't like that Deric. I hear he's still pushing the Obama agenda."[196]

The Obama agenda? No, I was simply honoring the law that said that the Affordable Care Act, minus the independent mandate that required people who didn't opt to buy insurance to pay a tax, was still federal law, despite untold attempts and promises by the GOP to "repeal and replace" it, including three attempts before the Supreme Court.[197]

We also focused on key administration priority areas, including rural health, opioids and other substance abuse disorders (SUDs), workforce development (more nurses, pharmacists, physicians, and med techs in at-risk and sparsely populated areas), telehealth and broadband concerns, and reducing drug costs.

Fortunately for me, my boss at the time, Acting Region IV Director John McGough, who concurrently was managing Region I, which included Boston, one of the initial COVID-19 epicenters in the U.S., totally understood and supported my position. In fact, he showed his confidence in my judgment and ability by assigning me as the point person to communicate with numerous elected officials, including Cobb County (where Dobbins was located) Commission Chair Mike Boyce, a former Marine. Boyce and I spoke every other day or so, as our ASPR office managed the quarantined residents at Dobbins, or if a situation or concern came up. I also served as the initial point person for elected officials in Florida who were struggling with COVID concerns, one of whom was Tampa Mayor Jane Castor.

On at least two occasions, I received early morning calls from Castor's chief of staff, John Bennett, with concerns over a lack of COVID testing sites in their communities. Castor, a one-time Republican and former police officer who joined the Democratic party in 2015, was also on the calls. She was highly upset with what she saw as a lack of urgency by the Trump administration to provide COVID testing, as she saw her city's numbers spiking.[198] Castor, whose governor, Ron DeSantis, was a COVID denier who constantly minimized the impact of rising death numbers in favor of keeping businesses open while battling with his health department to suppress the real numbers of deaths and infections, sought relief through the mechanism she believed should be responsive to her concerns, the HHS regional director's office. Unfortunately, our office was ill-equipped to deal with the problem. I alerted McGough to Castor's concerns, but did not get direction regarding how we could respond. The problem, I ascertained, was that the HHS (CDC and ASPR) were ill-prepared to adequately respond to increased testing at the time, largely due to Trump's policy of denial of the deadly nature of the disease, coupled with CDC Director Robert Redfield's inability to share scientific realities with the American public, possibly because of a lack of courage, or because he was under extreme political pressure to look the other way.

Bob Carter was perhaps best known as a climate change skeptic. However, what he will really be memorialized for is once upon a time saying: "Poor planning on your part does not necessitate an emergency on mine."[199] Well, if you work for the federal government in a regional office for a political appointee, that's exactly what it means. As I like to say, when they told us to "jump," we were expected to ask, "how high?"

In the fall of 2018, Shannon Royce and my RD, Renee Ellmers, discussed the possibility of her office making its first major foray into a region to share the priorities and hear from the stakeholders of her organization, the Center for Faith-Based and Neighborhood Partnerships. I saw this as a great opportunity, due to my years as our office's faith-based lead and my considerable connections to the religious community, including the Evangelical crowd. After several meetings, Royce and her public affairs specialist, Heidi Christensen, sent us an initial invite list and told us to build on it. Karen Jordan and I immediately jumped on it, reaching out to corral numbers and contacts for a broad range of faith leaders, including Sikhs, Muslims, Jews, Catholics, Buddhists, Mormons – you name it. Frankly, though many were difficult to reach, several expressed great excitement about the possibility of meeting with someone from headquarters who was representing the Trump administration. In addition to hearing our priorities, the forum was designed to allow them to share their main concerns, which included suicide, opioids, and other substance abuses.

Prior to building the list, I shared with Ellmers that I had a deep respect for a local Evangelical pastor of national significance, Rev. Bryant Wright of Johnson Ferry Baptist

Church in Roswell, a suburb of Atlanta. He was a well-known author and creator of a daily motivation vignette on radio called *Wright from the Heart*, which had long been a favorite of mine. I called his office following an email to alert him of who I was and of the upcoming HHS visit, and I brokered a meeting with him, Ellmers, and myself. Wright, former president of the Southern Baptist Conference, was a gracious host who said he'd be happy to provide a luncheon at his church for Royce and her team. He also said that while he applauded Trump's selection of conservative judges, he could not "vote for the man" due to his personal witness and behavioral failures. After submitting our list to Royce for her consideration, which included the Evangelical Covenant Church of America's superintendent for the southeastern conference, as well as his incoming successor, we were later to find out that only one of our suggested guests, from lists we had spent two weeks compiling, was invited. Also, when Ellmers and I reached the luncheon, which was beautifully catered, only half the people Royce had invited showed up, pissing me off because of all the people we had to disappoint who were excited about interacting with HHS. The following day, we had a highly productive visit at the Davis Direction Foundation, a full-service center founded by a mom who lost her son, which helps people get sober, find employment, and turn their lives around, as well as another meeting we set up. My problem with the two-day excursion was that it provided a stellar opportunity for the administration to share its mission, hear from its constituents, and perhaps gain a new level of trust and respect, yet Royce blew it because she only wanted to meet with a certain kind of people. Ironically, roughly a year later, the center finally decided to broaden its reach and speak to more varied constituencies. For me and my office, however, their snub created a rift and a loss of goodwill with those we would need to continue working with long after Trump was gone. Unfortunately, that's often how Washington – on both sides of the aisle – operates. Despite all your work and planning, it is not uncommon to be left explaining cancellations and snubs to strategic partners that regional staff will continue to work with long after the bigwigs have moved on to their next stop.

Dealing with IEA was always tricky, a delicate dance at best, especially in the midst of a crisis. Consistent whispers out of headquarters also indicated that Darcie Johnston was far less diplomatic than IEA leadership and the regional directors expected us to be. When preparing for and ultimately visiting Anniston, Alabama, in hopes of negotiating a deal for the local community to accept and host COVID-19-infected passengers from the *Diamond Princess* cruise ship, Darcie, not unexpectedly, ruffled her share of feathers. In fact, legend has it that she rode into communities IEA wanted to partner with on sensitive issues such as housing UACs like John Wayne telling the locals what was going to happen, totally abandoning the Republican mantra of states' rights.[200]

"I was shocked," said Anniston mayor Jack Draper. "I was shocked by the lack of planning. I was shocked by the manner in which it was presented to us."[201] A similar observation was made by other officials, including in Florida, where our office was directed to reach out to certain elected officials, while other departments "owned" the communications with certain officials. IEA was seeking to set up another UAC center to house the children separated at the borders from their parents and attendees in the Orlando area when local officials and our office were directed to send letters written by Darcie to specific officials. One official in particular, State Senator Linda Stewart, received the email, while some city officials said they didn't, prompting her to say the entire process seemed highly disorganized.[202]

Sadly, this was indicative of much of the direction that came out of IEA during the Trump administration. Jack Kalavritinos, who came back to help out after serving a similar role in the Bush administration, was not known as being disorganized and messy, but instead frantic and unsettled. Working for Trump, who, as everyone may remember, communicated almost exclusively in written form via Twitter, Kalavritinos expected his regional staff to do the same. Forget the fact that Trump's tweets were frequently untrue, divisive, demeaning, or misguided. Kalavritinos expected his regional staff to follow suit. For me personally, this was a challenge, not only because I didn't believe much of the drivel, but because I was old school and had few or no social media skills. A few of my seasoned colleagues were in similar positions, but in each case, they had younger counterparts who could assume the social media lead. Our five-person offices had been designed to have two public affairs officers each. Mine, the largest in the country, with responsibility for eight states, was one of the few where the opening created by the departure of April Washington, who was a social media pro, had not been filled.

On one particular occasion in 2018, when Ellmers was still the RD, headquarters was frantic about booking interviews for a senior official, Eric Hargan, then deputy secretary of HHS, over a controversial topic. Calling dozens of my key media contacts across the region, I was getting no commitments. In the meantime, Kalavritinos, one of those former lobbyists Trump said he would ban, was calling seemingly on the hour harassing Ellmers (and other RDs), evidence that he was under great pressure for his regional staff to produce for this initiative.[203] Finally, a Black radio station in south Florida committed to the interview, even after expressing skepticism because very little positive news had come from the administration concerning Black America. Before the time of the scheduled interview, which had been arranged largely because of prior relationships, headquarters canceled it. This action, of course, "validated" the station's concern that the administration wasn't earnest in its attempt to bring important information to the Black community and, at the same time, made my job more difficult in the future. This happened, frankly, several times, in effect burning both relationships and contacts. Though it was not unique to this administration, the damage was more severe in the Trump administration due to its overall shaky relationship with mainstream media.

had been arranged illegally because of prior relationships, headquarters cancelled it. This action of course, revindicated the station's concern that the administration wasn't correct in its attempt to obtain important information in the Black community and, despite solid long range planning, more difficulties in the future functioning troubles would ensue in laying out in both relationships made more difficult by not changing the way things are. The new reviews more sense of the French identification due to its growth with credibility for vital journalism in India.

Chapter 16: Be Careful What You Ask For

"I don't take responsibility at all for the testing failures."
President Donald J. Trump

Situations or circumstances we encountered throughout the region, especially in staunchly rural communities, proved the complexity of providing consistent, quality service to those who had few options.

"We are constantly being asked, 'You aren't going to leave, are you?'" recalled Mountain Area Health Education Center (MAHEC) Dr. Suzanne Dixon, who traveled many hours each week from Asheville, NC, through the mountains to serve rural patients in Franklin, NC, and had to continually assure her patients that she, too, wouldn't abandon them.[204] The problem is extensive in Region IV, the eight southeastern states in which I served, which included North Carolina. My colleague, Region IV ORD Executive Officer Natalia Cales, who utilized a doula for her own son's birth, served as national HHS co-coordinator in addressing the maternal health crisis due to the preponderance of challenges in Region IV. This was a major priority area in the Biden administration, along with expanding Medicaid, the scurry to re-enroll people on Medicaid after the end of the PHE (Public Health Emergency), fighting supply chain issues that shrank the infant formula access, monkey pox and, of course, ever-expanding COVID strains.

At HHS, and at the regional office, more specifically, we had prepared for some sort of pandemic from almost the time I arrived in 1998. The first time was in 1999 when I took a three-day training at the COOP (Continuity of Operations Plan) site, as we learned about situations that would require donning hazmat suits in a secret location and how we could continue to ensure the government ran, even if we were displaced from our office by some disruption, such as a saran gas attack, a foreign adversary, or anything else. Little did we know at that time, that by 2020, we would almost all be working remotely due to a raging COVID pandemic that took over a thousand lives per day. I also took CERC (Crisis Emergency Risk Communication) training eight years later that could be applied to avian (bird) flu, bioterrorism, a shutdown impacted by Y2K, or some other threat to public health. The six principles of CERC include Be First, Be Right, Be Credible, Express Empathy, Promote Action, and Show Respect.

On January 22, a case of coronavirus was reported for the first time in the U.S. ... China alerted the U.S. on January 3. "We have it under control. It will be just fine," Trump said. Soon, however, daily briefings began adding information about the danger of the virus sweeping the U.S.

White House aides met with Trump on January 27, pleading with him to pay more attention to the coronavirus. Peter Navarro, on January 29, wrote the first of two memos, warning of the potential dire threat of the virus. He raised the question of a travel ban for those coming from China. On January 31, Trump imposed a travel ban.

"By the way, the virus, they're working hard on it," Trump assured the American public. "Looks like by April, in theory, it gets warmer, it miraculously goes away," said Trump. However, on February 23, Navarro wrote a second memo, warning that at least a million Americans could die from the virus.

In March 2020, CNN Analyst Dr. Sanjay Gupta said we needed 250,000 ICU beds in the event of an emergency. Problematically, the U.S. has only about 100,000, thus the importance of "spreading out the cases, rather than have 200,000 of them, for instance, flood the system at the same time." That's why, as a public health professional, I felt like someone who was watching a catastrophic crash unfold in front of me in slow motion as we careened toward an unavoidable object. On March 13, the day before Trump declared a national emergency due to the virus, WH reporter Yamiche Alcindor asked him this: "You said you don't take responsibility, but you disbanded the WH pandemic office, and the officials that were working in that office left abruptly.[205] What do you say to that?"

"I just think it's a nasty question," replied Trump. "When you say me, I didn't do it. We have a group of people. I could ask, perhaps. I can perhaps ask Tony [Fauci] about it. I didn't know anything about it.[206]

POTUS was also challenged by NBC's Kristen Welker on his level of responsibility for the lack of testing, as well as questioning when testing would be available.

"I don't take responsibility at all for the testing failures," Trump said. "Because we were given a set of circumstances and rules, regulations, and specifications for responsibilities at different times."[207]

And don't underestimate this key fact: Trump mentioned, as he dropped in on a coronavirus press conference run by Pence and featuring Dr. Fauci and White House Coronavirus Coordinator Dr. Deborah Birx, Trump's leadership team, that he had been tested. However, though it was reported a few hours later that Trump was coronavirus-free, the vast majority of media outlets reported that "the WH said that the president was not infected by the virus." That distinction is important because, sadly, our ability to believe the president and the White House had been tragically compromised, at best, and permanently fractured, at worst.

"Her [Dr. Deborah Birx's] explanations are weak. They're woefully insufficient. They're an insult after 400,000 people have died," said CNN News Central host Brianna Keilar. "If they don't stand up for science when it counts, when lives are on the line, their reputation can be wiped away. All it takes is a little bleach and, in her case, a small ray of sunlight."[208]

"This should have been done a month ago," critiqued Democratic California Rep. Ro Khanna. "If POTUS can get 500,000 tests done a day, why wasn't this done a month ago?"[209]

Meanwhile, that same day, the number of evacuees from the Grand Princess cruise ship taken from Oakland to Dobbins AFB in Marietta, Georgia, had ballooned from 200 to 497.[210] The problem, as of March 14, at least, was that while the number of quarantined citizens tripled during the week, the number of public health care professionals monitoring, assessing, and caring for them as part of the ASPR team, stayed the same. Like many other inadequate systems thwarted by an administration that cut agencies and their funding like the CDC, NIH, and EPA, and refused to staff critical positions when decades of intellectual capital walked out the door, this one was straining at the seams when help was most needed. Still, in the spirit of American ingenuity and grit, they battled valiantly to do a good job, despite the odds.

I remember the day governors from Ohio, California, and Illinois moved to close all bars and restaurants in response to the coronavirus. More than a dozen states had already declared that all schools would be closed the same weekend. In the meantime, the long-awaited test kits promised by the administration were missing in action.

"I'm so sick of this guy, I don't know what to do," one millennial said as Trump's administration struggled to get a grip on the COVID pandemic. Mocking Democratic candidate Joe Biden, she intoned: "'We don't want a revolution, we want results!' Hell no! I want a revolution. We need to tear the whole [political] system down and start over."[211] Clearly, many Americans under 40 struggled to connect with Biden or Trump.

The more we found out, the more we discovered how critical areas were recklessly mismanaged by the Trump administration. All administrations receive briefings regarding national security as they prepare to take office. Chris Lu, former Deputy Secretary of Labor, details how a group of perhaps 30 Obama officials briefed 30 members of the incoming Trump administration in January 2017 regarding the possible emergency preparedness scenarios. One of them was a strain of the flu, according to Lu. Nevertheless, Trump, who has said that "he and he alone" knew what was best, refused to pay attention to emergency preparedness, even to the point of disbanding the office. Natalia Cales, the executive officer in my office, had led our team's training and coordination around a broadscale emergency preparedness for a public health emergency and attended a national tabletop exercise months earlier designed to combat a strain of the coronavirus.

Though some Trump officials insist the National Security Council office for emergency preparedness had become bloated and unmanageable, the entity's first director disagreed. "One year later, I was mystified when the White House dissolved the office, leaving the country less prepared for pandemics like COVID-19," Beth Cameron, the first director of the unit, wrote in an op-ed in *The Washington Post*.[212] Dr. Anthony Fauci, America's leading scientific voice – and the man who had the kahunas to contradict Trump's message that this would all go away soon – diplomatically told Congress, "It would be nice if the office was still there."[213]

We did other things besides managing COVID, though for a period of months, I was part of three calls a day capturing key developments or choke points for COVID supplies, testing equipment sites, and personnel. In early March 2020, we received an alert to conduct vigorous mayoral outreach in a variety of our key cities. For Region IV, that largely meant places like Miami, Ft. Lauderdale, Atlanta, Orlando, Tampa, Charlotte, Raleigh, Montgomery, Birmingham, Memphis, Nashville, Columbia, Charleston, Louisville, Lexington, and Mobile. After creating the templates, we would report back to headquarters that we had done so. Largely, this was political theater, especially since we were moving toward the teeth of the presidential election season that would kick into full throttle in just a few months. Trump, of course, was seeking re-election, but he was going to receive little support from most of the mayors of major Southern cities. That's because we had not communicated with most of them – except for during hurricane season or, perhaps, to alert them regarding a UAC (Unaccompanied Alien Children) center, or a very rare visit from our regional director, or another senior official. This administration, more than any I had worked for, had approached its work in a cloistered, shuttered manner, seeking instead to engage with an ultra-conservative movement, like ALEC, while prioritizing outreach to Evangelicals and other conservative Christians, keying on child adoption, opioids and other SUDs, rural health, workforce development, and issues that focused more on rural communities, Trump's base voters.

On March 23, 2020, the very day U.S. cases of the coronavirus topped 100,000, with nearly 550 total deaths, America experienced another, much more life-giving anniversary: the 10th anniversary of the passage of the Affordable Care Act. And while the vast majority of Americans were trying to come to grips with the deadliest pandemic the world had seen in 100 years, Trump's surrogates were trying to snuff the life out of the ACA, or ObamaCare, the flawed, but lifegiving health care act that provided a level of health care insurance for 27 million Americans, many of whom had never before been insured. That figure skyrocketed by 2023 after Biden restored funding for enrollment assisters, advertising, and regional staff support after those key elements had been drastically reduced during Trump's four years in office.

Meanwhile, the Trump administration continued to struggle to explain why so few test kits had reached the nation, despite the fact that other countries had tested hundreds of thousands of people. Michigan Governor Gretchen Whitmer put it this way: "We just received our allotment of PPE (Personal Protective Equipment) from the federal government's national strategic stockpile. The allotment of PPE for one of our hospitals is barely enough to cover one shift at that hospital."[214]

"That is the issue here. These front-line workers have to act as if every person they see has the virus. We've known this for some time," said CNN medical expert Dr. Sanjay Gupta. "We've known that we would need at least three billion masks."

"How bad it gets depends on the action we each take. We should act as if each of us has coronavirus. It's hard to ask people to do all they can if we don't see the federal government stepping up to do all it can," said Dr. Leana Wen, emergency room physician and head of the Baltimore health department. New Orleans Mayor LaToya Cantrell said she would have canceled Mardi Gras had she had better guidance from the White House, which in February of 2020 called the virus "under control."

In late March, the Trump administration ordered 10,000 ventilators. "I'm sure it's [COVID] contained. Aren't you?" said Trump spokesperson and adviser Kellyanne Conway.[215]

Trump says states should be "more appreciative" than to criticize The Feds' response to the pandemic. "I want them to be more appreciative. I say Mike [VP Pence], don't call the governor in Washington," said Trump. "You're wasting your time with them... Don't call that woman in Michigan."

"Three days ago, Florida's beaches were open," said General Russell Honoré, pointing out the hypocrisy of Florida's wacky anti-masking, anti-social distancing policies. Now they want to quarantine. Be careful what you ask for. Once you quarantine somewhere, people will not want to go there."[216]

The CDC, the leading health agency in the world, clearly had its once stellar reputation battered and bruised during the Trump administration, as Director Dr. Robert Redfield was consistently muzzled and compromised regarding his ability to speak the scientific truths about the dangers of COVID in an ever-evolving landscape.

"I find it concerning that the CDC director has not been outspoken when there have been instances of clear political interference in the interpretation of science," said Richard Besser, a former acting CDC director and now president of the Robert Wood Johnson Foundation. "I think it would be very helpful if the federal government could be more assertive and aggressive and more organized in helping us acquire these systems."

By April 1 – ironically, April Fool's Day – virtually every one of the resistant states, almost all Republican, had finally acquiesced and decided to lock down, effectively issuing "stay-at-home" orders to all its citizens, except those with essential duties. Georgia and, most notably, Florida, already in the top six in terms of cases, grudgingly cried "uncle." Kemp, seemingly in a daze, called the CDC's proclamation that one-fourth of those with the disease were asymptomatic or had no symptoms a "revelation and a game-changer."[217] Numerous public officials seized on his comments, including Chrissy Teigen, entertainer John Legend's wife, who tweeted, "I am very dumb, and I knew this," on a video of Kemp's remarks.[218] Even more piercing were Minnesota Senator Amy Klobuchar's comments regarding Kemp as the state's leader due to a highly questionable, razor-thin election victory: "If they had better election laws, Stacey Abrams would be governor of Georgia. Brian Kemp's negligence could cost Americans thousands of lives."[219]

*

DeSantis, who, before announcing a run for president himself in 2024, was a regular text buddy of Trump's, had allowed the beaches and bars to stay open until only days before. In two weeks, the U.S. case count had skyrocketed from 7,700 to more than 205,000. One month before March 1, 2020, the U.S. announced its first death from the virus. As of April 1, the U.S. death toll soared to 4,633. Both DeSantis and Kemp, as well as several others, had ignored the science for weeks – like their leader – and instead, feared the loss of jobs of those hourly workers and the impact on the economy more than the loss of life their states would experience by delaying social distancing.[220] I contend it was because the people who were dying, many of those in service industry jobs – Black, brown, and poor people who oftentimes were uninsured – were considered collateral damage in a thriving economy.

One week, Trump suggested "we" reopen the country for business by Easter. The next week, however, he had finally been convinced by the brilliant – though hamstrung – doctors and scientists surrounding him, to inform the nation that everyone should shelter in place until the end of April. Then, New York Governor Andrew Cuomo, who had become the voice of states under assault in what had become clearly the epicenter of the U.S. virus, called the state of affairs "beyond staggering," near the end of March 2020. By April 1, over 2,000 New Yorkers had died, a new death being registered every three minutes in the nation's crown jewel city. Some doctors were being told to use single-use masks for an entire week, even while many were struggling to obtain something as simple as Tylenol.

The New York Times put it this way: "Under the best case scenario ... Trump will see more Americans die ... than Presidents Harry S. Truman, Dwight D. Eisenhower, John F. Kennedy, Lyndon B. Johnson, and Richard M. Nixon saw die in the Korean and Vietnam wars combined."[221]

"The governor [DeSantis] was stubborn, and he has to own that, as do many of the other 49 governors," said former GOP Chairman Michael Steele.[222]

That is a stark comparison to new governor Andy Beshear of Kentucky, who announced strict stay-at-home orders on March 6, one day before New York's Cuomo and a full week before Trump would first suggest it nationally.

Ever seen anyone throw a rock and hide the hand? That's exactly what the administration did until virtually April of 2020, when Trump, in particular, pooh-poohed the epidemic, saying we would be back to business momentarily, while his minion governors followed in lockstep when federal leadership was staunchly needed. Pence, in the daily side show called the coronavirus press conference, deftly deflected:

"The WH Coronavirus Task Force continues to take the posture that we will defer to state and local health authorities on any measures that they deem appropriate."

U.S. Surgeon General Jerome Adams, perhaps taking into account that many of those dying would be the uninsured, the elderly, and those least positioned to protect themselves because of a porous safety net crippled, in part, by Trump's dogged, persistent attack on ObamaCare, was much more direct and honest regarding the crisis. Adams told Fox News: "We are at a critical inflection point in this country, people. We are where Italy was two weeks ago in terms of our numbers. When you look at the projections, there's every chance that we could be Italy." Italy had vaulted from 1,700 cases and 34 deaths to 25,000 cases and 18,000 deaths in only two weeks.[223]

In late March, the Trump administration ordered 10,000 ventilators. "We cannot let the cure be worse than the problem itself," Trump tweeted in mid-March. "My advice to America is that these guidelines are a national stay-at-home order."

Amy Klobuchar reminded the American public: "He told us, he and he alone can fix this."

There's an old, tried and true statement: Lead, follow, or get out of the way. Well, Trump damned sure didn't lead ... except perhaps right into the nation's most tragic catastrophe. And except for a few forward-thinking governors, Jay Inslee of Washington, Gavin Newsom of California, Andrew Cuomo of New York, Gina Raimondo of Rhode Island, and Phil Murphy of New Jersey, too many were slurping the Kool-Aid.

Editorial boards and investigative journalists across the country sounded the alarm on Trump's glaring inadequacies to lead in the midst of a crisis. The *Boston Globe*, with a sub-headline that read, "*Much of the suffering and death coming was preventable. The president has blood on his hands,*" was scathing in its condemnation. "The months the administration wasted with prevarication about the threat and its subsequent missteps will amount to exponentially more COVID-19 cases than were necessary. In other words, the president has blood on his hands."[224]

Yes, I was deeply ashamed for my department, my nation, and the president who refused to lead because he simply didn't care about the hundreds of thousands of vulnerable people he had pledged to protect and the millions of American families who trusted him to do so. From my perspective, as someone who sat in on at least three regional and national calls a day and pored over a missive of internal briefings, it was like watching a massive train derailment in slow motion from a mile away and being able to do absolutely nothing to stop it.

Chapter 17: An Unspeakable Cruelty to At-Risk Communities of Color

"I certainly hope black people don't fall for the okey-doke and go out and get their hair and nails done. Shrinking the minority voting pool. . . ."

Anonymous Texan

As word continued to seep out, first with quiet whispers, then, eventually, shouts and cries of agony, the coronavirus was ravaging Black and brown communities. In New Orleans, officials said that 70 percent of the cases and deaths were in the African American communities. In the nation's heartland of Chicago, which boasts a 30 percent African American population, the percentage of COVID-19 cases ravaging the Black community was even higher, according to Mayor Lori Lightfoot.

"We told the president this was going to be a problem back on January 23," said Congressman Ami Bera of California, a physician.[225]

Anecdotally, some things were painfully obvious, based oftentimes on zip code, social standing, and class. For instance, someone I know conducted a social experiment on March 28 in Dekalb County, GA. At a time when things like soap, hand sanitizer, and toilet paper were at a premium, she visited higher-end stores like Publix, Sprouts, and Target, in the wealthier neighborhoods of Dekalb, finding that the stores were well-stocked, but struggling to find toilet paper. She next visited stores in a more middle-class neighborhood where no employees wore gloves; no one at Kroger or Dollar General did, though they did have toilet paper. Apparently, many poor and middle-class Blacks were not hoarding toilet paper, either because they didn't have the money, or because they didn't realize the enormity of the situation.

In Georgia, Governor Kemp, who held off on issuing a shelter-in-place order until April 1, when he felt he had no choice, another conflicting national instruction didn't line up with a statewide mandate. Dr. Anthony Fauci and the Surgeon General, Jerome Adams, advised all Americans to wear a mask when going out in public. But in Georgia, and perhaps many other places, there was a deep concern about Black men going out in public wearing masks, due to historical bias and stereotyping. If white 25-year-old Johnny showed up at virtually any facility wearing a mask, no harm, no foul. If, instead, Black Joshua did the same, at least in some cases, alarm bells would go off, hair on the back of the neck of proprietors and security guards, especially in primarily white neighborhoods, would – consciously or unconsciously – quickly go into a state of heightened alert.

*

Andy Slavitt, largely credited for righting the ship that was the woefully painful launch of the Health Insurance Marketplace website under ObamaCare, pointed out, once again, how Trump's obsession with destroying "all things Obama" likely cost hundreds of lives in nursing homes and senior centers when the pandemic reared its ugly head.

Approximately a million and a half people live in nursing homes today in about 15,000 facilities. Among people over 80, many served in the Korean War, and some lived through the Great Depression. Our system, including our VA, has been flawed for many years. It made me remember the case of my own father, a Korean and Vietnam War veteran, who came here from the system in Shreveport, LA, where he had two hip replacements and apparently high-quality care. After living in Georgia for almost six months, however, my younger sister, who was visiting, noticed his inability to fully use one arm. At the VA, he was diagnosed as having had a mini-stroke. Though he walked into the hospital, he came out in a wheelchair, having to rehabilitate even to walk again – and that was under the Obama administration.

In 2016, in fact, President Obama put into place regulations that were wholesale meant to address nursing home infection control, overuse of psychotics, nursing home safety, all of these things. But sadly, in 2017, the Trump administration got rid of all the safety measures and said they were not going to enforce them.[226] This turned out to be the root of a lot of the challenges during COVID-19. "The time to have dealt with this is not in the middle of a pandemic," said Slavitt.

Overruled by her Republican-dominated Legislative Coordinating Council, Kansas Governor Laura Kelly had to make a last-minute appeal to the Kansas Supreme Court to re-enact her rule that no one could gather in groups of ten or more on Easter morning, including the churches that were determined to do so anyway, despite her statewide edict.[227]

Holy Week, the days preceding the death and resurrection of Jesus Christ in the Christian faith, was unlike any other in March of 2020. Whereas my small church would normally gather for Maundy Thursday, Good Friday, then in the garden of our local park for sunrise service on Easter Sunday, we, like millions of others, engaged in tele-church, learning to mute and unmute when speaking, straining to adapt to the "new normal." Oftentimes, we don't think about the fact that some people in our lives live alone. In this unprecedented era, we suddenly became more aware of them and their mental and spiritual health. Equally, or even more at risk were the people who were locked in with spouses, parents, siblings, uncles, and grandparents, who – intentionally, or out of a sense of frustration and desperation – battled those they supposedly love. Child and spousal abuse soared, as people who normally got a break from each other, were trapped. As someone close to me always says, "hurt people hurt people."

The CDC, Trump's and the world's premier health entity, had briefed him, "It's not so much a question of if this will happen anymore, but rather more a question of exactly when this will happen," in a February 25 event.

Trump, however, continued to defy the scientists and experts. "I don't believe it's inevitable," he said. "I think that there's a chance that it could get worse. There's a chance that it could get fairly worse."

Anybody that wants a test can have a test, POTUS proclaimed. Still, on April 12, nearly 100 days into the pandemic that had taken 22,000 American lives and almost two years after he had disbanded the pandemic task force, the U.S. had tested only two million people, less than one percent of the nation's population.[228]

Unaware of, or oblivious to cultural differences, a drive-up testing site was set up in a vulnerable community in Brooklyn, NY. Unfortunately, the site was ill-suited for the area, since it was set up for Black, inner-city residents, many of whom don't drive cars.

Day after day, the numbers rolled in. Due to a host of co-morbidities, including obesity, asthma, and diabetes, not to mention inherent ills like poverty, homelessness, and a lack of insurance, African Americans were dying at an alarming rate from the coronavirus. In fact, in Chicago, 68% of the city's COVID deaths were suffered in the African

American community, which soon climbed to 70%, though only 30% of Chicagoans are Black.

*

Like everyone else, I struggled to develop a workable rhythm while working from home. Following 26 straight days of work, as we monitored hot spots, PPE shortages, cruise ships that were and were not allowed to land, as well as comments and executive orders implemented by mayors and governors, I started to develop a groove. While many of my normal practices were curtailed, like those of everyone else, I did increase my head-clearing daily walks in the spring of 2020 from perhaps three to four times per week, to five or six.

Hearing people like Dr. Anthony Fauci, the nation's leading pandemic advisor, warn Americans that we should likely abandon the centuries-old habit of shaking hands, was certainly unnerving. And California Governor Gavin Newsom who, like New York's Andrew Cuomo and others, refused to be bullied by Trump regarding when to reopen the country and the economy, warned that the new normal might include going to restaurants where the waiter wears gloves and likely a mask.

All at once, it struck me. Since at HHS, I have been at the center of two of the most impactful events of the last century: 1) the rollout and implementation of the Affordable Care and Patient Protection Act by the nation's first Black president, and 2) the COVID-19 pandemic. The first, the ACA, gave more African Americans health insurance than at any other time since we were marched off the slave ships in 1619. The second, the coronavirus, was now cruelly and discriminately taking Black lives to a degree and with a deftness that Black-on-Black crime, and even the crack epidemic, never did. In both instances, working in the middle of the Stroke Belt, the Black Belt, the area of the country where Blacks suffered from every "ism" under the sun, along with the blight of poverty and overall poor education, I saw and rubbed shoulders with those people oftentimes most impacted by the shifts and challenges that swept our nation. As my old boss, Dr. Lowery, famously said, "When white America gets a cold, black America gets pneumonia." COVID-19's ruthless, concentrated attack on the African American community highlighted those disparities like little else could.

That's why, as I monitored the case and death counts daily, especially where I lived – in Dekalb County, Georgia, an Atlanta suburb and one of the top two biggest, Blackest counties in the state – I watched with apprehension each day for the death rate to spike in the county and wondered when it did not. On April 14, Dekalb County, GA, had 1,144 known cases, yet only 15 deaths from the disease. The rate of 1.5 percent was far below the national average and one-tenth of the state total of 14,578 cases and 524 deaths. In Dekalb, the fourth most populous county in the state, with 750,000 people, and the Blackest big county, people were out everywhere and, until the point when grocery stores began to enforce social distancing, people stood in close quarters in the checkout lines and shopping aisles. God only knows how many of them had coronavirus, especially since less than one percent of the nation's citizens had been tested, and if you were young and had credible, persistent symptoms, it was nearly impossible to get tested. April 14 was also the same day that New York recognized that it had undercounted its COVID deaths by 3,000, pushing the state's total to an astounding 10,000 deaths and the nation's count to over 29,000, only six weeks after the first death in a Washington nursing home. In New Jersey, the backlog for getting test results was two weeks, according to MSNBC's Rachel Maddow.

Governor Kemp did some things right. By April 16, he had dispatched the National Guard to sanitize 270 Georgia nursing homes, which certainly saved lives. He simply took too long to do it. Though he broke ranks with Trump on overturning the election, he was in lockstep with him as a COVID denier, instead preferring to value the Georgia economy over the lives of his most vulnerable citizens. Case in point: It was late April 2020, before the Georgia governor announced that anyone with COVID symptoms could *finally* get tested. Even then, however, the state's public health department had only 5,000 test kits on hand, a tiny fraction of the number that experts said was needed to track and contain the virus.[229]

President Obama famously said, leading to the launch of the ACA, "If you want to keep your health insurance, you can." Clearly, his statement proved to be wrong, or, as his conservative foes would put it, a lie. President Trump said in March of 2020, if you want a test [for coronavirus], you can get one." This, too, proved to be untrue. In fact, even as late as April 17, 2020, the U.S. was testing only 150,000 people a day nationwide. With only 3.5 million Americans tested – about one percent of the population – many who were sick, yet not elderly, were being told to go home and isolate. Millions of others were likely walking around asymptomatic, therefore not showing signs of illness, yet infecting others. So, while both of the last two presidents were wrong in their infamous statements (Obama's caused discomfort and pissed off a lot of people who wanted to keep their pre-ObamaCare insurance, yet couldn't), Trump's was more lethal. His proclamation, which proved false, meant people who were indeed deathly ill did indeed go on to die, as well as infect others. That was one helluva difference.

As of April 17, 2020, the U.S. had tested approximately 3.4 million people and was testing approximately 145,000 people per day. Sadly, that's less than one percent of the nation's 380 million people and, according to experts, less than one-third of the testing that should have been going on, at a minimum.

At one point, while COVID cases and deaths were so numerous and growing day by day, regional directors, who served as the secretary's representatives in the states they managed, had little control over the issues of testing, supply chains, messaging, and vaccination availability. In fact, about all they could do in states dominated by Republican governors who refused to impose restrictions on businesses and gatherings was "play whack a mole." VP Pence, certainly feeling the heat from Trump, called up *at least* one regional director late at night to issue a terse threat. "You and [Secretary] Azar better get your shit together," he said.[230]

On April 26, 2020, at the end of the weekend, as Kemp reopened Georgia's barber and beauty shops and tattoo parlors, Atlanta Mayor Bottoms said the state was up 32% in death count and 26% in cases from the week before. The following day, restaurants and other establishments were scheduled to open statewide, as well as in Oklahoma, Alabama, South Carolina, Mississippi, and several other states. Georgia and Florida, as bad as they looked, were not alone. Nineteen states reopened on some level as of April.

CNN, when interviewing Atlanta Mayor Keisha Lance Bottoms, aired footage of a virtually empty downtown Atlanta, showing that people there leaned on the advice of the mayor far more than they did on that of Governor Shotgun, who had been one of the last to issue stay-at-home orders, then became the first to proclaim the state's reopening on April 24. (Kemp had touted his anti-immigration cred when running for office by brandishing his shotgun and pickup truck to imply he'd use them to round up non-documented people.) Even Trump, likely at the insistence of his inner circle, voiced his disapproval of Kemp's decision, which clearly ran against the CDC's guidance that only after a 14-day drop in the percentage of new cases, should any government consider a phase one reopening.[231] As one of my Omega fraternity brothers in Texas, another state struggling with an abysmal response to the COVID pandemic, including a testing rate of 48th among 50 states, said: "How are you all out there in the ATL? I certainly hope black people don't fall for the okey-doke and go out and get their hair and nails done. Shrinking the minority voting pool. ..."[232]

I don't generally consider myself a conspiracy theorist, but with a high percentage of essential workers being Black and Latino, not to mention underinsured, Kemp's decision to reopen makes one wonder. If my antennas were unnecessarily up, I wasn't the only one. Black leaders throughout Georgia expressed both alarm and distrust, from Rep. Calvin Smyre, the most senior member of the Georgia House, to rapper T.I.

"I see an agenda, ya dig," said T.I., the award-winning rapper and Atlanta native. "And I'm sure everyone can see it. It ain't subtle, it ain't sophisticated, it's no mind-manipulated warcraft. It's real simple."[233] Many people were genuinely scared, and hundreds I personally knew, including the elderly and the medically vulnerable, had stopped gathering and fraternizing, even going to church. In addition, many people who had the luxury of doing so, had worked from home for the past two years.

When you earnestly look at the history of America utilizing people of color as guinea pigs, or tests for any number of deadly viruses, or in the name of medical advancement, the evidence is damning. The Tuskegee Experiment, perhaps the most famous, resulted in Black Americans being told they were being treated for syphilis beginning in 1932, though they were being given only placebos and aspirin, even after it was determined that penicillin effectively treated the disease.[234] Another gut-wrenching example was the way Dr. James Sims, the so-called father of gynecology, used slave women to experiment on techniques to find cures for childbirth complications by dehumanizing them while withholding anesthesia, as well as prescribing unproven medicine for children in Los Angeles that had killed Black children in Brazil and on the African continent, which was meticulously documented by Dr. Harriet Washington in her book *Medical Apartheid*.[235] The family of Henrietta Lacks, the poor Black woman whose illegally harvested HeLa genes from 70 years ago moved modern medicine ahead by decades, was finally awarded a $216 billion settlement from Thermo Fisher Scientific for her abuse in August of 2023.[236] It's worth noting that perhaps white America's first use of bioterrorism was the 1763 mission to infect Native Americans with smallpox by giving infected blankets as "gifts" after Shawnee and Mingo warriors assaulted Fort Pitt.[237] And for those of us who believe that discrimination in medicine is a thing of the past, 2020 studies show that physicians, often due to implicit bias, are less likely to treat Blacks equally for cardiovascular diseases and overall prefer white patients.[238] Those are just a few of the reasons that the implementation of the Affordable Care Act, which provided millions of poor and minority citizens their first health insurance ever, was such a monumental step forward, even though it was flawed.

Chapter 18: Hydroxychloroquine or Kool-Aid

"I will not give a single penny to any school that has a vaccine mandate or a mask mandate."

Donald Trump, campaigning in Wisconsin, June 19, 2024

These controversial business reopenings came on the heels of a week in which Trump, referencing some trials allegedly conducted by Homeland Security, suggested ingesting cleansers and disinfectants like Lysol and bombarding the body with heat, in yet another desperate attempt to stop the spread of the COVID virus. This came after several cases where the hydroxychloroquine and Ivermectin that the president had touted as possible cures, poisoned dozens of people across the country who took him at his word.[239] By Sunday, poison control centers in several states reported a rash of calls inquiring about gargling with, or ingesting different concoctions, including in Maryland, prompting GOP Governor Larry Hogan to say, "stick to the facts."

"People are buying over-the-counter Ivermectin, which is packaged to treat parasites in large animals like horses and cattle," explained Dr. Christopher Painter, an ER physician at BayCare Clinic in Green Bay, Wisconsin. "The animal preparations can be very dangerous. The dosing for a 1,200-pound animal is dramatically different than it would be for a human being. Even when used correctly, there can be some side effects, and those are much more likely to occur when users add significantly increased doses."[240]

Primarily due to the politicization of COVID, Republican lawmakers in at least four states (New Hampshire, Kansas, Tennessee, and Ohio) have continued to flout FDA and CDC directives, even two years after Trump left office.[241]

As the numbers began to escalate, from mid-April on, my boss, HHS Secretary Alex Azar, Trump's second HHS secretary, would end up being the scapegoat for the economic and human casualties of the novel coronavirus pandemic. Of course, that's what happens when you continue to "feed the beast." As denials continued to counter the rumors, growing into a rumble, my expectations of an impending Azar departure mounted. To his credit, however, he stuck around until the end.

By late April 2020, scientists determined that of the roughly 14 antibody tests available, only three were providing consistently reliable results. At the same time, April 26 proved to be the U.S.'s highest testing day – roughly 300,000 tests – which was still woefully short of the million or so per day needed, minimum. Even as late as April 28, Trump and VP bragged about having tested more people than any other country in the world, even as the U.S. also was branded with the label of having nearly 1,000,000 active cases, nearly four times as much as any other nation and more than the next four combined.

One of the most asinine statements and greatest spins in history took place at a news conference on April 26. John Karl, ABC News correspondent and president of the White House press corps, asked Pence what lessons had been learned since early March when Pence said there would be four million tests distributed to Americans by "next week." Pence, a marvelous second-in-charge, said, in essence, that the tests were distributed, but had not been administered or accounted for. As my friend Tony Renfrow would say, who does that make sense to? On April 27, Trump stood at the podium, boasting that the nation had tested five million people, "more than any other country in the world." What the hell happened to the nearly seven weeks in between?

Paul Romer, a Nobel Prize winner in economic sciences, said we should be spending $100 billion on testing, since the economy was losing $500 billion per month due to closure. Harvard claimed that the U.S. needed to test five million people per day in order to reopen safely, getting to five million a day by mid-summer (4/30/20), as U.S. coronavirus cases topped one million, with 58,000 deaths, a higher toll than America experienced during the grueling Vietnam War. In the meantime, Georgia's death count topped 1,000, while its total case count neared 25,000.

There were recoveries that certainly showed us the value of a single life. One example is Rodrigo Saval, who emerged from his 53-day hospital stay at Mount Sinai West Hospital in New York City, one of the hardest-hit municipalities in the nation. Saval, who spent half his time at Mount Sinai on a ventilator, was its first coronavirus patient.[242] April 29th saw dancing and unbridled joy on the part of the nurses and doctors, as well as his loved ones.

Assistant Secretary of Health (ASH) Dr. Admiral Brett Giroir, the administration's official in charge of testing, on April 27th threw cold water on claims of testing five million Americans a day after Trump said they'd meet that benchmark. "We're going to be there very soon," Trump told NBC Reporter Kristen Welker.

Giroir responded, "There's absolutely no way on earth, on this planet, or any other planet, that we can do 20 million tests per day, or even five million tests a day," in seemingly one of the few moments of truth voiced by the Trump administration regarding COVID. [243]

That truth, I contend, was exactly what Americans desperately needed and craved, both medically and politically: just tell us the truth, and we will deal with it.

The challenge, of course, was to engineer a way millions of Americans would not go bankrupt, or figure out how to keep the lights on and feed their families in the midst of the worst retail freefall since 1980, as more than a dozen states moved to reopen businesses, and even malls. Forty-three thousand health care workers lost their jobs in March, in large part due to the necessary cancellation of tens of thousands of elective surgeries. In Florida, as late as May 7, incredibly, only 28% of the 1.2 million people who had applied for unemployment benefits had received them from a "broken system." Congresswoman Val Demings said the governor had been warned about a year ago.[244] Chandi Bozeman, a beauty shop owner in Dayton, Ohio, had never filed for unemployment before. Denied a small business PPE loan, she tried to keep her family afloat, while refusing to allow her son to work during the pandemic. Bozeman is one of the 25% of American heads of households – the largest percentage in the world – that were single parents.[245] In most instances, these proud, resilient people, often leaders in their industries and valuable contributors to society, struggled mightily, both emotionally and mentally with their inability to care for themselves. And when a system they had paid into for years wasn't there for them, it could not help but shake confidence in our nation.

Once again, the poor, the uneducated, white, but mostly Black, brown, and yellow, paid the highest price.

"We are poor, and we need money, and we have no choice," a heartbroken daughter anguished over her mother, hospitalized and on a ventilator after contracting the disease at a meat plant in Colorado. "My mom says we don't have a choice. If they tell us to work, we have to work. We have a lot of bills to pay. My mom is a hard worker."[246]

Another, in line at a food bank in Long Island, NY, along with their seven-year-old, said, "It's a lot. I'm a single parent. I have a car note, and I have a mortgage. So, you kind of think, what's [my] priority right now? Do I pay the mortgage, or do I go grocery shopping?"[247]

Seventeen percent of mothers with young children said their children were not getting enough to eat, a figure twice that of the 2008 recession.

There were many heroes and "sheroes," however, like Yolanda Fisher, a cafeteria manager at T. W. Browne Middle School in Dallas, who continued to come to the closed school to pass out a week's worth of breakfasts to all the school's parents who showed up.

"I knew a lot of kids. This was the only meal they were getting every day," said Fisher, who had distributed 60,000 meals by the first week of May. Fisher began as a cafeteria worker who earned only $19,000 a year when she started. "Some of them have expressed shame, but I let them know there's no reason to go hungry if we're out here feeding."[248]

On May 8, it was reported that Katie Miller, press secretary for VP Pence and wife of Trump's white nationalist/anti-immigration/red meat-tossing attack dog Stephen Miller, had tested positive for COVID-19.[249] Her husband, one of Trump's leading policy influencers, praised Hitler's immigration policies, criticized the removal of the Confederate flag following the slaughter of nine Black parishioners in Mother Emanuel AME Church in Charleston, and was even labeled a white nationalist by a former right-wing Breitbart editor.[250] His uncle, who, like Miller, is Jewish, calls him an "immigration hypocrite." Part of me, I must admit, wanted to hear that she gave the virus to her race-baiting husband, not to kill him, but to make him deathly ill. As a Christian, I can't justify anyone dying from the horrific virus, but if I did have a short list ...

In April of 2020, I needed a root canal. Struggling with the decision due to COVID, I put it off at first, at the urging of my wife. Later, as the swelling and sensitivity intensified, I prayed and then went to get it done. My dentist, who pointed out that dentists and their assistants are the most afflicted among healthcare providers, told me she prays every time she goes into her office.

In New York, 80 percent of those arrested for failing to follow the social distance ruling were Black. Most cases shown on national news, which could, of course, be biased, was a blatant case of violence against Blacks. One man was repeatedly punched by one of Gotham's finest while on his back, trying to protect himself.[251] A woman, who allegedly became belligerent while refusing to wear a mask in a store, was body-slammed, sadly, by a Black off-duty cop. If we won't respect our own women – people – it makes it a helluva lot tougher to demand that others do.[252]

There was pushback. Color of Change was one group of young activists calling for justice and an end to America's willingness to sacrifice the poor, people of color, and the vulnerable.

Finally, on May 10, the White House determined that all employees and visitors needed to wear masks, a full 40 days, and three Trump-inner-circle infections after the CDC advised all Americans to wear masks when in the presence of others.[253]

CMS also used the occasion to announce that it was moving to provide COVID-19 testing to all nursing home residents and staff. Uh-oh, I thought. NOW you decide to do it, despite the fact that 1/3 of all deaths in the U.S. are related to nursing home infections. Just damn!

In an effort to help the lagging personal protective equipment (PPE) efforts, Alabama National Guard (ALNG) parachute riggers from the 20th Special Forces Group shifted from producing life-saving parachutes to life-saving surgical masks. The riggers had used their training time, materials, and skills to produce more than 2,000 masks thus far for #COVID19 responders. #TogetherAL

The evening of May 12, 2020, after having received a request from Congressman David Scott's office to help explore and locate a venue to do testing in Cobb County, a metro Atlanta suburb, I was shocked, a few hours later, to see a very familiar document highlighted on the *Rachel Maddow Show* on MSNBC. No, it was not me. Providing such highly-classified information to a national meeting in a time of crisis would be, as Dr. Fauci said while testifying before a House committee on education that very same morning when asked about the probability of vaccination by the start of the 2020 school term, "a bridge too far." That comment, of course, ticked Trump off and led him to repudiate the nation's leading infectious disease expert, who was already walking a political tightrope that would make the Flying Wallendas proud.[254] Early Indicators, the highly internal document that lists a series of cities and communities across the country where numbers of cases are skyrocketing – far above the national average and eons away from the 14-day leveling-off indicators that green-light reopenings of communities – was on the screen, in living color. Maddow acknowledged that someone had slipped the information to her. In one sense, mortified – in another, exceedingly thankful that I was not the party guilty of breaking protocol and sharing highly sensitive, internal documents in real time – the revelation was a confirmation that the desire to "sound the alarm" was more widespread than I had thought.

A Black doctor pointed out that COVID-19 didn't create a massive gap in life expectancy and vulnerability for African Americans. It simply exposed it. Dr. Foluso Fakorede, who is Nigerian, moved from New Jersey in 2015 to the Mississippi Delta, one of the poorest Black pockets in America, to make a difference. "My work involves saving limbs and saving lives," said Fakorede, whose parents were both diabetics. Poor Black people are referred for amputations at 3-4 times everyone else. They deserve a chance to be taught how to eat right to live right.[255] The same should be said for those living on reservations, in prisons, barrios, nursing homes, and food deserts.

Chapter 19: Being Black or Brown in America Should Not Be a Death Sentence

"The humblest peasant is as free in the sight of God as the proudest monarch that ever swayed a scepter. Liberty is a spirit sent from God and, like its great Author, is no respecter of persons."

Minister Henry Highland Garnet

On May 25, 2020, George Floyd was arrested and taken from his car. "Please, please, I can't breathe," gasped Floyd, as the officer leaned his entire weight on Floyd's neck for nine minutes and 29 seconds, according to the video. Transfixed, I watched the video, and even as my stomach turned, I could not swallow, and my heart broke. I could not intellectually grasp what I was watching, and yet, though deeply traumatized, I could not look away. This is the plight of being Black in America, the land of the free and the home of the brave. Once again, not long after the riots following the beating of Rodney King in Los Angeles, the police shooting of Michael Brown in Ferguson, Missouri, and the execution of Trayvon Martin, the sad saga repeated itself in the final days of May 2020. It was, tragically, "A Rage in Harlem" all over again.

Minneapolis Mayor Jacob Frey, even as his police department was under great scrutiny, said all the right things. "When you hear someone calling for help, you are supposed to help," said Frey. "This officer failed in the most basic sense. He was the person with the gun, the empowered." Floyd was the one being asked to trust a flawed system that privileges police officers, the good, the bad, and the ugly. Far too often, whether police officers do the right thing, or the wrong thing, they are rarely held accountable, especially when they take a Black life.

Ironically, or tragically, the last time I was in Minneapolis, my family and I stumbled into a large downtown protest. Thurman J. Blevins, 31, had been fatally shot days earlier, possibly armed and running away from police. Seeking lunch before heading to the airport following our denomination's annual meeting, Gather, we were surprised to run smack dab into a spirited protest taking up a major street in downtown Minneapolis. This was in June of 2018.[256] The death of Blevins took place just over two years and less than ten miles away from the killing of unarmed Philando Castile, allegedly stopped for driving a car with a taillight out. Castile was shot and killed in his car as his girlfriend and her four-year-old daughter watched and recorded the shooting.[257] Nearly a year following the Castile killing, Hispanic Officer Jeronimo Yanez was found not guilty of manslaughter after pumping five rounds into his unarmed victim. As bad as people talk about the South, Minneapolis, which has more interracial relationships per capita than anywhere else in the U.S., may be a more notorious killing field for young Black men.[258]

As frustration, righteous indignation, anger – and yes, opportunism – boiled into a rage, the peaceful protests, often stoked by police abuse and extreme force, at times erupted into riots. Beginning in Minneapolis, where the crowd watched in horror as cop Derek Chauvin put his full weight on the handcuffed Floyd for a full nine minutes and 29 seconds,[259] protests followed in Memphis, Chicago, Los Angeles, and elsewhere. Yes, it was ugly, and shameful. It cost good people their lives and livelihoods. It made me cringe watching it, people gleefully stealing whatever they could carry in response to the senseless killing of someone who looked like them, likely only because they looked like them. It was, to a much greater degree, the way I feel when I walk past a bus stop in a Black community, with trash cans on both sides of the benches, yet trash strewn across the place. Or my beautiful young brothers, with pants hanging down half their butts, not knowing why they wear them that way, or that their forced gait will lead to back problems. Or watching videos of young Black people performing smash and grabs, utilizing their genius and ingenuity for evil, not good. Yet, as bad as any of that is, it certainly was not as ruthless and inhumane as intensely kneeing a handcuffed man who had supplied little or no resistance – even as he cried "Mama!" and "I can't breathe," all the way up until he couldn't. The cop, in a position of power, coldly and without conscience, choked the life out of a helpless man. Yes, they rioted. They looted … and they were wrong. However, as Dr. King so eloquently framed the issue more than 50 years ago, "A riot," King said, "is the language of the unheard."[260] People who are desperate, people who are marginalized, people viewed as – and treated – as the Other, or less than, can reach a boiling point. People can and will, at least in some instances, revert to the very kind of reprehensible, animalistic, inhumane behavior that they were subjected to. I understand this behavior, even though I detest it. It is a transformation of the powerless seizing power for a brief moment in time, likely never to be repeated. The inevitable result of the world watching an execution of yet another innocent Black man: "A Rage in Harlem." This rash of Black killings, from Breanna Taylor and Botham Jean, in their own homes, Philando Castile, just down the road, Eric Garner and George Floyd, both choked out by the police in broad daylight and living color. Again, tragically, all this in the country that boasts, "we hold these truths to be self-evident, that all men are created equal, with certain inalienable rights to life, liberty and the pursuit of happiness." Bullshit. Dr. King hit the nail on the head in 1962 when he wrote *Why We Can't Wait*.[261]

Meanwhile, in 2023, for at least the second day in a row, a young white man, Peter Manfredonia, was on the run after allegedly murdering two men in separate incidents in Connecticut, including an elderly man who tried to help him and a former associate. Known to have struggled with mental health issues, Manfredonia had been identified on film as he fled along the railroad tracks.[262] During a month that the Black community had seen jogger Ahmaud Arbery tracked down like a runaway slave by three white men and shot point-blank because he was a suspected burglar, the killing of unarmed George Floyd by an officer who applied enough pressure on the unarmed man's neck with his knee to choke him out, someone I lived with simply couldn't take it anymore. Assessing the dual Americas confronting Black folk and the unequal justice that defined the home of the brave and the land of the free, she muttered, "I just can't." Watching the news segment on the fleeing Manfredonia, she commented: "I bet they take him alive." Indeed, they did.[263] Why can a young white man – who clearly has killed two in cold blood and kidnapped another – peaceably give himself up for arrest, while a Black man, simply out for a jog and committing no crime, and another under the knee of a cop for over nine minutes in broad daylight, be openly murdered? How many others, we must ask ourselves if we really want to deal with reality, die out of sight of a camera, or video? When will this country truly face a day of reckoning, the poor, the Black, the brown, and the oppressed ask every time this happens?

On the very same day, May 26, 2020, that the nation was within a whisper of reaching the profound number of 100,000 deaths from the coronavirus, a video surfaced about the heinous and blatant play on the race card by a privileged white woman in New York's Central Park. Illegally walking her dog without a leash, Amy Cooper was apparently courteously asked by a Black man, Christian Cooper (no relation), to put the dog on a leash. Mr. Cooper, a bird watcher, was adamantly told "no" by Ms. Cooper, who threatened to call the cops and tell them she was being threatened by a Black man if he insisted on asking her to leash the dog. Mr. Cooper continued to film her as she called 911 and said, "There's an African American man in Central Park. He's recording me and threatening me and my dog. I'm being threatened by a man in the bramble. Please call the cops immediately."[264] White pomposity!

Her employer, Franklin Templeton, after seeing the tape, fired her immediately. "We do not tolerate racism of any kind," the statement said. Ms. Cooper later apologized, saying she was scared because she was alone in Central Park.[265]

"She'll leave [Templeton] with a really nice separation package," a colleague of mine said, brimming with disgust.

On the same night, a Black man, Archie Charles Williams, was featured on *America's Got Talent*. He had been wrongly imprisoned for 37 years. Somehow, he still had his voice and, more importantly, his sanity and a belief that life was worth living, even though more than half of his had been stolen by a flawed and racially insensitive justice system.[266]

In Mississippi, where African Americans are 38% of the population, they are also 52% of the COVID cases, with an even higher percentage of deaths, due largely to lack of health care, poverty, and access.

Why, I thought, in a moment of deep despair, do we always have to be the ones understanding, forgiving, and keeping our heads and hearts up and open, even in the midst of our misery?

In 2018, approximately 9.2 million adults lived with co-occurring mental and substance use disorders. Those who misuse any substances are more likely to experience serious mental health conditions. The pressure of staying inside, isolated from family and friends, weighed more heavily on some than others. Those more susceptible to succumbing to addictive behaviors, often did so. The pandemic also opened numerous opportunities for human traffickers and predators prone to domestic violence to abuse their victims more easily, who were often unable to communicate with those who might help. To the Trump administration's credit, we did a tremendous amount of work communicating with and learning from domestic violence shelters, substance abuse centers, and other entities that focused on adoption, recovery, counseling, social services, and HIV treatment.[267]

Atlanta was also in play, as two major protest groups amassed in downtown Atlanta the day Trump tweeted this critique of the Minneapolis protests: "These THUGS are dishonoring the memory of George Floyd, and I won't let that happen." Trump added that he had spoken to Gov. Tim Walz and told him that "the Military is with him all the way. If there is any difficulty, we will assume control, but when the looting starts, the shooting starts. Thank you!"[268]

One young white girl, wearing a mask and helmet, came from mostly conservative Athens, home of the University of Georgia, two hours away, to join the Atlanta protest, along with her mother, who was on the front lines, face-to-face with police. "I'm here because I'm tired of young black men being killed for walking the streets," she said. Atlanta Police Chief Erika Shields, a small, white brunette, waded into the irate crowd, backed by one of her officers. Getting nose-to-nose with angry protesters who asked her how she was going to improve race relations in

Atlanta, Shields didn't back down, insisting she didn't represent Trump. "I don't want to be arresting young black people, especially young black men," she explained to a group of young protesters. "I want to arrest people with guns who are shooting people. I don't want to arrest people for stupid shit like smoking marijuana."[269] After that, the young Black men and women were defused, turning their frustration elsewhere.

"Violence is never the answer," said Rev. Bernice King, who noted that, like George Floyd's daughter, she lost her father to senseless violence as a little girl. "We must as a nation deal with racism and white supremacy. We must utilize non-violence. Violence never solved anything."

Cornell William Brooks, former NAACP president and Harvard professor, put it this way. "Yes, there are provocateurs [on both sides]. Let's be clear about this. It appears then, and it appears now, we have people coming in from outside the community, intent on fomenting chaos, anarchy, and violence. The issue is not left or right provocateurs, but right or wrong. It is wrong to attempt to loot or commit acts of violence in other people's community, or any community.

"In [Minneapolis] on a street corner where I stood, literally, two white supremacists came in from outside and shot five people within 24 hours of my standing there," Brooks continued. "But let's not tar the whole and the many protesters with terms like terrorists. They're [the protesters] doing what the constitution allows them to do, and their conscience compels them to do."[270]

Perhaps, in a way, the heartache, fear, desperation, angst, anger, loss, and heartbreak experienced in the Black community can be summed up by the rock group The Police: "Every move you make, every step you take, I'll be watching you."[271] While the masterful musicians meant it in a totally different way, as Black Americans – especially young Blacks, and particularly Black men – there's absolutely no way NOT to feel like you're under the microscope every day of your life. In fact, far too often for most white Americans to believe or understand, in confrontations with people in authority, Black Americans face a gun, a whisper, a stare, or a smart retort, in interactions and confrontations that may determine whether you live or die. This lived reality and the classic words to "My Country, 'tis of Thee"[272] simply don't line up for much of America, especially, though not exclusively, for young Black men and women:

> *My country, 'tis of thee,*
> *Sweet land of liberty,*
> *Of thee, I sing;*
> *The land where my fathers died,*
> *Land of the pilgrims' pride,*
> *From ev'ry mountainside*
> *Let freedom ring!*

"This is so much bigger than her," said Tamika Palmer, the mother of Breonna Taylor, a first responder shot and killed in her own home by a group of plainclothes police in Louisville. During one of several subsequent protest marches sparked by her killing, seven people were shot and one person killed on May 31.[273]

"This is exhaustive," a young protester in Atlanta said. "I have to protest my right to not be killed."

Finally, after days of silence, except for offensive tweets, Trump held a call with the governors on June 1, challenging them to "dominate" the protesters, or continue to look weak. Using the term "dominate" at least four times, he was challenged by at least two governors, including J. B. Pritzker of Illinois, who told him his rhetoric wasn't helping anything and that "people were hurting." Trump, like a petulant child, retorted that he didn't like Pritzker's rhetoric either.

"It's [the protests] about years and years of not having access to justice, a lack of accountability on the part of police departments, it's about good police officers not calling out the bad ones," said Sadiqa Reynolds, president of the Louisville Urban League. "This is about black people believing their lives don't matter. This is about white people not hearing us and feeling our pain."[274]

Protests blossomed in London, Paris, Amsterdam, and elsewhere within a week of the Floyd murder. Even in Saudi Arabia, a beautiful mural of Floyd was created.

Chapter 20: White Pomposity

White Pomposity: The unfair, unearned, and privileged expectation that allows some white people, as well as those who see themselves as white, to assume that this country and earth belong to them and that people of color who happen to be in what they perceive as their spaces, can be demanded, or asked to move aside, with every expectation that they will submit or comply, without question or resistance.

This country, it must be noted, was built on protest and the fight for agency and independence. The first and most enduring symbol of American independence from the world's most powerful nation, England, was immortalized by American "patriots" dumping 342 barrels of the tea off the good ship *Eleanor* in Griffin's Harbor in Boston in 1773.[275] What was "Mother" England's crime? Taxation without representation is the same thing the District of Columbia complained about in 2023, more than 225 years later.[276] The irony should not be lost on any of us that Crispus Attucks, a mulatto of Black and Native American descent, was the first person to be killed in the Boston Massacre.[277] Yes, European, white Americans took the country from the Indians, the First Nation folk, built it on the back of African slaves, and then saw the first person martyred in the revolution, a person of color, represent both ravaged races. Just damn!

Approximately 1.25 million Americans fought or supported the monumental efforts of World War II. The U.S. entered the war after Pearl Harbor was bombed to help tip the balance toward the Allies and away from Germany's push for Aryan world dominance, eventually breaking the iron grip of Hitler's Germany and Japan.

Many of the Black soldiers were cooks and handled tasks no one else wanted to do. However, there were others who fought valiantly, including the legendary Tuskegee Airmen, who proved to be among the best fighter pilots in the world, as well as the 761st tank battalion, cited by Major General Willard S. Paul for special commendation.[278] Meanwhile, German soldiers, captured in the war while striving for world domination, were granted privileges and treated better than the Black soldiers, who were forced to live and work under segregated conditions as they fought and died for their country. One example is the nation's oldest World War II vet, 110-year-old Louisiana native Lawrence Brooks. Drafted at age 31 in 1940, Brooks was shipped to Australia, where he cleaned uniforms, shined shoes for three officers, and was not allowed to carry a gun. His reality, socially, while serving in the Pacific theatre from 1941-1945, was a breath of fresh air. "I was treated so much better in Australia than I was by my own white people," he recalls.[279] His plight, however, was much more positive than that of many, including Isaac Woodard, 26, who was returning home to Winnsboro, South Carolina, on February 26, 1946, after three years of meritorious service fighting for his country in the Philippines. In uniform, Woodward asked the driver, who refused, to allow him to stop and use the bathroom. Instead, the driver called ahead to the Batesville police department. When the bus stopped, Batesville Police Chief Lynnwood Shull accosted him, beating him so badly, he blinded him.[280] Unfortunately, his story was not unique.

Less than a decade later, Rosa Parks and Dr. Martin Luther King, Jr. would burst onto the scene through the 381-day Montgomery Bus Boycott, one of the first major economic collaborations by Black people to challenge discrimination and spark systemic change. Choosing to walk, often for many miles, and coordinating their own illegal, ad hoc ride service, Parks and King were joined by Alabama State University professor Jo Ann Robinson, head of the Women's Political Council, Rev. Ralph Abernathy, and NAACP President E. D. Nixon. Together, they spearheaded a fierce resistance to a racist transportation system that treated them as second-class citizens. Though not the first successful bus boycott by Blacks in the U.S. – Baton Rouge and Tallahassee were fruitful earlier – this was the one that reverberated across the nation and helped launch the 27-year-old King toward immortality. Protest is as American as jazz, baseball, and apple pie. American independence from England was born out of protest. However, protests against violence enacted on Black Americans were discouraged and oftentimes met with violence and repression that included state-sanctioned authoritarianism, even when the protesters were peaceful and included white citizens.

"People are losing their lives, so we have to be willing to risk our lives to bring about progress," one 50-something-year-old Black woman said at a protest in D.C.

The call for justice reverberated worldwide, from London, Australia, South Korea, Mexico, and Germany. "No justice, no peace" and "Black Lives Matter," marchers proclaimed across the globe. Acknowledging the injustice, California and Minneapolis banned chokeholds and demanded that officers step in when they see abuse by other cops.

White pomposity? How about Anthony Brennan III, a lawyer, assaulting and intimidating three white teens on a Maryland bike trail? They had been posting anti-police brutality posters in response to the George Floyd murder that read: "Killer cops will not go free. Text 'Floyd' to 55156.

Do not live in ignorance. Use your privilege for good." His punishment? Three years' probation and anger management class requirements.[281] Roughhousing the teens like a modern-day gangsta-bully while they did their part to forward the national discussion over police brutality and over-policing, the married father of three allegedly called the shocked white teens "deviants" and accused them of "causing riots."[282]

Brennan, clearly playing on his white privilege and proudly proclaiming his white pomposity as a successful business executive, was shocked when he was immediately fired by his employer, Made to Order, where he served as an executive vice president, upon being identified as the assailant. I wonder what the former executive would have thought if one of his three children had been accosted by an overzealous 60-year-old, while striving to do their part toward righting centuries-old wrongs? What would he have said or done had someone confronted and threatened his own kids? This incident, much like the case of Amy Cooper in Central Park, reeked of white pomposity. Even more telling, his assault was perpetrated on white kids. Thank God they were white kids, though no one should be traumatized for demanding justice. Had they been Black kids, however, what kind of justice would they have received?

*

June 2, 2020, was a monumental day. Attorney General Bill Barr, at the direction of Trump, had federalized troops on horseback and in full riot gear, armed with clubs, tear gas, and rubber bullets to bum-rush peaceful protesters. Why? So Trump could stroll across the street from the White House to D.C.'s revered St. John's Episcopal Church for a photo op, pathetically holding the Holy Bible as a prop. The shameless ploy shocked some clergy and others who believed the church was a sacred place, not a political tool.

Heck, even some Evangelicals, 80 percent of whom supported him, were outraged. The moves also drew the ire of both the nation's most respected retired generals and even Presidents Bush, Clinton, and Obama, who had struggled mightily to stay quiet as Trump worked to destroy so much that Americans viewed sacred. Former Army Joint Chiefs of Staff Chairman Mark Milley, who built a meritorious career and is doggedly against the military being used for political purposes, later said his involvement was one of the most regrettable moments of his career. Reacting to Trump's brazen, federal-troop-clearing-of-protesters stroll to St. John's, down the street from the White House, the bishop of Washington said, "He's welcome as anyone is welcome to pray, to kneel before God in humility and to rededicate themselves to the task for which they were elected. He's not entitled to use the spiritual symbolism of our sacred spaces and our sacred text to promote or to justify an entirely different message."[283]

The next day, when the three other officers in the Floyd killing were finally arrested, tears were shed and protesters cheered, yet they vowed to continue to protest, pushing for reform. Angered by the latest Trump catastrophe – the bush league move at the church – while the violence and looting nearly dissipated, the protests grew larger, not smaller.

On the day of Floyd's funeral, June 4, 2020, another high-profile case went to court. The three people arrested for killing Ahmaud Arbery were front and center. Detailing the deadly minutes, detectives, testifying under oath, said the three men in two trucks chased him, one even running into him to keep him from getting away. Hemmed in, confronted by Travis, who was armed with a shotgun, Arbery fought back, getting a few licks in on Travis, who shot him, once in the wrist, then twice in the chest, apparently, as his father yelled, "Don't shoot!" Afterward, according to the third assailant, who hit Arbery with the truck; shooter Travis stood over the dying man, proclaiming, "F_____g Nigger!" Just like slave bounty hunters had 200 years before, the vigilantes tracked him down, executed him, and then cursed his very existence, even in broad daylight. Again, thank God for cameras, but damn white pomposity!

That same day, in Buffalo, New York, a tall, distinguished white man, Martin Gugino, 75, stood his ground as he took part in a Floyd murder protest, gesturing to approaching guardsmen in riot gear, rightfully expecting to be given the respect he certainly deserved. Instead, shockingly, without allowing him to explain anything, one guardsman abruptly shoved the older man, who was shocked and fell back, struggling to maintain his balance but crashing to the sidewalk, his head snapping as he hit the pavement, blood pouring out. Gugino was apparently out cold.[284] Immediately after the suspension of the two officers was announced, 57 Buffalo police resigned in protest, even though the first report from the police had erroneously claimed Gugino tripped.[285] The problem was not that any elderly American should have been given more respect than the gentleman was afforded, but that, as a white man, he fully expected it and was shocked to not get it. Instead, the officer who pushed him pulled another officer, who sought to render aid to the man who was lying on the pavement out cold, bleeding from the ears, away from the seriously injured elder. This particular protest, which, frankly, was controversial because it was based on the issue of race, police brutality, and an unequal justice system, was even victimizing white people.

During the leadup to the 2020 election, former President Obama ushered a frank warning, saying: "I believe a lot of young people have been activated in ways they haven't been before. But if we are slack, let our guards down. ..."[286]

Meanwhile, though numbers were slowing overall, 108,000 Americans had died from the coronavirus in less than four months, with some states reopening casinos, bars, beaches, waterparks, and restaurants to large, unmasked, or under-masked crowds. Was Trump right, or was he wrong, regarding his gamble to push to reopen the businesses that fuel the economy, despite half of America failing to read his own CDC's reopening guidelines? Was Trump really willing to pull the GOP national convention from Charlotte because Democratic Governor Roy Cooper insisted that social distancing must take place at the convention and that 50,000 unmasked people, though bringing big convention dollars with them, would not be able to cram inside the Charlotte Convention Center, August 24-27? By June 15, we would have a real indication. COVID and the economy were already twin barrels that were deemed to determine whether a second term would be granted. Suddenly, thanks to a 12-minute video and an excruciating nine-minute, 29-second execution of a handcuffed man in a video that went viral, Trump had aimed a third gun at himself. Unable to summon up any real semblance of empathy, the ever-defiant president seemed determined to stand his ground, much like George Rodriguez, but wielding the weapon of Twitter and a bully pulpit, not a .357 Magnum.

Everybody shouldn't be a cop, just as everybody shouldn't be a pastor, a teacher, a guidance counselor, or even ... the president. For me and my officemates, all of whom are Black, we were not officially impacted by the horrific string of shootings and killings of Black people, which challenged the nation's psyche and purportedly lofty ideals. However, Trump's relentless support of the police in virtually all instances, his calls for maximum aggressiveness against protesters, and his heightened criticism of minorities and strong women, were a constant drain on our enthusiasm and pride in our jobs.

Chapter 21: You Say You Want a Revolution

"The Lord who told me to take care of my people meant me to do it just as long as I live, and so I did what he told me."

Underground Railroad Conductor Harriet Tubman

I'll admit it. Gladly. Unashamedly, even. I was simultaneously deeply distressed and forever scarred by the trauma the George Floyd murder invoked, yet stunningly inspired by my country's response. Never in my lifetime did I expect, or even hope to see, the sort of revolution the public, filmed-in-broad-daylight execution by a state-sanctioned public official of George "Perry" Floyd on a Minneapolis street would provoke in the United States of America, much less the world. The choking out by cop knee, which took 9:29 minutes and was watched in living color by at least a dozen people, then shown across the globe, again and again, ignited a movement and sparked a revolution. The shameful event, another deadly, daunting example of white pomposity, reminded me of two quotes by the great Freedom Fighter Frederick Douglass: "Power concedes nothing without a demand. It never did and it never will" and "Without a struggle, there can be no progress."[287] The shame of it all was that it took a nearly 10-minute public execution to activate Americans to stand up for justice for unarmed Black men. Unfortunately, the horror of Floyd's death and the activism it sparked, is that it didn't last. Though white Americans turned out by the thousands across the nation and the world, the constant assault from the right labeling liberal whites "snowflakes" and "woke," along with gruffness and sometimes a threatening and even violent response from police, gradually thinned the crowds and quieted the outrage. Today, the element of white America who lives and breathes white pomposity continues to rage. Even in 2023, blatant examples emerge. In Montgomery, Alabama, once the home of the Confederacy, when Damien Pickett, assistant riverboat captain of the *Harriott II* tour boat, asked a party group of white boaters to move their craft a few feet to accommodate the incoming vessel so it could dock at its assigned spot, he was viciously attacked by five white people. Pickett, who is Black, had asked several times as those on the ship watched the assault unfold and several filmed it.

"This whole thing is just because these guys were being assholes," Capt. Jim Kittrell, who is white, told *The Daily Beast*. Pickett explained, "I was nice as a peach when I was talking to them at first: 'Please, help me out here, fellas. Move the boat up a little bit.'" Soon, Black patrons on the dock joined in the fracas to help the overwhelmed Black man, who was being pummeled as he lay on the ground. In the end, four whites and one chair-wielding Black man were arrested.

"The white guys that attacked my deckhand – and he was a senior deckhand first mate – I can't think of any other reason they attacked him other than it being racially motivated," Kittrell said. "All he did was move their boat up three feet. It makes no sense to have six people try to beat the snot out of you just because you moved their boat up a few feet. In my opinion, the attack on Damien was racially motivated."[288] It was yet another example of too much white pomposity and too much liquid courage. Many white people are simply unwilling to have people tell them what to do.

Black people like me have been simmering, even burning, like hot cauldrons for years at the injustice and systemic racism. How do we sometimes express it in destructive manners? Drugs, alcohol, overeating, high blood pressure, heart disease, induced self-hate, strokes, depression, domestic and child violence. You name it, many of us have sought ways to escape, to ease the pressure, to pretend like it wasn't as bad as we knew it really was, or, as in my case, "keep hope alive" that the pressures of racism are temporary, and that it will eventually get better.

      An eternal optimist who always wanted to believe the best about humanity, I was finally caught in the depths of despair. The date was June 13, 2013, another muggy evening in Atlanta. Although I was transfixed with the trial of George Zimmerman and, like much of America, awaiting the verdict, I had just taken our son, Jamal, to downtown Atlanta, where he was the videographer for an event that evening. As I dropped him off and whipped the car around to get back onto the highway and return home, unexpectedly, the jury returned, and I listened as the verdict was read on the radio. Community night watchman Zimmerman, despite being told by authorities not to pursue the youth, had been found not guilty by a six-woman jury, nearly 16 months after killing Trayvon Martin. It took only three days for a jury of his peers to acquit him of second-degree murder.[289] For one of the few times in my life, I was stunned. Looking for a place to pull over as soon as possible, I cut over in front of another driver, urgently trying to get to the side of the road. Though not in a place where it was particularly safe, I let the windows down, straining to grab a breath, my heart beating furiously, like a Congolese drum. Gasping, I fought back tears, even as they streamed down my cheeks, trying – desperately trying – to comprehend how the nation I loved so dearly could betray me so completely, so cavalierly. Martin, a 17-year-old, unarmed Black kid in a hoodie, was simply trying to get home from the store where he bought a bag of Skittles. Against police dispatch instructions, Zimmerman, armed with a Glock and the Castle doctrine, went after Martin. After being tracked like a runaway slave,

Martin fought back fiercely. As the teenager was whipping the grown man's ass, the cowardly Zimmerman shot him in the chest point-blank, instead of simply taking the ass whipping he had begged for. This verdict, perhaps more than any other, was more than I could bear. Broken, I leaned my head against the steering wheel, weeping bitterly until I could cry no more. It was at this point in my life that I felt most alienated, most distrustful of white America, even my beloved white friends. That next Sunday, even my white friends in my justice-conscious, multi-cultural church, which I love and believe gets it right almost all the time, were miles away from the depth of pain I carried from the acquittal.

After the death of Martin, 16, the nation erupted in protest following the killing by a St. Louis County cop of 18-year-old Michael Brown in Ferguson, Missouri on August 9, 2014. The shooting took place following an incident that Brown was involved in at a local grocery store. In the end, after the policeman followed Brown and got out of his car following a scuffle with Brown on the sidewalk, some witness accounts say that Brown, who was to head off to college in a few days, charged the officer, who shot him six times. Though the circumstances of the shooting were starkly different, Brown's body lay in the street in the sweltering heat for four hours.[290]

One month before the shooting of Brown, in July of 2014, New York police choked the life out of Eric Garner as he gasped, "I can't breathe." His crime? Selling single cigarettes. Just a few months later, 12-year-old Tamir Rice was alone, playing in the park with a toy gun. After receiving a call from an alarmed white person, police roared up to a bewildered Rice. Less than ten seconds later, hardly by the time the police car had screeched to a halt, Rice lay dead, shot from less than 10 feet away.

Why do I recount these tragic killings of unarmed Black boys and men nearly a decade later, two years before Trump even took office? The violence against unarmed Black men was certainly nothing new. However, there was clearly a backlash against Obama's election, which didn't sit well with certain elements of white America. Four times as many guns were purchased as there were babies born during Obama's first term, an absurdly unprecedented number.[291] It's worth remembering that South Carolina Congressman Joe Wilson, a son of the Confederacy who fought tooth and nail against removing his state's Confederate flag, broke decorum in an unprecedented manner by yelling, "You lie," at Obama during the State of the Union address.[292] Because I contend Trump's divisive, inflammatory, often hateful rhetoric targeted virtually all non-white, non-male people in America, making us unsafe as he weaponized lone wolves to terrorize in schools, stores, houses of worship, bars, and neighborhoods. I certainly didn't feel secure with him running the country and declaring there were "good people on both sides" as white nationalists chanted, "Jews will not replace us" in Charlottesville, where they sparked violent clashes that caused three deaths and injured at least 19,[293] nor when he criticized several city leaders' desire to remove monuments to slaveholders and insurrectionists who tried to overthrow the U.S. government over 150 years earlier when many of today's American citizens would have had no rights or agency. Congressman John Lewis, who represented the district in which our Atlanta HHS office was housed, was one of them. Trump lambasted those Black-run cities as "crime-ridden" and "falling apart" while pointing out that Lewis didn't attend his inauguration as a rationale for not taking part in the events where the deceased Lewis was being honored.[294] Instead of trying to understand the plight of those offended by the Lost Cause narrative and all it stands for in an increasingly multicultural America, Trump couldn't even pretend to be a unifier, but instead chose to throw gasoline onto the fire, exhorting the white nationalists to sow violence and chaos.

In 1998, I had heard anguished horror stories about James Byrd being offered a ride, then dragged alive by a trio of racists for three miles along an asphalt road in Jasper, Texas, likely alive until his body hit a curb, which decapitated him. This occurred just before I left my role as national communications director for the SCLC and moved to become the first public affairs representative for a political appointee in the regional office of the U.S. Department of Health and Human Services in the Region IV office in Atlanta. Unthinkably, John William King, one of three men who dragged Byrd until he was decapitated, became the first white man sentenced to death in Texas for killing a Black man.[295] That means that the hundreds who had done so before that heinous act had all gone unpunished. In 2009, President Obama named a hate crime bill after James Byrd, Jr. ... Why am I retelling these stories a quarter-century later? Because they have not stopped, nor become less horrific. White pomposity is still alive and well, some 70 years after the alleged deaths of Jim and Jane Crow. [296]

This brief but devastating list doesn't include Sandra Bland, Darrius Stewart, Kendrick Johnson, Philando Castile, Terence Crutcher, Walter Scott, and Elijah McClain, all unarmed and killed at the hands of police since 2008. Or Kathryn Johnston, 92, living in inner city Atlanta, who was shot by a "Red Dog" team with a no-knock warrant, or Breonna Taylor who, in 2020, suffered a similar death.

Thirteen days after the Floyd protests began, word leaked out that Trump had ordered 10,000 U.S. troops out to control and, in his words, "dominate" American citizens standing up for their rights. How, I ask myself and the rest of the country, can someone we trust to lead us, to protect us, to inspire us, dare to send an Army of our military combatants to control law-abiding American citizens exerting their rights to peacefully protest?

A sign in London read *White silence is violence, Silence is complicity*. Similar signs and campaigns were spotted in Sydney, Australia; South Korea; Berlin; and throughout the world. "Being a black man in America, we all feel the pressure to survive," said Joshua Lee, a recent college graduate marching in our nation's capital.

None of the pushback moved Trump, however. In fact, it seemed that every time he opened his mouth, he pushed his size 12 foot further into it.

By June 6th – day 12 of the protests across the United States – the sporadic vandalism, looting, and violence by protesters had slowed to a crawl. Instead, a determined rainbow of U.S. citizens striving to create change in America's 400-year history of mistreatment of people of color, flooded the streets. The goal was to challenge the inbred double standard framed by white supremacy and the dehumanization of people of color, especially Black people.

"George Floyd is going to change the arc of this nation," said Texas Governor Greg Abbott. "His death was not in vain."[297] That was mighty white of Abbott – the governor who in 2023 shipped scared, confused immigrants who sometimes had traveled thousands of miles to get to the Texas border – to northern cities like Chicago, New York, and Washington, D.C., as political puppets. He's also the same governor who, in the summer of 2023, established a barrier of large, floating orange balls in the middle of the Rio Grande, where several immigrants were cut by the barbed wire surrounding the balls, and at least two were found dead, caught on the wires.[298] A Texas border patrol officer called the treatment of the immigrants "inhumane" in a July 3, 2023 email. In his charges, he recounted that a four-year-old girl passed out from heat exhaustion as she was pushed back by

Texas state troopers when she tried to navigate the barriers.[299] White pomposity, I tell you, or as Dr. King would say, "Man's inhumanity to man is not only perpetrated by the vitriolic actions of those who are bad. It is also perpetrated by the vitiating inaction of those who are good."[300]

Bubba Wallace, the Black NASCAR driver who admitted he was still learning all about the underlying reasons for the Black Lives Matter movement, said his goal was to remove all Confederate flags from NASCAR events because they make some people uncomfortable. Love the sentiment, I thought at the time, but good damn luck with that one. I was proven wrong, but this time, in a good way.

"Bringing people together around a love for racing and the community that it creates is what makes our fans and sport special," NASCAR said in a statement. "The display of the Confederate flag will be prohibited from all NASCAR events and properties."[301] However, two days after Wallace called for a ban on the flags, and NASCAR (seemingly agreeably) complied, a noose was found in his garage stall at the Talladega Superspeedway.[302] So even though NASCAR's corporate leadership may have been fully on board, clearly someone else wasn't.

Speaking in broad terms about the 2020 social movement that galvanized the nation and spread to much of the world, former Republican Congressman Joe Scarborough of MSNBC's Morning Joe posited: "This isn't about Trump. … This is about 400 years of racial injustice."

"We're headed for a fight with the police union relative to all of the transformative measures we've seen put on the table," said Redditt Hudson, a former St. Louis police officer. "The police can't investigate themselves."[303] Let's think about that statement rationally, can we? Do any of the rest of us get to investigate ourselves?

Speaking before the congressional House hearing on June 10, Floyd's younger brother, Philonise, said this: "My brother didn't deserve to die for twenty dollars. I'm asking you, 'Is that what a black man's life is worth?' He still called him sir as he pleaded for his life. You don't even do that to an animal."[304]

Republicans, on most occasions, continued to remain mum on numerous key issues, as the high profile of unarmed Black males killed by white men in authority continued to rise. Trump posited that the 75-year-old white protester in Buffalo approaching the police to have a conversation was injured in a "set up," when officers pushed him backward, causing him to fall and crack his head. Trump's tweet suggested Martin Gugino, a long-time peace activist, was an "ANTIFA provocateur."[305] For any police officer to believe they could brazenly push a 75-year-old white man to the ground is an example of unmitigated white pomposity, regardless of the color of the officers. Gutless wonders. Attorney General Bill Barr and Economic Advisor Larry Kudlow took it to an even higher level of white pomposity. Asked whether they believed the United States was plagued with systemic racism, with a straight face and apparent earnestness – despite all that we have seen and the nearly ten other African Americans who we now know died while saying "I can't breathe" – Barr and Kudlow both insisted, "I don't believe there is systemic racism."

Perhaps Judy Scott, mother of unarmed Walter Scott, 50, who was shot in the back *running away* from Officer Michael Slager, put it best: "There's a lot of Georgie Floyds, and my son was one of them."[306] Scott, guided by her faith, almost unbelievably forgave Slager at his trial.

*

The image was branded into my brain, even my subconscious. It turned my stomach, yet I could not turn away. The nine minutes and 29 seconds were burned into my soul. Watching, my gut churned like a cauldron, my spirit crushed and all but broken. I tossed and turned all night, consumed by the image of Chauvin's knee in George Floyd's neck as he pleaded for mercy. I tell myself I would not have stood watching and instead would have slowly approached the officers, reasoning with them, hands outstretched, palms up, prayerfully giving the rest of the anguished bystanders some courage to come along with me. If ineffective, I would charge Chauvin. They wouldn't shoot us all … could they … would they? I wanted to believe I'd do the right thing. I see myself as nobody's hero. But I am older now. I had seen so many Black men murdered, so many Black women abused and disrespected. So many proud people were reduced to living beneath their abilities, shunned by a system they undergirded and sustained; but in the end, I couldn't be sure. On other occasions, I had failed to stand up, instead counting the cost.

Chapter 22: Trump's Twisted Juneteenth

"This isn't about Trump. This is about 400 years of racial injustice."

Former GOP Congressman Joe Scarborough, Morning Joe, MSNBC

Clearly, Trump determined that he and his cadre of conservative governors were more than willing to sacrifice tens of thousands of American lives for the sake of reopening the nation's businesses and putting Americans back to work. To that end, the week of June 6-9, 2020, resulted in U.S. infection rates spiking by 36 percent, according to the WHO, though it had misspoken earlier in the week when it said asymptomatic people weren't likely to spread the virus. At the same time, as the U.S. moved toward mid-June of 2020, 12 states that had opened earlier than their more cautious colleagues, saw a rise of COVID cases by 25 percent.

What a week. Trump insisted he didn't choose Juneteenth, the holiday commemorating the day when slaves were finally told that Lincoln had declared them free, to hold his post-COVID-shutdown coming-out event in Tulsa, perhaps the site of the worst atrocity white Americans ever perpetrated on their Black neighboring citizens. Torching the famed "Black Wall Street" in 1921, white marauders and mobs killed hundreds of Black citizens, and approximately 190 Black businesses and 1,000 homes went up in flames.[307] Of all the places for Trump to reemerge after having had virtually nothing to say about the death of George Floyd and the broadest, most sweeping social revolution since the

1960s, he chose Tulsa. Trump, of course, insisted there was no intentionality in the choice of cities. Yeah, right.

The historic city was quite likely the place that Herman Cain, one of Trump's most visible and high-profile African American allies, along with a group of other Black supporters, attended the rally without wearing a mask – against the advice of the county's health director – contracted COVID and died, five weeks later.[308] Cain, an uber-successful businessman and a model of Black excellence, whether you believed in his politics or not, briefly led the pack of 2016 GOP presidential candidates. Yet another sacrificial lamb to Trump mania, Cain became the highest profile casualty of the inner circle anti-mask brigade. Fatefully, the same day Trump arrived for his rally, the June 16, 2020, *Tulsa World's* headline read "New Cases Surpass Peak," while the banner headline read, "Trump in Tulsa." How reckless, yet how routine, in the age of Trumpism.

*

Ironically, or was it fate, that in the same city, Tulsa, two cops arrested and handcuffed two Black teens, who by all accounts were respectable, for jaywalking. The very same week, Tulsa police commander Travis Yates nonchalantly proclaimed that according to studies, police should shoot 24% more Black people than they actually do.[309] Who says something like that in 2020? Only someone drunk with white pomposity. If "Officer Tinsley" said it, certainly millions more Americans think it. Not that Trump would know this – though I wouldn't put it past his minions – but Tulsa was also the city where "nervous Nelly" Officer Betty Jo Shelton, who was clearly spooked, shot a single bullet into the chest of unarmed Terence Crutcher, as he stood next to his SUV, on September 16, 2016.[310] Shelton was acquitted of manslaughter. At the time, in 2017, *The New York Times* detailed 15 killings of Blacks by police, netting only three convictions. Same old story, same old song. The unarmed Black man, and occasionally the Black woman, like Sandra Bland, Breonna Taylor, and Kathryn Johnston, almost always loses.[311]

Black Tulsans, where the destruction of one of America's most prosperous Black communities occurred in 1921, have lived through ongoing trauma from the event for more than 100 years. In October of 2022, 10 coffins of unmarked graves were discovered; another 19 were discovered in the same cemetery, then 24 more in October of 2022, including those of several children. In June of 2024, the Oklahoma Supreme Court dismissed the case of the last two survivors of the Tulsa Race Massacre, Viola Fletcher, 110, and Lessie Benningfield Randle, 109, who both remember the terror of the event.

The conservative court said their "grievance with the social and economic inequities created by the Tulsa Race Massacre is legitimate and worthy of merit," yet the court dismissed the case, deeming the suit a "political" question that is beyond the purview of the Court.[312]

Dozens of Black business owners who filed insurance claims were denied, along with thousands of homeowners. Black people are often told, "You can't receive reparations because you weren't the ones harmed." In this case, these two women, as well as the third plaintiff, who died in 2023, were alive during the 1921 terrorizing event, which lasted 16 hours. Yet another example of the Trump-led, ultra-conservative wing of the Republican Party at work in the judicial system. Where's the justice in that?

That wasn't the case, I'm eternally thankful, for the shooting by cop Amber Guyger of Botham Jean; Guyger was convicted and sentenced to 10 years.[313] During Guyger's trial, I experienced something that perhaps neither I, nor modern America had ever seen before. Jean's younger brother, Brandt Jean, during a riveting moment right after the verdict was read, asked Judge Tammy Kemp if he could give Guyger, the woman who admitted to killing his big brother in his own apartment, a hug. "Please, can I give her a hug," he asked a second time, his voice trembling as he spoke. Judge Kemp, a Black woman, agreed as the breathless courtroom watched on.[314] Kemp, too, was moved by her humanity, as the profound forgiveness displayed by Brandt Jean, who admitted that, for a while, he hated Guyger and wanted to kill her himself, to avenge his brother. However, his love and relationship with Jesus Christ overruled his desire for revenge.

Mocked by some on Black radio – even those who professed their belief in Jesus Christ – Brandt was called a chump, a sell-out, weak, and worse. But I saw him as courageous, probably more than I could have been, yet someone with incredible strength and love. Only 17, he exemplified far more compassion for someone he could easily have hated than Zimmerman, or the countless police officers who felt little or no remorse for gunning down unarmed Black men, women, and boys. Brandt Jean was, at least in this instance, like Martin Luther King, Jr., C.T. Vivian, Lula Williams, Viola Liuzzo, Minister James Reeb, Rev. Jonathan Daniels, J.T. Johnson, Andy Young, veteran Jimmie Lee Jackson, Fred Temple, Carl Cooper, Alton Sterling, Corporal Roman Duckworth Jr., Samuel Ephesians Hammond Jr., Delano Herman Middleton, Henry Ezekial Smith, and countless others, who chose sacrificial love over violence and hate.[315] This, of course, stands in stark contrast to the murderers of Cheney, Goodman, and Schwerner, abused and killed by lawmen in Mississippi; Sandra Bland, "mysteriously" found dead in a Texas jail; or Laquan McDonald, shot 16 times *walking away* from police on a Chicago street. The real question is, in primarily white

America, where power, prestige, and presumed honor are largely relegated to our lighter brothers and sisters who have surveyed the scene from a position of power since soon after they arrived on the American shores, do Black lives really matter?[316]

Sadly, alas, typically, it took the deaths of white people standing up for freedom, justice, and equality when it absolutely wasn't popular, to move the needle in the modern civil rights struggle. That's a damn shame, isn't it? And yes, it happened again in 2020 when white protesters were killed in Kenosha, Wisconsin,[317] and Dallas, Texas.[318] However it had to happen, putrid and demoralizing in the end, I'm glad it happened, even though the blood of untold numbers of Black men, women, boys, and girls also cry out from the grave.

Chapter 23: So I Said to My People, Slow the Testing Down

"Some Americans are wearing masks because they don't like me."

President Donald J. Trump

Before mid-June of 2020, roughly three weeks after reopening, 12 states experienced an increase of 25 percent in COVID-19 cases, with two more reporting spikes of 40 percent or more. Four months after the nation's first death, the victim list had reached 115,000, with two million infections.

"So I said to my people, 'slow the testing down!'" Trump crowed on June 20th, exactly seven months before what would become his last day as president.[319] Meanwhile, Dr. Deborah Birx continued to soft-shoe Trump's statements on injecting bleach as a cure to COVID as his "musings."

"The state has preempted local governments from hitting the brakes," said Houston Mayor Sylvester Turner, after Texas Governor Greg Abbott insisted on moving to stage three for reopening, despite reporting four straight days of new case highs. Overall, the nation experienced a 36% surge in new cases. The vast majority of the governors pushing for full reopening were Republican. Clearly, like Trump, they took the position that a few hundred thousand lives lost across the nation were worth less than getting their economies back on track. Meanwhile, Trump had effectively muzzled the CDC, the nation's foremost authority on infectious diseases. As the legendary O'Jays reminded us in their 1973 classic song, "For the Love of Money," people will steal from their own mothers. "For the love of money, people don't care who they hurt or beat. ... For a small piece of paper, it carries a lot of weight. ... Almighty dollar."[320]

*

"I think the concept of chokeholds sounds so innocent, so perfect," Trump began, sending mixed messages so as to seem politically acceptable. "Then you realize if it's one-on-one. If it's two-on-one, that's a bit of a different story, depending. With that being said, I think that overall, it would be a very good thing if that was ended."[321]

Perhaps, as devastating as any of the police killings, was the case of Louisville police, in plainclothes, bursting into the home of first responder Breonna Taylor, allegedly seeking someone involved in trafficking drugs. It would turn out later that the police already had the suspect in jail. Why did they break in on Taylor and her boyfriend? More unbelievable, despite the fact she was shot eight times, the police report, finally released in mid-June, said that she had no injuries.[322] Who the hell could even fix their mouth to submit such a report, with the world in turmoil? Even white citizens who had heretofore been quiet as mice pissing on cotton, *en masse* began to *at least* give lip service to the Black Lives Matter movement. And while many tweeted their support, apologized to Black associates, and ordered books about racial reconciliation and the Black struggle, tens of thousands of white protesters – young, old, men, women, and children – filled the streets, along with their fellow Black, Latino and Asian brothers and sisters, in unprecedented solidarity for an American minority population.

Patrick Hutchinson, a leader of a BLM protest in London, may have said it best: "This is a happy day. If you look around, this [protest] is multi-cultural. The solution is with white people."[323] Truer words were never spoken. This nation will never address the deep-rooted issues of racial injustice in health care, housing, the criminal justice system, education, the long-term impacts of slavery, the realities of implicit bias, and structural racism, until white people decide to honestly explore and confront these critical issues – and that doesn't even include patriarchy and gender bias.[324] The truth hurts, but it also heals.

Rev. Jesse Jackson, who founded Operation PUSH and was a seminal figure in the Civil Rights Movement of the latter half of the 20th century, loved to say Black people "can't ride to freedom on pharaoh's chariot." That's probably true. But to earnestly pursue justice and equality in this nation, it's going to take more than Black, brown, Jewish, Palestinians, young people, and those discriminated against based on gender.

There were heroes and "sheroes" of all hues in the protests around the world who stood with Americans protesting the over-policing of Black people in the U.S., as well as villains and provocateurs like Trump.

"I have no idea who that man was. I just know he was up to no good," said Patrick Hutchinson, who scooped up a scared, bald-headed white man who was injured as his crew clashed with BLM protesters in London. "He was there with some football hooligans and football thugs. I think he was a fallen man who got left behind. That's something your police officers over there could take a lesson from. Just because a man is up to no good, you don't have to kill him."[325] Whoa.

Larry Kudlow and Attorney General Bill Barr both insisted there was no institutional racism inherent in policing and police culture, though, at least Barr did acknowledge that racism still exists. How in the world would they know, I asked myself? I almost guarantee they had never been racially profiled, or harassed by police. More unbelievable was the fact that Housing Secretary Ben Carson, one of only two prominent Black leaders in the Trump administration, was quick to point out that the June 12 police shooting of Rayshard Brooks in Atlanta was less "clear cut" than the police killing of George Floyd. Yes, true. The whole world watched as Floyd was summarily executed in broad daylight without resisting arrest. Brooks fought back, in fact, was whipping ass when he took an officer's taser and bolted. Still, in Georgia, a Taser is not a lethal weapon. And Brooks was *running away* from the officers when he was shot. So yes, the situation was different, yet, no less unjustified.

Carson, a brilliant surgeon who immersed himself in the cloak of privilege after overcoming a tough childhood, today rejects his Blackness. Remember, he was the very Negro who had the unmitigated audacity to call slavery the first form of immigration.[326] What a bootlicking sycophant. Is it any wonder that Trump is totally off the rails, with virtually no one who's really in touch with the challenges, struggles, fears, and life chances of the Black community in his inner circle? Carson and his fellow right-wing powerhouse, Supreme Court Justice Clarence Thomas, are sad examples of Black folk themselves invoking the principle of white pomposity, likely because they have reached elite status. The marvelous documentary about the great writer-activist James Baldwin is entitled, *I Am Not Your Negro*.[327] Indeed, for those who subscribe to the belief that there is no inequity, explicit bias, or institutional racism still staining the fabric of our nation, Thomas and Carson are both *your* Negro.

Oftentimes, many white people in America do not want to be told what to do. Take the case during the pandemic in Orange County, California, where a law was passed requiring a mask, then rescinded when the blowback came. "We are imprisoned by lockdowns; masks over our faces, mouths, and nose," one resident read at a public meeting on the issue, which ultimately led to the resignation of the county's top public official, who had pushed for the adherence to CDC guidelines calling for citizens to wear masks. "We don't like people telling us what we can and what we can't do," he said ... and other citizens along Huntington Beach proclaimed, "We like our freedoms."[328]

Yeah, that's mighty white of you. What about all the Black folk locked up for long sentences for smoking marijuana or crack cocaine, while our white brethren were ignored, or at least received much lesser sentences for snorting powdered cocaine? What about all the indigent people arrested for loitering and other petty crimes, who can't get out of jail because they can't post bond? What about the list as long as my arm of Black and white Americans killed protesting for all to have the right to live, eat, and shop wherever they wanted, the right to vote, the right to be tried by a jury of their peers, the right for political representation, the right to be stopped by a cop and not incur a death sentence, or vile and vicious threats? The right to be at home and not be confronted by armed policemen invoking no-knock warrants in the middle of the night? (Breonna Taylor) The right to not be tracked down like a runaway slave because we are out on a jog and stop at a house – get a drink of water, then continue, only to be hunted, cornered, and ultimately shot down like a dog? (Ahmaud Arbery) How about the right to walk the street and not be harassed (or killed) because I "look suspicious"? (Elijah McClain). Or the right to go into a store and not be trailed as a theft suspect, simply because of the color of my skin, or even the clothes I wear? Or my right to be in a park or live in an upscale condo or neighborhood because I don't look like you? What about my right to take a nap in the common room of an Ivy League school, where I bust my butt to succeed, only to be accused of being an intruder because I don't fit the mold of what you think I should look like? And don't let me even go back to Reconstruction,[329] when much of America revolted because 12 Blacks, less than 10 years out of slavery, had ascended to prominent elected offices, like congressmen of the United States, only to see the KKK rear its ugly head and say, "hell no, nigger, not here, not now."[330] "Segregation today, segregation tomorrow, segregation forever," declared Alabama Governor George Wallace nearly a century later.[331] So, hell yes, I resent the fact that in the midst of a pandemic the world has not witnessed in any of our lifetimes, some want to invoke their white privilege of not being told what they can or can't do, while Black, brown, mentally fragile, meat packing plant workers, factory workers, the elderly, and our beautiful, brave frontline health care workers, are dying at alarming rates. Why sugarcoat it? Why not simply say, "You're expendable, and I'm not?" Yes, former President Trump, you reek of white pomposity, and your overwhelming hubris won't even allow you to recognize it. And while spewing his venom, Trump empowers and emboldens those on the fringes to act out his words, as he calls judges, prosecutors, and witnesses he doesn't like, "racists" and "nasty," "unfair," and worse.[332]

"This is exactly why I don't want to have kids," a Gen Xer I know told me. "Every Black woman my age feels the same way. It would be irresponsible to bring someone into this world, as messed up as it is. I'm terrified. They're born with a target on their backs. I'm trying to survive my darn self."

Once again, Trump rolled out an initiative, this one, intolerably late, focused on reforming policing, which much of the nation has been crying out for overwhelmingly, at least since the killing of George Floyd. Speaking in the Rose Garden, Trump was, characteristically, flanked by a group of white men, except for one Black police officer, even though the nationwide protests were triggered by unequal and unjust treatment of Black men and women *by* police.

"What Americans want is law and order," said Trump. Sure, Trump, Americans want safety and justice performed uniformly, regardless of the race, sex, or gender of those people involved in police encounters. What Americans *of every hue* are marching in the streets for, enduring tear gas, physical abuse, and risking contracting the most contagious virus in a century, is an end to police brutality and over-policing of Black people, especially Black men. The futility of it all brought me back to one of my favorite songs, "The Boxer," performed by one of my all-time favorite groups, Simon and Garfunkel.

> I am just a poor boy
> Though my story's seldom told
> I have squandered my resistance
> For a pocketful of mumbles
> Such are promises
> All lies and jest
> *Still, a man hears what he wants to hear*
> *And disregards the rest* [Emphasis added]

On May 4, 2020, the day the state reopened, Florida reported 819 new cases. On June 13th, the figure had skyrocketed to 2,581 new cases, even fewer than California's record 3,000 new infections per day. Sixteen other states reported new highs, even as New Jersey and New York, which shut down extensively, were recording new lows.

"This [masking, social distancing, and vaccines] isn't about health or economics," said Tom Frieden, former CDC director. "Health is the road to a better economy."[333]

"Some Americans are wearing masks because they don't like me," Trump proclaimed. Of course, it would be too much to expect our president, Trump, the leader of the free world, to set an example for all Americans and promote safe habits by wearing a mask. Instead, he promoted defiance and independence, not interdependence, even as cities like Albany, Georgia, and Montgomery, Alabama, the cradle of the Confederacy, were ravaged by the disease. But, of course, as Trump said about the protesters across the nation, "those are not my people." In Montgomery, 72 percent of the cases were African American, and an astounding 60 percent of the deaths in a city almost at full capacity in the ICUs.[334] Among Albany's population, the percentages of deaths and infections were similar, sparked by attendance at a funeral.[335] Still, the Montgomery city council voted down a requirement for citizens to wear masks, one councilman calling the requirement "an overreach." Fortunately, Black Mayor Steven Reed overruled the council. It makes me wonder: what would it be like to live life proclaiming, "I care about other human beings" while, in fact, I really only care about myself and those who are like me? In the end, I realize while it would certainly be different and provide a level of freedom I've never been privileged to know, it's an arrogance I do not want to experience. I personally prefer the unease of being Black, to white pomposity because it requires a level of humanity that many others never experience.

As the protests and proof of bias in policing continued to emerge, one veteran journalist, NBC commentator Harry Smith, put it this way: "Many of us whites have felt black history month, the MLK holiday, Juneteenth, was for blacks. But perhaps, like Saul in the bible, we are beginning to see that it's just the opposite. Those stories, that history, our privilege; by choice, we have been blind too long.[336]

"My Administration has done more for the Black Community than any President since Abraham Lincoln," Trump tweeted on June 5, 2020. What you've done for me, I muttered, is raise my blood pressure by continuing to say things so ridiculous that I am no longer surprised.

Trump said he should get credit for "making Juneteenth famous. Nobody had ever heard of it," he said, despite his own administration's sending out news of the event the past three years. Trump did acknowledge there was "some" systemic racism in the country, yet also said that taking the names of Confederate soldiers off U.S. military bases would split the country apart.[337] At the same time, Nike, Uber, Twitter, and numerous city and state governments (including New York), have or are moving to make Juneteenth a paid holiday.

African American Mary Elizabeth Taylor, Assistant Secretary of State for Legislative Affairs, announced her resignation.[338] "Moments of upheaval can change you, shift the trajectory of your life, and mold your character. The President's comments and actions surrounding racial injustice and Black Americans cut sharply against my core values and convictions," she said, following Trump's handling of the Floyd murder and other responses to racial unrest.[339] For me and thousands of other justice-conscious Black folks who worked for the federal government, this was a moment of quiet hope and inspiration. There were indeed a few conscionable members of the administration who were appalled by Trump's rhetoric and willing to take a stand to say so.

Eight months after the no-knock shooting of Breonna Taylor, the city of Louisville, which touts an overwhelmingly white police force, finally moved to fire one of the three officers who broke into her apartment early in the morning. While the shootings of Rayshard Brooks, Ahmaud Arbery, and others were filmed, along with the excruciating execution, by the knee, of George Floyd, the killing by cop of Breonna Taylor was not. Again, Black women, the most educated community in America, got the short end of the stick.

"When you test more people, you're going to find more people," Trump said to a robust but less-than-full Bok Center in Tulsa, after claiming 800,000 were on a waiting list to attend. "So I told my people, 'slow the testing down,'" said Trump.[340] White House staff quickly interjected that he "was joking," though what idiot would joke about anything that had killed 118,000 Americans and infected two million in less than six months, even as the previous day produced a record 150,000 new COVID infections worldwide, as U.S. cases skyrocketed in 22 states?

Before arriving in Tulsa, Trump tweeted this: "Any protesters, anarchists, agitators, looters, or lowlifes who are going to Oklahoma, please understand, you will not be treated like you have been in New York, Seattle, or Minneapolis. It will be a much different scene!"[341] Despite all the Trump bluster, even though the facility holds 19,000, the Tulsa Fire Department reported that approximately 6,000 were in attendance.[342]

"Whenever white America feels like it's losing its grip, violence follows," said Princeton University's Dr. Eddie Glaude following Trump's rally in Tulsa on June 20. "He was stoking hate all night."[343]

Like many before him, Billy Graham, perhaps America's foremost evangelist, was MIA (missing in action) when it came to standing up, speaking out, and leading by example as oppressed Blacks pushed and cried out for equity and justice during the '50s, '60s, and '70s. Sure, he made token entrees toward reconciliation, but acknowledged, "I think I made a mistake when I didn't go to Selma." [344] Instead, he stayed in the safe lane, preaching evangelism, but ignoring all the social aspects of his beloved Gospel that didn't speak to people who looked like him. In the end, the excuse for not collaborating with King in his non-violent protests was as weak as water, and his vaunted place in history must include this glaring sin of omission. White people have the luxury of deciding when to opt in and when to opt out of including people of color in a full share of the American dream. Black and brown people, as well as some others, live and feel the struggle for equality and acceptance every moment of our lives. Likewise, his son, Rev. Franklin Graham, was deathly silent about the injustices of over-policing the Black and brown communities. Instead, Graham, a leading Trump evangelical cheerleader, pointed the finger at Antifa when Trump supporters stormed the Capitol, even though there was no evidence to support it.[345] Graham was also quiet when it came to condemning the police violence. On the other hand, televangelist Joel Osteen, pastor of mega-church Lakewood in Houston, took part in the marches there, declaring, "We need to stand against injustice and stand with our black brothers and sisters."[346] The action of so-called righteous Christians who stayed on the sidelines, or failed to criticize police, reminded me of what King said about those in Birmingham: "He who passively accepts evil is as much involved in it as he who helps to perpetrate it. He who accepts evil without protesting it is really cooperating with it."[347]

The woeful silence of both Grahams reminded me of former Alabama Governor George Wallace's decision to meet with SCLC President Joseph Lowery at St. Jude's in Montgomery at the conclusion of the 30th anniversary of the Selma to Montgomery March in 1995, at which I was honored to promote and participate in. Wallace, a staunch segregationist who refused to meet with Lowery and the SCLC before the historic 1965 march that led to the passage of the Voting Rights Act, this time did meet with the marchers in an attempt to make amends.[348] Many of us wondered if the meeting was simply an opportunity for the aging Wallace (by then confined to a wheelchair from an assassination attempt when he ran for president in 1972), to move to the right side of history. Perhaps that's what some of the Evangelical leaders of today will do years from now.

Chapter 24: MIA

"It takes two to speak the truth – one to speak and another to hear."

Henry David Thoreau, American philosopher

Had they been soldiers of war, instead of the puppeteers who decided when and where marching orders were enacted, Pence and Trump could have been brought up on dereliction of duty charges. Pence, whom I believed to be primarily a traditional Republican, allowed himself to be sucked down the MAGA drain, like many of the others, who actually *knew* better, but couldn't manage to help themselves. I think he was genuinely embarrassed by much of Trump's antics and the rhetoric and vitriol Trump constantly spewed.

Texas and Florida, both with Republican governors, chose to open their states back up weeks before other states, against CDC guidelines. Those guidelines would have likely been much stricter and more consistent had Trump and Azar not restricted the CDC's ability to make scientific, not political, advisements and updates on the impact of COVID.

"These were places that opened when they [COVID cases and deaths] were still increasing. Opening while you're still increasing is kind of like leaning into a left hook," explained Dr. Thomas Frieden, former director of the CDC. "You're gonna get hit."[349] In the meantime, California, which had shut down earlier than most states, was still experiencing soaring new caseloads, along with Arizona and Nevada, which suffered record new highs.

Three months earlier, in fact, I fielded a call from John Bennett, chief of staff for Tampa Mayor Jane Castor, who called early one morning in March of 2020, following our outreach to big city Florida leaders regarding their state plans and preparation to control COVID-19. I was designated as the principal point of contact by my Acting Regional Director, John McGough, who simultaneously managed the Boston region, which included six states. Following a brief, cordial conversation I had with Bennett and Castor, during which they expressed concern over not having enough testing sites, I requested they put their concerns in an email to me that I could forward to headquarters.

Bennett wrote in an email:

"The City is interested in knowing if and when remote COVID-19 testing sites can be established in our city. Hospitals are [allegedly] turning away patients with symptoms, and without being tested, we would have a limited understanding of what our local risks would be and evolve to. Finally, we would appreciate a response as soon as possible as we need as much decision support in the response realm as possible to be more preventative, mitigative, and adaptive."[350]

Thanks in advance.

John Bennett

One week later, after not getting an adequate response from a government trying to put out fires everywhere and woefully behind on its promises to supply testing equipment and PPE for hospitals and first responders, Castor pushed back.

"As I have said before," Castor, who spent 31 years in emergency management and law enforcement, said, "this is the highest level of unpreparedness from the federal government that I have ever seen in any type of an emergency."[351] She continued, "I can understand everyone was caught, to a degree, by surprise, but we've been at this for a month now. And not being able to produce some of these items by this time is very, very surprising."[352]

In the midst of the biggest public health crisis in 100 years, Trump moved – once again – to scuttle the ACA, which provides health insurance for as many as 23 million Americans, many already traumatized by COVID-19. That was on the heels of a Trump rally in Tulsa, where signs denoting social distancing between seats were allegedly removed by campaign staffers. Also, Pence, leading his first coronavirus task force press conference after nearly 70,000 more deaths in two months, again showed up minus a mask, while all the others, the CDC, Fauci, Birx, and Azar, wore theirs. His position? Americans were simply exercising their First Amendment rights. The rest of us be damned.[353]

Occasionally, during one of the strangest years in both U.S. and world history, there was good news. Princeton removed the name of Woodrow Wilson from its public policy school, as well as one of its residential buildings, over his racist views. Serving as U.S. president from 1913 to 1921, Wilson insisted on a segregated military and later prevented Black students from attending Princeton when he served as its president.[354] The state of Mississippi, the heart of the Confederacy, moved to change its state flag from the stars and bars. It must be noted that the Confederate flag wasn't added to the Mississippi state flag until 30 years *after* the end of the Civil War when segregationists fought to blunt Reconstruction. NASCAR banned the Confederate flag from being flown at its races. Cities across the nation moved to pass laws against police using chokeholds. Statues of Confederate generals and even U.S. presidents who owned slaves, were taken down across the nation. What next? A host of locusts? Oh yes, they were swarming in late June in parts of Africa and South America, so thick, they blotted out the sun. And let's not forget the Godzilla dust cloud blanketing half of the U.S., the largest in at least 50 years to reach the U.S.

Chapter 25: For the Love of Money

"I urge you to answer the highest calling of your heart and stand up for what you truly believe."

John Robert Lewis, Congressman, and freedom fighter

As a scientist, an epidemiologist, and yes, the nation's doctor, U.S. Surgeon General Dr. Jerome Adams issued a haunting warning to the U.S. on March 18, 2020. We watched on the evening news in horror as Italy, once the center of the world, suffered thousands of coronavirus deaths each day in a nightmare that only seemed to get worse.

"We have the same number of cases now that Italy had two weeks ago, and we have a choice to make," said Adams, the highest profile, most respected Black person in the Trump administration. "Do we want to lean into social distancing and mitigation strategies and flatten the curve, or do we want to continue going on as business as usual and end up *being* Italy?"[355] One hundred days later, Italy had indeed flattened the curve, and finally, on June 23, the U.S. reached a peak of testing 500,000 per day – some seven months after the initial warning of the impending epidemic and was in the vortex as the virus threatened to careen totally out of control. The nation's biggest states – Florida, Texas, and California – produced record new cases daily for over a week as young people, who had been social distancing for well over a month, threw caution to the wind, heading for the beaches, bars, restaurants and parks – sans masks! But really, how could we expect our young people, or anyone else, to take the epidemic seriously, if our leaders didn't?

Finally, after months, Pence, the man "allegedly" running the coronavirus task force, encouraged U.S. citizens to wear masks on June 25.[356] This belated gesture came despite Trump's suggestion, in an interview with *The Wall Street Journal* days earlier, that some people might wear masks to "signal disapproval" of him.

"We are aware that there are 'embers' that need to be put out," parroted Kayleigh McEnany, who sank to perhaps a new low for her, instead pivoting to brag about the marginal benefits of Remdesivir to reduce mortality, even as 31 U.S. states reached all-time coronavirus case highs, with several at, or near, ICU bed capacity.[357]

Assessing the impending tsunami, Dr. Peter Hotez, dean for the National School of Tropical Medicine at Baylor University, called it a humanitarian catastrophe, noting that he was confident that when all was said and done, the bulk of the deaths and infections would be suffered by the poor, minority, and marginalized people.[358] True dat, Dr. Hotez, who was just as straight-up and plain-spoken as pulmonologist Dr. Vin Gupta, both of whom warned Americans to "wake up."

Meanwhile, Trump continued to stoke the racial fires, retweeting two vile tweets in a day. The first featured a white, wealthy couple, a pair of attorneys standing on the porch of a palatial abode situated down the road from the mayor of St. Louis, pointing guns at protesters as they marched toward the mayor's house.

"The only thing that stopped the crowd from approaching the house was when I had that rifle," Mark McCloskey said in a June 29, 2020, interview. "[It was] the only thing that stemmed the tide."[359] There was no indication, however, that protesters approached, or threatened the armed couple. The other tweet from the same day featured a group of pro-Trump protesters riding golf carts near *The Villages*, a massive senior citizen complex in

Florida, past a group protesting against police violence toward Black and brown people. One of the Trump supporters, his golf cart adorned in MAGA signage, shouted "white power" as he rode past the line of justice protesters. The tweet was retweeted by Trump, but was soon pulled down after it received widespread criticism. Trump, of course, as well as his sycophant press secretary, insisted he didn't hear the driver raise his fist and shout "white power," only that he saw the signage on the cart of one of his supporters.[360] And through it all, Trump has the nerve to court Black and brown voters and, amazingly, attract millions! Just damn! I'd rather run through a fire with gasoline drawers on!

Days later, Trump tweeted that Black Lives Matter was a "symbol of hate," as he bemoaned the fact that his hometown, New York City, was painting "Black Lives Matter" in front of Trump Towers on 5th Avenue.[361] Ironically, this was the same 5th Avenue about which Trump proclaimed in 2016 that he could walk down the street and shoot someone and "wouldn't lose any votes."[362]

Ever hopeful – or delusional – Trump said the same week, "I think we're going to be very good about the coronavirus. At some point, I believe it's going to just disappear, I hope."[363] His partner in crime, Florida Governor DeSantis, who won a hotly contested election against Andrew Gilliam to prevent Florida from electing its first African American governor, continued to insist he would not close businesses in the state, even as the state careened out of control with new cases. "I heard a lot of people in your profession who waxed poetically for weeks and weeks about how Florida was going to become just like New York. Wait two weeks. Wait two weeks," DeSantis crowed. "Hell, we're eight weeks away from that, and it hasn't happened."[364] On July 1, the state recorded another new record, this time 10,000 new cases, as several Florida cities moved to shut down beaches, bars, and restaurants, though the *government* continued to resist.

"Governor DeSantis abdicated any pretense of effective leadership in Florida," according to University of Washington pulmonologist Dr. Vin Gupta. "He's acting irresponsibly. DeSantis dispatched the National Guard to quell protests, but he hasn't done so to bolster ICU capacity in hospitals statewide. That should tell you where his priorities lie." Like DeSantis (who even withheld federal funds from schools that installed mask mandates), "Texas Governor Abbott finally invoked a state mask mandate in November 2020 that he should have done weeks ago," Dr. Gupta said.[365]

Less than one month after seeking to distance our work from the COVID-19 response and responsibility and Florida registering 11,000 new cases per day and its death toll on the verge of 130,000; our headquarters held its bi-weekly national conference and conducted Indian County COVID calls the first week in July 2020.[366] Laura Rigas from headquarters announced she would be MIA for the foreseeable future as she looked forward to taking leave to have her baby. The announcement made me all-but gasp over the irony. At some point in 2019, Rigas, who was new to the department, was overheard saying at a departmental gathering that she "didn't like Deric [Gilliard]" because she had "heard that he was pushing the Obama agenda when Trump took office." Yes, this was the same appointee that our all-Black office had pulled a tall order coup for, securing 16 major hospital CEOs for conversations with IEA from mid-November, when many were off on vacation until the end of January. No other region had delivered like ours did, and we were the only region in the nation with eight states. When I first heard that she had made those comments about me months earlier, I shook my head in wonder. Now, hearing her announcement, I couldn't help but think to myself: Yeah, it's just fine for you to go on leave, using your top-of-the-line federal government insurance to have your Polly Purebred white baby at taxpayers' expense. Yet, you have disdain for me because I continued to communicate with ACA navigators, stakeholders, and citizens concerned about the future of their coverage, which Trump castigated – without, I might add, a plan to replace it – while the ACA was still the law of the land. Just damn! Obama often talked about the Audacity of Hope. Well, this was just plain ole white pomposity.

Roughly 43% of those in grocery stores, meat packing plants, sanitation workers, food servers, valets, hair stylists, nail salon experts, etc., are Black, Asian-American/Pacific Islander, and brown, thus most vulnerable to the disease. They are, sadly, also the most expendable, based on how American society devalues their lives and contributions to our everyday existence.

On the social justice and race front, five people of color were found hanged in the weeks following the killing of George Floyd.[367] On July 4, another Black man, Vauhxx Booker, a member of the Monroe County Human Rights Commission, was grabbed and threatened by a host of whites accusing him of trespassing, along with his white friend, en route to watch a lunar eclipse in Indiana.[368] Thankfully, both Miller and those around him were filming as he was tied to a tree, and shouts for a noose were heard. Again, Frederick Douglass's timeless, *What to the Slave is the Fourth of July?*[369] speech, from exactly 168 years before, showed that while Black folk are no longer slaves in America, they certainly haven't achieved full-class citizenship in the eyes of all Americans, even 157 years after the signing of the Emancipation Proclamation, and 56 years after the Civil Rights Act of 1964 "allowed" Black folk to live, eat, shop, and play anywhere anybody else could. It was, indeed, another glaring case of white pomposity.

Chapter 26: McCarthy, Wallace and Donald J. Trump: Race Baiting

"Black Lives Matter is a 'symbol of hate.'"
President Donald Trump

I categorically deny the characterization by far too many that the protests were primarily riots, not the assertion of First Amendment rights to challenge what millions see as injustice, racism, over-policing, or implicit bias.[370] That right should be every bit as fundamental as the promise of "life, liberty, and the pursuit of happiness."[371] Certainly, there have been riotous acts that have emerged from the protests, including looting, destruction of police cars and buildings, and even attacks on people. However, they are very limited in the width and breadth of a movement that was ignited across the country, galvanizing whites, young, old, Asians, Latinos, the LGBTQ+ community, justice-seeking elders, and many other communities who were prepared to push back on the over-policing of Black and brown people. Classifying them as riots, frankly, is not only disingenuous and inflammatory, but a total dismissal of the fundamental issues of police brutality and over-policing that ignited a nation and the world.

Taken from Trump's playbook, the best way to distract from the real issue is to focus on the ancillary results, not the rotten, endemic causes at the core of the problem.

Why earnestly examine the fact that police don't see Black and brown men as fully human, when you can instead point to sporadic acts of violence, and thus misclassify an entire movement – the most broad-based movement in a century – as a thug-directed plot to overthrow our nation, rob, and pillage and, eventually, rape our women? Sadly, this is the same old story, the same old song. These attitudes and tropes were inflamed, refined, and perfected by Donald J. Trump in an imperialist manner that built on the racist mantra of Wisconsin Senator Joseph McCarthy, master of the Red Scare,[372] and white nationalist Alabama Governor George Wallace.[373]

Remember, the people on the front lines of the COVID pandemic are largely people of color: migrants, Black, brown, and Asian, as well as a host of uneducated and undereducated Anglos. They are, as Ta-Nehisi Coates calls them, the "expendables."[374] How do poor and working families, living on the margins figure out childcare for kids who are in school for two or three days and out of school, supposedly doing virtual learning, the rest of the week? How many bosses in retail establishments, restaurants, grocery stores, sanitation, and mass transit stations, can afford or navigate such a slippery slope? It's very different from someone who can sit at home and work in front of a computer. Privileged people – and far too often, the high-income shot callers who push the buttons and make the decisions – are often clueless about the complications of families who live in Atlanta's English Avenue, Chicago's Lawndale, and Kansas City's Prospect neighborhoods.

Attorney General Bill Barr, after literally day after day, week after week, of seeing cases of unarmed Black men assaulted, criminalized, and killed at the hands of police – the very people who are sworn to protect and serve – had to admit that America does indeed have a problem. "I do think there is a widespread phenomenon that African American males, particularly, are treated with extra suspicion and not given the benefit of the doubt," Barr said.[375] During the same interview, however, he expressed a concern that voter fraud, which could be possible if all Americans were allowed to mail in their ballots, outweighed the imminent threat that millions would risk by standing in crowded lines in order to exercise their rights to vote November 3. White pomposity, I tell you.

How many times have we seen the rich, elite, or at the very least, privileged, denigrate others, either for wearing masks or, in some way, being complicit in bringing COVID-19 to American shores? YET ANOTHER incident took place July 8, when tech company CEO Michael Lofthouse harangued and chastised the Asian families out to celebrate at a restaurant. Thank God, this family had a cell phone as Lofthouse yelled, "f____g Asians!" The family patriarch, who has lived in the U.S. for over 25 years was gracious, saying he forgave the privileged white man. How many incidents of racism, hate, and discrimination were directed toward Asian Americans in 2020? The count is dizzying, I assure you. The very same day, the Black man who was threatened by a white woman, Amy Cooper, who said she'd call the police and accuse her fellow bird watcher – yes, I said that correctly, bird watcher – of assault, was brought up on charges of filing a false police report. Dude rancher Christian Cooper graciously declined to press charges. Again, why and how is it that minorities, and especially Black people, are consistently forgiving and understanding? Is that what's required, even for those whom white Americans consider the "good Negroes," to be accepted? Cooper accepted her apology, even as her lawyer was parading the "cancel culture" excuse. Where the hell was the tweeter-in-chief when THIS incident happened in Central Park? ... unlike the one he still refuses to acknowledge he was wrong about, the horrific injustice against the Central Park 5, whom he called to receive the death penalty. If so, just damn! Twice again, white pomposity rears its ugly head!

How do Black people ever catch a break? We're taught from birth that we all deserve a trial by a jury of our peers. How, then, is it that the system too often fails us? Part of the reason is that Trump and people like him perpetuate racist stereotypes and fear tactics that continue to frame people of color, especially Black and brown people, as the "Other."

"They're [Black people] prosecuted more, arrested more, arrested more, prosecuted more," said Oakland Public Defender Brandon Woods. And very few people who actually look like them sit on juries. Woods pointed to a Black co-worker who has had over 20 cases, "yet she can count the number of black jurors she's had on one hand. Black people, rightfully so, have a distrust of law enforcement." A new study showed prosecutors "striking," or eliminating, Black jurors 72 percent of the time for reasons such as wearing dreadlocks, slouching, or wearing blinged-out sandals. What is the percentage of whites "struck" or excluded from jury duty? Less than one percent.[376]

Meanwhile, one-third of the nation's COVID cases were in the Latino communities, where the majority were either front-line service workers or food producers who had little choice but to go to work. If 19% of the nation produces 33 percent of the cases, how can anyone deny the disparities in our system?

While race and justice continued to be major themes during the Trump administration, often fueled by his divisive tweets and anti-immigrant rhetoric, the world's once most respected health agency, the CDC, was being effectively muzzled, if not neutered. The CDC Director Robert Redfield, saddled with the enormous weight of a President and HHS secretary unwilling or unable to deal with the realistic and growing pressures of a global pandemic, became a spineless Trump lapdog, just like a litany of other appointees. They, however, were not charged with protecting the nation's health and wellness. Redfield was.

*

Finally, on a hot July day in 2020, at the famed Walter Reed Army Hospital, President Trump, for the very first time, donned a black mask in public in a very carefully orchestrated stroll down the hallway, knowing the camera and the world were watching. Almost six months after the nation diagnosed its first confirmed COVID-19 case, on January 20, 2020,[377] Trump openly, though certainly grudgingly, put on the mask that his top public health officials had been imploring the general public to do for months.[378]

"I think when you're in a hospital, especially in that particular setting, where you're talking to a lot of soldiers and people that, in some cases, just got off the operating tables, I think it's a great thing to wear a mask," the president told reporters. "I've never been against masks, but I do believe they have a time and a place."[379] Never mind that his federal staff had to get vaccinated, file validation papers, and practice social distancing, while he held numerous public events without masking while unvaccinated. Finally, his position had publicly (at least) changed, months after millions of his flock had followed his previous advice and contracted the debilitating disease, or even died.

On July 16, 2020, Trump was questioned as to why Black men continued to be killed by the police. As usual, oblivious, or in full denial of the facts, he simply lashed back at the reporter, telling her it was a terrible question because more white people were killed by police than Black people. Of course, he failed to note that six times as many white people live in the U.S., yet police kill three times as many

Blacks as whites. Furthermore, far too many Black people are unarmed and sometimes even running away from the police. The further tragic irony of the moment was that it was five years to the day that an unarmed Eric Garner, the father of six, was choked to death by a host of police as he gasped several times, "I can't breathe, I can't breathe." Garner's dying words became piercing daggers that have now been recorded being uttered by more than a dozen Black and brown men from Colorado to Phoenix to Minneapolis and several other cities across the country who each experienced death by choking at the hands of police officers.[380]

Meanwhile, the COVID treatment and response system, which I, among other Feds, monitored three times a day for the eight southeastern states to provide continuous intel to my regional director, showed glaring inadequacies and inconsistencies. For example, one Miami nurse noted that it was taking "14 days, sometimes 18," to get COVID test results.[381] Oklahoma's governor, Kevin Stitt, showed up at Trump's infamous Tulsa rally, like the rest, maskless. Result: he became the first governor to contract the virus, though he insists it didn't happen at the rally.[382] Right. In the meantime, his buddy, the equally inflexible Georgia Governor Lyin' Brian Kemp, had the nerve to sue several Georgia cities, including Savannah, Athens, Dunwoody, and Decatur, because they instituted a mask policy. This happened the very day half the nation's governors had invoked a mask requirement, while the governors from the crown jewels of the south, Florida and Texas, only dug in deeper. Meanwhile, South Carolina recorded its daily record death rate, along with soaring cases and hospitalizations. Still, incredibly, people doubted that the disease was real.

What kind of alternative universe am I living in, I asked myself, as governors in the heart of Trump country, like Abbott of Texas and Ivey of Alabama, at least had the common sense to reverse course and admit they were wrong as their states spiraled out of control, setting new COVID case and death records, seemingly every other day. Admitting you were wrong isn't rocket science. Believe me, I've had to do it more times than I care to admit. Try and tell that to Kemp and DeSantis, however, who, like their "hero," instead doubled down and found a way to dig a deeper hole, not only for themselves but, more importantly, for the very people they were sworn to protect and serve. I ask myself, is this Hollywood? But no, this is worse. Even on my best day, I couldn't have conceived a scenario so bizarre. How bizarre? On July 12, 2020, Trump retweeted talk show host Chuck Woolery, saying, "The most outrageous lies are the ones about Covid 19. Everyone is lying, the CDC, media, democrats. Our doctors." The disease, I'll remind you, primarily impacted the working poor, the elderly, minorities, and the gullible. White pomposity, once again, was promoted and encouraged by the leader of the free world, who was elected to protect and guide us. On July 16, Woolery deleted his account after acknowledging that his son had contracted the disease. I ask you, who in da hell could make this shit up?

Something is deadly wrong in this sick society we live in. First, a young Latina woman who enlisted in the Army to better the life chances of her family and open a world of possibilities, was murdered by a fellow soldier and dismembered. Only weeks later, another bright light, paratrooper Enrique Martinez, who mysteriously disappeared while camping with his buddies on leave from Ft. Bragg, N.C., was also dismembered.[383] Don't try to tell me that these things just happen when we lose our best and brightest mysteriously.

*

July 18, 2020, was a landmark day in American history. Word came that civil rights giant C.T. Vivian passed away at age 95. Vivian integrated the beaches in St. Augustine, helped coordinate the Selma movement, was a key component in integrating Nashville, and was an SCLC leader in "Project C" and the landmark Birmingham movement.[384] Less than 24 hours later, we lost Rev. John Robert Lewis. Son of a sharecropper and America's living saint, Lewis, a Georgia congressman for 30 years, was beaten as he and Rev. Hosea Williams co-led the famous march at the Edmund Pettus Bridge in Selma. Leader of the Student Nonviolent Coordinating Committee (SNCC), he represented the radical element at the iconic 1963 March on Washington.[385] Only months earlier, another of America's most influential 20th-century Black leaders, Dr. Joseph E. Lowery, one of the founders of the SCLC and the "Dean of the Civil Rights Movement," died at 98. Three civil rights giants, all from Atlanta, were lost in a single year.[386] This was a time I felt the pain and isolation that compounded the sense of personal, profound loss when I and thousands of others were denied the opportunity to attend the funerals and celebrate the lives of Lowery and Vivian due to COVID restrictions and the danger of creating super-spreaders. Lowery, whom I had worked for and traveled the country with, was someone I considered one of the most significant leaders of the second half of the 20th century. Vivian, who was likely a key player in more civil rights campaigns than anyone in the modern Civil Rights Movement, was a treasured mentor. In some ways, the loss to COVID of my much newer friend, Kelly Draheim, a white colleague who was moving fast toward becoming a powerful, equipped ally in the fight for social justice, was more painful. He was just beginning his justice journey, while Lowery and Vivian had already made profound impacts. And Kelly, much more than the other two, was my friend. The inability to gather, hug colleagues, and share precious memories, gave me a small glimpse of what those had experienced while being prohibited from visiting hospitals and nursing homes, getting on planes, or driving cross country to spend final moments and say last goodbyes to mothers and father, sisters and brothers, wives and husbands. COVID, a vicious and unforgiving foe, allowed for no do-overs.

On the same day, 18 states in the red zone would be rolling back reopening efforts. Those states were included in Region IV, except for Kentucky. Georgia Governor Kemp, leader of one of those states, declared that "Atlanta Mayor Keisha Lance Bottoms' mask mandate is unenforceable. Her decision to shutter businesses and undermine economic growth is devastating." Pushing back, the eighth-straight Black mayor to lead her city since Maynard Jackson was elected in 1973 retorted: "The governor has simply overstepped his bounds and his authority, and we will see him in court."[387]

Chapter 27: The "Resistance" Strikes Back

"Wrong is wrong, no matter who does it or who says it."
Malcolm X

Maryland Governor Larry Hogan, a moderate Republican I respected, who moved independently to get the Personal Protective Equipment (PPE) his state needed when Trump was slow-walking the federal COVID response, said this:

"I've watched as the president downplayed the outbreak's severity and as the White House failed to issue a public warning, draw up a 50-state strategy, or dispatch medical gear or lifesaving ventilators from the national stockpile to American hospitals," said Hogan. "Governors were being told we were on our own. It was sink or swim. And if I didn't do something dramatic, we simply would not come close to having enough tests in Maryland.[388] As Hogan said, "It was clear that waiting around for the president to run the nation's response was hopeless; if we delayed any longer, we'd be condemning more of our citizens to suffer and death."

At the same time, Trump, with a 1960s understanding of who now makes up most big-city suburbs, said this at a Rose Garden speech: "The Democrats in D.C. have been and want to, at a much higher level, abolish our beautiful and successful suburbs by placing far left Washington bureaucrats in charge of local zoning decisions. Your home will go down in value, and crime rates will rapidly rise. What will be the end result is you will destroy the beautiful suburbs."³⁸⁹ Trump's veiled reference was to the Obama administration's 2015 Fair Housing Rule, aimed at ending racial discrimination in housing.³⁹⁰

"Suburbs equal white. Hey white people, if you vote for Joe Biden, you're gonna get a lot of Black people showing up in your neighborhood," explained national analyst John Heilemann on MSNBC's *Morning Joe*. "This is like standard 1970s Wallace-Nixon fare. We've made those comparisons in the past. That's the card he is playing." ³⁹¹

Ironically, the very same year, yet another attempt to right a decades-old wrong about accommodations, once again aimed at Black people, took place in Rock Hill, South Carolina. There, Judge Mark Hayes vacated the sentences of Friendship 9, who had been convicted in 1961 of trespassing and breach of peace.³⁹² Their crime? Eight students and Congress on Racial Equality (CORE) activist Thomas Gaither, sat in at a segregated lunch counter at McCrory's. Given the choice to pay a $100 fine, or spend 30 days in jail, they chose hard labor and jail, sparking a "jail not bail" movement within a movement for nonviolent activists.³⁹³

The activists, eight college students, and Gaither and their families, finally received justice 54 years after the fact, though one had died in the meantime. "We cannot rewrite history, but we can right history," said Judge Hayes, pointing out the activists had been prosecuted "solely based on their race."³⁹⁴

*

Dave Aronberg, a Florida state attorney based in Palm Beach, minced no words in framing Governor Kemp's callous, profit-above-all approach to managing the pandemic in Georgia:

"Remember, it was the most devious kind of voter suppression that got Kemp elected in the first place," said Aronberg. "So we shouldn't be surprised he's trying to politicize this pandemic. Even when his neighboring governor, Kay Ivey, of Alabama, issued a mandatory mask order. When your policies are so regressive that they make Alabama look progressive, you've got a problem."[395]

Another bright light in the midst of travail and madness was the anthem "March March" by The Chicks. Despite attacks from notable Trump fall guys Ted Cruz and Sean Spicer, The Chicks, who once drew flack for criticizing President George W. Bush and the United States' invasion of Iraq over alleged nuclear weapons, had the sensitivity and decency to change their band name from the Dixie Chicks, something they said they had been considering for some time anyway. Noting on *The Late Show with Stephen Colbert* that their most enriching experience had been the women's march right after the election in 2016, their unapologetic social justice perspective was refreshing, especially for a group with a sound that leans toward southern and rural. Despite its costing them legions of fans, this move, along with that of Lady Antebellum, follows a trend that speaks to the nation's leading white feminist voices putting their money and their reputations on the line to push for change.[396] The Chicks' beautiful requiem "March March" honors the LBGTQ+ movement, women's rights, Black Lives Matter, anti-lynching, environmental justice, job equity, and more. Listing the names of Black lives taken, they proudly promote #endwhitesilence. Say what you want, I, for one, will now seek out their music and support their progress. This was the type of bold, unapologetic statement that turns one from an ally to an advocate, regardless of the personal financial cost. This uncompromising boldness is what moves the justice needle. At some point, for some cause or reason, each of us is called to make a stand for something we fervently believe in that is righteous. As Dr. King famously said, "There are some things so dear, some things so precious, some things so eternally true, that they are worth dying for. And I submit to you that if a man has not discovered something that he will die for, he isn't fit to live."[397]

*

First-term congresswoman Ilhan Omar, part of "the Squad," the group of four progressive women of color who took the House by storm in the blue wave of 2018, talked of the impact John Lewis had made on her. An immigrant from Somalia, she, like Alexandria Ocasio-Cortez (AOC), Ayanna Pressley, and Rashida Tlaib, represents the American dream, even when she says things that offend some, and starkly speaks against racism in earnest, raw ways that those who preceded her, like Edward Brooke, Charles Diggs, Adam Clayton Powell, Shirley Chisolm, and Barbara Jordan, had less room to do.[398] Tlaib, speaking to a progressive group, Moveon, about her victory celebration, shared this story: "And when your son looks at you and says, 'Mama look, you won. Bullies don't win,' and I said, 'Baby, they don't,' because we're gonna go in there, and we're going to impeach the motherf****r."[399] I'm not with Tlaib's language here (though I do employ some pretty salty language myself), but I do stand by her right to say it, as much as South Carolina's Congressman Joe Wilson asserted his by standing and shouting, "You lie!" as President Obama addressed Congress.[400]

John Lewis, on his final journey, lay in state at Troy State University, the very institution that denied him admission in 1957.[401] Congressman James Clyburn, Lewis's friend for 60 years, and the man who saved Biden's 2020 election bid by rallying the troops for a decisive win in the second-Blackest state in the union, his native South Carolina, honored John Lewis thusly: "I do believe as the sun set on John Lewis' life last night, the sun rises on a movement that will never die. Thank you, John. Rest in peace, my brother."

The chorus, including Martin Luther King, III, son of America's Black prophet, continued to lobby to change the name of Selma's Edmund Pettus Bridge, where Lewis and dozens of unarmed Black marchers were beaten on Bloody Sunday in 1965, to that of Alabama civil rights hero Lewis.[402] At the time, Selma "would've been a place where names were about [Black people's] degradation," says Alabama historian Wayne Flynt. "It's a sort of in-your-face reminder of who runs this place." Pettus, who called Selma home, was a former senator, slave owner, Confederate general, and leader in the Alabama KKK. I can assure you that such a move would not only turn Trump orange, but blazing red.

*

Once again, in 2020, other countries violated our election system. This time, instead of Russia's Fancy Bear and the GRU, radical Islamic ISIS was tampering with our elections by infiltrating Facebook as early as the summer of 2000.[403]

As we as a nation grappled with a chaotic election season and the twin-demic of COVID and the flu, forty percent of LGBTQ+ young people considered suicide during 2020, according to the Trevor Project.[404] CEO Amit Paley, later drummed out of the organization for his role in the opioid epidemic, pointed out a federal attack on the community, based on Trump's declaration in 2017, via tweet, that trans soldiers could no longer join the military, as he commonly communicated, over the objections of his Secretary of Defense, Jim Mattis.[405]

"Unfortunately, our hospital rooms look like war zones," said Judge Richard Cortez from Hidalgo County, Texas, who issued a shelter-at-home order on July 21, pointing out that he had had an average of 22 deaths per day in the previous eight days. New CDC data released on July 22 said that as many as 13 times more people might be infected in the nation than previously thought. Meanwhile, California passed the 400,000-case mark, while Florida Governor DeSantis and the largest Florida Education Association battled over the governor's insistence that they reopen schools on time and in person, despite the safety concerns of teachers and other personnel. That all took place as infections in Florida's nursing homes rose 153% for residents and 126% for staff in the first three weeks of July. Sixty percent of Miami-Dade's hospitals reported one or fewer available ICU beds.[406]

At the same time, there were 4,000 COVID cases involving children in Dallas alone. "She's [Department of Education Secretary Betsy DeVos] trying to increase allocation disproportionately for private schools over public schools in the midst of the debate over whether or not schools should reopen," charged NAACP President Derrick Johnson in a lawsuit against the DOE Secretary, the same one who has never attended a public school in her life. "It's horrific what she's doing. What will happen is you further take money away from children who are financially in need, to benefit high-wealth children."[407]

As the sun set on the final week of the $600 unemployment add-on for those who lost their jobs during COVID, it was estimated that as many as 12 million Americans were in danger of being evicted from their homes. Visiting Massachusetts on July 24, where half a million people were losing their unemployment benefits, VP Pence assured Governor Charlie Baker that "we're going to make sure that families in this state, businesses in this state, and your administration, have the resources to move forward."[408]

In Portland, Day 56 of the protests, a wall of veterans, many wearing Black Lives Matter shirts and insignia, locked arms in confrontations with Trump-directed and -placed military personnel firing tear gas, pepper balls, and other projectiles at protesters, as federal troops captured and arrested protesters.

Farm workers in California wine country, Napa County, were a classic example of the pandemic's ravaging of Latinos, who count for 57% of the cases, though only 35% of the state's population was especially vulnerable to COVID. According to Ceja Vineyards CEO Amelia Ceja, who previously worked at the vineyards herself, "this pandemic has exposed the need for affordable housing. The workers who allow us to make this world-famous wine need to be able to live where they work."[409] Too many of them pack vans and travel two hours from Fairfield, where they can afford to live, to Napa Valley, where only nine percent of the housing is deemed affordable. In Napa, a two-bedroom can cost $2,500 per month.[410]

One week after Trump grudgingly donned a mask for only the second time and suggested that wearing a mask was "patriotic," the nation endured its fourth straight day of 1,000 or more deaths, just as the federal ban preventing evictions ran out July 25. At the same time, Florida passed New York, as California had days earlier, to rank first and second in COVID cases. The same day, Hurricane Hanna began battering Nueces County in the Texas Rio Grande, which only days earlier had reported that 85 babies had contracted COVID.

"We put it [COVID] out instantaneously, and we feel great," said Trump, miraculously. "Then you start getting phone calls [asking] 'Did you really say that?'"

Was anyone surprised? As of July 26, 2020, six months before the election, 63% of Americans believed

Biden cared more about their children's health in terms of the decision to send them back into the classroom with COVID raging, as opposed to Trump, who polled at 48%.[411] Hundreds of teachers refused to return to the classrooms, mainly due to autoimmune diseases, pre-existing conditions, and a concern that children would find consistent mask-wearing and social distancing an impossibility. In Florida, cases among children soared to over 10,000 in ten days. In Alabama, 40 maskless parishioners tested positive after attending a Baptist revival two weeks *after* Governor Kay Ivey lifted the COVID state of emergency.[412]

Regarding race and justice, 24% of Trump supporters saw the issue as important, compared to 76% of Biden's. "When people proudly have their confederate flag, they're not talking about racism. They love their flag. It represents the south," opined Trump on April 23, 2020. "It's basically an appeal to racism," countered *New York Times* columnist Eugene Robinson. "It's an appeal to those who are worried, who are freaked out by the increasing diversity of this country."[413]

In Oakland, as an arm of the peaceful protest threatened to spin out of control, one of the BLM activists, armed with a megaphone, urged: "If you're about black lives, come with us," he admonished. "If you're about breaking glass and confronting police ... stay with them."[414] In Portland, more of the same: "They started gassing us, so we came back with respirators," explained local organizer Mac Smiff. "They started shooting us, so we came back with vests. Who's escalating this? It's not us."[415] Indeed, several of the protests involved the burning of buildings and forced entry of federal property. Were these protesters run amok, imbedded anarchists, or white supremacists seeking to stoke racial fires and promulgate Trump's agenda? History will no doubt show that it was, unfortunately, a combination of them all, which diluted the purity of the purpose of the move toward racial justice and a stop to police brutality against Blacks. Certainly, a third of America buys into the "law and order" concept and the inflammatory Willie Lynch-type tropes dominating the Trump commercials and campaign … whether they admit it or not.

In Savannah, Georgia, one of the oldest, loveliest cities in the U.S., a clinical trial volunteer for Moderna was vaccinated on July 27th, the same day that the nation entered Phase 3. The volunteer, Dawn Baker, an anchor at WTOC in Savannah, is a Black woman. Praise God for her, as we certainly desperately need Black volunteers, especially since Black folk were dying from COVID at three times the rate as whites, and Latinos two times the rate. Baker said, "This is really, to me, very empowering that I could be that person who could help save some lives. It's been very heartbreaking to hear about people who've lost their lives because of this. I never thought that I'd do something like this."[416]

Based on Black America's history with vaccinations and medical abuse, coupled with the callous disregard for Black health overall, at that time, I muttered to myself, "It damn sure wouldn't be me unless I was in dire straits."

Meanwhile, Trump sent more troops into Portland and Kansas City and threatened to do the same in Chicago, Seattle, and elsewhere. Seattle Mayor Jenny Durkan, leader of what Trump called the "Democrat-led cities," laid out why the leader of the free world was leaning into fascism and totalitarianism by sending in federal troops without local agreement or consent.

"We had weeks of peace in Seattle," a city with few Blacks, yet a protest hotbed, explained Durkan. "We've seen millions of people turn out in the streets of America, raising their voices and challenging our government, including me, to be better. First Amendment rights must be protected. There's a balance that police will have to strike to make sure that they can protect public safety, not see the type of destruction we saw in Seattle this weekend and last week. We had weeks of peace in Seattle. We had really been focused on the hard, substantive change; but when Portland started to escalate, things escalated in Seattle. Person after person, when interviewed Saturday, said they were there because of what the president [Trump] was doing."[417]

Just when you think Trump had turned a corner, after grudgingly donning a mask and calling doing so "patriotic," in some quarters, he did an about-face, again glorifying a group of doctors promoting hydroxychloroquine as a cure for COVID. Mind you, I know a doctor who does believe it is effective, though its most widely acknowledged use is as a treatment for malaria. However, Trump retweeted and endorsed the findings of Stella Immanuel, an African physician, no less, who pointed to aliens having sex with humans to spread COVID. At that point, even if there was a valid argument for treatment, though not rogue use by uninformed and untrained trusting people, most credibility was destroyed by the claims of the "demon sperm" doctor.[418] For me, as I watched the clip in horror and disbelief, this was a classic example of "collective shame" that I, as a Black American, sometimes feel when Black folk do things many see as deeply distressing. I have a similar reaction when gangs of organized thugs, who utilize all their brilliance to rob and steal, descend on a high-end store in L.A., D.C., Atlanta, Chicago, and elsewhere to deftly and efficiently steal thousands of dollars of expensive goods within two minutes, tops. Why not use that brilliant timing and execution to code, engineer, start a business, or choreograph? White people, as far as I can tell, do not feel "collective shame" at the criminal acts their people perform. Perhaps the world would be a better place if they did.

Ohio, Indiana, Kentucky, and Tennessee, mid-south and mid-north states in the heart of Trump country, were suddenly declared dangerous COVID hotspots that could quickly spiral out of control, much like Florida, Texas, and California, each of which recorded new daily death or case counts on July 29, as the nation hit its fifth-straight day of 1,000 deaths.

"If you're not getting your arms around and suppressing that surge that's coming up two to three weeks down the road, you're in trouble," said Dr. Fauci, who politely disputed Trump's claim that hydroxychloroquine was a safe, effective cure for COVID. I personally identified with and understood Dr. Fauci's consistent but careful repudiation of Trump's baseless claims. Though infinitely more powerful and protected, Dr. Fauci chose to stay through the MAGA-madness and strived to be the adult in the room at the upper levels of the administration. To me, and no doubt to millions of other Americans, he was a voice of calm and moderation, not unlike the role I sought to play in the regional office, though certainly on a much lesser stage. Dr. Fauci's correction of Trump's statement came as 21 states were declared red zone states, with a minimum of 100 new cases per day, at his $100k-per-person campaign dinner. The first coronavirus death in the U.S. was noted exactly five months earlier. The death toll rose above 150,000 – more than 50 times the number of lives taken on 9/11.

"I really do believe that governors should be opening a lot of states that aren't open," said Trump on July 27, 2020. He also, once again, erroneously and with very little perspective, insisted that the U.S. led the world in testing. Trump's continued denial of the deathly impact of COVID cost 36,000 lives because he failed to promote social distancing, according to a study by Columbia University in May of 2020. The study also noted that the U.S. went from 500 COVID infections on March 8, 2020, to 2,000 a week later, indicating that implementing social distancing even a week earlier, would have saved thousands of lives.[419]

On July 30th, former President Obama eulogized Freedom Fighter and Georgia Congressman John Lewis in Ebenezer Baptist Church the home church of America's prophet, Dr. King. Ebenezer is also the church pastored by Rev. Raphael Warnock, who, six months later, would become a huge thorn in Trump's side as he and John Ossoff would both be elected to the U.S. Senate and play a major role in the election that booted Trump from office and gave Biden a slender majority in the Senate.

Giving the eulogy at Lewis' service, Obama said this: "The life of John Lewis was, in so many ways, exceptional. It vindicated the faith in our founding, redeemed that faith, that most American of ideas; that idea that any of us ordinary people without rank, or wealth, or title, or fame, can somehow point out the imperfections of this nation, and come together, and challenge the status quo, and decide that it is in our power to remake this country that we love until it more closely aligns with our highest ideals. What a radical idea? What a revolutionary notion? This idea that any of us, ordinary people, a young kid from Troy [AL], can stand up to the powers and principalities and say, no, this isn't right, this isn't true, this isn't just. We can do better. On the battlefield of justice, Americans like John, Americans like the Reverend Lowery, and C.T. Vivian, two other patriots that we lost this year, liberated all of us in many ways that many Americans came to take for granted."[420]

George Wallace might be gone, Lewis had reminded us, but we can witness our federal government sending agents to use tear gas and batons against peaceful demonstrators.

Lewis, whose final public act was taking a photo on the Black Lives Matter Plaza in front of what was then known as Trump Tower, frequently reminded justice seekers that "Emmett Till was my George Floyd, he was my Rayshard Brooks, Sandra Bland, and Breonna Taylor."[421] The genius move to paint the street in front of Trump's hotel by D.C. Mayor Muriel Bowser was clearly an affront to Trump, who disparaged and demonized the BLM Movement as he did Asians and Latinos, and also as former President G.W. Bush used Willie Horton in the presidential election of 1988.[422]

The same day Lewis was eulogized, on July 30, 2020, Trump, in yet another tweet, proclaimed that "with universal mail-in voting (not absentee voting, which is good), 2020 will be a great embarrassment to the USA." He continued that instead, we should "delay the election until people can properly, securely and safely vote."[423]

There was an occasional ray of good news for the country, though. Black billionaire and media magnate Oprah Winfrey made history when, for the first time in its 20-year history, she did not appear on the cover of her prestigious magazine, *O*, but instead, chose to feature Breonna Taylor, the EMT who was killed in Louisville during a no-knock raid.[424]

Chapter 28: Protecting Our Mental Health in the Height of COVID

"You're right. People are dying. It is what it is."
President Trump

      Like most Americans, I found it necessary to carve out some level of normalcy during COVID, if only to protect my psyche and mental health. One of the things I did to clear my head and infuse my spirit was walking the steep hills in my neighborhood. On a particular walk during COVID, I stopped at my usual place, a bus stop about 1.5 miles from my house. Approaching the stop, I noticed a slight figure, a girl, perhaps 10-12, by herself at the stop. Usually, in the throbbing summer heat, I check my phone, wipe my brow, and take a deep pull from my water bottle. This time, however, as I'd left a little later than usual, it was dark, nearly 9:10 in the evening. Alarmed that this girl was too young to be coming from a job, and with few businesses open where a child could be served by herself, I found myself concerned. Waiting longer than usual, I glanced from time to time in her direction as she was sitting at the stop across the street. Finally, seeing no movement, I called 911, explaining that it wasn't an emergency that I was calling about, but in the hopes of avoiding one. What if I walked away and something happened to that precious little girl? And yet, if I walked across the street to check on her and make sure she was waiting on someone or the bus, I could be seen as a pedophile or a predator. Deeply troubled, yet unsure what to do, I waited about ten minutes, hoping a police car would come. Ten minutes later, resigned and anguished, I left, praying she would be safe. Things were so different when I grew up in the sixties, when you were not only your parents', auntie's, and grandma's child, but the neighborhood's. Today, concerns about lawsuits, or being seen as having bad intentions, have stolen too much of our humanity. In that way, I long for the good old days.

Lest we forget: Eternal vigilance is the price of freedom. Some attribute it to founding father Thomas Jefferson, but with no clear conclusion. That's good because brother-in-law, slave-owning Jefferson just doesn't work for me.

In some ways, Georgia, especially Atlanta, was one of the epicenters of change in 2020. We lost the bold, intellectual, and spiritual leadership of civil rights giants Lowery, Vivian, and Lewis. Ahmaud Arbery and Rayshard Brooks, both unarmed, were killed by police in high-profile "incidents," and Mayor Keisha Lance Bottoms and Governor Kemp battled over masking. Also, the nation's leading disease experts, the CDC, proved inconsistent and shaky, while the nation's most famous and enduring cable news company, CNN, saw its iconic logo desecrated by angry protesters following the murder of George Floyd.[425] The irony is that while CNN is broadly considered center-left, at best, by conservatives, much of the world considers it the U.S.'s standard-bearing news source.

Meanwhile, tens of thousands of young, uninformed, and defiant Americans continued to party like it was 1999. "It's hard to put your life on pause for a minute for a virus, especially if you're young and stupid," a young man acknowledged on July 31, 2020, as parties of as many as 700 people were being regularly broken up across the country.[426]

By late summer 2020, 75% of test results were coming back in five days, according to HHS. At least 6,600

COVID cases were connected to students set to return to college, according to a *New York Times* survey.

There were also over 4.5 million confirmed COVID cases in the U.S. Florida recording its fourth straight day of record deaths, climbing from 186, 216, 153 to 257 to close out July, just as it announced a shuttering of its testing sites in the new U.S. epicenter, South Florida, as Hurricane Irma charged toward it. Meanwhile, Trump visited Florida for the 47th time since taking office, this time Tampa. Pence, testing leader Giroir, Surgeon General Adams, and other top officials had beaten a well-worn path to Florida over the past few months. In another hotbed, California, Latinos made up over half of the nearly half a million cases. At the same time, irrational behavior, allegedly sparked by a belief that being required to wear a mask equaled an assault on personal rights, continued across the nation. One of the latest examples was at a Staples in New Jersey, where a younger woman grabbed the cane of a frail, elderly woman and slung her to the ground, breaking her leg, allegedly after being told to don a mask.[427] When did Americans become so callous about the health and wellness of the sick and frail? When did parents stop teaching respect and kindness?

As the virus raged, Trump was focused on seemingly much less consequential things, like proclaiming an intention to ban TikTok and crowing about Operation Legend's success in controlling and stamping out violence and protests in major U.S. cities like Portland and Kansas City, where he and his deputized armed troops snatched people off the streets and, in too many instances, assaulted, tear-gassed, and brutalized them. After suggesting the election be postponed, which GOP leaders largely agreed to, Trump said, "This is going to be the greatest election disaster in history. It'll be fixed, it'll be rigged; it could go on forever." At the same time, Trump appointee Postmaster General Louis DeJoy, a major Trump donor and head of the

U.S. Postal Service, made major cuts in postal drop boxes and sorting machines, often in poor and urban areas, claiming waste.[428]

When he delivered the eulogy for fallen leader John Lewis, Obama elicited his most stinging warning about his successor: "There are those in power who are doing their darndest to discourage people from voting, even undermining the postal service in the run-up to an election that will be dependent on mail-in ballots so people don't get sick."

Kelly Loeffler, whose husband owns part of the New York Stock Exchange, was appointed by Governor Brian Kemp to finish the term of Georgia Senator Johnny Isakson, who retired early due to health concerns. Loeffler, a former basketball player, was also an owner of the predominantly Black Atlanta Dream, a WNBA team. As an extremely wealthy and privileged white woman, she criticized the BLM and the protests, clearly in a move to pander to her rural, Anglo, small-town Georgia voters, who were bound to face a difficult choice between her and Trump attack dog Doug Collins, who was also running to fill the seat, permanently. Loeffler knew she was facing a wide-open race with 18 other candidates, while Collins was endorsed by Trump. So, what did she do? Loeffler went whole hog, brandishing her ultra-conservative colors, and promoted her interview with Jack Posobiec, who has strong ties with Unite the Right leader Richard Spencer, whose group marched, fought with protesters, and chanted "Jews will not replace us," during the deadly Charlottesville encounter that injured several and cost Heather Heyer her life.

"I joined @JackPosobiec on @OANN to discuss why I had to call out the BLM political organization – and why the woke mob is trying to cancel me," she wrote in one tweet. "WATCH the full interview here."[429]

So Loeffler had the nerve to own a mostly Black WNBA team in a mostly Black city and rail against the greatest social movement and awakening in over 50 years, and not understand the outrage and insult she has caused? Again, white pomposity, this time on steroids.

Dr. Bernard Ashby, head of the Florida Committee to Protect Medicare, said this: "The fact that I'm having to respond to Trump on clinical medicine is insane. He needs to stay in his lane," said Ashby, a Cornell University graduate. "We are pissed off. We want Homey to stay in his lane and not talk about clinical-based medicine, if he doesn't understand it."[430]

Barron Trump, the president's youngest son, couldn't even attend his posh private school. Why? Because it was closed due to the coronavirus, unlike the thousands of schools across the country that TRUMP insisted needed to open.

Many of these children who couldn't attend school are in multi-generational households. The children might not have gotten sick, but they could bring it home, and vulnerable people were going to die. Meanwhile, Trump and his minions were in court trying to take healthcare access through the ACA, or ObamaCare, away from millions of people.[431] Certainly, those children who were prevented from going to school suffered academic and social setbacks and often struggled with mental and behavioral health issues. Those are challenges that need to be addressed and dealt with, especially since we now know that COVID will be with us for the foreseeable future. As uncomfortable and inconvenient as staying home was, it did prevent thousands of kids from debilitating disease and death.

In July, more than 40 percent of the nation's 4.5 million cases were confirmed. The steady fire had turned into a raging, scorched earth affair for rural America. Some states, like Mississippi, where the nation's highest percentage of Black folk live, were unprepared and out of control.

"I want to be clear," explained COVID Task Force leader Dr. Deborah Birx. "What we're seeing now is different than March and April. This is extraordinarily widespread." Yes, because you and Trump refused to sound the alarm early on, so tens of thousands of lives could have been saved. Chicago schools had planned on a hybrid model between in-class and virtual learning. That soon changed, like in Los Angeles, where distance learning alone quickly ruled the day.

Trump, clearly unhappy with her long-awaited truth-telling, called Birx "pathetic" after she claimed the pandemic was "extraordinarily widespread."

While Black Americans and Latinos were suffering far higher COVID death rates than Anglos, Native American populations were also disproportionately impacted. They were 2.8 times more likely to die of COVID than whites, according to the Princeton School of Public and International Affairs.[432] One of the six federally recognized tribes our office worked directly with, the Mississippi Band of Choctaw Indians, lost 81 members to COVID.[433]

Forty million Americans were out of work by the fall, the number growing by the week, even as their health care through the ACA was being chipped away in court by Trump. Five million of those jobs were in the hospitality industry, highly populated by Black and brown people, who comprise nearly 55 percent of the nation's front-line workers.

Colorado is off the hook. A Black woman, Brittany Gilliam, with four girls, including two nieces and a six-year-old daughter, was stopped by police in Aurora en route to a nail salon, handcuffed face down, and detained because she had the same license plates as a reported stolen vehicle. The problem? They were in a van, and the stolen vehicle was a motorcycle from another state.[434] Do you believe, even in your wildest imagination – or nightmare – that this would ever happen to a white woman and four girls? Not for one damn minute! Who knows what, even in this era of heightened white sensitivity to the injustice and double standard of over-policing, it will take for white Americans in authority to see Black folk like they see their neighbors, the people on their children's sports teams, or the same friends they have barbeques and attend church with, instead of the "Other?"

One of the four children placed face down cried out in the anger and frustration many Black Americans have felt over the years: "It's like they don't care," said 14-year-old Tariana Thomas, niece. "Who am I going to call when my life is in danger?"[435] Aurora, Colorado, is the same city where unarmed 23-year-old Elijah McClain was killed by police while walking home from the convenience store.[436] Just damn! White pomposity.

Rep. Gohmert, another Trump sycophant and unrepentant mask denier who contracted COVID and likely gave it to Rep. Raul Grijalva at a meeting when he should have been quarantined, still may be in a Trump trance, but not his daughter. Caroline Brooks tweeted: "My father ignored medical expertise, and now he has COVID. ... It's not worth following a president who has no remorse for leading his followers to an early grave."[437]

"You're right. People are dying. It is what it is," Trump said in an interview.[438] On the same day, it was reported that the death rate from coronavirus had topped 156,000. More alarming, the percentage of deaths had climbed 24% in the past week, even as daily cases dropped by eight percent (CBS News). Twenty-four percent over the previous two weeks, and Mississippi was on pace to become number one in COVID cases per capita.

"Come into my ICU," said Dr. Brad Spellberg of the LAC-USC Medical Center when questioned whether COVID is as severe as the media portrays it. "What we're seeing is the working poor being wiped out."[439]

"Early on, the president ignored the warnings that were coming from the intelligence community, ignoring the warnings that were coming from the international health community," said Ron Klain, Ebola czar in the Obama administration. "He [Trump] stood in front of the American people, told people it would go away, it would be like a miracle. There were more new cases of COVID yesterday in Paris, Texas than in Paris, France." So, I mean, this is a singular failure of the Trump administration.[440]

Because of research on the social determinants of health that have been decades in the making, the evidence was clear that African Americans and other minorities have at least five times the hospitalizations as Caucasians, according to COVID Czar Dr. Anthony Fauci of the National Institutes of Health (NIH). Speaking at the Harvard School of Public Health, Fauci said it is "unacceptable" that some people still couldn't get COVID tests as late as the summer of 2020.[441]

In an appeal to Evangelicals as to why he was better for them as president than the Roman Catholic Joe Biden, Trump said Biden would "hurt the Bible." Meanwhile, COVID cases in the U.S. under Trump's administration soared, and 160,000 Americans had died from the disease we were told only a week ago would "go away." One American died every second during the first week of August 2020, even as tens of thousands of young people gathered for parties and impromptu events after months of cabin fever, regardless of the costs. This all took place as the

Center for Public Integrity warned that Portland, the California Central Valley, Boston, Detroit, Baltimore, Washington, D.C., Atlanta, and heartland cities Omaha, Chicago, and Kansas City were all in dire danger of an eruption of COVID cases and deaths.

Just like the coming COVID tsunami that began to gain momentum in February and March of 2020, even a blind dog with a note in his mouth could see what was going to happen when Trump and the gullible governors rushed back to school. In Georgia, for example, in outlying Paulding and Forsyth counties, students proudly posted shots of the senior class in front of the school on opening day. In Paulding, student Hannah Watters took a photo of a very crowded hallway as kids changed classes. Again, very few wearing masks. Watters was suspended, and both schools reported new cases on day one.[442] Acknowledging she broke three school rules in the process, Watters, whose suspension was later overturned when the media got hold of the story, was confident she did the right thing in the spirit of Freedom Fighter John Lewis.

"I'd like to say this is some good and necessary trouble," Watters said. "My biggest concern is not only about me being safe. It's about everyone being safe because behind every teacher, student, and staff member, there is a family, there are friends, and I would just want to keep everyone safe."[443]

A teacher and 20 students were sent home from one Cherokee County (GA) school after a positive test, with 65 being quarantined, including a first and second grader, along with a kindergarten teacher. All this happened as Trump insisted that young kids were immune from COVID. In Paulding, a staff member, several teachers, and numerous members of the football team tested positive for COVID.

"People are just terrified about going back into brick and mortar schools right now because we cannot keep them safe," said Fredrick Ingram, president of the Florida Education Teacher's Union. "We know that our schools were made for social interaction, not social distancing."[444]

Challenge trials or a journey into the absurd? The UK's University of Oxford sought to vaccinate volunteers, then *intentionally* infect them with coronavirus. The study was funded by the Welcome Fund.[445]

"Yes, I'm confident they will be approved," said Adrian Hill, who directed the study. "A lot of people feel very passionately that they should be and that the tiny risk is worth it for the benefit of developing a vaccine, or a drug, faster."[446] Let me say this with a straight face and all sincerity. There are people in the world who love their fellow men and women, feel strong and healthy, and are willing to put their lives on the line to move humanity forward. In many ways, I liken them to those in the military who volunteer to fight with the significant chance they will return home with some sort of physical or psychological scars, even in a body bag, like some U.S. vets who died fighting for Ukraine's sovereignty. From a more personal perspective, I liken these people, though not as famous or individually significant, to the civil rights gladiators like Amzie Moore, Fannie Lou Hamer, James Zwerg, Andrew Young, Fred Bennett, Willy Leventhal, Medgar Evers, James Peck, the Rev. Fred Shuttlesworth and countless others, who were willing to put their lives on the line to move society and their race further toward racial righteousness and equality. God bless them and protect them, I say.

Meanwhile, the same week, a group of Daphne, Alabama (a burg near the Gulf with a Black population of 15%) cheerleaders posed with a Confederate flag that said, "I love redneck boys." When the two Black cheerleaders protested, teammates, coaches, school officials, and fellow white cheerleaders moved ahead as if nothing were wrong. For the six white girls who posed with the flag and t-shirt, it may have all been harmless fun, indeed, a display of their "southern heritage." For the Black cheerleader, Reagan (yeah, I know) Coleman, the shirts were an affront, as the flag stands for a defeated nation that built its wealth and Jim Crow society on slavery, dehumanization, and domination of people who looked like her. For the feckless white cheerleaders and their defenders, this is just another case of white pomposity.

"I immediately see hate," said Coleman, who quit the team after the July 4th photo was published. "There's no 'two sides' to that flag. That means hatred," explained Reagan's mother, Latitiah. "That's what it stands for [for] us. We were oppressed with that flag."[447]

Sadly, this is just another example of being marginalized, ignored, and dismissed as a Black person living in a strange land called America. I can only imagine, but the experience might be something akin to the victims of Jeffrey Epstein hearing Trump say that he "wished Ghislaine Maxwell" the best as she headed off to prison for her alleged complicity in sexually assaulting dozens of underage girls.

Dr. Stephen Hahn, head of the FDA and the person who refused to answer a single question on his position on the vaping crisis during his confirmation hearings, assured the public in a tweet that he would not compromise safety by rushing out a coronavirus vaccine.[448] At the same time, the polls revealed that only 42% of Americans said they would trust the vaccine if it came out before the election, down from 55% who said they would get the vaccine in May, questioning the safety and efficacy of a vaccine developed at "warp speed."[449]

Of course, the "wills" and "won'ts" of getting vaccinated were largely split around party lines. My question is, for those people who read and follow what they insist are scientists and "fake news," did they see what happened to former GOP presidential frontrunner Herman Cain and the warnings from the daughter of Texas anti-masker Rep. Louie Gohmert, who contracted the disease and likely gave it to several of his House of Representative colleagues?[450] Well, as for me and my house – barring, God forbid, someone being on their death bed – I damn sure won't be taking the first vaccine rushed out of the lab at warp speed, I thought at the time. A few months later, however, my perspective changed, largely because of a conversation our office had with a longtime colleague I trusted, who happens to be Anglo. Public Health Service Rear Admiral Tom Bowman explained the efficacy of the Pfizer and Moderna vaccines to my Black career colleagues, Natalia Cales and Karen Jordan, in the HHS Office of the Regional Director and convinced us. After weeks of trying, I got my first COVID shot as soon as I could get it scheduled.

"Our right to not wear a mask is going to kill us," California ER physician Dr. Desmond Carson said the day the U.S. pushed past 160,000 deaths, noting that "only" 60,000 people died in World War II. "That bullshit is going to kill us. How am I going to differentiate flu from corona?"[451]

Black and brown people are more reliant on public transportation in urban areas, more likely to live in food deserts, and less likely to have health insurance. Is it any wonder Blacks in America were dying at 74 per 100,000, Native Americans, Hispanics, and Latinos at 40, Asians at 31, and Anglos at 30 per 100,000?[452]

"We recognize the impacts of behaviors on our health, like smoking, drinking, even loneliness, so why not recognize the impacts of racism, too?" said epidemiologist Dr. Shawnita Sealy-Jefferson. "We have a lot of data on individuals' experience with racism and individuals' experience with discrimination, and we have linked that to poor health and mortality."

Liz Plank, a Canadian journalist and the host of *Positive Spin*, noted several glaring disparities. There are 1.5 million missing Black men in America, Black mothers are up to six times more likely to die during childbirth, Black women in D.C. have a maternity death rate twice that of women in Syria, and six Black trans women were found dead in July alone.

Front-line workers were more than three times as likely to contract the virus, even with the right gloves, gowns, and face protection. Black and Latino health care workers were at an even higher risk: five times more likely to test positive for COVID-19 than their white coworkers, according to the Kings College of London study.[453]

Nerves were frayed, and people acting out became more and more common as COVID turned life, as we knew it, upside down for most communities. I understand that police officers were affected, too, by this "new normal." However, when an officer in Waycross, Georgia, shot at a group of Black kids ages 9, 12, 14, 15, and 16 … *That* crossed the line. "At least seven shots were fired by the officer," the nine-year-old boy told WJXT. The children's outraged father, Dominique Goodman said, "They shot at a car full of unarmed minors. A car full of unarmed children. Like who in the world can't see that this is a nine-year-old? Who can't see that this is a child? They look like children," he told WJXT. Would they have shot at a car with a bunch of white teens in it? This was unjustified, the 59th officer-involved shooting in Georgia, and it was only August.[454] White pomposity and seeing Black people as the Other, yet again.

As of June 8, 2020, there were five million cases and 163,000 COVID-related deaths in the U.S., one fatality every 83 seconds over the previous week, even as the virus "[was] disappearing," according to POTUS. Nationwide, 97,000 children were infected in the last two weeks of July, contrary to Trump's insistence that kids were "virtually immune" from the virus. One man infected 90 people at a church service, even as PPE, vaccines, test kits, and other tools were still scarce in the U.S. At that point, 300,000 kids were infected by COVID, including over 100,000 in the previous two weeks. Ninety-three children died from COVID in 2020, with a 90% increased infection rate treated in children in the previous two weeks.

"How do you, Dr. Anthony Fauci, walk the fine line of telling the truth – warning the masses – while not pissing off the boss, thus risking the boot and eliminating one of the most honest voices the nation respects, while constantly serving as the whipping boy of the far right?" I often asked myself during the daily grind of gathering statements from elected officials, collecting anecdotal evidence, and assessing COVID-related statistics.

By August 10, 2020, there were 20 million coronavirus cases worldwide, an astonishing five million in the U.S. Among those were nearly 165,000 deaths. One day later, Florida, which had set an all-time death record of 246 the day before, reported 276 deaths the next day.

Again, in the strangest of worlds, two more shocking, earth-shattering events took place. The presumed Democratic nominee, former Vice President Joe Biden, announced Kamala Harris, daughter of immigrants, a Black Jamaican and an Indian scholar, as the first woman of color chosen to run for VP on a major ticket. In a vastly different arena, two of the vaunted Power Five NCAA conferences, the Big Ten and the PAC 12, announced they would cancel all fall sports due to the coronavirus.

As a white southerner, political consultant-author, and Lincoln Project advisor, Stuart Stevens may have put it best: "You don't have to be a racist to support Donald Trump, but ultimately, you have to be comfortable with having a racist as president. There's something you think you're getting from him being president [that] is more important than him being a racist. And that's increasingly difficult to deny, every hour, as we go forward."[455] But what else could we have expected from a president who told U.S. veterans not to believe our lying eyes?[456] Not to be outdone, Trump's 2016 campaign manager and another of his deft snake oil saleswomen, Kellyanne Conway, had introduced the term "alternative facts" when justifying White House spokesperson Sean Spicer's lies about the size of Trump's inauguration crowd, as well as a number of other issues.[457] Most of Trump's spokespersons were very talented, yet deeply whorish in their willingness to unashamedly state what they knew were lies.

So, as Rome burned and Trump fiddled, at least two significant landmarks happened on August 12, 2020. U.S. Surgeon General Jerome Adams, perhaps the most honest task force doctor during the coronavirus, announced via Twitter that day that for the first time, 90 percent of COVID tests in the U.S. were being returned as either positive or negative, within three days. Rapid turnaround testing, along with "if you want a test, you can get a test," had been promised since May, so at long last, there were key signs of progress. On the same day, it was also reported that the U.S., which had experienced 17 straight days of 1,000-plus deaths, had the day before lost more lives (1,468) to COVID in one day than at any time since mid-May, three months earlier.[458]

How could this be happening in the richest, most technologically savvy, freest nation on the planet? Contributing mightily to the bad numbers, Florida Governor DeSantis and Georgia's Kemp, neither of whom required masks in their states, insisted that their vulnerable children should go back to school for in-person learning, on time.

Hmm…was it a coincidence, or more likely a direct correlation, to the fact that Florida and Georgia, as of August 12, 2020, were ranked No. 1 and 2, respectively, in per capita cases in the nation? Yep, if you're going down a cliff and unwilling to put on the brakes and change course, Donald Trump, clearly, you are not alone, followed near cultishly by Tweedledee and Tweedledum. The late, great songwriter David Bowie poignantly wrote in a summer classic, "Fame," released 45 years before the pandemic, when U.S. citizens were dying at *four times* the rate of people in any other country, "Is it any wonder, I reject you first? Is it any wonder you're too cool to fool?"[459]

Fame

Fame (fame) makes a man take things over.
Fame (fame) lets him loose, hard to swallow.
Fame (fame) puts you there where things are hollow.
Fame (fame)

Fame, it's not your brain, it's just the flame
That burns your change to keep you in … sane (sane)
Fame (fame)

Fame, (fame) what you like is in the limo.
Fame, (fame) what you get is no tomorrow.
Fame, (fame) what you need you have to borrow.
Fame (fame)

Fame, "Nein! It's mine!" is just his line
To bind your time, it drives you to … crime.
Fame (fame)
Could it be the best, could it be?
Really be, really, babe?
Could it be, my babe, could it, babe?
Could it, babe? Could it, babe?

> Is it any wonder I reject you first?
> Fame, (fame) fame, fame, fame (fame)
> Is it any wonder you are too cool to fool
> Fame (fame)
>
> Fame, bully for you, chilly for me
> Got to get a rain check on ... pain (pain)
>
> Fame

"We believe many school systems can open and open up safely," insisted Trump,[460] even as at least three Georgia high schools closed, with 1,000 students and faculty on quarantine. And Georgia was far from the only trouble spot. In Elizabeth, New Jersey, 400 teachers filed for medical exemptions, declaring that going back into the classroom compromised their health.

I get why parents wanted to get their children back in school. I volunteer and serve on the board at an afterschool program. Socialization, one-on-one help, and reconnecting with friends and humanity, coupled with, for many, the best meals they will receive, are critical to growth and normalcy. Those are vital reasons to get kids back in school, especially for the five million ESL (English as Second Language) Spanish-speaking children in the country. But let's be honest: There is also a segment of parents, generally white and privileged, who simply don't want to be inconvenienced by having their children at home all days, or most days, and the responsibility that comes along with ensuring they are studying and engaged. Sure, some simply don't have the education or background to make it work. I get it. If I'm brutally honest, however, I understand it on an even more visceral level for the migrant farmer mom, the inner-city mother who works in her service industry, low-paying job, or whose children go meatless and struggle to get enough to eat. Sadly, I know many such families. All too often, they are undereducated, relatively unskilled, struggling to scratch out a living and provide opportunities for their children under normal circumstances, fighting drugs and crime, and too few role models for their children's futures. For them, the choices are bleak. Conversely, for many other privileged parents and families, solid choices do exist. Most have the choice to either hire tutors, create learning pods, or work with the children, themselves, to keep them on track. Legions protest, however, because, frankly, they believe it is their right to send their children to schools, even at the risk of their children, their elders and teachers, and families of classmates. That, whether we want to acknowledge it or not, epitomizes white privilege in its basest form and white pomposity at its core.

"If we think things are bad now, wait until mid-September, when school children have had greater opportunity to relax and consort, then take whatever they contract back home to at-risk elders and other compromised loved ones," I thought at the time. "If you think things are ugly today, August 12," I said to myself, "just give it a few weeks." Once again, there was a colossal train wreck waiting to happen. As usual, those who would suffer the brunt of the carnage were poor Black and brown people who have limited choices, not those who have top-notch health care, numerous options, and are among the nation's privileged.

Chapter 29: Don't Make Us Write Obituaries

"All you keep hearing about is [white] fear. It's amazing," said Rivers, "why do we keep loving this country, and this country does not love us back? You don't have to be black to be outraged."

NBA coach and former star Glenn "Doc" Rivers

Trump claimed suburban dwellers were afraid that minorities would come in and erect low-income housing. He said 30 percent of suburban residents are Black, and they threaten to take over. Fearmongering and age-old tropes tended to be his weapon of choice. Meanwhile, New Jersey Governor Phil Murphy authorized a remote-only learning option for its schools after 400 teachers from Elizabethtown opted out of teaching via medical exemptions.

"How will you keep a mask on a little six-year-old?" asked Marie Tichenor, one of the teachers, who has an immune-compromised husband. "What do I do when a child cries, or needs a shoe tied? How do I tell them I can't comfort you because we have to be six feet apart?"[461]

August 13th was also exactly five months after paramedic Breonna Taylor was shot and killed by three Louisville cops serving a no-knock warrant. Despite the cops breaking into the wrong house and shooting her multiple times, no one except her boyfriend, at home with her asleep, had been arrested for shooting back at police. Taylor's death sparked months of protests and calls for wide-scale reform.[462]

"Somehow, they can't figure out how to charge some cops who murdered a black woman," one activist said. Oprah Winfrey launched a massive campaign, funding 26 billboards around Louisville in honor of each of the years of her life. It's also worth noting that at least 44 trans-Black women have been murdered during 2020. Tragically, there has been very little coverage of that.[463] The Divider-in-Chief's constant rhetoric and caustic name-calling made LBGTQ+ Americans, as well as Blacks, Jews, the disabled, women, Latinos, and Asians, casual, yet constant, victims of hate.

White pomposity? Our privileged president, a wanna-be autocrat, openly proclaimed that he wanted to minimize absentee voting because he was convinced it privileges Democrats and leads to an abundance of cheating, despite the fact that historically, Republicans vote absentee by a huge percentage. There was, of course, no significant evidence that supported his claim. Even crazier, Trump and his wife, the very same day, requested their own absentee ballots for his home in Florida.[464] White pomposity on steroids.

Even the previously reticent Obama, who I realized was working overtime to not criticize his successor, couldn't keep silent after this assault on freedom and equality. Obama said, "What we've never seen before is a president say, 'I'm going to try and actively kneecap the postal service to encourage voting.'"

A leaked document dated August 9 from the Coronavirus Task Force criticized Trump and "strongly recommended" a statewide mask mandate because of Kemp's open bars, restaurants, and gyms and the as-expected continued rise in COVID case numbers. Governor Kemp, initially, of course, refused to address the report.[465]

As California shut down early, yet had topped 600,000 cases by August 14, Dr. Fauci warned that not following guidelines would ultimately fuel and extend the virus's death, destruction, and disruption.

"Absolutely, we should have universal wearing of masks," said Fauci, who rarely shared a stage with Trump after May 2020. "In your understandable zeal to quickly get back to normal and revive the economy, you can do it if you do it in a measured, prudent way. To think that you can ignore the biologic, it's just not going to happen."[466] Somewhat relenting to continued pressure and ridicule, Kemp finally issued a partial mask mandate on August 15.[467] Damn shame it took over 2,000 quarantined Georgia students and teachers, and a leaked report from the White House Coronavirus Task Force that characterized the state as having "widespread and expanding community viral spread," to make it happen.[468] No damn wonder Northerners think Southerners are yahoos – for damn sure, too many of our governors and senators, almost exclusively ultra-conservative old white men, are.

Both infections and testing began trending down, possibly as much as 17%, even as the U.S. posted 20,000 new cases over the previous two weeks, as of the middle of August 2020.

Many Americans actually didn't believe campaigning could be any more bizarre than when POTUS insisted that Obama wasn't an American, and thus ineligible to be president on March 23, 2011. Obama, at the Democratic National Convention in 2016, returned the favor in his description of Trump, who would be elected a few months later, and was prophetic in his warning about the threat Trump would soon become:

"In remarkably strong language, Obama suggested Trump was a 'homegrown demagogue' who 'threatens our values,' much like 'fascists,' 'communists,' and 'jihadists' do, and who could imperil 'this great American experiment in self-government.'"[469] We saw that play out at the end of 2023, when Trump declared during a rally that immigrants were "poisoning the blood of our country. They poison mental institutions and prisons all over the world, not just in South America, but all over the world. They're coming into our country from Africa, from Asia. ..."[470] Some in his party, like Alabama Senator Tommy Tuberville, who held dozens of military promotions to protest pro-abortion laws, said, "I'm mad he [Trump] wasn't tougher than that" in his condemnation of immigrants.

 I do not personally believe in burning the flag. My father served 27 years, including two tours in Nam and one in Korea, finally retiring after being shot down out of a helicopter. He and his five brothers served, as well as their father and grandfather. To me, Old Glory is sacred. However, as much as I respect the flag, I will not deny the racist and misogynistic nature of the nation's founding, nor of its founding fathers. And never will I accept the premise that the flag is more important than the people it was designed to unite and represent. The flag, however, would soon become another "prop," or symbol that Trump would misuse and misrepresent to the nation to divert from the real issue, police mistreatment and abuse of unarmed Black men in America.

 Of special concern: COVID cases in children, yeah, the little ones Trump said were essentially immune – continued to rise, with as many as 45% of them projected to be asymptomatic. Among universities, Notre Dame, Villanova, and the University of North Carolina were some of the schools that were impacted by outbreaks the first week of school. In Georgia, where 31% of the population is Black, 51% of all reported cases were Black, according to Dr. Jeff Hines of WellStar in Atlanta.

In Alabama, two physicians, Brian Richardson and Jeff Nix, braved tradition to start a new standard, wearing black scrubs, instead of the traditional blue or green, in honor of the Black Lives Matter movement. Why was this important? In Alabama, Blacks accounted for 26% of the population, but 45% of the state's COVID-19 deaths. "We recognized that if there are health care disparities, then yes, black lives matter most right now," said Richardson. [471] How damn refreshing to hear a white physician say that!

When his son reached his twenties, Nix, who is white, envisioned his now ten-year-old Black son asking him, "Dad, what'd you do? What'd you do when that was going on?" Nix said if he told his son, "'I just did my job,' I don't think he'd be okay with that."[472] On August 28, the 57th anniversary of the March on Washington and King's iconic *"I Have a Dream"* speech, the docs initiated a National Day of Unity with the hashtag #blackscrubs.

Instructed to wear masks, close bars, decrease indoor dining, and increase outdoor dining, colleges were still partying, including East Carolina University, which closed down 20 parties, including one with 400 attendees. The University of North Carolina reported four clusters, and LSU, Oklahoma State University, Notre Dame, and others were all flagged for outbreaks. Teachers resisted all across the country, fearful for their lives and for their families. Duh! Yes, many parents are incapable, unwilling, or not privileged enough to manage and process remote learning – and even more so for those who have special needs children, including those who are autistic and require very special skills and aptitudes. "To shut it all down to [go] virtual, that's ridiculous," one parent proclaimed. "You need that interaction between teachers and students." And then there's the other side, which was aptly articulated by another parent: "This is not worth losing a child over. I have nine grandkids, and I do not want to see them die."[473]

In Chicago, Blacks accounted for 71% of the COVID deaths through April of 2020, even though they represented about 30% of the population. Only 22% of North Carolinians are Black, yet in the first five months of 2020, they comprised 37% of the state's COVID deaths.[474] Through the first five months of 2020, with 41 states reporting, though Black Americans represented 13.4% of the nation's population, they accounted for more than half of all COVID cases and over 60% of the virus's related deaths, largely influenced by diabetes, asthma, and heart disease. Well-earned mistrust of the medical profession, lack of access and insurance, and medical bias were also factors. This is not an equal opportunity disease, nor a pandemic, but one that devours the weak and vulnerable.[475]

It was disclosed that the federal government was not tracking COVID numbers in school systems across the country. Hmm ... I wonder why. Could it be that the Trump administration was so concerned with getting the country back to normal (which meant children going to school so parents could go to work) that they were trying to suppress the news about infections and outbreaks, so that parents would send their children back into the schools, whether they could be protected or not?

A report announced findings that young people under 22 carry higher levels of the virus than older infected people. Fourteen colleges, including Syracuse University, reported extensive cases of COVID on August 20, prompting more schools to send students home and move to virtual learning, exclusively.

On August 21, as COVID deaths in the U.S. topped 175,000, one of the pandemic's youngest victims, a six-year-old Florida girl, perished. That same day at the University of Notre Dame, one of many across the country that had insisted on opening in person – incredibly, expecting college students to social distance and wear masks – the school editor wrote a searing editorial:

"Don't make us write obituaries," the headline shouted, as Nelisha Silva, a member of *The Observer*'s editorial board, explained. "It's on all of us. If we don't change our actions and policies now, people might die. People will die."[476]

At the University of Maryland, the school newspaper accused the school of "willful ignorance," claiming the university was "overly reliant on housing revenue."[477]

Pre-pandemic, approximately seven million children nationwide received special education services in public schools. Sadly, only approximately 40 percent of all U.S. schools have on-site nurses. Seven million U.S. children require special education services, bringing fear and anxiety to the parents who insisted their children were falling further behind due to social isolation and remote learning. Though the law provides for special education staffing and programming, the likelihood of it happening was dim in a flourishing COVID environment. In addition, John Eisenberg of the National Association of Special Education warned that when COVID eased, and children returned to the classroom, there would be little chance they could count on the IEP (Individual Education Plan) that they would need to keep up and flourish.

Deaths were predicted to soar to 200,000 by mid-September, as outbreaks surged on reopening college campuses full of students who had lived relatively pent-up existences for the first time in their lives and were yearning to get back to as normal an environment as possible. Meanwhile, Trump continued to insist he "did the right thing and we have to reopen the schools," even as Kenneth Coffey, a lawyer representing the Florida Teachers Union and suing to prevent in-class learning, said, "Pouring these kids into them [schools] is pouring and packing our most precious human value, our children, into a disease factory."[478]

Postmaster General Louis DeJoy insisted the hundreds of mailboxes and sorting machines he removed within 100 days of the biggest election in U.S. history were unneeded. DeJoy, a Trump donor who had been in his position only two months, acknowledged slowdowns, yet insisted the cost-cutting measures were worth it. Meantime, however, millions of Americans with limited transportation and work flexibility were left with fewer options to cast their votes, many of whom were poor minorities from the inner cities, typically not Trump's voting bloc.[479]

David Williams, a senior postal official who testified before Congress, resigned in April because he feared the Postal Service had been politicized by granting decision-making authority to Treasury Secretary Steven Mnuchin.

"You don't save money by breaking down machines and putting them in storage," said Williams. "Transfer of our decision-making power to him was illegal."[480] Frankly, it could be argued that many acts and policies initiated under the Trump administration were, if not illegal, certainly immoral.

Who would believe that a major American city like Baltimore would have 40% of its homes without internet access? In fact, over nine million U.S. homes are in that situation, providing deep deficits for many rural and inner-city children. Wi-Fi is a blessing that far too many Americans don't have, and too many of us take it for granted.

What makes America great? Success stories like Russell Ledet of Lake Charles, LA. A security guard at a hospital a decade ago, Ledet approached a physician, Dr. Patrick Greiffenstein, the chief surgery resident at Baton Rouge General Medical Center, who took the young security guard under his wing. Ten years and two degrees later, including a Ph.D. in molecular oncology, Ledet, a Navy vet and father of two, returned to the same hospital to begin doing rounds. Ledet, 34, who wants to be a "beacon of light" for his community, while specializing in pediatrics, is also the founder of The 15 White Coats, a non-profit that focuses on raising funds for hopeful med students.[481] "God has brought me so far," said Ledet. "If I didn't see any black doctors growing up, I need to be that example." [482]

Doc Rivers, an NBA standout in the nineties and coach of the Los Angeles Clippers, who were playing the Milwaukee Bucks – who live and play not far from Kenosha, Wisconsin, where Jacob Blake was shot seven times in the back moving away from police – expressed as raw an emotional response from a Black man of privilege as I have ever seen after his players decided to boycott a playoff game in a call for justice: "It's amazing why we keep loving this country, and this country does not love us back. ... You don't need to be black to be outraged. You need to be American and outraged."[483] It is indeed a question for the ages: How and why do Black Americans continue to love a nation that refuses to love us back?

Noted Anglo historian Jon Meacham said, "White expectations and white fears take up too much of our mind space, take up too much of our public space. We're beyond conversation. There has to be recognition of reality and then the work of reconciliation. We're being led to that by these very brave voices of protesters who are reminding us that America is not supposed to be just for one group, but for everybody. ... Having a president that refuses to acknowledge the plain facts of the matter about structural racism and the prevalence of injustice is a central stumbling block. We need a president who sees the world as it is and can lead us to a place where we want it to be."[484]

"You get mad when 'we' start destroying things?" said a young Black man at the protest in Kenosha. One Black woman said in the smoldering ruins of Kenosha, Wisconsin, "It's heartbreaking. How can you destroy your city, your home?" How can frustrated Black folk sometimes destroy their own communities, even as the cops invade their communities and they are blocked from encroaching wealthy white communities? Protests and riots are indeed the language of the oppressed, as King said six decades ago.

Dr. King wrote 60 years ago in his piercing *"Letter from Birmingham Jail"*: "First, I must confess that over the past few years I have been gravely disappointed with the white moderate. I have almost reached the regrettable conclusion that the Negro's great stumbling block in his stride toward freedom is not the White Citizen's Counciler or the Ku Klux Klanner, but the white moderate, who is more devoted to 'order' than to justice; who prefers a negative peace, which is the absence of tension, to a positive peace which is the presence of justice."[485] In the age of Donald Trump, white Evangelicals and boundless, fear-filled parroting criticism of "wokeism" and CRT, we may be as culturally and generationally divided today as we were 60 years ago. How sad. White America, unlike even South Africa, which finally acknowledged its sordid, racist past through its 1995 Truth and Reconciliation Commission,[486] as well as the others that preceded it, simply refuses to repent of its ugly, checkered, racist past. That attitude of resistance is steeled by the fiery, inflammatory, racist rhetoric of former president Trump, who calls anyone who opposes him derogatory names that incite his rabid followers and prompts those already on the edge of violence or rage to act out violently. An analysis by *The Washington Post* reveals that counties that hosted a 2016 Trump rally had a 225% increase in violence there.[487] Additionally, since he left office in early 2021, we hear seemingly weekly about hate crimes perpetrated by white racist radicals, as Trump uses vile tropes against Black female prosecutors, judges, and anyone else who challenges his actions and autocratic positions.

White journalist-activist Anne Braden met King at the legendary Highlander Folk School, now known as The Highlander Research and Education Center, in Tennessee in 1957. Her husband, Carl, was charged with sedition for buying a house to sell to a Black family in segregated Louisville in 1954, which led to a sentence in the Atlanta federal prison. Anne said decades ago that white America has yet to honestly deal with its hegemony.[488]

"Whites always resist facing up to racism," she said. "You think of every excuse. You tried to sweep it under the rug. You say 'it's outside agitators' causing it because you don't want to face your own society being wrong, your own government being wrong. It's [repentance] painful, but it's not destructive. And once you do [repent], you're free. [America] needs to turn itself inside out and turn its policy upside down, and so far, it hasn't done that. It's just picked around the edges of the problem. And that's just not going to work."[489]

On August 25, 2020, 17-year-old Trump zealot Kyle Rittenhouse was arrested for shooting three white protesters, killing two, in Kenosha. The same day, one of the nation's fiercest hurricanes, Category 4 Laura, bore down on Lake Charles, LA, and the Gulf Coast in what was called an "un-survivable storm surge," in one of the least populated sections of the Coast. People on the path of the hurricane expressed fear of going to a shelter, or better conditions, because of COVID. How does someone shoot three people, kill two, walk down the middle of the street, his automatic weapon slung around his shoulder, with arms held high as to surrender, and even approach a police vehicle, as two armored cop vehicles roll past? The kid seemed to be trying to surrender, yet he was not arrested, even though protesters shouted to police that he had shot several people. Not only did he drive from out of state to be part of the melee – allegedly protecting property and community, even though it wasn't his – but he wasn't even old enough to own the weapon he used to take the lives of two people and damage another. How does it happen? Because Rittenhouse was a privileged young white boy, who got caught up in the moment. You can imagine what would have happened had he been Black. This case reminded me of the story of one of my GOP regional directors whose son owned an assault weapon because it "was fun." It was all fun and games until the teen failed to secure the weapon, and it was stolen. Rittenhouse's story embodies white pomposity, once again.

Frederick Douglass, the great emancipator, challenged us to understand that "there is no progress without struggle." In the era of Trump, a half-century after the passage of the Civil Rights Act of 1965, never have I seen so many grown Black men, strong and virile, welling up with fear, frustration, and exhaustion about their own lives, but even more so, those of their Black sons.

"If you want to show America what the problem is, that someone with a long rifle, [about whom] people are yelling 'he just shot somebody,' and police yell at him to 'step back on the sidewalk,'" said then-CNN talk show host Chris Cuomo, in the aftermath of the Rittenhouse shootings.[490]

"Daddy, I love you so much," Jacob Blake told his father the first time he was able to speak to him following coming out of a coma after being shot by police in the back seven times in Kenosha, Wisconsin. "Why did they shoot me so many times?"[491]

There is a knee on the neck of democracy, the righteous indignation that sparked millions of white Americans to go into the streets in a multi-cultural, multi-gender, unified outrage after a rash of killings of unarmed Blacks, similar to the seminal Civil Rights Movement of the sixties. Immediately following the amazing summer of 2020, however, the movement, galvanized by young people, began to lose steam after the predictable right-wing backlash and retrenchment.

Up until that point, I had become more encouraged in 2020 about both the passion of young people and the nation's response to the over-policing of Black bodies than I had at any other point in my life. We shouldn't have to risk our lives to cast our vote, I told myself in despair, as COVID cases from protests spiked, yet people still insisted on standing in long lines to vote. All Americans need to be able to do what President Trump does and vote by mail. We need to use this moment to expand this movement.

Elizabeth Neumann, former Assistant Secretary for Threat Prevention in Trump's Department of Homeland Security, left the Trump administration after three years, partly because of a lack of will to address anti-Semitism, domestic white terrorism, and gun violence. "He uses rhetoric to scare people," said Neumann, who backed Biden in the 2020 election. "This is a known psychological tactic that if you get people to fear, they tend to follow you to the solution of 'How are we going to save ourselves?' And his [Trump's] answer is, 'It's me. If you vote for me, I will save you,'" she [said]. "Well, for some people, the way that they think they need to protect themselves is more than just a vote for a president. It's 'let me go kill people.'"[492] Thank God she said it. We need to hear it from Trump's political appointees, especially white women, since only Will Hurd, Asa Hutchinson, and Chris Christie, among Trump's legion of 2020 presidential candidate opponents, called him out for his racist, divisive tactics. The rest are sniveling cowards who have no chance of winning the nomination, unless Trump was wearing an orange jumpsuit, or crippled because of the imminence of it.

By this point, at least 30 human vaccine trials across the world raced to be first to find a proven vaccine. On August 25, 2020, Dr. Fauci said: "The one thing you would not want to see with a vaccine is getting an EUA [Emergency Use Authorization] before you have a signal of efficacy."[493]

As I watched excerpts of the 57th anniversary of March on Washington, I welled up with pride for my people. Strong, proud, resilient; bloody, battered, yet heads unbowed. Tens of thousands gathered from all over the country, including the mother of Ahmaud Arbery, the father of Jacob Blake, and a contingent of relatives of George Floyd donning black shirts that said in big numbers, 8:46, representing the elongated, torturous time the video shows a heartless, inhumane policeman kneeling on Floyd's neck until he could gasp for breath no more.

Congresswoman Ayanna Pressley, full of grace and presence, Martin Luther King, III, and his daughter, Yolanda Renee, each, in their own way, urged this country to "rise up and live out the true meaning of its creed: 'We hold these truths to be self-evident, that all men are created equal,'" as King challenged in 1963 in, perhaps, the most significant speech in American history.

On the same day, August 28, 2020, the state of Iowa posted an astounding 79% COVID-19 positivity rate for those tested. Governor Reynolds, who spoke at the GOP convention the same week, announced that one Democrat county's push for absentee ballots through the mail had been disallowed by the Iowa Supreme Court. To reopen schools, the CDC suggested that the COVID positivity rate should be no more than 5%, yet in Iowa, Democratic counties were prevented from voting by absentee ballots. Who does that make sense to? Sadly, however, this was a practice being repeated in many conservative-leaning states throughout the nation.

Minnesota Senator Amy Klobuchar, who ran for president herself in 2020, may have had one of the tweets of the week. As Trump accepted the nomination in a flag-filled, donor-littered, you-and-me funded, three-hour, campaign ad/dog-and-pony show that pimped the willing – and unwilling – Black folk like nothing I can ever remember seeing a white man so shamelessly do, Klobuchar tweeted: "Get off our lawn. Yes, the White House is the people's house, not the domain and enduring stage of a dictator or a demagogue." Not me, not ever. I prayed that night in the United States of America. Kiss the ring or kiss the ass. Indeed, I refuse to do either!

"They are trying to muzzle their career public servants" who wanted to tell the truth about the dangers and impact of COVID, noted Rep. Raja Krishnamoorthi of Illinois. True dat, I thought, shaking my head, after my role in working with the assister community had put our three-person regional office, the only all-Black career servant regional office, I might add, directly under the bright, white Trump administration microscope, since the fall of 2017.

In 2018, following the arrest of five young Black people after a car theft and subsequent crash, Kenosha Sheriff David Beth said this at the news conference a day after the incident, according to CNN affiliate WTMJ: "I'm to the point that I think society has to come to a threshold where there are some people that aren't worth saving. We need to build warehouses, put these people into it, and lock them away for the rest of their lives. We put them away for the rest of their lives so that the rest of us can be better," Beth said.[494] Beth's comments came after the arrest of five teens, including a 16-year-old driver who robbed a Tommy Hilfiger store and then led police on a high-speed chase that resulted in arrests and injuries from a crash into another car with a 16-year-old driver and her mother.

Let me take a minute to unpack that. Under no circumstances do I excuse or rationalize thuggery. Hell, like you, I've seen instance after instance where young people – too often Black and Latino – use their obvious genius and planning skills to descend on a store and ravage it in 60 seconds, leaving with hundreds of thousands of top-end stolen goods. Inexcusable and despicable from any direction. But to say that "those people aren't worth saving"? Would Beth, under any circumstance, have said that about white youth? Hell no. At least, to his credit, he'd said in advance that he wasn't being "politically correct." He simply said what far too many white people think almost every day, especially when crime and violence rear their ugly heads: Black people simply aren't as valuable as we are; in fact, they are expendable. Beth is the same sheriff whose officer shot unarmed Jacob Blake seven times in the back two-and-a-half years later, paralyzing him. White pomposity.

Chapter 30: America's Biggest Terroristic Threat: Young Angry White Men

"Whenever white America feels like it's losing its grip, violence follows."
Princeton professor and MSNBC Contributor Dr. Eddie Glaude

In Georgia – wouldn't you know it – a case study analyzed ballots that were rejected because of an alleged lack of ability to confirm the signature. Nationally, the average is 1.2 percent of ballots. However, the study showed that for African Americans, the percentage of rejections was 1.6 percent, Latinos 1.9 percent, and Asians 2.4 percent, while Anglo ballots were rejected at only .09 percent. All told, more than 550,000 votes were disallowed over signature verification in 2018.[495] Metro Atlanta, which produces 46 percent of all of Georgia's voters, yet boasts only 38 percent of the voting places, sometimes left frustrated voters waiting ten hours to exercise their democracy.[496]

I'd realized that Michael Caputo, HHS's chief communications director, the Assistant Secretary of Public Affairs (ASPA), was a strange bird and, like his friend and boss, Trump, highly combative and determined to fight the media, not work with them. Never before in my 23 years at HHS had I seen an ASPA who so frequently tweeted taunts and challenges toward the media after it called out his boss on exaggerations, inconsistencies, or outright lies. By this time, leaked memos disclosed that Caputo was demanding to "clear" CDC MMWR (Morbidity and Mortality Weekly Reports) documents, considered the gold standard for the world, before their release, so that if the documents contradicted Trump's positions, they were held up. Caputo, mind you, has no health or scientific background.[497] In fact, his biggest claim to fame may have been as a Putin sycophant, paid to spread and spew misinformation. This time, however, he may have "out-alarmed" the president, promising that if Trump won the 2020 election, opposing forces, including the deep state, would demand he vacate the White House, sparking a domestic war.

    Caputo accused scientists at the CDC of sedition, claiming there was a "resistance unit" at the CDC committed to undermining the president. "Can they actually keep the coronavirus concern ball in the air long enough to drive enough destruction of our economy for them to win?" Caputo asked on his podcast, though the question was quickly deleted. "Our intention is to make sure that evidence, science-based data drives policy through this pandemic, not ulterior deep state motives in the bowels of the CDC."[498] Hell, Caputo wouldn't recognize science-based data if it walked up and pimp-slapped him. The problem was, as he and those blinded by Trump loyalty refused, or were unable to see, every time the economy had a chance to turn the corner, POTUS was insisting the Big 10 and NFL play football, and our precious children go back to school, only to infect their teachers and come home and infect their compromised families. So, though he wanted to move forward, he was much like the addict who swore they wanted sobriety, but naturally, when left to their own devices, he couldn't help the allure of the drug and continued to overdose time and time again.

    Trump wanted to win re-election so badly that he could not see that families who had lost loved ones, had seen the impact on long-haulers, like Chris Cuomo, who still felt the effects of the illness months later, were real people who needed and deserved empathy, concern, and support, as well as a path forward. Instead, in Trump's mind, based on his actions, a roaring economy heals all wounds and makes the nearly 200,000 American lives lost inconsequential. Of course, there are so many problems with that picture. One of the most glaring is the fact that a high percentage of those deaths were people not in the stock market. They were those on the front line, whether they delivered food, served food, processed the meat, drove trucks, taught our children, or treated the afflicted. On another key issue, Trump gambled that more Americans were concerned with law and order, than social justice. He also believed the suburbs were the ones June and Wally Cleaver inhabited, while the cities were strictly represented by the Evanses from *Good Times,* or John Singleton's *Boyz n the Hood*. Or that Americans who aren't white, rural, and predominantly Southern, still buy into the myth that the Confederate monuments primarily represented Southern pride, not hegemony and racism.

Responding to Caputo's rambling rant, Richard Besser, the former CDC director said, "The idea that politics would change what was in there totally undercuts the value of the [CDC] document. That sort of behavior will cost lives."[499] Another former CDC director, Tom Frieden, who held the job before Redfield, was even clearer: Frieden termed the White House's intervention to change the guidance of the CDC, determined as a result of rigorous science and years of education, "unjustifiable. It's putting people's lives at risk."[500] In an irony of ironies, Caputo accused CDC officials of "sedition," when at least four of the Proud Boys, whom Trump earlier told to "stand down and stand by," have been convicted of sedition for the roles in the January 6th attempt to keep him in power.[501] Talk about the pot calling the kettle black!

POTUS has continually said the U.S. has a high case rate because it does "too much testing." So when Trump's White House pressured the highly respected CDC to change its guidance to say that those who were asymptomatic, even though they had come into contact with someone who had been infected, didn't need to be tested, someone leaked the tampering, as often happened in the Trump White House. "This is basically an abuse of power," continued Frieden, pointing out that the CDC objections to the changes in the advice had been overruled. "It's an overriding of science by politics." Following intense pressure, the White House backed down, and the policy was reversed.[502] With Trump and Pence at the wheel, the CDC, Fauci, and Birx had become unwilling yo-yos, with us, who served in the regional offices, also dangling in the unpredictable winds. Never in my then-20 years in government had I – or my experienced colleagues – seen so many anti-government government appointees, many of whom were far from qualified for their roles. Virtually every morning, as I woke up, I wondered what level of lunacy we would be confronted with next.

On September 15, 2020, Trump traveled west on a trip designed for campaign stops in Nevada and Arizona, coupled with an opportunity to tour the damage caused by the worst fires in California history.

"It'll start getting cooler, you just watch," Trump assured Wade Crowfoot, California National Resource Secretary, who told POTUS that climate change was real and pointed to the raging fires throughout the western U.S. as proof that the earth was heating up and its citizens paying the price. Meanwhile, Biden, who had been accused of being too low-key or too passive on the campaign trail, continued to zero in on Trump's vulnerabilities, labeling him a "climate arsonist."[503]

With 71 major fires raging across the west, 33 people killed, and more missing, the Southeast faced the most active and strongest hurricane season in 50 years, with six named storms currently churning over warm waters. The denier-in-chief, however, whose administration rolled back rule after rule and act after act to benefit business and allow compromise of the environment, insisted the scientists had it wrong.

FBI Director Christopher Wray, unwilling to compromise over who is America's biggest threat, did something unprecedented in the history of American government – he warned of the growing threat of white, armed domestic terrorism in the U.S. "I would certainly say, as I think I've said consistently in the past, that racially motivated violent extremism specifically, of the sort that advocates for the superiority of the white race, is a persistent evolving threat," Wray said. "It's the biggest chunk of our racially motivated violent extremism cases for sure, and racially motivated violent extremism is the biggest chunk of our domestic terrorism portfolio."[504]

"Within the domestic terrorism bucket, as a whole, racially motivated violence extremism is, I think, the largest bucket within that group and within the racially motivated extremist," said Wray. "But people subscribing to some sort of white supremacist ideology is certainly the biggest bucket of that."[505]

Olivia Troye, Homeland Security advisor for Vice President Pence, resigned over Trump's disingenuous response to the virus. "It was shocking to hear the president saying that the virus was a hoax, that everything's okay when we know that it's not," she said. "The truth is that he doesn't actually care about anybody else but himself."[506]

Two weeks after Labor Day weekend, 2020, 16 states, most in the upper Midwest and Southeast, saw dramatic spikes in cases and deaths. How could anyone be surprised? Think college students, many of whom think they are invincible anyway, after having been on at least "semi-lockdown," while staying at home with parents for the summer, wouldn't throw caution to the wind when returning to school? For many of them, contracting COVID was not much more than a personal inconvenience, causing them to be isolated for a few days and maybe feeling relatively bad. But who else might they impact, especially those who were asymptomatic and might have gone home, or elsewhere and infected more vulnerable loved ones or others?

As the coronavirus hit a major milestone of 200,000 deaths on September 21, the CDC, fast losing credibility based on Caspar Milquetoast's leadership that bowed to Trump pressure, like Congress and many others, made another huge blunder. Posting guidance that warned that the virus was spread airborne easily at distances far greater than six feet, it again reversed course hours later, insisting the guidance was "only a draft" and incorrect, even as opponent Biden dug in, insisting Trump "failed to act."[507]

Meanwhile, the people I personally know and respect at the CDC readily admitted that the once highly respected agency was suffering deep morale problems and growing outraged that science was being minimalized under the weight of immense political pressure. Simultaneously, a few weeks after the reopening of schools and Labor Day, when reopenings and beach parties were being promoted, 33 states showed an increase in cases over the week before and greater than a five percent infection rate. The president, of course, consistent since the beginning, again gave himself an "A-plus" for his handling of the virus, though he did say his public relations positioning grade was a "D."

"Is this a nightmare," I asked myself for seemingly the 50th time in 2020, "or have I been transported to some alien universe?" Richard Besser, CNN Medical analyst, pediatrician, and former acting director of the CDC, put it this way: "It should be up there in some form. When you put something up and then have to pull it down, every time it happens, it begs the question, why did that happen?" Regarding the push to reopen the schools and the fact that most are poorly ventilated, more so in poor neighborhoods, Besser asked: "How do we value black and brown children? How do we show that if we're not providing the same resources that we are in wealthier neighborhoods?" Noting that the disease doesn't hit all communities equally, with a far higher burden being carried by Black, brown, and poor communities, he asked, "What does it say about us as a nation if we say not all lives carry equal value?" [508]

Duh, that's exactly what Black Lives Matter, Colin Kaepernick, the good people of Louisville, and even the hundreds of thousands of citizens, including mostly white people, have been marching in the streets for much of 2020 and beyond. Apparently, everybody who wants to, can see the stark contrast in access to resources, including health care, in the U.S. – all except those benefiting most from the sacrifice. In the third decade of the 21st century, people under 40 are now the majority in America. Let's face it. Most think and see the world differently from Baby Boomers like me. How long do the Republicans believe that they can hold onto power as their numbers crumble and their philosophy – at least for the near future – atrophies? It is now apparent that the GOP will do whatever it takes to hold onto power until it is ripped from their cold, dead hands. Trump, an opportunist, not a real Republican, gets it: "This is the most important election of our lifetime," he proclaimed again and again in 2020. Damn skippy. At least until the 2024 election.

Reluctant to condemn right-wing and white supremacist groups, while constantly pointing out Antifa and Black Lives Matter as terrorist groups, when pressed, Trump told the Proud Boys to "stand back and stand by."

In Texas, voter suppression was put in place by Governor Greg Abbott, who declared there could be only one election ballot drop-off point in each county, a ridiculous limitation for a state as big as Texas, with massive counties, like Harris County, which includes sprawling Houston, the nation's fourth most populous city.

Airlines laid off 40,000 workers at the end of September, after Congress failed to agree on a stimulus package, even though the Democrat-dominated House put forth two proposals. The president never met with Speaker Pelosi and the Senate Minority leader, even as 837,000 new people filed for unemployment benefits.

Over four days, a white man, Michael Frederick, 24, shot into the home of a Black family, consisting of Candace and Eddie Hall, both Army vets, and their children, and then tagged their car with a swastika, slashed their tires, and committed other despicable acts, seeking to terrorize them in Warren County, Michigan. (Warren, Michigan, was previously a "sundown town," a place where Black folk were warned not to be after sundown.) They were his neighbors. He fired into their home, flattened their tires, and wrote racist threats on their house, where a Black Lives Matter poster was displayed. He later asked for forgiveness, saying he acted out of character.[509] The Halls, both people of deep faith, forgave Frederick, telling him he wasn't a bad person. "This wasn't about the color of their skin," said Frederick, who has a $200,000 bond and has been charged with nine criminal counts. Police said Frederick's father tried to take apart and hide the gun his son used. Still, the Black parents, followers of Christ, somehow, inexplicably, publicly forgave him. "If he finds God in this, that was the purpose of all this," said Candace Hall.[510] If not "about race," what the hell was it about, then? White pomposity that a Black family of faith that had served their country with honor would declare that they, too, are American?

"They never have to grow up," a young sister said, pointing out obvious and painful differences between how the law looks at Black people versus white people. "You're [Black people] an adult at 10, but they always have an excuse." Damn skippy! Think that excuse would even be considered if the shooter/terrorist were Black?

They also have to go over the law with a study, pointing out obvious and painful differences between how the law treats an black people versus white people. You're "Black people an adult at 40, but they always have an excuse." Damn skippy! Think 'not excuse' would not be considered it in an order reporter was like...

Chapter 31: Denier-in-Chief

"Don't let it (COVID) dominate you. Don't be afraid of it. You're going to beat it."
Tweet by President Trump

On Friday, October 2, just a month before the 2020 presidential election, after numerous people whom he had been in close, unmasked contact with tested positive for COVID, Trump reluctantly admitted that he and his wife had contracted the virus. This happened at the same time at least 20 White House officials came down with COVID, only a few days following what had been termed a "super spreader" event, the Rose Garden coming out party for Supreme Court nominee Amy Coney Barrett. Three days later, at prime time, of course, Trump, who received a COVID treatment cocktail cure unlike anyone else in the world, was released from the hospital. He then refused to participate in the scheduled debate with Biden because it would have to be virtual, due to his contracting COVID.

The beat goes on. Not only were 34 people from the White House infected with COVID-19, but also nine four-star U.S. generals.[511] The tweeter-in-chief, who said he wanted to pass a stimulus bill during his four-day "visit" to Walter Reed after contracting COVID, got out Monday and, by Tuesday, reversed course, vowing to not negotiate another stimulus package for tens of millions of jobless, hungry, and increasingly homeless Americans.

"Don't let it dominate you. Don't be afraid of it. You're going to beat it," Trump tweeted, again comparing

COVID-19 to the flu, to the horror and outrage of the friends and families of 211,000 Americans who lost their lives to the deadly virus. In fact, tell that to the Berg family, where seven of eight family members contracted the disease, with the parents dying just before celebrating their 56th anniversary.[512] What about their family, their friends, their neighbors, and bridge partners? Twitter flagged the tweet as violating its rules about harmful information, while Facebook removed it. Dr. Fauci, the nation's leading infectious disease expert, also vehemently disagreed. "The potential for what COVID can do is very different from influenza," said Fauci. "You don't get a pandemic that kills a million people – and it isn't even over yet – with influenza. So it is not correct to say that it is the same as the flu."[513] The 208-year-old venerable *New England Journal of Medicine,* which had never before made a political statement, said the Trump administration had bungled their response to the pandemic so badly that they "have taken a crisis and turned it into a tragedy."[514]

Once again, our commander-in-chief proved he was untruthful and untrustworthy. In fact, on October 5, with five polls taken, 67% of registered voters said Trump likely would not have been infected had he taken the disease more seriously, and 52% of those polled by Yahoo/YouGov didn't trust him to provide accurate information about his own health and treatment.[515] Brian Morgenstern, the White House spokesman, refused to say when Trump's last negative test was during an October 9 press conference.

Truth be told, by January 28, 2020, Trump and the administration were fully aware of what the virus would and could do. In November 2019, a colleague of mine went to D.C. to take part in an emergency preparedness tabletop exercise specifically focused on the looming crisis of COVID-19.

Instead of debating, however, six days after going into the hospital and five after getting out, Trump hosted an event with as many as 2,000 people outside the White House. His doctor, Ronnie Jackson, who had been sketchy with his non-answers and evasiveness regarding POTUS's condition, gave him the "all clear" sign to resume campaigning, though he wouldn't say he was "COVID-free."

CDC Director Redfield, finally deciding to grow a pair late in the administration, allowed or directed a CDC edict calling for an order that would have mandated that both passengers and employees wear face coverings on planes, trains, buses, subways, in airports, stations, and depots. Trump and the White House, of course, shot it down. Drafted a month earlier by CDC officials under the agency's "quarantine powers," it was approved by HHS Secretary Alex Azar, whom I worked for. However, the White House Coronavirus Task Force, led by Vice President Pence, declined to even discuss it.[516] Certainly, Pence felt the weight of the world as COVID cases mushroomed, and Trump undoubtedly pushed him to fix what he himself had failed to address for six months. This is the same Pence who, in the end, upheld the Constitution. He's also the same one who called up at least one of the HHS regional directors late one night as the pressure mounted and tersely told him, "You and Azar better get your shit together."

The denier-in-chief simply doesn't get it. In fact, he never did. Very early Friday morning, he tweeted that he was sick with COVID, the very disease he had been telling Americans all year would simply go away and was no big deal. Yep, the same deadly disease that, up to that point, had killed 210,000 Americans, at least a quarter of them his supporters. Trump could have stayed put, taken his time getting better, and told the American people he now realized the destructive nature of COVID and more clearly understood the pain and anxiety their families and the nation faced. He could have. He should have. But he didn't. Instead, Trump forced his doctors to release him three days after entering the hospital, then five days later, hosted an event for 2,000 people at the White House.

Trump's response to a well-conceived, multi-pronged plot to kidnap and try Michigan Governor Gretchen Whitmer because they thought her policies on masking and staged shutdowns of the economy were too extreme? Well, POTUS called her "that woman" and criticized her for not thanking him for the fact that the plot was discovered and thwarted by the same FBI that he refused to believe regarding Russian interference in our election, or the increasing threat of white domestic terrorism. What did he have to say about the 13 militia members arrested, and others on the run? Crickets. As far as I can tell, he was about as silent as a mouse pissing on cotton. As in the case of Kyle Rittenhouse, who gunned down two white protesters while going with other militia members to Milwaukee to "protect businesses," Trump never condemned the young white kid; instead, he only said he was scared for his life while telling his staffers to openly make a case that Rittenhouse was only defending himself.

Should we be surprised Trump called the Michigan governor "that woman"? I think not. No president in modern history has been more openly abusive, dismissive, and demeaning to women.

"She was threatened, and she blamed me," Trump railed at a rally at a church in Nevada, following the botched plot to kidnap Whitmer, whom Trump's senior advisor/daughter-in-law Lara also called "this woman."

"A decent human being would have picked up the phone and said, 'are you okay?'" said Whitmer. She noted that after Trump referred to her as "that woman," she saw an increase in hateful language aimed at her on social media.[517] Brandon Caserta, one of the men tried, but not convicted in the plot against Whitmer, seemed to be no fan of Trump, either. "Every single person that works in government is your enemy," Caserta said. Several of the very same militia members accused in the plot had occupied the Michigan state house a few months earlier in protest of restrictions requiring masks, social distancing, and, in some instances, closures.

Dennis Plowden Jr., of Philadelphia, who had driven away from police after a stop, was apparently sitting on the sidewalk after he crashed the car. Witnesses said Plowden had one hand in the air, the other on the ground when he was shot by an officer within six to eight seconds of arriving. This time, however, Officer Eric Ruch, Jr., 34, was charged and convicted of murdering Plowden after a police chase.[518]

Back on the road again on October 12, 2020, Trump's first campaign stop was in Sanford, Florida. Sound vaguely familiar? That's because Sanford played hand in hand with his "law and order" platform. Sanford, in 2012, was the very city where night watchman George Zimmerman killed Trayvon Martin. Unsurprisingly, Trump chose sites of gut-wrenching Black angst, including Tulsa, where the devastation of Black Wall Street took place, and Sanford, Florida, where the "stand your ground" killing of unarmed Martin rocked the nation. It is worth noting that in places where Trump held campaign rallies in 2016, racial violence increased 226%.[519]

As Lebron James won his 4th NBA title on October 12, making my eldest son's evening, Trump's doctors declared he had tested negative for COVID two days in a row. With Americans rushing to the polls beginning October 11th, the Northeast portion of the country, which was the USA's hotspot for the first three to four months of the pandemic, before becoming a model for reducing both death rates and infections, erupted again. This time, cases rose by 40%, feeding the new national rates of 50,000 infections per day.

In Denver, a supposed security guard for a right-wing television crew shot and killed an unarmed protester. If this protester, Lee Keltner, a 49-year-old white man, was shot down by another white man while protesting a "Patriot rally," what sense of comfort and justice should I, a Black man, take in my ability to peacefully protest over-policing and injustice?[520]

"Looks like I'm immune, maybe for a long time or a short time," Trump proclaimed. The administration, using COVID as a rationale had, as of October 2020, deported 160,000 Mexican refugees back across the border without the hearings the law says they are entitled to.[521]

"I never imagined crossing the border with my son," said a female journalist, Angelina Estrada, who had fled from Venezuela, and was interviewed while caged with dozens of other mothers and children. "But as a mother, you can do anything."

Chapter 32: Despicable Disparities

Black Americans are 75% more likely to live near toxic pollution and suffer 38% more from air pollution than white Americans.

NAACP & Clean Air Task Force

In many communities of color, wait times in lines to vote were six times that of white communities during the 2018 voting experience, according to the Bipartisan Policy Center in November 2019. "What we're trying to do is drive some combination of 80 percent of the voters to vote before election day," said Richard Barron, head of voting in Fulton County, Georgia.[522]

In Europe, Italy and Spain showed rates of infection that had not been seen since March. Remember what Surgeon General Adams said back in the spring of 2020? If we're not careful, we'll be Italy in three weeks.

"This isn't Donald Trump's country. It is yours," tweeted Minnesota Senator Amy Klobuchar on October 12, days before the hearings for Supreme Court nominee Amy Coney Barrett. "This shouldn't be Donald Trump's judge. It should be yours."[523] At that point, 215,000 Americans had died, with 15 states producing COVID highs, many in the conservative upper Midwest.

How can the GOP distribute ballot drop boxes in California and declare them to be official in October 2020, leading up to the most consequential election in U.S. history? In what kind of alternate universe is that possible?

According to Tom Hiltachk, the GOP's general counsel, the boxes complied with California's "ballot harvesting" law, allowing "people" to collect ballots from voters and return them to county election offices to be counted.[524] God only knows who put ballots in those boxes and what happened to them. What would the GOP do next, create a slate of "alternate" electors? Of course, though I worked in an office for a political appointee, we never discussed these things with our regional director since we were career staff, though I had no choice but to think about the ramifications all the time.

"Suburban women, will you please like me?" Trump pleaded in Pennsylvania. Iowa, a state he won handily in 2016, yet one reeling with 100,000 COVID infections, was one of nearly a dozen states still too early to call. Three weeks before the election, one Wisconsin hospital saw a 500% increase in COVID admissions, another factor in the state standing up a COVID field hospital. Before October, the highest daily casualty reported was 22 on May 27. By mid-October, 34 were reported in one day.

"People are dying every night, and there's nothing we can do about it," said beleaguered nurse Carolyn Sienko of Aspirus Hospital in Wausau, Wisconsin. "We're trying. We're doing everything we can."[525]

On October 14, with Oklahoma City reporting no open ICU beds, Utah having a soaring infection rate, Iowa in unknown territory, and one-third of the states reaching new records, Trump hit the road to make his case for a second term. With 281,000 dead, the U.S. roared within a whisker of 8,000,000 COVID-19 cases.

"I may not be able to change my father's mind, but together, we can vote this toxic administration out of office," said Caroline Rose, Rudy Giuliani's daughter, who urged Americans to vote for the Biden-Harris ticket.[526]

The U.S. recorded one million new COVID-19 cases in three weeks, as of October 17, 2020, just over two weeks before the 2020 election. COVID case numbers hit all-time highs in at least 15 states, with 38 states showing increases. The nation had over eight million cases and was on the verge of 220 million deaths. Yet, we continued to hear that we were over the hump and the virus was under control. "We are rounding the corner," proclaimed Trump, even as women marched against him and his policies in 400 U.S. cities.[527] Is there any wonder that Americans – especially women – were flooding polling places, standing in long lines, most often to repudiate the madness that was the Trump administration?

There were more than 63,000 new cases in one day – the most since July – with hospitals in some places, like Kansas City, turning patients away. By mid-October, the U.S. had reached eight million COVID cases and topped 218,000 deaths. Still, Trump insisted as he raced from state to state, seeking to salvage a sinking campaign, that the U.S. was "rounding the corner" in conquering COVID. New Mexico, Ohio, Iowa, and five other states recorded record case numbers.

"I think as we enter the fall and winter [2020], every part of the nation will be lit up by infection," said former Trump FDA Administrator Scott Gottlieb, one of the very few truth-tellers in the Trump administration.[528] Texas, where the governor sued to reduce the number of ballot boxes to turn in votes to only one per county, and Florida, where Governor DeSantis moved to allow teams to have full attendance at stadiums, clearly decided that thousands of people must die so that the economy could thrive.

"There's a red tide flowing all over the state of Ohio," acknowledged GOP Governor Mike DeWine. A conservative-leaning investment group, its leadership strongly supportive of Trump and MAGA platforms, shared late nights emails and IMs on the night of October 21.

Among the strange assertions were that California Congresswoman Maxine Waters would be arrested, Trump would override the authority of governors and go into states to quell violence – which, I believe, he already had done – and that Democratic presidential candidate Joe Biden would be dropping out of the race 13 days before the election. Unfortunately, this was an example of the bizarre Qanon echo chamber in which millions of Trump followers were immersed.

By debate night, October 23, 2020, 53.7% of the total U.S. COVID cases and 36% of the total deaths had occurred since March 20th, when Trump proclaimed the virus would float away. The same day, the nation recorded over 71,000 new cases, the fourth most since COVID hit U.S. shores.

"I don't want to hurt him. He's been there for about 350 years," explained Trump, who continued to point the finger after calling Dr. Fauci, the nation's top infectious disease official, a "disaster."[529] Trump, like a pampered-only child, whined that "the American people are tired already with this!"

His opponent, Biden, agreed. "The American people are tired," he said. "They're tired of your lies about this virus. They're tired of watching more Americans die, and more people lose their jobs because you refuse to take this pandemic seriously."[530]

On the economic horizon, things were also grim; as of mid-October, 55 million Americans were living in poverty, eight million more than were on that list in May.

Trump wanted to leave the impression that all the violence and attacks were enacted by far-left groups. However, on October 23, the FBI announced an arrest of one of the Boogaloo Boys for the attack on a Minneapolis police precinct in the midst of the George Floyd protests.[531]

Meanwhile, the rich got richer, the educated and computer-literate could often work remotely, and the poor people of all colors remained voiceless and victimized. Case in point: The Black folk living on former slave land in Cancer Alley St. James Parish, Louisiana, where citizens fought against the Taiwanese company, Formosa Plasma, which was erecting a $9.4 billion, nine-acre plastic company assured of bringing more industrial pollution.

"Because we're black and we're poor, and they think they can shove anything down our throats, and our public officials allow it," said a defiant Sharon Lavigne, whose family has lived on the land for nine generations. Black Americans are 75% more likely to live near toxic pollution and suffer 38% more from air pollution than white Americans.[532] When you couple that with the fact that Black Americans are far less likely to be insured and many are faced with the threat of Trump striking down the ACA, which insured 20 million Americans, there's little question why skepticism exists. Benzene, formaldehyde, and ethylene oxide will be heavily utilized in a community already wracked by high death rates of cancer, and asthma rates that are three times that of white America. "I would tell the state, if they don't have a problem putting it in my neighborhood, put it in their neighborhood."[533]

For people of color, front-line workers like food service, EMTs (emergency medical technicians), gig workers, or poor people, health care – or the lack thereof – is much like money, or even white privilege, to most Anglo Americans and other middle- and upper-class Americans. The insured rarely have to think about health care beyond using precautions, social distancing, and commonsense steps all people are urged to take. The wealthy, and even many of the middle- and upper-middle class, take health care and food security for granted, much like my white friends and church members, who acknowledge that they don't worry or think about confrontations with police when their sons and daughters leave the house. That's white privilege. But the poor and undereducated certainly have even less privilege than I, an educated Black man, do.

In another example of collateral damage, it was learned that 545 children remained separated from their parents at the southern border, the bulk of whom have been deported, even as late as June 2020. The ACLU was trying to track down the parents, while the administration said the parents had been contacted and refused to be reunited with their children. Many are younger than five. A few months later, "The Squad," Congresswomen Talib, Omar, Ocasio-Cortez, and Pressley, led 170 elected officials who called on the United Nations to investigate the Department of Homeland Security's role in alleged forced medical procedures on migrant women. The request was triggered by a whistleblower complaint filed by a nurse at the Irwin County Detention Center in Ocilla, Georgia, which reported "jarring medical neglect" and alleged "high rates of hysterectomies done to immigrant women." At least 19 women alleged being pressured to submit to questionable surgeries.[534]

Chapter 33: 80,000 New COVID Cases a Day: A New U.S. Record

"What we're seeing is historic decimation of the Hispanic community by this virus. It's hitting Hispanics in their forties, fifties, and sixties, but what it really means is it's robbing families of this whole generation of their fathers, mothers, and brothers and sisters."

Dr. Peter Hotez, Founding Dean of the National School of Tropical Medicine at Baylor College of Medicine[535]

Everyone had some vulnerability to the various never-before-encountered COVID variants. However, the elderly, the very young, those with co-morbidities, and, among ethnicities, Native Americans, African Americans, and Latinos, were especially vulnerable to the debilitating disease. COVID oftentimes crippled those families, killing the mothers, fathers, and grandchildren, not only ravaging breadwinners, but generations of matriarchs and patriarchs.

In one Milwaukee hospital, many of the most critically ill patients were in their 30s and 40s, unlike 45's claim that young people were virtually immune. Remdesivir was approved by the FDA on October 22, the same day seven states reported all-time COVID case records.

By late October 2020, the U.S. recorded its all-time daily tally of record-breaking COVID cases, soaring to over 80,000 on the 23rd, shattering the previous record of 77,362 on July 16. The day before, October 22, 71,671 cases were reported, even as winter approached, with predictable gatherings at Thanksgiving and Christmas, coupled with more people staying inside, and pneumonia complicating matters. More than 30 states reported upticks, especially in the plains and upper Midwest, even as a maskless POTUS campaigned vigorously in the ravaged upper Midwest. The average daily death rate hit 763, rising steadily.

"From the outset of the COVID-19 pandemic, the administration has taken decisive actions to engage scientists and health professionals in academia, industry, and government to understand, treat and defeat the disease."[536] This outlandish missive was released by the White House on October 28, the very day that 78,000 more cases were recorded. As one of his field staff charged with disseminating Trump's embellishments and misinformation, I could only cringe and shake my head as I hit the "send" button on the release that I knew would be viewed as disingenuous by many of my media contacts.

"Who do you know that's getting on a plane and going on Christmas vacation?" asked Stephanie Ruhle, subbing as host of MSNBC's *The 11th Hour*. "I don't," she added, noting that Chicago was set to suspend in-restaurant dining on October 31, 2020, and 800,000 Americans had fallen into poverty under Trump's watch.[537]

Out of the beltway and into rural America, Dr. Deborah Birx, while visiting North Dakota on October 26, said she saw fewer masks being worn than in any other state in the country, even as a Grand Forks newspaper said that if the state were a country, it would have the world's worst confirmed COVID-19 outbreak.[538] Meanwhile, North Carolina, Georgia, and Texas recorded record voter activation and millions flooding to the polls, despite many standing in line for up to ten hours to exercise their sacred right.

"This is not only the most important election in our lifetime, but the most important election in the modern era of this country," asserted Senator Bernie Sanders.

A new COVID case was reported in the U.S. every 1.2 seconds, with someone dying every 90 seconds. "It's not just a function of testing," countered Giroir. "Yes, we're getting more cases identified, but cases are going up. And deaths are increasing."

"He's turned the White House into a hot zone," quipped President Obama.

"He is enacting a coup by undermining our very election system," said Pulitzer Prize winner Carl Bernstein, who, along with Bob Woodward, broke the Watergate scandal during the Nixon administration. "We've never seen anything like this in our history. We've never had a president trying to suppress votes. We haven't seen anything like this since Dixiecrat southern democrats tried to keep black people from voting."[539]

It may not have been illegal for Georgia Senator David Perdue to buy medical equipment and vaccine stock while getting rid of casino stock right after a January 24 United States Senate classified briefing on COVID; but if not illegal, it damn sure was slimy. You and I couldn't do it and get away with it. It was, at a minimum, the height of hypocrisy, especially as Perdue insisted that COVID was not serious and was about to go away, mimicking his beloved leader, Trump. So, when former federal official and investigative reporter Jon Ossoff, who was running neck and neck with Perdue, cleaned his clock at a debate when he confronted Perdue about his financial dealings, as well as the fact that he voted against preserving health insurance for those with pre-existing conditions at least four times; Perdue slunk away, declining to participate in the next senatorial debate.

Twelve thousand counties, nearly one-third of all U.S. counties, were listed as COVID hotspots, according to Dr. Birx, who crisscrossed the nation warning rural communities that they were in a "new phase" of COVID. Unfortunately, she waited until November to do so, instead of challenging Trump in the spring and summer, when he insisted that the pandemic was overblown and not a real threat. Finally, in late November, Birx told Americans who gathered for Thanksgiving they should "assume" they were infected and get tested.[540] She had far more detailed information than the sit-reps (situation reports) I saw several times a day. It would have been nice if she had stepped up and challenged Pence and Trump's faulty guidance, and called for proactive measures six months earlier.

On October 29, 2020, the U.S. recorded more than a COVID case per second, as nine million people had contracted the disease, and nearly 230,000 had died, including nearly 1,004 that very day.

"Trump cares about feeding his ego. Joe cares about keeping you and your family safe," said Obama. "The idea that this president has done anything else but screw this pandemic up is nonsense."

"I just don't believe that the sacrifices that are asked to be made [masks, social distancing] are as big as the sacrifice of losing a family member," said Lauren Williams, whose father, Gary Gavin, died from COVID. He was one of 230,000 Americans lost as October 30 registered nearly 99,000 new cases for the day.[541]

"He's [Trump] privileged," said Lucero Martinez Felipe, whose Latina mother died in New York. Though only 18% of the population, Hispanics and Latinos account for 24% of the nation's COVID deaths. "Did every single person who lost their lives receive the same treatment he [Trump] did? They didn't. He had all these resources that none of us did."[542]

"What we're seeing is historic decimation of the Hispanic community by this virus," said Dr. Peter Hotez. "It's hitting Hispanics in their forties, fifties, and sixties, but what it really means is it's robbing families of this whole generation of their fathers, mothers, and brothers and sisters."[543]

"This is the invisible workforce that kind of uplifts the country, but yet the country doesn't uplift them," said legendary Latinx rights activist Dolores Huerta. "We must start to change our mentality to think that these are the farmworkers who feed us. They need to come first. They need to be the first in line to get the help and resources they need."[544]

In Wisconsin, the positivity rate hit 30 percent, with desperate pleas for retired health workers to return to the front lines. In South Dakota, deaths skyrocketed 52 percent, while in El Paso, they ordered their fourth mobile morgue.

Chapter 34: COVID: Is There an End in Sight?

"We've never seen anything like this in our history. We've never had a president trying to suppress votes. We haven't seen anything like this since Dixiecrat southern democrats tried to keep black people from voting."

Pulitzer Prize winner Carl Bernstein

"Suburban women, would you please like me? I saved your damn neighborhood, okay?" Trump pleaded several times, including on his final day of campaigning before November 3, as he skipped through a maddening five-state blitz.[545]

On pins and needles in Georgia, as we awaited both presidential and senatorial results a full two days after the November 3 official election day, a sea change occurred. Forsyth County, Georgia, the once sundown county where white nationalists ran aging Freedom Fighter Hosea Williams out of town in 1987, after he and his fellow civil rights activists showed up to celebrate Dr. King's birthday, delivered only 30 more absentee votes to Donald Trump than Joe Biden.[546] This is the same Forsyth County, an hour from Atlanta, where white citizens lynched a Black man in 1912 they had accused of murdering a white woman before hanging a second man, then driving the entire Black community out of the county.[547] Again, what sort of alien universe is this, or is Georgia really the cutting edge of the progressive New South? Trump's slender statewide lead climbed to 1,805 after hours of massive lead bleeding. Though optimistic, admittedly, I was battered by the 2018 close-but-no-cigar gubernatorial race of Stacey Abrams, whose quest to become the nation's first Black female governor, was narrowly defeated by Kemp.

"If you count the legal votes, I easily win," said Trump on November 4, as the election lay in the balance. "If you count the illegal votes, they can try to steal the election from us. We were up by over 700,000 votes in Pennsylvania. We won Pennsylvania by a lot. We were winning in all key locations by a lot, actually. Then our numbers started miraculously getting whittled away, in secret. And they wouldn't allow legally permissible observers."[548] While dismissing Trump's case, that he all but called frivolous, U.S. District Court Judge Matthew Brann said Trump was attempting to overturn the results with "strained legal arguments without merit and speculative accusations ... unsupported by evidence."[549] Trump twisted and disputed the truth so often, so consistently, that if you didn't listen to anyone not connected to his echo chamber, not married to his administration's "alternative facts," parroted by spokesperson and counselor to the president Kellyanne Conway, you could easily be deceived.

Friday, three days after the Nov. 3rd election, the U.S. soared to another new one-day case record: 122,365 COVID cases; 235,000 dead, including 1,300 in one day. Beginning on Nov. 3rd, the U.S. broke all-time COVID case records for 42 days in a row, despite POTUS insisting that "after November 3rd, no one would still be talking about COVID." As an additional apropos irony, White House Chief-of-Staff Mark Meadows was at home trying to recover from COVID.

In Georgia, the heart of the New South, we went to bed Tuesday night with Biden/Harris trailing POTUS by 372,000 votes. The deficit was confusing, as many of us lost sight of the fact that for days, we had been told that the day-of-voting was assured of showing Trump as the leader in the battle for the presidency. To some, being down by so little a margin was a win. After all, in ruby-red Georgia, the Dems hadn't won the presidency since Clinton did so in 1992, but even then, that was with third-party candidate Ross Perot winning 19% of the vote. Wednesday morning, however, the deficit had shrunk to 72,000 votes. The following morning, November 5, Biden crept past the president by the narrowest of margins.

"Where are the military ballots in Georgia?" a desperate POTUS tweeted.

As Biden's slender lead began to grow, some Republicans cried foul, while others crunched the numbers. "There simply is not any evidence that anybody has shown me, or anybody I'm aware of, any evidence of any kind of widespread corruption or fraud," said Rhode Island Republican Senator Pat Toomey.[550]

"Frankly, I think what the president needs to do is put on his big boy pants and needs to acknowledge that he lost," said Philadelphia Mayor Jim Kenney on November 6. "This is not a victory for a candidate or for a party. This is truly a victory for our democracy."[551]

Finally, after waiting what seemed like a lifetime, NBC called Pennsylvania for Biden at 11 a.m. on November 7, catapulting him into the presidency, and triggering both massive, spontaneous celebrations across the nation and the world, as well as pockets of despair in red and rural America.

Watching the crowd in Wilmington, Delaware, as the anticipation grew for Biden's first speech following the morning call on November 7, that he had secured the 270 electoral votes to become president-elect of the United States, I, like probably 55% of the nation, had a great sense of relief. I didn't think that Biden-Harris would be the answer to all the nation's ills, including COVID-19, the economy, the southern border, racial strife, those desperate for a stimulus package, and a gaping, raw, Trump-inspired divide over whether American voters had chosen Biden in a fair and open election. I felt relief – like a 100-pound weight had been lifted from my chest – because I believed Biden would move us beyond the childish rants, the unpresidential actions and demeanor, the vicious rancor, race baiting, and loathing for American values.

Before the election, our focus in the regional office had been human trafficking, SUDs (substance abuse disorders), and HIV. Since May, we had essentially bailed on the overall office response to COVID, though Acting Regional Director John McGough had still been heavily invested. The election results finally became clear as we headed back into the office on Monday, November 9. We were all interested in finding out how our office's focus might change, or whether we would stay the course until the January 20th transition. And political appointee McGough and others in the Trump administration were looking for their next position, as they knew they would not be retained by the Biden administration.

By this point, 122,000 lives had been lost to COVID. Is there an end in sight, I wondered? How far, deep, and wide can COVID go in ravaging our nation and world, as Texas, the country's second most populous state, had *by itself* just hit one million COVID cases? The disease is far more than numbers, however. In Texas, five-year-old Tagan Drone became one of the state's youngest victims. "This doctor told us our child would be fine," said father Quincy Drone. "[But] she didn't even make it twenty-four hours. Our daughter died within the next fifteen hours."[552]

Talk about eating your own. On November 9, as Georgia crawled toward a final count for what would prove to be a razor-thin Biden victory in the only purple state in the deep red South, sitting Senators Loeffler and Perdue called for fellow Republican Brad Raffensperger to resign his position as Georgia's Secretary of State. Why? Despite nobody offering any credible evidence, Loeffler, appointed to fill the term of retired Senator Johnny Isakson, and Perdue insisted, "There have been too many failures in Georgia elections this year, and the most recent election has shined a national light on the problems."

The crime? The insult? The egregious offense? The fact that Raffensperger, the Secretary of State, his staff, and even Governor Kemp insisted the election was fair and accurate after *two* recounts.

In a joint statement, Perdue and Loeffler cited "mismanagement and lack of transparency" as the reasons for their demand, while failing to provide any specific examples.[553] Frankly, they were simply seeking to hide their shame at failing to defend their seats against Jon Ossoff,[554] who became the youngest U.S. senator after Perdue refused to debate him, and Reverend Raphael Warnock, a successor to Dr. King at perhaps America's most famous church, who became Georgia's first Black senator and only the 11th in U.S. history.[555] Perdue had been investigated for questionable stock deals that reeked of insider trading, and Loeffler, the one-time owner of the WNBA Atlanta Dream, a mostly Black women's pro basketball team, criticized the league's support of the Black Lives Matter movement because of what she called its "Marxist leanings."[556] Good riddance, I thought, on both counts. Too many MAGA Republicans fail to realize, certainly if you hold or aspire to statewide offices in diverse states, that culture wars are simply not a winning ticket.

Meanwhile, COVID cases in the U.S. topped 10,000,000 on the same day Pfizer announced its drug had an amazing 90% efficacy rate. The initial hope, according to epidemiologists, was that we could roll out a drug with a 50-60% rate of preventing the disease. The vaccine required everyone to get two shots, three weeks apart. A second vaccine maker, Moderna, produced a similar product shortly thereafter; welcome news as 1,000 people a day were dying and 100,000 new cases were being recorded. Still, only half of Americans were ready and willing to take the vaccine on day one. The reason? The tardy and massive mishandling of the COVID response.

"A mask is not a political statement," said President-elect Biden on November 9th. "But it is a good way to pull the country together."

Again, in the height of irony, David Bossie, chosen to lead Trump's quest to prove voting irregularities in the states he lost and needed to win re-election, contracted COVID the same day, November 9th, that HUD Secretary Carson and three other White House staffers were also diagnosed positive. Both had been seen at a White House election night event without masks.

More than 60,000 Americans packed crowded hospitals due to COVID, as the virus continued ravaging the upper Midwest, where colder weather was already closing in. Dr. Anthony Fauci predicted as many as 20,000 more people could die before the end of November 2020. "Do not be surprised when we reach 200,000 cases per day," said newly appointed Biden Coronavirus Task Force member Dr. Michael Osterholm, Director of the Center for Infectious Disease Research and Policy at the University of Minnesota. Only a week earlier, 100,000 cases per day seemed unbelievable, yet November 10th was the seventh straight day with at least 100,000 new cases.

November produced one million new COVID cases in the first 10 days – unprecedented numbers so numbing that we couldn't quite seem to grasp it as we vaguely remembered that Trump declared that once Election Day came, nobody would still be talking about COVID. There were sixty-two million new COVID hospitalizations on November 11, with 152,000 new COVID cases and over

1,400 new deaths. In North Dakota, the fight for staff at the overloaded hospitals was in such a state of crisis that asymptomatic COVID-19-infected health care workers were still staffing patients and hospitals. Texas, the nation's leader, topped 1,000,000 cases *by itself*, with El Paso (where they kept running out of mobile morgues) as the new epicenter. At the same time, the *nation* of Italy, once the COVID epicenter, also topped one million cases.

"Our worst nightmare right now is having to choose between a patient with COVID and a patient from a car accident," said Dr. Julie Watson, chief medical officer at Integris Health in Oklahoma City.[557]

"We didn't invest early on in manufacturing, so we're not going to have enough doses for all the people who could benefit from these medicines," said former Trump FDA Commissioner Dr. Scott Gottlieb, one of the very few Trump officials who had been honest with consumers all along.[558] That reality was a fatal consequence for tens of thousands of Americans who died as a result of Trump's failure to acknowledge and act on the deadly nature of the disease in the early phase instead of insisting it would simply "disappear."

Meantime, kicking and screaming, hoping against hope that he could overturn the election results, crybaby-in-chief Trump refused to allow president-elect Biden the customary access to intel and other benefits of an incoming president. According to former GOP House Republican Conference Chair Liz Cheney, over 60 judges reviewed and rejected his claims of voter fraud in states Trump lost.

*

By November 12, the dam seemed to be breaking wide open. Arizona was declared a win for Biden after Trump lawyers acknowledged they had no real case to challenge the election. The following day, Georgia was declared for Biden, the first time the increasingly progressive capital of the New South had gone blue since 1992, and then, with third-party candidate Ross Perot splitting the vote. Chicago Mayor Lori Lightfoot proclaimed that people could only go to work, school, and out for essential needs, beginning November 16. By November 13, every U.S. state was surging with coronavirus, as 193,000 cases ravaged the nation. El Paso, Texas, reported a higher rate of COVID than any city in the nation. In early September of 2020, Wisconsin was registering about 900 new COVID cases per day. By November 13, that figure had catapulted to 6,000.

Despite all the president's charges of voter fraud and cheating, Trump's Department of Homeland Security cybersecurity head, Chris Krebs, called the 2020 presidential election the "most secure in American history. There is no evidence that any voting system deleted or lost votes, changed votes, or was in any way compromised," said Krebs.[559] At least 12 judges agreed, throwing out cases, or having Trump lawyers pull their filings. Meanwhile, according to *The Washington Post*, as many as 130 of Trump's Secret Service staff may have been infected while traveling with, and securing POTUS. White House press secretary Kayleigh McEnany? What a disgrace to the profession. Trump has a way of turning his spokespersons into high-priced charlatans who will say almost anything to sell his message. Alyssa Farah Griffin, once Trump's strategic communications director, described her colleague as a "smart woman," at the same time pointing out her conniving ways in the House January 6th Committee testimony.

"She [McEnany] knew we lost the [2020] election, but she made a calculation that she wanted to have a certain life post-Trump that required staying in his good graces," said Griffin. "And that was more important to her than telling the truth to the American public."[560]

Trump and the MAGA crowd's elongated foot-dragging was particularly designed to disenfranchise Black, brown, and young people, though it also impacted millions of Americans who consider themselves independents and progressives, while at the same time sucking in millions of vulnerable Trump followers.

"Everywhere we've seen lawsuits, we've seen this as a direct assault on black voters," said NAACP President Derrick Johnson.[561]

"This is just Jim Crow modern tactics of trying to take away the right to vote, by powerful people from black people," said Stuart Stevens, chief advisor of the Lincoln Project. "If one of the issues is how do you motivate African Americans in a runoff, I think Republicans have played this hand disastrously. They [Republicans] know that Donald Trump is going to lose, and they're still afraid of him."[562]

Back in Georgia – that's newly minted Blue Georgia, I'll remind you – the deep stain of abject racism still runs deep, especially in south Georgia, and outside the metropolitan areas. That lone, solid blue state in the southeast corner of the map was about the sweetest thing I'd seen in a long while! I say that as someone who, 20 years earlier, had campaigned and voted for Black Republican candidates in the state.

The roots of white pomposity are inherently ingrained in many parts of the country, including Georgia, which the two new progressive senators call home. Example: Seeking bond in the murder case of jogger Ahmaud Arbery, Travis McMichael, whom a video clearly shows as the shooter, retweeted to his friend about "crackhead gold-teeth wearing black people," which the friend insisted wasn't racist. Zachary Lincoln, McMichael's friend, admitted under oath that they frequently exchanged such tropes, including calling Asians "slant-eyed fu__ks."[563] According to William

"Roddie" Bryan, who filmed the heinous event and used his truck to help corner Arbery, whom they tracked down like a runaway slave, McMichael called Arbery a "f__king nigger" after shooting him three times at close range. "Ahmaud wasn't allowed to go home," said the victim's mother, Wanda Cooper Jones. "So, them going home would be totally unfair."[564]

In another example of white pomposity, a couple in Jacksonville, Florida, a Black female labor attorney, Abina Horton, and a white artist, Alex Horton, tried to refinance their home. When the appraisal came back shockingly low, a revelation suddenly hit the Black woman. The appraiser was reacting to the pictures of Black people all around the house. Taking down all evidence of being a biracial home, the couple arranged for another agent to give an appraisal, but Abina was absent. This time, the price of the home came back $100,000 higher. The couple filed a lawsuit against Fair Housing.[565] The problem is that this is very similar to a study conducted by Diane Sawyer and ABC News nearly 30 years ago, in 1991. It also mirrors a study in Chicago done in the 1960s featuring two "Alices," one Black and one white, designed to root out unfair housing practices.[566] When, I must ask, as a Black man whose parents couldn't vote when I was a child, and someone who personally faced the degradation of using substandard, segregated facilities growing up, can I expect to be treated and respected like white Americans are?

For those open to honest interrogation, there is ample evidence that racial and ethnic hate and terrorism against Asians, Jews, African Americans, Latinos, and the LGBTQ+ community have increased dramatically in the age of Trump.[567]

"White power. It's a cancer to American society," said former Clinton Chief of Staff Leon Panetta. At least 20 hate crime suspects cited President Trump as their motivation for committing racist, or homophobic acts of aggression. In comparison, the president was never cited by anyone arrested for hate crimes during either the Bush II, or Obama administrations.

On November 16, Trump's White House Coronavirus Task Force member, Dr. Scott Atlas, told Michiganders to "rise up" against their governor because she urged people to celebrate Thanksgiving with their nuclear families, not at large gatherings. How does a doctor who has sworn an oath to "do no harm," urge a radical element, in a state where far-right groups plotted to kidnap and execute the governor, to "rise up" because she is trying to protect them?[568] The reason is that he, like POTUS, is strictly concerned about himself, even as the U.S. added one million new COVID cases in not a month, but a single week! That same day, lawsuits challenging COVID restrictions were filed in Wisconsin, Georgia, Nevada, and Arizona – each case dismissed.

Secretary Azar, an extremely intelligent man, still refused in meetings with his HHS career staff to acknowledge that he and his boss would be out the door on January 20. Talk about living in the 51st state of denial! "Every single person in Washington, including Senator Cruz, knew the reality of the situation. This election was over a long time ago," said former senior Obama advisor David Axelrod. "They're playing this out because that's what their boss demands of them."[569]

After reviewing Trump's post-campaign literature and soliciting more donations, it quickly became apparent why he wouldn't give up. ... "60% of each contribution goes first to Save America," Trump's new political action committee, one of his solicitations said in fine print.[570]

Chapter 35: The Highly Effective Vaccines Produced by Operation Warp Speed

"You just feel defeated. Am I making a difference anymore? I'm here, and there is this patient in the ICU who is clearly confused about how real COVID is."

Nurse Ashley Bartholomew, El Paso, TX

Finally, there was good news as two vaccines, Pfizer and Moderna, both reported efficacy rates of more than 90%, with Moderna, in fact, saying its vaccine had a 95% efficacy rate. Game changer? Lord only knows, I thought at the time. We all hoped and prayed that this was so, as the stock market soared and Donald Trump played golf, lauding the highly impressive Operation Warp Speed's initial results; yet, saying nothing about the skyrocketing virus infection numbers that pushed the U.S. over 11,000,000, with nearly 275,000 deaths. As of November 15, the U.S. was averaging 150,000 new cases per day. That's more than 101 new COVID cases per minute. Over one million children, the very people Trump insisted were virtually immune from the virus, had been infected by mid-November. It was only a few weeks earlier that the concept of reaching 100,000 daily cases was unfathomable. With every state registering climbing case numbers and death rates, there was no predicting how high the daily counts could go before the end of a torturous 2020. God only knows how many of those cases could have been avoided, and how many lives could have been saved had Trump acted back in January, instead of waiting until March to provide tepid, COVID response leadership and reluctant focus on the deadly disease. Finally, after nearly nine months, 35 states had *finally* invoked some sort of mask mandate. Meanwhile, operating in a vacuum, a clearly defeated Trump continued to withhold key intel and briefings to President-elect Biden, due to his refusing to concede he lost. The Republican governor of Iowa, Kim Reynolds, who chided mask-wearing as a "feel good measure," finally mandated mask-wearing on November 16th, with 73,000 new people in her state hospitalized with COVID.[571]

The same day, just before the deadline, 93,000 former Boy Scouts filed suits of sexual misconduct against the legendary organization and their scout leaders for decades of hidden abuse and shame. The Boy Scouts were as American as the flag, baseball, and apple pie. Had it not been for the fact that the nation was uber-tense over a highly contested election, and was finally provided access to effective vaccines that could slow the global pandemic that was infecting 100,000 Americans a day and nearing 300,000 deaths, this would have been the major story of the day. Safety continued to be a huge concern for engaged parents, whether it be in scouting, the designation of bathroom use, or social media.

*

On his way out the door – reluctantly, I might add – Trump, like the petulant child he is, was determined to do all the damage he could. First and foremost, he cried foul, insisting the voting process – the same one virtually all of his top security chiefs at Homeland Security, FBI, and CIA said was the safest, most closely monitored in U.S. history – was deeply flawed and that he had been cheated. A poor loser, even after his loss was abundantly clear to anyone not drinking the Trump Kool-Aid, he summoned his faithful to protest and push back. Perhaps, most importantly, he cast a deep and enduring pall of doubt over the psyche of many Americans that they could ever again truly trust the election process, *even if they were white*. Next, he pulled troops out of Afghanistan and Iraq, both strategically critical to the balance of world power, against the advice of his senior military leadership. He also fired several key people, including Chris Krebs, who oversaw cybersecurity for Homeland Security, and declared that there was no systematic cheating in the 2020 election.[572] Trump also continued a series of frivolous lawsuits, having 12 either withdrawn or dismissed by a range of judges, both liberal and conservative, who said they were meritless. Why? Because he simply doesn't know how to graciously lose. And perhaps the worst insult of all, during a pandemic spiraling out of control, Trump never commented on the crisis, only promoting the fact that two highly efficacious vaccines were developed under his watch.

"The vaccines are soon on the way," Trump said. However, compounding his total lack of leadership and empathy for the colossal grief and loss of life, Trump continued to withhold the intelligence always provided to the president-elect that could have saved thousands of lives. As a friend and mentor of mine, Tony Renfrow, says, "who does that make sense to?" Meanwhile, the delays continued to have a devastating effect on front-line workers.

"You just feel defeated. Am I making a difference anymore? I'm here, and there is this patient in the ICU who is clearly confused about how real COVID is," said nurse Ashley Bartholomew, who quit her job in El Paso, where prisoners were being paid two dollars per hour to load bodies of those who died from COVID into refrigerated trailer morgues.[573]

The first two weeks in November produced 250,000 new COVID cases in children. Overall, the first three weeks in November produced one-fourth of all the COVID cases in the U.S. since March of 2020, as Americans, fatigued from staying inside and "masking up," gathered and traveled over Thanksgiving, despite the dire warnings. As 1,600 people a day were dying from COVID, and more than 200,000 people were contracting the disease each day, Trump never said a mumbling word about the suffering and pain of his fellow Americans. Instead, he tweeted incessantly that he had won the election and that he was the victim of a massive fraud campaign.

"Frankly, the president's legal team has been a national disaster," said Trump confidant and former New Jersey Governor Chris Christie, almost a full two years before he hammered Trump's record and decision-making as a candidate himself for the 2024 presidency.

As tension in the medical community continued to rise, the frustration over the highly-charged political discourse and acrimony also spiked. "I'm surprised at some of the vitriol, and outright lies, at some of the threats you get," acknowledged Georgia Secretary of State Brad Raffensperger, whose office was under constant attack because it insisted Trump, Perdue, and Loeffler actually lost their elections. "I would think Republicans are better than that."[574]

Days before Thanksgiving and two weeks after the election, Thomas Donohue, CEO of the U.S. Chamber of Commerce and a supporter of the Trump agenda, said the president "should not delay the transition a moment longer."[575]

After traveling the South extensively for years, especially during the first five years following the implementation of the Affordable Care Act, I had a good idea of how fragile the health care system was in many small, poor, rural communities. At least 149 hospitals, the primary job source in many of those communities, have been forced to close, or seriously scale back over the past decade, especially in the deep South, where every single governor except Kentucky's refused to expand Medicaid when the ACA was rolled out.[576] The worst year in a decade was 2019. For that reason, as well as struggling economies in depressed areas, I was braced for the imminent aftershocks as COVID began ravaging big cities like Seattle, Boston, New York, Chicago, Detroit, and others in the spring and early summer of 2020. Though it absolutely should not matter, these were virtually all cities in Democrat strongholds, places Trump routinely labeled "blue states" while calling them rat-infested, poorly managed, and slum-ridden. Atlanta talk show host Dana Barrett, who is white, called Trump the "bigot-in-chief," because of his attack on predominantly Black cities like Atlanta and Baltimore.[577] Characteristically, he frequently sparred with their leaders, like Congressman Elijah Cummings, Congressman John Lewis, former Chicago Mayor Lori Lightfoot, and Seattle's Jenny Durkan. However, I, along with many others who had driven the rural highways and byways, traversing the country roads that compose the bulk of the 3,119,884 square miles of the continental United States, knew something Trump clearly did not. The people who trusted and believed in him most, those who believed in fighting abortion, standing tough on crime, hard work, and traditional values, yet all too often also lived in largely white, homogeneous communities, were squarely in the COVID crosshairs. And these were overwhelmingly "his" people. Too often believing Trump's proclamation that the virus was a hoax, and that masks and social distancing were a waste of time and energy, many relaxed, as they saw their fellow big city neighbors sometimes lose dozens, even hundreds, of loved ones each day. Not all his followers were Christians, but thousands flocked to his rallies, soaking in his evangelistic fervor as they sported MAGA gear. Many of them traveled to venues known as previous havens of hate, like Tulsa,

Oklahoma, on June 20th, the first place Trump visited after COVID placed a grip on the throat of a nation, as well as the site of one of the greatest racial massacres in American history. Was it a coincidence that Trump chose to resume his Make America Great Again tour there? I think not. How about Leesburg, Virginia, which native Josh Stack insisted has a long, sordid history of racism?[578] Trump held a campaign rally there two days before the 2020 election, and his daughter was featured at an event in Leesburg at Trump National Golf Club.[579]

Trump flew into Waukegan, Wisconsin, where police shot an unarmed Jacob Blake in the back three times, paralyzing him. He spoke at Kenosha, on the site of a burned-out store attacked by an angry protest where one of his young followers joined the Proud Boys to "protect property," yet panicked and ended up shooting and killing two white protesters.[580] On October 12th, 2020, a week after getting out of the hospital because of callously contracting COVID-19, Trump, to prove himself strong and COVID-free, took his Make America Great Again tour to, of all places, Sanford, Florida. Why was that important? Though rarely noted, Sanford was the place where grown man/neighborhood watchman George Zimmerman tracked down 17-year-old Trayvon Martin and killed him. So why did Trump choose to visit Sanford? Was it the same reason he took his rally to Tulsa? Rarely, if ever, did Trump express sincere compassion and empathy for those killed in righteous protests against the over-policing of unarmed Black men. Instead, he increased his call for more law and order, more force, and more authoritarianism.

In the end, it was inevitable that COVID would reach rural America. First, in the great Midwest and Western states of Montana, the Dakotas, Iowa, Nebraska, and Utah, the autumn cold chased misinformed, unmasked, unvaccinated people inside into closer quarters – but eventually, it reached the rural South. Outside of their big cities, hospitals were few and far apart, often small and understaffed, frequently ill-equipped to deal with acute care patients like those struck with coronavirus. It was in those places, more than others, where nurse after nurse, doctor after doctor, told tales of direly sick patients waking up, disoriented, insisting that "this can't be real" because coronavirus is a hoax, only to die soon after. Surely, COVID was bound to spread the globe and reach our shores. But ill-prepared, untruthful, and ambivalent Trump was determined to take the road of least resistance, dooming hundreds of thousands of Americans to a wretched death they didn't have to endure. In the process, he deepened the political and cultural divide in this country into a chasm that might not be healed for at least a generation.

Chapter 36: Repudiation

A Wisconsin judge dismissed Trump's suit to overturn the election as a "thin claim, like Frankenstein's monster, haphazardly put together based on strained legal arguments and speculative observations."[581]

Reserve Judge Stephen Simanek

Let's be clear about the landmark 2020 elections. It was unequivocally a repudiation of Donald J. Trump. Why? Because down-ballot-endangered Republicans, like Maine's Susan Collins, North Carolina's Richard Burr, Alaska's Lisa Murkowski, and several others who challenged Trump's assertions, won. It was Trump, in fact, who weighed down the ticket. His bluster, lack of empathy for those suffering and dying in the greatest health crisis in a century, putting kids in cages and separating them from their parents, promoting racial and gender insensitivity, dismissing obvious cases of police brutality, and his blatant distinction between red states and blue states, were simply too much to stomach for nearly 80 million Americans. Disrupting the tried-and-true democratic process, Trump wanted and still wants to be an autocrat. He has clearly proclaimed that if he returns to office in 2024, any federal employee who refuses to take a pledge to him will lose their job.[582] Is this still the United States of America, or are we becoming *CSA: The Confederate States of America,* the mockumentary by filmmaker Kevin Willmott?[583] If this country desires to be known as a democratic republic, it will not remain so under another Trump presidency, or that of anyone who later tries and succeeds at what he is attempting to do in 2024.

By November 20, 2020, as the nation was mired in political tension – its progressive wing celebrating a Biden victory, while conservatives cried foul in disbelief that Trump lost – 51% of parents reported skipping meals in order to feed their children, with almost 40% not paying bills to buy food. In addition, millions of Americans were braced to see their extended unemployment benefits expire right after Christmas.[584]

Also on November 20, Kyle Rittenhouse was released on a $2 million bail bond, paid by an anonymous source. His release was facilitated by conservative attorney Lin Wood, and Trump associate, MyPillow® CEO Mike Lindell. Rittenhouse, who had a friend buy him an AR-15, crossed state lines to allegedly protect property in Kenosha, Wisconsin, and then, while apparently fleeing, shot three unarmed protesters, killing two. Those people shot, it must be noted, were white activists. We have gotten to the point that white men masquerading as defenders of the breach can even kill unarmed *white people*. A group calling itself the Kenosha Guard had issued a call to arms that drew Rittenhouse: "Any patriots willing to take up arms and defend our city tonight from the evil thugs?" the group had written on Facebook. "No doubt they are currently planning on the next part of the city to burn tonight."[585]

"We're setting records today and breaking them tomorrow," noted Dr. Leana Wen, former health director for the city of Baltimore. "Rural hospitals are being overwhelmed and have nowhere to send their patients."[586]

Dr. Deborah Birx, once a fixture with the Coronavirus Task Force, made her first visit back to the group, which hadn't had a press conference in four months. "More than half the counties in the country are in what we consider the red zone," said Birx. "Unfortunately, the worst is yet to come."[587]

On November 22, one Wisconsin judge called the Trump lawsuits aimed at overturning the state's razor-thin Biden victory a "thin claim, like Frankenstein's monster, haphazardly put together based on strained legal arguments and speculative observations." On the same day, then Maryland Governor Larry Hogan, no fan of Trump's, called on Trump to "stop golfing and concede."[588]

In Atlanta, Black media mogul Tyler Perry fed 5,000 at-risk families on November 22, one of the legions of bright lights in the midst of one of the dreariest periods of American history.

That same Thanksgiving week in 2020, a Black dad, Corey Robinson, fearful of his son's ability to grow into manhood in this magnified era of tragic police encounters with young Black men, organized a sharing session between the Black community and police in Roswell, Georgia, an Atlanta suburb.

"I can't sleep at night when he just drives to the high school," said Robinson, referring to his 17-year-old son, also named Corey. "If I'm honest, I want our police force to know who our children are. I want police to show them what they should do."[589] What that said to me was that in addition to the national trauma over the deadly spread of COVID, the threat millions faced over food and housing insecurity, and the tense atmosphere over the 2020 election results, Black families like the Robinsons faced the daily fear that their children might be victims of what should be a routine, harmless police encounter. This constant fear and pressure are both gut-wrenching and very real in comparison to the "white fragility" expressed by some parents because their children could be taught the ugly side of American history, including the virtual expulsion and eradication of the First Nation population that was here when Anglos arrived, the Japanese internment camps, the Chinese Exclusion Act, and the horrors of slavery and lynchings for Black America.[590]

As Thanksgiving approached, and the three vaccine manufacturers confirmed amazing results with their products, each with success rates over 90%, Americans, shaken by interference by the Trump administration, with the FDA and CDC slow to issue full-throated affirmations. In fact, front-line nurses weren't even in agreement, as 34% said they would get the vaccine when available, 36% said "no," and 31% were undecided.[591] Undoubtedly, when the Trump administration finally moved forward to protect Americans from COVID, it did indeed move at warp-speed, producing three potentially remarkable products in a record nine months.

As one African American colleague of mine in another regional office said, "I certainly wasn't going to be a guinea pig for a vaccine they rushed out in months when they should have been working on it for the last year."

After a sordid history, especially targeting people of color, and an administration unfamiliar with truth-telling, many insisted on seeing proof. It didn't help when the word of under-disclosed side effects, including high fever, body aches, bad headaches, daylong exhaustion, and other symptoms after receiving COVID shots leaked, as opposed to being openly disclosed.[592] Perhaps even more egregious, ICE detainees, those with little representation and even less of a voice, were alleged victims of unneeded and unwanted surgeries while incarcerated.[593] Jamaican immigrant Wendy Dove, who had lived illegally in the U.S. for 20 years, says she was awakened from her cellblock in rural Irwin County, GA, and told she needed surgery to stop menstrual cramping. Later, Dawn Woodard, a nurse at the facility, filed a whistleblower complaint that several women at the facility had had their uteruses removed without consent, or full understanding of what they were facing. At least 16 were treated by Dr. Mahendra Amin, who ICE officials noted was the facility's primary gynecologist. That is exactly the kind of predatory, illegal, and inhumane behavior that makes marginalized people of color wary of the medical community.

Unbelievable, right?

On November 25th, 2,380 Americans died of COVID-19-related illnesses. It was the 15th straight day of new records of hospitalized coronavirus cases, with no end in sight as 50 million Americans hit the road to celebrate Thanksgiving with loved ones. In all, more than 250,000 Americans had died from COVID-19.

"We are in a humanitarian crisis right now," said Dr. John Brownstein, chief innovation officer at Boston's Children's Hospital.[594]

As President-elect Biden made historic cabinet picks, including Alejandro Mayorkas, the first Cuban American Homeland Security Secretary; Deb Haaland, the first Native American Secretary of the Interior; Janet Yellen, the first woman to serve as U.S. Treasury director; and Michael Regan, the first Black EPA administrator,[595] Trump's actions were damaging, not affirming. Trump, who hadn't offered a word of comfort or care for the millions suffering from the loss of friends and loved ones, instead pardoned his first national security advisor, Michael Flynn, who had been convicted of lying to The Feds about his involvement with Russia.[596] Meanwhile, Trump, ever an elitist, failed to pardon a single one of the more than a thousand charged, and hundreds of his avid followers who received prison sentences after he urged them to go to the Capitol and "fight like hell."

Food scarcity for those living on the margins continued to increase, with the looming end of the CARES Act assistance at the end of 2020. An estimated 50 million Americans faced food insecurity, including 17 million kids.[597]

"I don't know what is going to happen," said Trump, in one of his first public comments in the three weeks since the outcome of the 2020 presidential election. "I do know one thing: Joe Biden did not get 80 million votes. It's going to be a very hard thing to concede because we know there was massive fraud."[598]

On November 28, a delusional Trump tweeted that "Biden can only enter the White House as president if he can prove that his ridiculous '80,000,000 votes' were not fraudulently or illegally obtained. When you see what happened in Detroit, Atlanta, Philadelphia, and Milwaukee, massive voter fraud, he's got a big unsolvable problem!"[599] Again, I asked myself and anyone else who would listen: "What alien universe am I living in, or why can't I wake up from this dreadful nightmare when a man who lost the electoral count, and earned seven million fewer votes than his opponent, refuses to concede an election?"

"Calling an election unfair does not make it so," wrote the U.S. Court of Appeals for the Third Circuit Judge Stephanos Bibas, a Republican appointee. "Charges require specific allegations and then proof. We have neither here."[600]

Trump, who insisted he didn't believe the results then, and wouldn't in six months, said, "This election was rigged. This election was a total fraud, and it continues to be, as they hide – and the problem [is] we have to go to judges, and people don't want to get involved."[601]

And while Trump fumed and tweeted incessantly about voter fraud and cheating, some scientists insisted that the cases of those infected were as many as eight times higher than diagnosed. But Trump obviously didn't care about the suffering of Americans.

How was it that two-thirds of America's nurses had never been tested, while professional athletes were tested several times a week? Something was clearly wrong with this picture. [602] Where was the justice in that?

Pfizer and Moderna applied for EUAs (Emergency Use Authorization), as four million Americans were infected with COVID-19 in November alone. Both required two doses, but Pfizer's vaccine had to be preserved in "cold boxes" at 94 degrees below zero. "Hospital capacity is the top concern," warned New York's Governor Cuomo. Some doctors reported having worked over 250 straight days to treat the ill.

November of 2020 saw a jaw-dropping 36,000 Americans die from COVID, with another 100,000-plus hospitalized. Half the states in the country reported supply shortages to deal with COVID patients, 93,000 of whom filled hospital beds.

The U.S. topped 13 million COVID cases a few days after Thanksgiving, with 265,000 American lives lost, as experts warned the turkey day gatherings almost ensured a surge on top of the surge. Meanwhile, in the political world, Trump threw away $3 million to challenge the Wisconsin presidential results, only to see that not only were Biden's votes not taken away, but that Biden's final lead was a little higher.

"Why won't Governor @BrianKempGA, the hapless governor of Georgia, use his emergency power, which can be easily done, to overrule his obstinate secretary of state and do a match of signatures on envelopes? It will be a "goldmine" of fraud, and we will easily win the state. ..." Trump tweeted.[603]

"I just wish Trump would stop, quite frankly," said GOP fundraiser Dan Eberhart, who worried that the president's insistence he had been cheated would hurt Republican senate candidates in Georgia. "Acting like a sore loser is plain not helpful."[604]

"He's an enemy of the people," Trump called Georgia Secretary of State Raffensperger.

"My family voted for him, donated to him, and are now being thrown under the bus by him," said Raffensperger, who received death threats, along with other members of his family.[605] Raffensperger, a staunch Christian, said he leaned into Psalm 37 to get him through, even as his home was under 24/7 protection. By December 2, no systemic voter fraud was found in 47 cases filed by GOP and Trump sympathizers.

Meanwhile, the vaccine rollout, Operation Warp Speed, as uneven as it was, became the largest government operation since World War II.

Brad Parscale, a former Trump campaign manager who was relieved of duty in July 2020, was starkly honest about one of the key reasons Trump lost in 2020.

"We lost suburban families," Parscale said. "I think that goes to one thing: the decision on COVID to go for opening the economy, versus public empathy. ... I think if he had been publicly empathetic, he would have won."[606]

"Lin Wood and Sidney Powell are totally destructive," tweeted Newt Gingrich, former speaker of the House and architect of the Reagan Revolution, as America prepared for the seismic run-off in Georgia that would determine control of the U.S. Senate. "Every Georgia conservative who cares about America MUST vote in the runoff. The 'don't vote' strategy will cripple America."[607]

Remember the Devil Went Down to Georgia?[608]

Soon, there were fourteen million *active* COVID cases in the U.S., 2,887 deaths in one day, and one American dying every 30 seconds. Equally startling, over 100,000 people were hospitalized, fighting COVID for their very lives. Over 192,000 new cases were recorded on December 3. More than half of all coronavirus cases were transmitted by people who had no symptoms.

"The cavalry [Biden administration] is on the way," I told one of my healthcare.gov enrollment state navigators, who was complaining that she saw extensive radio, television, and newspaper commercials promoting Medicare.gov, yet nothing on healthcare.gov for the health insurance marketplace. She was right, of course, after Trump had slashed ACA funding by three-fourths when he arrived in office in a budgetary effort to kill the Obama signature landmark legislation he could not destroy via the vote or the law.

Remember the top GOP priority when America's first Black president took office? Mitch McConnell was quoted saying in the National Journal in 2010, "The single most important thing we want to achieve is for President Obama to be a one-term president."[609] Though the GOP was unsuccessful in limiting Obama to one term, they relentlessly continued to overturn his signature legislation, the Affordable Care Act, in what I, and many other Black people believed was an attempt to destroy his legacy.

As the year closed, 712,000 filed for unemployment, with 17 million more behind on mortgages and rent, and scheduled to lose their lodgings at the end of the year when the mortgage forgiveness ran out.

In a show of true American nationalism and solidarity, three former presidents, Bush, Clinton, and Obama, volunteered to be first to take the new COVID vaccines, even promising to do so on television in order to boost national confidence in the science. According to released information, 30% of Pfizer trial participants and 37% of Moderna's were from minority groups.[610] A host of the nation's top Black doctors,[611] including Dr. Valerie Montgomery Rice, president of Morehouse School of Medicine, and Dr. Victoria Smith of the prestigious Ochsner Health, were among the first to volunteer for the trials and co-signed onto the validity of the vaccine's science and its efficacy, particularly for minorities. "We need to be very transparent with patients," said Smith.[612] "One of the reasons why I wanted to participate was to be a model of participation for the safety of the vaccine and the process."

Understanding the painful history of Black folk and medical science, including the travesty endured by Fannie Lou Hamer, the Tuskegee Experiment, the testing done on Puerto Ricans at Vieques island, and the countless cases cited in the book *Medical Apartheid*, I was initially skeptical.[613] However, the validation provided by these documents was comforting for me, as I have worked in the public health sphere for the past 23 years. In decades past, Black physicians had very little voice, or agency in what ambitious physicians and scientists chose to inflict on poor and minority communities, too often making them guinea pigs, or sacrificial lambs in the name of medical advancement.

Listen, I get it, totally. Black, brown, indigenous, and other people, including Puerto Ricans on Vieques, are among the Americans who have been used and abused for medical experimentation in ways that were cruel, opportunistic, and inhumane.[614] This time, however, it would be different. People of color, including Chairwoman Dr. Marcella Nunez-Smith, would be at the forefront of the COVID-19 Health Equity Task Force.[615]

"This nation is severely unprepared for this pandemic, and I think we have to call it the way it is," acknowledged CDC Director Redfield in a startling, way-too-late admission.[616] I'm not sure where Redfield's courage was before it became apparent that Trump was on the way out the door, but the admission only verified what hundreds of hours of calls HHS tasked me with monitoring what supply chain suppliers, public health officials, elected officials, and other front-line workers, federal, state and local, had clearly shown me over the previous nine months.

In Illinois, four of every five ICU beds were full by December 4. In Wisconsin, another state at the breaking point, Democrat Governor Tony Evers wrote, "As vaccine distribution gets underway, our state cannot afford to have this pattern of failed promises repeat."[617]

Our leaders, however, continued to send mixed messages. Trump lapdog Congressman Matt Gaetz partied with about 150 young Republicans in New Jersey, with very few wearing masks. Denver Mayor Michael Hancock, San Francisco's London Breed, and California Governor Gavin Newsom, were among several high-profile leaders who were caught saying one thing about not traveling, or convening with others outside your house, yet doing another, over the holidays.[618]

As the world focused on health and political issues, 40,000 Americans languished in prison for marijuana use, with Black Americans four times more likely to be arrested for this offense. As *The Washington Post* put it, the Dow passed 30,000 for the first time ever, with Trump calling the number "sacred," yet lines of cars at food banks stretched for miles.[619]

As late as December 7, and even as late as 2023, I knew people who insisted that the Supreme Court would overturn Biden's election, that Rudy Giuliani was intentionally infected with COVID, that QAnon would trample the "deep state," and that Obama and Hillary were really under house arrest, and Trump would be reinstated any day. Go figure.[620] All this, frankly, reminds me of what I've read about the cult-like vises imposed by silver-tongued politicians like Joseph McCarthy, who raised the Red Scare that prohibited, or restricted many Black luminaries from earning a living. As a result, Josephine Baker, Dr. W.E.B. DuBois, Paul Robeson, Lena Horne, Dorothy Dandridge, James Baldwin, Kwame Ture (known to many as Stokely Carmichael), and a host of others accused of being Communists by the FBI, or the House Un-American Activities Committee (HUAC), either left the U.S., or strongly considered it.[621] These tactics, and more, are not only possible, but highly likely in a contentious, loyalty-demanding, autocratic, White Christian Nationalist-steeped second Trump administration. In the process, Trump would again lean into divisive dogma and culture wars – relating to race, ethnicity, and gender – that further separate America, while capitalizing on the demonization of the "Other."[622] By this point, clearly, we have no option but to acknowledge that's exactly who he is, even though one-third of the nation sees him as the next best thing to Jesus Christ.

California and its 33 million people went back to virtual lockdown as of December 7, ironically, Pearl Harbor Day, the gruesome day 79 years earlier when 2,403 Americans were killed in a sneak attack by the Japanese during World War II. That assault, surgical and decisive, was a blatant act of war. In 2020, however, we endured virtually the same number of lives lost every single day in the U.S. At Renown Regional Medical Center in Reno, they had to set up a field hospital next to the brick-and-mortar facility because of the overwhelming numbers of cases and intensive care patients.

Armed protesters paraded outside the home of Michigan Secretary of State Jocelyn Benson, while Georgia's Raffensperger and his family received ongoing death threats. Benson is a Democrat, and Raffensperger, who voted for, and wrote checks to the Trump campaign, is a lifelong Republican. On December 7, both re-certified the fact that Trump had indeed lost their states' presidential elections.

VMI (Virginia Military Institute), much to the disdain of Trump, moved its controversial statue of Confederate General Stonewall Jackson. Also happening on December 7, legendary songwriter Bob Dylan sold the rights to his amazing catalog for $200 million. To be sure, I thought, "the times they are a-changing."[623] Meanwhile, Trump lawyer Giuliani, older and less healthy than most of the staff and inner circle in the Trump orbit who had contracted COVID, remained in the hospital, though he insisted he was rapidly improving. Giuliani, like Trump before him, was assured of getting the finest of care, even as 90 fellow Americans were dying every hour. The nation topped a million new cases in the first week of December, even before the expected surge from Thanksgiving travel and interaction took effect. In Los Angeles, the number of infected health care workers doubled during the last week of November.

The vaccine, first administered to British residents on December 8, was touted to have minimum side effects, to work with people regardless of age, weight, or race, and to provide protection within 10 days. Promised to work at 95% effectiveness, many questioned why only 60% of Americans said they would readily take the vaccine. Why? Partially because the leader of the free world, more than a month after the election, still claimed he might be the next president and because he lied blatantly and incessantly during his four years in the White House about numerous topics, including the deadly nature of the disease and what was being done to combat it. "They've [vaccines] been severely politicized, especially in the U.S.," said Pfizer CEO Dr. Albert Bourla. "That makes people confused. They don't know who to believe and what to believe."[624]

If you don't believe it, listen to the friend of former Alabama GOP State Senator Larry Dixon, 78, who died after contracting COVID, along with his wife. "We messed up, we let our guard down," Dixon told his wife Gaynell on his deathbed, according to his good friend Dr. David Thrasher, a pulmonologist. Thrasher said Dixon contracted the disease while attending a social gathering with a few others. "Please tell everybody to be careful. This is real, and if you get diagnosed, get help immediately."[625]

Chapter 37: Life in the Real World Working for the Trump Administration

Whatever you do, work at it with all your heart, as working for the Lord, not for human masters, since you know that you will receive an inheritance from the Lord as a reward. It is the Lord Christ you are serving.

Colossians 3:23-24, New International Version

"They wanted her body, and they took her soul," said Debbie Robinson, suicide victim Morgan Robinson's mother. Robinson took her life after being gang-raped, then was refused help by the Army, who transferred her to another base without alerting the new commander of her traumatic abuse and fragile state of mind.[626] For me, a person whose great-grandfather, grandfather, father, and five uncles had all fought for their country, it was one of the few times I was personally and deeply ashamed of the institution. This atrocity was certainly not unique to the Trump administration, as far too many women who have believed in serving their nation have been harassed and assaulted, with little or no consequence. Trump has, though, time and time again, shown a disdain for the high calling of the U.S. military, labeling those who died "losers and suckers," while allegedly seeking to keep wounded vets out of sight during military parades.[627] Trump also failed to show up at a commemoration honoring fallen marines and soldiers from WWI in France due to "weather problems," though he was already in the country.[628] Pretty rich for someone who never served.

We live in a world where Florida police raid the home of a fired health official and whistleblower as a manner of intimidation, because she refused to falsify COVID numbers for the state. "It's time to speak up before another 17,000 people are dead," wrote scientist Rebecca Jones, formerly head of the Florida COVID tracking team. "You know this is wrong. You don't have to be a part of this. Be a hero. Speak out before it's too late." Granted, she accessed an account at an agency she no longer worked at, likely illegally. But did it warrant a swat team entering her home, guns drawn, at night, when her two children and husband were unsuspecting? Apparently not, at least according to a prominent Republican who resigned from a board he was appointed to, saying enough was enough.

"I have been increasingly alarmed by the governor's response to the COVID-19 pandemic," wrote Atty. Ron Filipkowski, former vice-chair of the 12th circuit Judicial Nominating Committee of Florida, the night after the raid on Jones's home surfaced. "I believe the policy of this state toward COVID is reckless and irresponsible … I have followed the events of Ms. Jones … and reviewed the search warrant that led to her home being raided. Based on what I have seen and read, I find these actions unconscionable."[629]

Tragically, on the same day, December 9, 2020, 3,064 people died from coronavirus-related illnesses, an all-time U.S. high.

Why did this rankle me to my core? Several reasons, but one was the fact that I, in my role as the regional public affairs specialist, felt constantly cloaked in a heavy pall because I knew my government, the country that I loved, should and could be doing more to protect its citizens, especially its most vulnerable. I stayed in government, in what I saw as a very special role for 25 years, because I cared about helping people gain access to health care, and become empowered to live better lives. It had become a calling.

Instead, we were caught up in a political morass that gave new meaning to Dr. Joseph E. Lowery's "51st State of Denial," and continued to lose precious lives each day that could have been saved.

Meanwhile, 17 states backed a Texas lawsuit to overturn elections in battleground states, including Georgia which, I proudly say daily, broke the seemingly impenetrable red wall of conservative states in the deep South. Utah, Montana, North Dakota, South Dakota, Nebraska, Kansas, Oklahoma, Missouri, Arkansas, Mississippi, Alabama, Tennessee, Indiana, West Virginia, South Carolina, and Florida, all vowing to support efforts to overturn elections in other states. What planet have you dropped me onto? I thought this was the United States of America, but surely I'm mistaken. I'm used to the United States being a structurally racist, sexist nation, but at least I recognized it and acted accordingly. But this is clearly Trumpland, or will be until we wretch it from his gnarly, arthritic hands. Trump even asked his former nemesis, Ted Cruz, whose father he accused of being part of the Kennedy assassination, to ask the Supreme Court to overturn those election results, if they agreed to hear the case. Cruz, by the way, called Trump a "sniveling coward," while Trump derisively called Cruz "Lyin' Ted." Former VP Al Gore might not have been widely respected until years after he became one of the first to warn about climate change, but unlike the 126 MAGA House Republicans in Congress in 2020, he graciously accepted his defeat in the razor-thin 2000 presidential election for the good of the country, which was decided, ultimately, by a few hanging chads.[630]

Fifteen thousand more people died in the U.S. in early December due to COVID. Also, with the initial global vaccination rollouts taking place in Britain, the first significant side effects surfaced: major reactions for people with allergies. This, quite frankly, is exactly why I had some hesitancy, though I intended to get a vaccination when it first became available to me within a few months. I'd rather know, as much as possible, what the pluses and minuses were. Eighty percent of U.S. counties reported more people traveling for Thanksgiving in 2020 than in 2019. That is understandable, as people were on lockdown for ten months of the year, though traveling was clearly still incredibly dangerous. COVID also continued to ravage Latino communities, as they served as a high percentage of the staff in meat packing plants and agriculture fields. They also often packed more people into vehicles, lived more people per square foot in close quarters, and were uninsured, often due to documentation issues. In Los Angeles, they were two times as likely as whites to get infected. Far too often in our society, we undervalue the hard-working manual and blue-collar laborers who do the work most of us are unwilling to do in order to provide benefits and services many of us take for granted until they disappear.

As Christmas 2020 approached, a Black dad, Chris Kennedy, erected a Black blowup Santa in his yard in an attempt to ensure that his daughter could "see herself" represented in every way positive.

"Please remove your Negro Santa Claus. You should not try to deceive children into believing that I am a Negro," an anonymous letter said. However, after Kennedy posted it on Facebook, neighbors in North Little Rock, Arkansas, responded positively, with many white families erecting their own Black Santas throughout the community.[631] Responses like these are what keep me hopeful about what I want to believe is the overall goodness and humanity of most Americans.

Suddenly finding his spine as the Trump administration was winding down and he knew his legacy would be impacted, CDC Director Robert Redfield began to speak plainly. "Probably for the next 60-90 days, we'll lose more people every day than we did [on] 9/11," Redfield said as 2020 drew to a close.

The case Trump called, "the most important in U.S. history" died with a whimper as the U.S. Supreme Court, including the three justices he appointed, determined that the case brought by the state of Texas, and co-signed by Missouri, Arkansas, Louisiana, Mississippi, South Carolina, and Utah, to overturn the election was rejected.[632] The court ruled that Texas "did not have standing" to overturn elections in Georgia, Michigan, Wisconsin, and Pennsylvania, which turned the tide for a Biden election.

Nearly 900,000 Americans filed for unemployment insurance the week of December 5. Over 19 million Americans were unemployed, with their checks set to expire the week after Christmas.

Also, on December 13, the same day UPS and FedEx were expected to begin rolling out vaccines to locations across the country, Mississippi announced it was out of ICU beds.

On December 13, more than one million vaccine doses were distributed to all 50 states, with shots expected to go into arms the next day, even as the U.S. death toll neared 300,000 and infections topped 16 million, including one million in the past four days. All this as eight million more Americans have slipped into a state of poverty since the summer of 2020.

On December 14, 2020, America's first health care workers began getting vaccinated, beginning in Queens, NY. All states and Puerto Rico were expected to receive their initial portion of the 2.9 million vaccine doses at 636 locations by the following Wednesday. Another 2.9 million Pfizer vaccines were expected to be delivered by Christmas week, perhaps one of the most cherished presents ever. It was also the eighth straight day of record-setting numbers of hospitalizations due to COVID. New Jersey recorded the highest COVID death rate in the nation, while Los Angeles County alone reported a 370% hospitalization increase in the last month. Simultaneously, due to the mixed messages coming from the Trump administration, not to mention a history of lack of transparency, 39% of Americans said they probably, or definitely, would not get vaccinated.[633] That is a painful example of the nation's sordid history with marginalized populations, the politicization of a pandemic, and the unintended consequences of the Trump administration's approach to a pandemic.

At the same time, Trump's White House, which had proclaimed that they would get the first vaccine, backed down on Tuesday, apparently shamed by their latest display of white pomposity. William Barr, perhaps the most caustic, dangerous, and dutifully damaging attorney general in modern history, announced his resignation.

"We need to spend every minute we have between now and vaccine availability building trust," said Dr. Richard Feifer, chief health officer at Genesis, which runs 300 nursing homes in 24 states.[634]

Mississippi and California were essentially out of ICU beds, even as California restaurants disobeyed state law, faced with the excruciating choice of saving others, or economically saving themselves.[635]

At the same time, our political world continued its free fall. What kind of "leader" fails to concede after being so soundly defeated while working his zealot followers into such a frenzy that the state of Michigan couldn't open its state house due to armed protesters threatening to overrun the building? In addition, Arizona disclosed its electoral vote in a secret location due to concerns about disruption or potential violence.

Nearly 180,000 children contracted COVID during the second week of December 2020. Mitch McConnell finally acknowledged Biden as president-elect on December 15, as world leaders continued to do, yet others, including Trump, defiantly refused to do so.

"I said two years ago that I do not believe this man intends to give up this office," pointed out South Carolina Congressman James Clyburn. "I have really been grappling with this, trying to figure out what allows independently elected officials to be co-opted this way. All of a sudden, elected officials seem to be unable to exert their constitutional responsibilities."[636]

On the same day, at least 12 states alerted The Feds that they did not have enough money to administer vaccines, or conduct contact tracing. Pointing to Operation Warp Speed, the effort to get an approved vaccine to all Americans: "It's as if we have invested in those aircraft, but we're unwilling to pay for the fuel to get them off the ground," said Lisa Macon Harrison of rural North Carolina's Granville-Vance District.[637]

In California, at least 60 morgue trailers were on stand-by, some located outside hospitals, as nurses were being warned they were in "disaster mode." At least 5,000 body bags were ordered, in addition to a request to the Department of Defense for 200 more medical personnel.[638]

In many ways, Operation Warp Speed was a colossal success. Securing agreements with nine different vaccine manufacturers, utilizing three different platforms, the U.S. invested $18.4 billion in vaccine development to protect its citizens, resulting in unprecedented lives saved and illnesses prevented. Alas, had this only been done a few months earlier, when the denier-in-chief was insisting COVID was not serious and would "disappear," we could have saved well over 100,000 American lives.[639]

In Chicago, another policing injustice finally came to light, nearly two years after it occurred. Anjanette Young, a Black social worker, said she had just returned home from working her shift at a hospital. She was undressing when 12 cops, led by white Sergeant Alex Wolinski, broke down her door and barged in, allegedly looking for drugs. Naked and handcuffed, she repeatedly told the all-male squad they had the wrong house. Eventually, they put a coat on her shoulders, yet left her front uncovered. Two hours later, they left, telling her they believed her story. The city only released the video after a judge ordered them to, nearly two years after the 2019 raid. Obviously, this would almost never happen to a white woman in an all-white neighborhood. Four years later, in 2023, the Chicago Police Board voted 5-3 to fire Wolinski.[640]

In December 2020, major league baseball finally chose to honor and "give" equal credence to the Negro Leagues, long after most of the stalwarts had died. The accomplishments of Cool Papa Bell, Satchel Paige, Josh Gibson, and others, will now be incorporated into the records, alongside those of Ty Cobb, Pete Rose, and Babe Ruth.[641]

By December 14, there were ten more consecutive days of record hospitalizations, with more than 112,000 COVID patients nationwide. The previous day – December 15 – 3,019 Americans died of COVID-related illnesses. Nevertheless, virulent protests across the country insisted that closures were wrong.

In Dodge City, Kansas, the mayor resigned because of threats to her life for implementing a mask mandate. Two years earlier, during the 2018 midterm elections, some Dodge City residents who were newly registered voters were directed outside of the city limits to vote, more than a mile from any bus stop. "I didn't know this could get worse, and it did: 'Hey, let's move the site and not tell new registrants where they are supposed to go,'" said Johnny Dunlap, chairman of the Ford County Democratic Party.[642]

Approximately 50 million Americans went hungry at Christmas 2020, and 19 million collected unemployment.

On December 17, 3,665 Americans died, 113,069 more were hospitalized, and there were 247,403 active cases. The total cases had *more than* doubled in the two months, from eight million on October 17, to 17 million on December 17. In southern California, there were zero ICU beds left. Patients were going into cardiac arrest in the hallways of some hospitals, dying before they could even get into a room with a bed. There were 100,000 new cases recorded in the previous 24 hours. The state had a goal of vaccinating 6,000 health care workers by Christmas. FEMA, along with others, rushed 80 health care workers to the state. We lost 17,000 Americans in the previous week, a record 3,600 on October 17, alone. Incomprehensible! Trump, meantime, continued to tout the anti-malarial drug hydroxychloroquine, which he called a "game changer," though it actually proved to have increased the chance of death for those who took it on six continents.[643]

There were hiccups to the life-saving drugs. A couple of health care professionals had extreme reactions to the Pfizer vaccine in Alaska. Several states, including Iowa, complained that they received as much as 30% less vaccine than they had been promised, though The Feds insisted that was not accurate.

"I'm not going to sugarcoat this: we are getting crushed," said USC Medical Center Chief Medical Officer Dr. Brad Spellberg. His facility, like many in Southern California, had no available hospital beds, and had patients either outside in the cold in tents, or waiting in ambulances, or hospital hallways to be treated.[644] In some hospitals, they even had to put patients in beds in the gift shops.

COVID, of course, was not the only public health emergency the nation was grappling with. In Fulton County, Georgia, home of Atlanta, one in six families faced food insecurity. The story was being repeated across the nation.

Remember that back in March 2020, POTUS, who said nothing in 700-plus tweets about the suffering and COVID-19 death angel ravaging his nation, finally told the unvarnished truth, "It is what it is."

"They [Americans] are dying, that's true," Trump said. "And you have … it is what it is. But that doesn't mean we aren't doing everything we can. It's under control as much as you can control it. This is a horrible plague."[645] Compounding matters, more states complained that they were being told by The Feds that their expected doses for the following week had been cut.

"I failed, I am adjusting, I am fixing, and we will move on from there," admitted General Gustave F. Perna in the midst of a herky-jerky rollout of COVID supplies, testing, and vaccine disbursement. Perna, a former four-star general, was appointed by Trump as the chief operating officer of Operation Warp Speed, the federal government's public-private partnership for the accelerated development, manufacturing, and distribution of the COVID-19 vaccines.[646]

A glimmer of light burst through the pall of death and despair, however. The state of Colorado, where two unarmed Black men had been killed in 2019, Elijah McClain and De'Von Bailey, passed the Enhance Law Enforcement Integrity Act. The bill was designed to hold rogue law enforcement officials in Colorado accountable, especially during encounters with young men of color, by eliminating the qualified immunity that provides virtual blanket protection for officer shootings.[647] The tragedy is that it took two more innocent Black lives to effect the change.

Fourteen million U.S. households faced eviction at the end of the year, including Cierra Senegal, 20, mother of a two-year-old. She lost her job in October due to COVID.[648]

Nationwide, at least 900 hospitals had hit 90% of capacity as of December 18. Nursing homes, though containing only about .004 percent of the nation's population, had endured an amazing 40% of all COVID deaths. The goal, with Moderna and Pfizer vaccines now available, was to have CVS and Walgreens vaccinate seven million nursing home residents and staff quickly and methodically, in over 75,000 facilities across the U.S.

By December 20, 2020, the CDC determined that the next priority group to get the COVID vaccine, following health care workers and nursing home residents and staff, would be seniors 75 and older. Moderna vaccines were shipped across the nation; but just when there was reason to exhale a bit, a new, more easily transmitted strain of COVID emerged in the United Kingdom and Denmark.

At least one major California hospital was running at 270% capacity. Even the famed Rose Bowl was officially relocated to Texas, due to COVID's devastating impact on California. Eighty-four million Americans were estimated to travel over the Christmas break. The same day, a $900 billion COVID relief bill was finally passed, supplying $600 for all adults, while extending the $300 per week unemployment checks. Assistance for renters, food relief, and help for small businesses were all part of the package.

South Carolina Congressman Jim Clyburn was interviewed after his subpoena of Azar and Redfield regarding documents obtained in December 2020 by the subcommittee. They revealed that over a period of four months, as coronavirus cases and deaths rose around the country, Trump administration appointees attempted to "interfere with scientific work conducted by career officials" at the CDC and "block at least 13 scientific reports related to the virus."⁶⁴⁹

Meanwhile, in the real world, life totally changed for almost every American citizen in terms of where they could go, and with whom. A young relative was asked, "Are you going to church, or watching it on TV?" The seven-year-old responded: "We're watching church on TV because some people are sick with the virus. Dad, does Jesus have the virus?"

"I would like African Americans to know that this [vaccination] is something that we must do," insisted Clyburn, while acknowledging the historical mistreatment and mistrust Black people harbored, with good reason, for the American medical system, after getting his own COVID shots.

"This [COVID] is another disaster waiting to happen," said then-New York Governor Andrew Cuomo. "Why are we doing nothing?"

"If you walk through my hospital, you would not feel like you were in America," said a California doctor, Armand Dorian, of USC Verdugo Hills Hospital.⁶⁵⁰

The first wave of the Moderna virus, according to HHS Secretary Azar, would go to 3,500 sites, more than the Pfizer vaccine.

Life is funny sometimes. I remember 60 years ago when I was ashamed of my Georgia roots. Yes, I was very naïve, viewing the state through youthful eyes. And now – though not for the first time – I'm fiercely proud of my home state, with the election of progressive candidates, Senators Raphael Warnock and Jon Ossoff, and President Biden. Georgia, long red, was now, at the very least, starkly purple.

I was sick and tired of the "radical" label Loeffler and Perdue placed on Ossoff and Warnock that I almost called

Earl (vomit) every time I saw them. The problem, frankly, especially for Warnock, is that Black men can't be honest about America's racist history in America. If they do, it's like committing political suicide. One commercial chastises Warnock for his criticism of Israel, saying he compared "our ally, Israel," to a racist country. Why? Because he insisted that "Palestinian Lives Matter." As we live through the near annihilation of Gaza in 2023, Warnock's – and much of young America's – contention that Palestinian lives do matter, as much as Israeli lives, has never rung truer.

The year 2020 became the deadliest in U.S. history. COVID deaths lagged only behind cancer and heart disease, with three million fatalities, more than 2,600 deaths every 24 hours. The U.S. recorded one million new COVID cases in only four days during the week of Christmas 2020. Tennessee, one of the eight states in Region IV of HHS, our region, had the highest infection rate in the country in late December.

"It's embarrassing that a country that routinely calls itself the wealthiest in the world [takes] nine months to come up with $600," said Christy Gatos of Delaware, referring to the proposed $600 stimulus check for Americans earning less than $75,000 a year. "Six hundred dollars is the amount of money rich people think poor people think is a lot of money."[651]

Three weeks after the Trump administration separated children from their parents at the various U.S. southern borders, 600-plus children still had not been reunited with their parents. A social services group, Seneca Family Agencies, sought to put the families back together, even as doctors say they will suffer "irreversible trauma." The Trump administration refused to fund the group, which provides mental health care to families, until a judge ordered them to do so. That, frankly, is just one of the myriad examples of why voters rejected Trump in 2020 for a more compassionate Biden, who liked him or not, believed him "too old" or not, earnestly showed empathy in sensitive situations. To Trump, the children separated from their families were political tools, not people to be treated with humanity and dignity, even as they laid it all on the line for a chance at a better life.

By the end of 2020, two in five Americans were experiencing mental health issues due to COVID.[652]

Dr. Susan Moore of Indiana charged her attending physician with racist treatment. "I was crushed. He made me feel like I was a drug addict, and he knew I was a physician."[653] Moore later died of COVID, largely because her doctor refused to believe her. This white doctor, exhibiting a total lack of respect for a fellow physician who was a Black woman, the most disrespected of Americans, is a clear and present example of white pomposity.

"This [Moore's death] was devastating, this was me. This speaks to the heart of implicit bias," said Dr. Matifadza Hlatshwayo Davis of the John Cochran VA Medical Center in St. Louis.[654]

A seventy-one-year-old Black man, Jethro Devane, was ordered out of his home, naked, at gun point in Rock Hill, South Carolina, by police who said they were looking for four teens. Demanding entry to the home at 4 a.m., Officer Vincent Mentesana cursed at DeVane and told him he "didn't want to talk to him."[655] White pomposity, I tell you ... even from those who want to be white. Would this have happened to an elderly white homeowner?

Affirming the compassion and goodwill that most Americans harbor, community fridges have popped up all over the country, storing extra food from restaurants for people to freely access.

*

Following Trump's pardons of convicted associates Roger Stone and John Manafort, one GOP senator was willing to call a spade a spade. "This is rotten to the core," said Republican Ben Sasse, pointing to Trump's pardon of 26 people on the way out the door, including QAnon provocateurs, who Sasse said "flagrantly and repeatedly violated the law and harmed Americans."[656]

Comic and social satirist Hasan Minaj asked Stacey Abrams (whose masterful organizing job, along with others', ushered in the election of both Warnock and Ossoff) if she was on a list of Biden vice presidential candidates. "There's no reason not to join the ticket as vice president if somebody asks you," she said.[657] The issue, for Abrams, had absolutely nothing to do with her expertise, political acumen, or credentials. Abrams' challenge, frankly, was being a strong, large, dark-skinned Black woman.

HHS's pledge on December 6 to vaccinate 20 million people by the end of December fell woefully short. As of December 28, nearly 9.5 million doses had been delivered throughout the U.S., but only one million had reached the arms of patients. Moncef Slaoui, chief scientific advisor of Operation Warp Speed, acknowledged that shots in the arm were moving "slower than we thought."[658]

At the end of 2020, there was another stark reminder of the difference between the U.S. and some other nations. New Zealand, about the size and population of South Carolina, suffered 25 COVID deaths after imposing a total shutdown. South Carolina, on the other hand, lost over 5,000 souls after admonitions and advice, but no strict rules.

White pomposity has not gone away, even with the Trump defeat in November 2020. In some ways, it has accelerated.

A young white woman accused the 14-year-old son of a jazz musician of stealing her cell phone at a hotel in New

York. The hotel manager accepted the white woman's interpretation of what happened, though the accuser had assaulted the stunned youth, who had not taken the cell phone, as was seen in the video.[659]

By the end of December, more than a month after Trump lost to Biden, a new strain of the virus, which emerged in England, and was supposedly 70% more transmissible, was producing hot spots in the U.S.

Trump promised 20 million vaccines by the end of 2020. There were 11 million delivered by the end of the year, but unbelievably, only two million doses had reached the arms of Americans. Meanwhile, 3,706 people died of COVID-related causes on December 29, and the nation roared toward 400,000 deaths, with COVID finishing as the third highest cause of American deaths, behind cancer. This was consistently an administration that over promised and under delivered.

In a stark contrast before the politicization of science, in New York City, they vaccinated six million people in one month in 1947, including 500,000 in a single day.[660] The difference? Vaccinations weren't politicized in those days; instead, they were a way to protect the nation and its citizens.

*

White pomposity: Trump – as late as 2023 – simply did not know how to lose like a gentleman, much less like a leader.

In late 2020, White House attorney Pat Cipollone told Trump, "There was no constitutional authority for [overturning the election] that was being discussed."[661] Attorneys Sidney Powell and John Eastman, among the group that VP Mike Pence would later call Trump's "gaggle of crackpot lawyers that kept telling him what his itching ears wanted to hear," disagreed.[662] Even Trump lapdog Bill

Barr, on his way out the door after protecting POTUS since assuming the job in 2018, said he believed Russia was behind the massive election hack of the U.S. He also said there was "no need" to enact martial law to further investigate the elections that went for Biden in four battleground states. By early December, despite scouring the contested elections, Barr announced, "We have seen no fraud that could overturn the results of the election."[663]

"The violence and elements of Trumpism [aren't] going to disappear," said Jason Johnson, MNSBC contributor and Morgan State professor, on the announcement that Josh Hawley would challenge the election of Biden on the Senate floor on January 6. "You can draw a straight line from Proud Boys to white nationalist violence, to an increasing segment of the GOP that does not believe in democracy. There is no democracy other than keeping Republicans in power. They do not believe in anything other than white minority rule. That's what the Republican Party has become."[664]

Wins and losses: Feds declined to prosecute police who killed 12-year-old Tamir Rice, who was holding a toy pellet gun on a playground when someone called the police.[665] As the police car roared into the park, the boy, who apparently reached into his waistband, according to the surveillance video, was shot within two seconds of their arrival. Police said Officer Tim Loehmann believed Tamir had a real gun. He had been released from his previous suburban police job after supervisors wrote that he "lacked the maturity" and displayed a "pattern of indiscretion and of not following instructions." Two officers, including Officer Joshua Janes, who is accused of lying about why they raided the home of Breonna Taylor, were fired nine months after she was killed. Biden Attorney, General Merrick Garland, charged four of the officers involved with civil rights violations.[666] Myles Cosgrove, the officer who fired the fatal shots in the early morning 2020, no-knock invasion, was fired from the Louisville Police Department for use-of-force violations. He now has another job in a nearby Carroll County department.[667] Policeman Adam Coy, who shot and killed Andre Hill, 47, in Columbus, Ohio, with a smartphone in his hand, was fired. Officers handcuffed him and offered no aid for five minutes. "Truth is the best friend of justice, and the grand jury here found the truth," said Ohio Attorney General Dave Yost. "Andre Hill should not be dead."[668] His family would later receive a $10 million settlement from the city. How many of these Black people would have been killed had they been white? I couldn't help but ask myself.

Inequities still abound in our nation at the conclusion of 2020, in many places, including counties lacking SANEs (Sexual Assault Nurse Examiners). In Texas, only 28% of the counties have SANEs, while in Washington, D.C., there are only nine in all. How do we expect assaulted women to come forward with these scant numbers and lack of accessibility to counselors?

In Petroglyph National Monument in Albuquerque, New Mexico, Daniel House was repeatedly tased because he left the trail to pray, which he said he regularly does. "I come here to pray and speak to my Pueblo ancestor relatives," House wrote in the caption to the video. "Here, you will see a white man abuse his power. Both men pulled tasers on me after the first one couldn't keep me down." House said the National Park Service officer violated his religious rights, and he promised to sue.[669]

On December 29, the nation recorded 3,740 COVID deaths, a U.S. record.

Politically astute, Trump tweeted that "unless they [Republicans] have a death wish," they'll vote for the $2,000 stimulus.

On New Year's Eve, we heard from a dear friend that the hospital had called and told the family to come and say their goodbyes to their husband and father. He had been there for less than a week before COVID claimed his life. This was the first person I was close to who succumbed to the deadly disease.

The deaths of our heroes simply added to the grief and loneliness brought on by COVID isolation and the unsettled nature of our political divide. Charlie Pride, Janet DuBois, Bonnie Pointer, Dawn Wells, Ellis Marsalis, Little Richard, Bob Gibson, Whitey Ford, Tom Seaver, Curley Neal, Lou Brock, Kobe Bryant, Kenny Rogers, Bill Withers, Johnny Nash, Joe Clark, David Dinkins, Katherine Johnson, Betty Wright, Helen Reddy, Olivia De Havilland, Kirk Douglas, Chadwick Bozeman, Hugh Downs, John Lewis, all had gone on to meet their maker in 2020.

As a new B.117 COVID strain emerged in the U.S., two national guardsmen were dispatched to Good Samaritan Society Nursing Home in Colorado, where all 26 residents, along with most of the staff, contracted COVID.[670]

"It's like a war zone, and we're asking for help, and help is not coming," a tearful California nurse said, as 230 people a day died, and infections skyrocketed from 1,200 per day at the end of November to 13,000 in December. She added, "People are dying like flies, we're full, we're at mass capacity."[671]

75% of adults 28-34 suffered from anxiety through the pandemic, with one in four having thoughts of suicide, according to the MMWR.[672]

Chapter 38: An American January for the Ages

"There's no way I lost Georgia. No way. Because of what you've done to the president, lots of people are not going to vote. They hate the governor, and they hate the secretary of state. Stacey Abrams is as dishonest as they come."

Trump's phone call to Georgia Secretary of State Brad Raffensperger

In the U.S., 344,000 Americans died of COVID-related illnesses in 2020, with over 3,700 on each of the last two days of the year. Fewer than three million doses went into American arms by the close of 2020, while 12.4 million doses were distributed, far below the promised 20 million doses. Operation Warp Speed became Operation Snail's Speed. "We really need to rethink, or think more intently, about how we're going to reach out and help the states," said Dr. Anthony Fauci, as Kansas, Mississippi, and Alabama had the lowest percentages of vaccine dose administration. Wisconsin, South Dakota, and New Mexico had the highest, as mayors and governors pleaded for more help and more funding.[673]

At the same time, one-third of all Americans who were out of work were in the travel and tourism business. Grocery stores, the heart of our critical supply line during the pandemic, experienced 20,070 grocery workers infected in 2020, including 850 in Los Angeles County during the last two months of 2020.

As 2021 dawned, the new strain of the coronavirus had reared its ugly head, just as California hospital CEO Robert Kim-Farley called the pandemic a "viral tsunami."[674]

Stephen Brandenberg, a self-proclaimed conspiracy theorist pharmacist in Wisconsin, admitted to intentionally spoiling up to 570 doses of the precious COVID vaccine. The people who were administered the vaccine, which was kept out of the highly calibrated freezers for two nights in a row, did not know whether the vaccines they received were any good, further shaking many Americans' trust in the process. Brandenburg, who told police he "believed the vaccine could harm people and change their DNA," was sentenced to three years supervised release, and required to pay $84,000 to the Aurora Medical Center for the ruined drugs.[675]

Some countries were told they might not get vaccines at all in 2021, unless they were being used as test subjects for new vaccines. It is still difficult to understand fully why a handful of the world's countries (14%), including the U.S. and Canada, controlled 53% of its global vaccine supply. Dozens of countries vaccinated most, or all of their populations, even before some poorer nations, including several in Africa, received a single dose.

Americans, in a time of great need, benefited from the love and care of good-hearted people. Gloria Scott, 73, who called an electrician to fix a light socket, ended up with a rebuilt house, thanks to John Kinney of Weymouth, MA, whose mission became a non-profit, Gloria's Gladiators, named after the first recipient.[676]

No rational case could be made that Georgia senatorial candidate Jon Ossoff took Black or young voters for granted. He hired 2,000 part-time mobilizers to focus on getting out the vote in the under-30 communities, with a special emphasis on minority Georgians. That, in addition to numerous other strong initiatives, helped to get 113,000 new voters to the polls days in advance of the November 5th runoff election that would determine the balance in the U.S. Senate. Thirty percent of those voters were under 30.

Trump pardoned former Prince George's, Maryland, police officer Stephanie Mohr after she unleashed an attack dog on an undocumented person.[677] This same Trump, two years later, warned Americans that immigrants were "poisoning the blood" of the nation in a speech that some likened to one from Adolph Hitler. "They come from Africa, they come from Asia, they come from South America," Trump said, lamenting what he said was a "border catastrophe."[678]

Twenty states bucked the trend of paying Americans a minimum wage of only $7.50 per hour by moving the bottom line to $10 in 26 jurisdictions to help the lowest-paid workers better navigate inflation and the ever-increasing cost of living.

In Tennessee, citizens lined up for hours for the vaccination, only to be turned away. In Florida, at *The Villages*, one of the nation's largest senior communities, seniors as old as 85 waited as many as nine hours to receive their first vaccinations.

In a case of sweet irony during an administration where the president's main issue was controlling immigration, Santiago Potes, from Columbia University, became the first DACA Rhodes Scholarship recipient, matriculating to Oxford University as Trump pushed for a second term.[679]

Houston had 750 doses of the vaccine, but their call center received 250,000 calls. In California, one hospital reported an eight-hour wait for space inside to unload COVID patients from ambulances waiting outside. Many states reported one in five of their health care workers were declining to take the vaccine when offered.

On January 2, three days before the most pivotal senate runoff in U.S. history, Trump called the Georgia Secretary of State and asked him to "just find 11,780 votes, which is one more than we have, because we won the state," in his illegal quest to to overturn his jarring loss to break the deep red wall of Southern states dominated by the GOP for a generation. During the hour-plus call, Trump reminded Raffensperger that "he's a Republican," while bringing up rumors about Dominion machines being swapped out and boxes of ballots missing. "We won by hundreds of thousands of votes. There's no way I lost Georgia. No way. Because of what you've done to the president, lots of people are not going to vote. They hate the governor, and they hate the secretary of state. Stacey Abrams is as dishonest as they come." [680]

Nobody likes to lose, especially the privileged and the great. But damn! Everybody loses sometimes, right? Trump said little or nothing about the 350,000 American lives lost, or the 20 million more infected. One in 16 Americans were at this point infected by COVID, up from one in every 1,000 a week earlier. As of January 3, 2021, roughly one in every 100 Americans had been diagnosed. Feeling desperate and pressured, Perna was now considering administering only a half-dose to people up to 55 years of age. Still, Trump fought desperately to overturn an election he decisively lost.

Republicans Loeffler and Perdue, working to paint Ossoff and Warnock as "too liberal for Georgia," took the rhetoric even a notch higher, insisting that if "we lose Georgia, we lose the country," in their dozens of television, radio, and print ads.

Personally, I'm deeply conflicted with my people who tell me they have never voted before. No, let me be totally honest. They piss me off. Somehow, they have failed to get the message chronicling all the lives and careers that have been sacrificed to ensure they have the right to vote. No excuse – including they no longer believe in the system – is good enough.

"Mr. President, the problem with the data that you have is [that it's] wrong," Raffensperger said, as Trump lost nearly 50 court cases trying to prove voter fraud.[681]

"I only need 11,000 votes. Fellas, I need 11,000 votes. Give me a break." Apparently, the 18th time [phone call] wasn't the charm. "There's nothing wrong with saying, ah, that you recalculated," pleaded Trump.[682]

Perhaps Mitt Romney, himself a Republican, said it best: "I could never have imagined seeing these things in the greatest democracy in the world. Has ambition so eclipsed principle?"

"I don't know why he still wants the job, [because] he doesn't want to do the work," said Biden. True that, prez.

D.C. planned to activate as many as 300 national guardsmen to ensure that protesters and activists – particularly ardent Trump supporters – didn't enact a reign of terror.

L.A. County, experiencing 25 deaths per day from COVID at Thanksgiving, saw those numbers soar to 133 deaths per day, only two weeks later. Nevertheless, sick and tired of being quarantined, 1.3 million Americans flew home on January 4.

Dr. King may not have said it first, but he is best known for it: "Truth crushed to earth will rise again."

It's hard to match the euphoria of Barack Obama in 2009, smiling triumphantly as he and his beautiful family took the stage, looking out at America from a position never before experienced by an African American, as he was just declared president of the United States. That moment was long overdue and, in some ways, a partial culmination toward the dream of full voter participation that had been a hallmark of the SCLC, the organization of a few dozen Black preachers, including Dr. King, Dr. Abernathy, Dr. Shuttlesworth, Dr. C.K. Steele, and Dr. Lowery, my old boss, co-founded and gave their lives to and for, in 1957.

Yet for me, I will tell you, the Biden victory that blasted a hole in the great red wall, followed by the stunning, grind-it-out victories of both Raphael Warnock, the first Black senator from the Deep South, and Jon Ossoff, a Jew who became the youngest U.S. senator, was every bit as relieving, as historic, as exhilarating. Exhaling, I thought, democracy is safe, at least for another four years. Bursting with pride, my family and I celebrated that night like when Obama won in 2008, or when the city of Atlanta was named host of the 1996 Centennial Olympic games.

From a professional, vocational perspective, it meant I would not have to walk into my building and my office, and look at the photo of a gloating Donald Trump anymore. Nor, beside it, would I see photos of people, including VP Pence, committed to the agenda of dismantling the law of the land, the ACA, or separating children from parents at the border.

I was also in the euphoria of the moment early Tuesday morning, January 6, 2009, despite GOP Senate leader Mitch McConnell's proclamation that his number one mission was to make the nation's first Black president, Barack Obama, a one-term president.

As I watched the votes continue to pile up and new states going either for Trump or Biden, while others seemed to languish in the balance, too close to call, I asked myself, knowing we had to work the next morning, "Should I go to sleep?" A more salient question was ... could I go to sleep?

"I'm going to wake some people up," I proclaimed in the wee hours of the night, as Dekalb County registered 9,100 new votes for Ossoff to vault him into the lead over Perdue, with still 10,000 votes to go. "They can cuss me out tomorrow!"

"Black votes matter! Black lives matter! Black people matter," one of my relatives said, triumphantly thrusting her arms into the air after Warnock was projected the winner in Georgia in the runoff election.

Euphoric, at about 2:20 a.m., we shouted, skyrocketed by the news that Ossoff had gone ahead by 9,300 votes in the latest batch of ballots in hometown Dekalb County. I couldn't help but sing out the words of a dearly departed soul favorite from the '70s, Sugarfoot of the Ohio Players: "It's over, it's over now!"

That night, I thought about my desire, some sixty years earlier, to escape Georgia and the South. Naive enough to not realize that racism and hegemony were not strictly a Southern thing, I wanted to get away from overt racism, hate, self-hate, brutality, and all that was encapsulated by Jim Crow.

By election day, for the two critical senate runoffs in Georgia, many eyes were focused on control of the Senate, not COVID, especially after the president tried days earlier to convince Secretary of State Raffensperger to "find him" 11,801 votes. COVID, however, had hardly gone away or even slowed down. In certain parts of the country, particularly out West, ambulance drivers who picked up COVID patients were told to make decisions regarding whether the patients who could not be revived within 10 minutes should be brought to the hospitals, where patients likely would wait up to eight hours before being seen.

Though doing better, by January 4, only 4.5 of the promised 20 million vaccines for the end of 2020 had been administered, even as 30% of all health care workers declined to be vaccinated.

One man, though he represented thousands, said he should have paid attention to the warnings. "I didn't wear a mask," said Chuck Stacey, an IT firm owner from Inlet, Florida, who was strapped to a ventilator, his eyes welling with tears. "I didn't. I believed this was just the flu. You don't want to end up like me. Do it for your children and your loved ones. Do it for yourself."[683]

"These folks have to decide whether they still believe in democracy," said Rick Wilson of the Lincoln Project, commenting on the Republicans' stunning loss of two senate seats in Georgia and the role of the Lincoln Project, a group of Republicans sick and tired of Trump, in the campaign to unseat him. "Every once in a while, you've got to take on the biggest bully in the barnyard."[684]

As the soon-to-be youngest U.S. Senator, Jon Ossoff, moved solidly ahead of rich guy incumbent David Perdue at about 5 a.m. on January 6th, and a defining end to exhausting run-off to settle the November 4th election, I crawled off to bed exhausted but elated. After all, my state, Georgia, and more specifically, my predominantly Black, well-educated, middle-class county, Dekalb, had delivered the clinching numbers to bring Ossoff from 20,000 votes behind, with 97% of the state total in at the 11th hour. That meant that both he and Raphael Warnock, a preacher and the 11th of twelve children, would win Senate seats and make history. Their historic elections, along with the shocking Biden victory over Trump on November 4, smashed a giant hole in the daunting Republican power structure in the South and gave Georgia two Democratic senators and a Democratic president for the first time in decades. So yes, after answering the door-to-election canvassers from

Pennsylvania, Ohio, North Carolina, Georgia, and New York for the past two months, not to mention all the calls that went to voice mail and the two trees' worth of mail that came daily, I was feeling about as well as a man could feel as I trudged off to bed, though I realized we were expecting some level of drama the next day as VP Pence oversaw the certification of the election for president, especially since his boss, 45, expected him to find a way to flip the script and name him the winner. In addition to the pride and exhilaration, I felt from knowing that people had been elected who *at least thought* that POCs should be treated as equal and who had to be somewhat accountable because of the broad range of progressives who had elected them, I was juiced about working for a more inclusive administration.

Little did I know, of course, what awaited the nation and the world on January 6th.

*

MSNBC's Joy Reid compared the kid gloves treatment of protesters who stormed the Capitol, breaking out windows and brandishing weapons inside, undeterred, to the police who strong-armed protesters in Baltimore protesting the treatment of Freddie Gray.

"What we see is that our system is more patient and indulgent with whiteness, while it criminalizes black behavior. What we see is that we have two different systems of justice and that they entirely depend on the color of your skin," said Sara Totonchi of the Southern Center for Human Rights.[685]

"Whose First Amendment rights are worthy of being respected and defended and whose First Amendment rights [are] constantly under attack?" asked Nse' Ufot of the New Georgia Project.[686]

Joy Reid said, "White Americans aren't afraid of the cops. They aren't even afraid of the cops when they commit insurrection. You aren't afraid of the police because the police are you."[687] This statement reminds me, frankly, of the age of the KKK and the White Citizens' Councils, who were sometimes policemen who carried their Klan gear in the trunk of their cars.

Claire McCaskill, former Missouri Senator and MSNBC political commentator, who knew she was sacrificing her seat, in part by voting against Supreme Court nominee Brett Kavanaugh, said this: "Can you imagine [how many lives would have been lost] had that been black people, or Black Lives Matter protesters, storming the Capitol today?" It was great, frankly, to hear a white conservative state the obvious truth: There would have been dozens, if not hundreds, slaughtered on January 6th, had the insurrectionists been Black. Others were blunter: "My mom said if you did this, you'd be shot," Beatrice Mando, who works for the district and attended BLM protests last year, said. "She is right. There would be hundreds dead, if not more, had this group been Black."[688] President-elect Biden, more politically correct, put it this way: "No one can tell me that if it had been a group of Black Lives Matter protesting yesterday, they wouldn't have been treated very, very differently from the mob of thugs that stormed the Capitol," he said.[689]

On January 8th, horrified by Trump's actions on January 6th, key Trump leaders, Labor Secretary Elaine Chao, the much-maligned (appropriately so) Education Secretary Betsy DeVos, former Chief of Staff Mick Mulvaney, and HHS' Elinore McCance-Katz, Assistant Secretary for the Substance Abuse and Mental Health Services Administration (SAMHSA), Matthew Pottinger, John Costello, Tyler Goodspeed, Stephanie Grisham, Rickie

Niceta, Sarah Matthews, and Eric Dreiband, all resigned. I guess even sycophants have their breaking point.

Others at HHS denounced the attempted coup of our government, but failed to rebuke the president, or leave their posts, even as President-elect Biden called the assault "one of the darkest days" in U.S. history. "These weren't protesters, don't dare call them protesters. They were a riotous mob, insurrectionists, domestic terrorists."[690]

Michelle Obama was equally pointed in her statement: The takeover of the U.S. Capitol "made it painfully clear that certain Americans are, in fact, allowed to denigrate the flag and symbols of our nation. They just got to look the right [white] way."[691]

None of us had ever seen such an assault on our regal Capitol – built, by the way, by Black slaves – which represents the heart and soul of democracy in the most esteemed country in the world. That's because an assault on the Capitol hadn't taken place since 1814, when the British burned it down.

The United States of America, known across the globe as the one nation where the peaceful transfer of power had never been questioned, or compromised, suddenly looked like a country in free fall. Much like back in 1964, when photos were sent across the world showing hotel manager James Brock pouring muriatic acid in the swimming pool as Black citizens sought to integrate St. Augustine, Florida's Munson Hotel, or 1963 when Birmingham unleashed water cannons and German Shepherds on children marching peacefully, the USA looked hypocritical, vulnerable, and ordinary. Or in 2019, when cameras caught police shooting a nonresistant and unarmed Philando Castile at a traffic stop, while his daughter and girlfriend watched in horror. Or when Derek Chauvin, using the entire force of his body, knelt on the neck of unarmed, prostrate George Floyd for 9:29 seconds, all on film, while mortified onlookers pleaded for the police to stop as Floyd hoarsely cried out, "I can't breathe." These instances stripped bare the long-held notion that the U.S. was the beacon of democracy, fairness, and opportunity for all Americans, with the Floyd, police-sanctioned execution launching a worldwide movement. The January 6th insurrection, in contrast, was a riot, as opposed to vulnerable, unarmed citizens asserting their agency and seeking to realize the rights the Constitution allegedly provided them. "Stop the steal, stop the steal," yelled hundreds of protesters, as they broke down the doors and windows and surged into the U.S. Capitol. Once inside, some even defecated on the floors. No rational American, on their worst day, could have envisioned what we witnessed and experienced on January 6th. This sacrilege was perpetrated and orchestrated by white people, or those who envisioned themselves as white, like Enrique Tarrio of the Proud Boys or John Earle Sullivan, who sought to blame Antifa for the carnage.[692] That, my friends, is white pomposity, perhaps at its worst.

Bill Barr said, "Orchestrating a mob to pressure Congress is inexcusable. The president's conduct yesterday was a betrayal of his office and supporters." Kind of like finding Jesus, huh? Where the hell was all this righteous indignation when you approved clearing the mall of BLM activists, so your then-boss could pose holding a Bible in front of a church?

"What I felt 24 hours ago in the Capitol behind us is something I hadn't felt since I was in Afghanistan," said Congressman Jason Crow, a former Army ranger. "To think that as a member of Congress, in 2021, in the U.S. Capitol, on the house floor, that I was preparing to fight my way out of the people's house against a mob, is beyond troubling."[693]

"Suppose this had been a Black Lives Matter rally?" asked Jeh Johnson, former Secretary of Homeland Security.

"Suppose this would have been people of color storming the Capitol?"

"When the looting starts, the shooting starts," Trump tweeted on May 29 when protests against the George Floyd execution took place in Milwaukee. Seven hours later, however, after finally being convinced by his staff that the January 6th insurrection was out of control, Trump tweeted: "Go home. We love you. You're very special."

QAnon had alerted its followers: Arm yourselves. January 6th is Independence Day! "[What] we saw in the Capitol was the internet come to life. We saw Proud Boys, QAnon followers, Militiamen, all assembling at the president's call," said NBC News reporter Brandy Zadrozny.[694]

"The intelligence was there that the threat was articulated and known," said former FBI Agent Frank Figliuzzi. You must ask yourselves, why those who counter[ed] the threat on the ground were not prepared to do so.[695]

At the same time that Americans were trying to understand if they still lived in the same nation they thought they knew only days earlier, epidemiologists determined that 59% of all new COVID cases were asymptomatic.[696] In California, hospitals began instituting Crisis Standards of Care, which included determining certain standards of treatment based on assessments of who had the best chance of survival. January 7 became the deadliest day of the pandemic, with 4,004 Americans claimed by the disease.

"We gather due to a selfish man's injured pride," said Utah Senator Mitt Romney, the day after the assault on the Capitol. "The best way we can show respect for the voters who were upset, is by telling them the truth."[697] The barrage of insurgents, a combination of Boogaloo Boys, Militiamen, Proud Boys, and others, including independent Trump loyalists, had made their intentions clear, as documented by the Anti-Defamation League three days earlier, known to anyone paying attention.[698] Trump's call to "march down to the Capitol and fight like hell," only stirred the frenzy to an unprecedented level.

Trump called the protesters of police injustice against unarmed Black Americans during the summer of 2020, those his troops sought to disperse with tear gas and pepper spray, "thugs." He called those who broke into and overran the U.S. Capitol, stole sensitive information, and desecrated one of the nation's most venerable spaces, resulting in the deaths of five people, "patriots." Our children, who watched the terror unfolding on television were traumatized. Hell, I had been in a war zone, and I was traumatized.

January 8, 2021

In the throes of the ever-worsening pandemic, overall unemployment stood at 6.7%, Latino unemployment at 9.3%, and Black unemployment at 9.9%, as 140,000 new jobs were lost in December 2020, making the overall figure almost 16 million jobs lost in 2020, including 372,000 eliminated.[699]

In the midst of the chaos in Washington, patients were forced to share oxygen in L.A. County, where at least a dozen refrigerated trucks were brought in to store bodies. Ambulances sometimes waited hours, because there were no beds.

January 10, 2021

It was learned that the New York Police Department, among others, sent specific, extensive information to the Capitol police, warning them of the impending danger and planned assault on the Capitol. The FBI, which also passed along warnings to the Capitol police, visited at least 12 known dissenters before January 6th, and warned them not to go to the Capitol.[700]

Twenty-two million doses were distributed, yet fewer than 7 million were administered, or placed into the arms of patients. In San Antonio, 9,000 slots for vaccines were filled in a span of only six minutes. In Georgia, the websites crashed as the 11,000 vaccines available at several metro Atlanta counties were snapped up in a New York minute. There were 3,091 deaths reported nationwide on January 10.

January 11, 2021

"This is what happens when people don't do what public health tells them to do," said Dr. Brad Spellberg, chief medical officer of Los Angeles County Hospital. We have no beds for them. We have not yet seen a post-Christmas surge. The system collapses."

"We need to acknowledge that it's not working," said former FDA Director Dr. Scott Gottlieb, as 22,000 Americans died within seven days and vaccinations lagged woefully behind distribution. "We need to hit the reset and adopt a new strategy to get this out to patients."[701]

Like many people of color before him, Black Capitol policeman Eugene Goodman stood in the gap, a fast-thinking hero, as dozens of anarchists stormed into the Capitol. The only officer around, Goodman warded off the crowd and then misdirected them away from the Senate chamber, so that the Senate chamber doors could be sealed. Otherwise, had the rabid crowd made it to where our lawmakers were unarmed and unprepared, who knows what might have happened.

Harry Dunn, a massive Black Capitol policeman, reflected on the bizarre nature of the day. "I work on the first responder's unit. I've always wanted to be a police officer, protecting and serving," said Dunn, a 14-year-veteran, who said he was called "nigger" several times that day. "Every day I see that building, I think it's beautiful. Slaves built that building. And here I am, 200 years later, a black man, protecting what they built."[702] Five people died as a result of the carnage on January 6th.

Unnamed, armed group calls for "storming" of government buildings and courthouses, if President Trump is removed before January 20, reported ABC News correspondent Pierre Thomas on January 11. There were multiple threats made against Biden, Harris, and Pelosi, among others.

January 12, 2021

The FBI acknowledged that it missed strong messages warning of the probability of violent protests and assaults on January 6th when the Senate was poised to confirm the election of Joe Biden as president, over the protestations of dozens of GOP lawmakers. What didn't make sense was the fact that months earlier, FBI Director Christopher Wray testified before Congress that the biggest, most dangerous collections of domestic terrorists in the U.S. were not Antifa, or Black Lives Matter, but violent white supremacist groups like the Proud Boys, the Militiamen, NSC-131, No White Guilt, the Oath Keepers, and others. Inexplicably, along with those who rampaged through the Capitol with an assault weapon and 100 rounds, one insurrectionist with a box full of Molotov cocktails and pipe bombs, was an Olympic gold medalist; another was a son of a Brooklyn judge. How much more un-American can it get than to try to overthrow the very country that you represented on the world stage?[703]

"There has never been a greater betrayal by a president of his office and his oath," declared Liz Cheney, the third-ranking Republican house member. The mob assault placed Congress in the painful position of invoking the 25th Amendment, declaring the president unfit for office, or making Trump the first president in U.S. history to be impeached twice. While cowering under benches and behind seats, at least three House members contracted COVID during close contact. Several GOP members refused to wear masks, while they were all together trying to stay safe, even as others tried to convince them to wear them.[704]

"Congress needs to hear glass breaking, doors being kicked in, and blood from their BLM and Antifa slave soldiers being spilled," wrote one insurrectionist in a call to rally others.[705]

"Get violent. … Go there, ready for war. We get our president, or we die," wrote another.[706]

The fallout not only continued after the assault on the Capitol but, in fact, grew to a fever pitch. Corporate giants, including Walmart, GM, and Hallmark, declared they would no longer support politicians who protested Biden's election and who called on anarchists to march on the Capitol. With his approval rating plummeting to an all-time low of 33 percent, Trump refused to accept any blame for the five lives lost, the battering of the United States' reputation around the world, and the shaken, bruised spirits, and morale of American citizens. Norfolk FBI warned: "War is coming." Live pipe bombs were placed at both the DNC and the RNC.

Far too late, on January 12, HHS Secretary Azar, who also yielded to incredible pressure from Trump and Pence to downplay vaccines and social distancing, announced they would release all of the vaccines, instead of holding back the second doses.[707] Disney World, State Farm Arena, New York Citi Field, and other giant venues, were announced as new vaccination sites, as less than one-fourth of the vaccines distributed had been administered. Only about 150,000 people had been fully vaccinated a year after COVID had reached our shores. Everyone 65 and above, as well as teachers, first responders, and those who worked in grocery stores and food service, were immediately eligible for vaccines. Meanwhile, more than half the states began collapsing under what some docs called a "medical tsunami." Deaths in California were up over 900% since November. From May to November, 5,364 children across the nation were reported hospitalized with COVID in 22 states.[708]

Trump, of course, said his speech exhorting his supporters to overrun the Capitol was "totally appropriate," just as he had claimed 10 days earlier in his infamous, taped call to Georgia Secretary of State Brad Raffensperger. Knowing his vice president was under assault, along with the rest of the Congress, Trump didn't reach out to check on his safety, even knowing that hundreds of insurgents had broken into the Capitol, and were roaming and desecrating "the people's house" and many yelled, "hang Mike Pence!" Trump had told VP Pence on January 6th, "You can either go down in history as a patriot, or you can go down in history as a pussy," as Pence headed to the Capitol, according to one of his staffers.[709]

Sedition? Benedict Arnold had nothing on these hooligans.[710] Let us not forget the takeover of the Michigan Capitol, and the plot to kidnap Governor Gretchen Whitmer.

"He should be totally ashamed of himself, and he should take that shame and turn it into a resignation," said former Secretary of State Colin Powell, a Republican and the first Black to serve in that position.[711]

"If we nominate Trump, we will get destroyed, and we will deserve it," Lindsey Graham had tweeted just over four years before the 2016 election.[712] The year before, when Graham still had a pair, he tweeted: "Joe Biden is as good a man as God ever created. Trump is a xenophobic, race-baiting bigot. You want to know how to make America great again. Tell Donald Trump to go to hell."[713]

*

Only one-third of the 27 million vaccine doses available had been injected into the arms of patients.

Liz Cheney, one of ten Republicans voting with the Democrats in favor of impeachment, said, "Enough is enough….The president of the United States summoned this mob, assembled this mob, and lit the flame of this attack. Everything that followed was of his doing. The president could have immediately and forcefully intervened to stop the violence. He did not. There has never been a greater betrayal by a president of the United States to his office and his oath to the constitution."[714]

That same day, 4,336 new COVID-related deaths were reported in the U.S.

January 15, 2021

As more and more information trickled in, it became increasingly clear that much planning had gone into a coordinated assault on the U.S. Capitol.

"This is an inside job. I'm sorry," documentarian Michael Moore said. "I've been to the Capitol a dozen times in the past decade, and I couldn't tell you how to get to Nancy Pelosi's office. They know exactly who the Republican members of Congress were who took them around and told them how to get where. What they do know is that dozens, or maybe more than dozens of police and ex-military men were there, part of the rally."[715]

Moore pointed out that when anarchists took over the Michigan state Capitol with long guns, there were no arrests. "I think that was the first mistake, and we made it in

Michigan," Moore said on MSNBC's The 11th Hour with Brian Williams.

January 14, 2021

By January 14, 2021, the U.S. had recorded 40,000 COVID deaths in the U.S., in just the first two weeks of the year.

The federal government had also identified 200 suspects in the January 6th insurrection. Our nation had clearly come under attack by its own citizens, mostly MAGA believers and radicalized white supremacists. We remember what happened when Black activists showed up armed in the 1960s, including Fred Hampton, chairman of the Chicago Chapter of the Black Panthers, who was shot and killed in a COINTEL-inspired raid as he slept next to his eight-month pregnant wife, along with a second member, Mark Clark.[716]

"Everybody in there is a murderous traitor. Death is the remedy," said Peter Stager, who beat a fallen officer with the U.S. flag on a pole on January 6th.

"Impeachment? If we go along with it [insurrection] as Republicans, we will destroy the Republican Party," acknowledged Senator Lindsey Graham. Does he prefer that we destroy the republic, I asked myself?

By January 14, 2020, one in three residents of L.A. County was believed to be infected, and nearly 1 million Americans filed for unemployment that week for the first time.

Historically, in this nation, white folk get the benefit of the doubt, while Black folk are victimized by a twisted presumed guilt. We danced around this very gingerly, even as the mob shouted, "Hang Mike Pence, hang Mike Pence." In the end, this isn't something people of color, particularly Black people, can solve. The key to a realignment toward a norm we can understand, and eventually justice, sits squarely at the feet of "good" white folk, those who acknowledge and are stirred by the injustice, but even more so, are then moved to challenge the wrongs, and insist on making it right.

I cannot help but draw on the emboldened courage to effect change that our beautiful white brothers and sisters, who were freedom fighters in the 1960s and beyond, demonstrated in standing with their marginalized brothers and sisters in Black America during the Jim Crow era.

"It is not debatable that the United States did this more poorly than any nation on earth," said Minnesota's newly-elected Democratic Governor Tim Walz, characterizing the Trump administration's response to COVID as an "abject failure." "We will continue to do what we have to do — clean up the mess that the federal government leaves us with."[717]

Four thousand Americans dying a day? Haven't we been told our whole lives, and for generations untold, that this is the greatest nation in the history of the world? How does this happen?

I do believe that this is the greatest nation in the world, perhaps the greatest in the history of the world. Yet, whether we admit it or not, we face a clear and present danger, and it is not Black unemployment or welfare babies, street violence, human trafficking, or the opioid epidemic, though all of these, as well as many others, are deep wounds inflicted on the body politic. In 2023, fueled by the "Jews will not replace us" mob at Charlottesville, the armed invasion of the Michigan State Capitol, or the temporary takeover of the people's house in Washington by thousands of insurgents called to arms and revolt by the former deceiver-in-chief, Donald J. Trump, we as a nation have a hot mess on our hands.

Following the madness of January 6th, four times the number of troops in Afghanistan, Syria, and Iraq combined was called upon to safeguard the upcoming inauguration, certainly unlike any in history, even as Trump enacted a grand military exit.

Elected officials, the 10 House Republicans who had the courage to call the assault on the Capitol what it was – treasonous – by voting to impeach Trump, were moving to buy body armor, fearing for their lives.

At this point, 30 million vaccinations had been delivered, yet only 10 million had reached the arms of anxious and desperate Americans. Is there any question that the states needed help in terms of personnel, strategy, and a national plan to utilize more current and retired health care professionals and other concerned citizens, in order to expedite the process?[718]

There were 21,000 National Guard troops in D.C., a city under siege, in order to preserve and protect the democratic process. At least a dozen U.S. cities were investigating their officers who were at the Trump insurgency rally, some filmed raging in the Capitol, or assaulting officers outside and in.

"To imagine that colleagues of mine could have aided and abetted this is incredibly offensive, and there's simply no way they can be allowed to continue to serve in Congress," said Rep. Mikie Sherrill of New Jersey, a former U.S. naval pilot.

Some members of Congress noted there was an unusually high number of groups touring the Capitol on January 5, the day before the insurrection, particularly since public tours of the building were suspended in March of 2020, due to COVID precautions.

"There's been a great deal of overpromising on timelines," said former CDC Director Dr. Julie Gerberding, who noted that more than 36,000 deaths had been reported in the first two weeks of January 2021.[719]

By mid-January, one in five senior citizens, or 5.3 million, faced a hunger crisis that was growing by the day.[720]

In California's Antelope Hospital, COVID patients, over capacity, pushed the hospital to set up 50-bed mobile units of emergency field hospitals, which normally only stood up during disaster scenarios, like hurricanes or tornados, or in war zones. However, they couldn't utilize them to treat and preserve patients, because the hospital could not acquire oxygen, which is a stark failure of the government, and a classic example of a lack of coordination and planning.

Biden's plan called for $160 million for vaccinations and testing, $130 million to reopen schools and safeguard staff and students, and another $1,400 payments to Americans.

Georgia reported the fourth worst COVID numbers in the nation the week of January 16.[721]

Showing callous disregard for some of his most vulnerable citizens, Michigan's former Governor, Rick Snyder, was charged with two counts of willful neglect after toxic levels of lead killed a minimum of 12 people, and likely compromised the health of a generation of children. Toxins poured out of the city water, which, to save money, was being pulled from the Flint River in the mostly Black city. Sadly, the Michigan Supreme Court threw the case out.

January 15, 2020

People started yelling, "Kill him with his own gun," recalled Capitol police officer Michael Fanone, who answered a distress call to the D.C. police on January 6th.

Fanone, who was dragged and beaten by the mob of insurrectionists who stormed the Capitol, suffered a minor heart attack during the event. He appealed to those beating him by telling them he had kids, which moved some to protect him, likely saving his life.[722]

One anarchist, Jennifer Leigh Ryan, a realtor from Texas who took a private jet to D.C. for the event, said this: "We are going to f----ing go in here. Life or death, it doesn't matter. Here we go."[723]

Jacob Chansley, the so-called "QAnon Shaman," after invading the vice president's chambers in the Capitol, left this message written on Pence's desk: "It's only a matter of time. Justice is coming."

Acknowledging something many state governors believed, HHS Secretary Alex Azar finally said it: "No. There's not a [COVID vaccine] reserve stockpile. We now have enough confidence that our ongoing production will be of high quality and available to provide the second dose for people, so we're not sitting on a reserve anymore."[724] Two million people had died worldwide, while the U.S. was losing over 2,000 people daily, one-fifth of the world's total pandemic death toll.[725] In Los Angeles County, someone was dying every six seconds, even as the more contagious COVID variant that began in Europe had been detected in at least 15 U.S. states. It was expected to be the dominant version of COVID in the U.S. by March.

"They were lying," said Minnesota Governor Tim Walz. "They don't have any doses that were held back." Though 31 million doses had been delivered and 12 million people had received a first dose, only 1.3 million, including first responders, had received their second dose.

As with the rollout of the Affordable Care Act in 2013, websites crashed across the country as citizens were told they could finally register for vaccines.

Meanwhile, Trump was on the way to becoming the only president to be impeached twice. The charge: incitement to insurrection.

Seeking to return to a sense of normalcy in government and a renewed belief in our democracy, Biden promised, "You have my word," touting a $2 million proposal, as well as a mask mandate, wherever he had the authority to do so. "We'll manage the hell out of this operation."

January 17, 2021

In Idaho, a white-hot 41% of all those tested came back as positive, with Iowa and Pennsylvania at 34% and Mississippi at 33%, followed by South Dakota at 31%. As the U.S. roared toward 400,000 deaths, and 24,000 Americans infected by inauguration day, January 20,[726] various countries, including the United Kingdom, demanded proof of testing negative before allowing American air travelers to enter the country.

"The party of Lincoln was once the party of civil rights," said outgoing DNC Party Chair Tom Perez. "I want a strong two-party system. [But] the party of Lincoln is dead."[727] I firmly agreed with Perez. America desperately needs at least two political choices, both with decent, honest people whose first and last priority is the people they are elected to serve, not themselves, their dogma, or wealth and power. It would seem that those days are gone for the foreseeable future.

Meantime, all this talk and chatter about the shadowy "cabal" was unnerving in 2020 and 2021 and wearisome, if not sad, in 2023. The nation was still awaiting the Obama and Clinton arrests, and transports to Gitmo that the QAnon faithful believed in, as well as a return to the 1976 provisions that called for a new government brought in by NESARA/GESARA.[728] Waiting for the unveiling of those things must be like my wife telling me how long I had been telling her I was going to retire, and that our proverbial "ship" was soon to dock.

As the sun set on the Trump administration, U.S. coronavirus cases topped 24 million. Just shy of 400,000 Americans had lost their lives to the unforgiving, opportunistic disease. As for Trump, he had disappeared from the public stage. He was spending his time determining whom he could pardon in the final two days of his administration, and deciding which of the persons on death row, most of whom suffered from mental illnesses or disabilities, he could execute on his way out the door. The final tally was 13, including five in 2020 when Trump authorized the execution of 10 people, more than three times as many people as had been executed by a president in the past six decades.[729]

Determined to hand out pardons to mostly bad people like M&M's to a sugar addict, pay a visit to his inglorious wall on the southern border, and planning a grand military salute to himself as his term ended, Trump focused on everything but the main thing. Two days before Biden's inauguration, Trump removed the travel ban for Europe and Brazil, two areas where the new strain of COVID was raging. Never in his final days, and hardly ever before, frankly, did the president offer true empathy or remorse for all the death and suffering. He did not create the COVID-19 virus, but he tragically mismanaged it, finally – months later – acknowledging that it was the defining health and economic crisis of the last century. Equally critical, he exhorted thousands of faithful, sometimes rabid, followers to storm the people's house, the revered United States Capitol, in an attempt to overturn his legitimate loss to Joe Biden. The assault, shown around the world, and gloated over by our enemies and agonized over by our friends and allies, sullied America's reputation and shattered the nation's image of who and what we are as Americans.

January 18, 2021

On Dr. Martin Luther King's birthday, a long day of service, brotherhood, and calling America to live up to the high ideals it has long claimed to exemplify, the nation was instead locked down, bracing for what Trump loyalists might do two days later to disrupt the peaceful transition of power that had been taken for granted for over 200 years. Who could have imagined that the Washington police would have to check our incoming National Guards and elite troops to ensure that they were not part of the radical insurgency devoted to overthrowing our government? Again, what kind of alternative universe are we living in, and will someone please wake me up from this nightmare?

"Ideas don't just win," said Thomas Friedman, "they require power to win," pointing to Nazism and fascism and Islamic radicalism. "There has to be a war of ideas within conservatism to root them out. What we're going to need here is for conservatives to take on these ideals."[730]

HHS Secretary Azar, my boss, ever loyal, even to a man who had no loyalty to him, stayed the party line right up until the bitter, disgraceful end, spinning the message every bit as good as Trump spin-masters Sarah Sanders, Kayleigh McEnany, and Kellyanne Conway.

As many as 1,000 people may have trampled their way into the Capitol on January 6th. One woman, Riley June Williams, 23, from Harrisburg, Pennsylvania, helped steal a laptop from Nancy Pelosi's office while they rattled through the desks of congressmen and congresswomen, taking pictures of their private papers and notes. Some even defecated in hallways and corners of the revered building. To their credit, many true patriots – not the radicals who would overthrow a legitimate government that, for 240 years has been virtually unshakable – turned in family members when they saw pictures of them ransacking the Capitol.

"It's like our democracy is starting fresh on the twentieth," said Minnesota Senator Amy Klobuchar.

Demonstrating unmitigated gall, many administration leaders lauded the contributions and the mission of Dr. King, despite consistently voting and standing against his principles and his ministry to the "least of these."

"We're certainly demanding answers from the Trump Administration," said Oregon Governor Kate Brown. "Their empty promises are literally playing with people's lives."

*

Twenty states had identified a new variant of the COVID virus by January 18, even as hospitalizations had finally begun to slow. In desperation, Washington Governor Jay Inslee was seeking to involve Starbucks in getting vaccinations. Disney opened its parking lot, and Uber offered free rides.

A caravan of people seeking a better life rambled toward the southern border. Overturning the Muslim ban, reentering the Paris Accord, extending student loan moratoriums, a living wage, and expanding economic relief, were priorities in the new administration.

January 19, 2021

On his final night as president, Trump listed in his accomplishments a proclamation that he was proud of not "starting" a war. On the international stage, he did not start a war. However, his isolationist, and "America first" ideology, prompted him to pull U.S. troops from Afghanistan, Somalia, and Germany, abandoning our allies, the Kurds, and allowing the Russians and Syrians to slaughter thousands.[731] His legacy also includes an elitist, whites-only nation, as promoted by his one-time Secretary of State, Mike Pompeo, who declared that "multiculturalism is not who America is."[732] Trump also proved to be the most divisive president of the last century, separating immigrant children from their parents, as well as the guy who proclaimed Mexico would pay for his ill-fated wall on the southern border. Meanwhile, on the home front, domestic terrorism, in some instances, radicalized Islamists, but, most often, white right-wing terrorists, who hung on his every word, flourished during the Trump era.

The day before Biden's inauguration, and after what had been the most tumultuous, tribal, cut-to-the-bone campaign season in my lifetime, I happened to read a headline where former Georgia Senator Kelly Loeffler described her brief time in the U.S. Senate as "the honor of a lifetime."

Arrogant, privileged elitist, I couldn't help but mutter under my breath. Had you been just a bit less divisive, more understanding of people who weren't rich and white, and less caustic in your attack against the BLM Movement and its supporters, you could easily have earned another term. But no, not you. You had to be as antagonistic as you could, even while owning a virtually all-Black WNBA team, the Atlanta Dream. It also didn't help that you claimed to be more conservative than Attila the Hun and clung to Trump like a three-month-old hangs on its mother.[733] Small wonder the wealthy white businesswoman would be upset in a Senate runoff with first-time candidate Rev. Raphael Warnock in an increasingly blue Georgia.

My old boss, Renee Ellmers, a Republican I thought well of, used to always say, "Elections have consequences." Damn skippy.

On January 19 – hours before the inauguration of the 46th president of the United States – Biden paid homage to the 400,000 Americans who had lost their lives to COVID in a somber, earnest tribute.

"To heal, we must remember," said Biden. "Sometimes it's hard to remember, but that's how we heal. It's hard to do that as a nation, but that's why we're here."

When Biden began his first day as president, he did so in a cathedral, accompanied by the two Republican and Democratic leaders of Congress. Twelve national guardsmen, summoned to protect at the presidential inauguration, were sent home due to potential threats they posed to the republic, as QAnon followers had been urged to pose as guardsmen to get access to the event.

The Oath Keepers' Thomas Caldwell, along with four other members, was convicted on two charges of obstruction and tampering with evidence in connection with the attack on the Capitol.[734]

Trump said, "We did what we came here to do, and so much more," in a videotaped goodbye. At the same time, Speaker Mitch McConnell, who would later soften his description of the insurrection, said this on January 19: "The mob was fed lies. ... They were provoked by the president and other powerful people."[735]

Over 51 years earlier, on March 30, 1968, four days before his assassination, Dr. King warned us, saying, "We must all learn to live together as brothers, or we will all perish together as fools. ... And it may well be that we will have to repent in this generation. Not merely for the vitriolic words and the violent actions of the bad people, but for the appalling silence and indifference of the good people who sit around and say, 'Wait on time.'"[736]

Immediately following the Trump-inspired insurrection, GOP House Leader Kevin McCarthy, Senate Speaker Mitch McConnell, and even South Carolina Senator Lindsey Graham offered full-throated condemnation of Trump and his role in the insurrection. As time rolled by, however, their voices muted, and Trump and his huge following were quietly welcomed back into the fold.

"I took on the tough battles, the hardest fights, the most difficult choices, because that's what you elected me to do," Trump said in a taped final message the night before Biden replaced him as president. "We restored the idea that in America, no one is forgotten because everyone matters and everyone has a voice."

This was, frankly, the biggest bowl of crap I ever heard. Those, not white, or wealthy, were routinely left out and marginalized. White pomposity, I say.

The UK variant of COVID was scheduled to be the dominant version of the virus in the U.S. by March, even as it had already reached nearly half of the country. California, the U.S. epicenter, had discovered three variants. Only one-third of the 30,000,000 vaccine doses had reached arms.

January 20, 2021

I recall how, on March 30, 2020, Trump said, "We are doing a great job," insisting the "15 cases would go to zero. It will go away. You know it will go away."

On inauguration day, January 20th, 4,131 Americans died of COVID-related illnesses, one every 21 seconds in the deadliest day yet of the pandemic. In all, 24 million Americans had been infected, and 405,000 had died, all in a single year.

Exactly one year before the passing of the torch from Trump to Biden, the first U.S. case of COVID-19 was identified after weeks of watching the disease ravage Europe, especially Italy. It was not, however, HHS's first indication of the disease, or its ability to ravage and reign. My colleague, the executive officer of the Office of the Secretary/Office of the Regional Director for HHS, Natalia Cales, as office leader for emergency preparedness, went to Washington specifically for a tabletop exercise to prepare and react to COVID-19 in November 2019. So, despite what the former president would have you believe, we were very clear-eyed regarding the sweeping potential of the deadly disease some four months before it began to ravage the U.S.

Exactly two weeks before the inauguration, Trump urged and exhorted the marchers he had called to the nation's capital from all across America to storm the Capitol in the most brazen, shocking affront to democracy this nation has ever endured. Perhaps only the attack of 9/11, though much more deadly, could possibly reach the levels of violation I and most of my fellow Americans felt on January 6th. Tragically, this mission to injure, destroy, and overthrow, did not come from plotters and terrorists from the Middle East, or Russia, but from right here within our own borders. Truly, we discovered what FBI Director Christopher Wray testified to months earlier, during the Red Summer of 2020: "The top domestic terrorism threat we face continues to be from DVEs we categorize as Racially or Ethnically Motivated Violent Extremists ("RMVEs"), including those who advocate for the superiority of the white race, who were the primary source of lethal attacks perpetrated by DVEs in recent years."[737]

On Trump's final day as president, 4,377 Americans died from COVID, not far from the 4,872 total death count in the entire country of Japan throughout the pandemic.

As Trump exited and Biden took center stage, the differences were stark. Biden's administration launched with a rendition of "The Hill We Climb" by poet Amanda

Gorman, a young, Harvard-educated Black woman and the youngest inaugural poet in history. She was brilliant. Author-enunciator of "The Hill We Climb," Gorman, who challenged and electrified the nation, would never have been given that stage within the Trump administration. It was, indeed, a new day.

Being American is more than a lifestyle we are privileged with, or the pride we inherit as citizens of the greatest nation in the history of the world. It's also America's checkered past we step into, and how we repair it. Much healing and restoration of our battered, disoriented, one-half discouraged, and the other half-hopeful nation, was desperately needed.

This beautiful Black sister, Amanda Gorman, who overcame a speech impediment, exemplifies the strength, brilliance, and unconquerable spirit of Black women, the sturdy backbone of the Democratic/progressive movement. They, along with millions of young people who have grown up in a society where they go to school, play sports, and even sometimes live in integrated neighborhoods, understand, much more than my parents' generation and mine, that we are more alike than we are different.

"There is always light if we are brave enough to see it. If only we're brave enough to be it," she extolled.[738]

California's first Hispanic senator, believe it or not, the first Black senator from the South since Reconstruction, and the youngest senator, Jewish American Jon Ossoff, the latter two from Georgia, joined the new Congress in January of 2021. Alex Padilla's ascension came as a result of Kamala Harris's selection as Biden's running mate, which adds up to two glass ceilings being shattered. The election of Warnock, running for office the very first time to become Georgia's first Black senator, and Ossoff, who had run for a House seat twice to lose tough, close elections, are all a glimpse into the future of a bolder, more inclusive new America. True, some of the brilliance of the shining city on a hill called the United States of America was gone. Yet, as Dr. King often declared, "hope crushed to earth shall rise again!"

So, screw you, Mike Pompeo, when you say, "multiculturalism is not what America is."[739] Take your cocky, delusional ass back to California, but please don't go back to Kansas. You are a disgrace to the legacy of the Sunflower State, Brown v. Topeka Board of Education, Gordon Parks, Bleeding Kansas, and true patriots John Brown and Arthur Fletcher, one of the fathers of affirmative action, a true Republican trailblazer. You and our former president, though your actions and mission have brought many progressive-thinking white, brown, Black, and yellow people together, have stoked division and discord that have set our nation back years.[740]

As you both ride off into the sunset, I and millions of other Americans rue the day Trump used the tool of promising conservative judges, to lure in Evangelicals and God-fearing people as a foil for spreading hate, racism, sexism, and a white power agenda.

Trump and his deniers are also credited with the fact that on the last day of his presidency, 4,229 people died from COVID, many of whom could still be alive. That's 400,000 lives in just one year, more than died in World War II. Had you called for national mandates and structures, moved far more quickly, worked more closely with the states to ensure they had the help they needed, and better communicated the critical nature of the deadly disease, instead of playing it off like it was just the flu and would go away by itself, America would be a much better, more united, safer place. People whom you led believed you and died because of it. You, Mr. Trump, own that.

Biden pointedly declared that white supremacy must be defeated. Never before has an American president been so bold and declarative about the need to achieve racial and ethnic equality. The next four years and beyond were going to be some ride, yet one I was all in for. Were you? For me, with my federal career of over 25 years nearing an end, I had determined I would need to find another job if Trump regained the White House in 2020. I'd felt that the great Congressman Jim Clyburn, who delivered South Carolina's bell-weather primary in 2020 to a Biden campaign on life support, had been disappointed in Biden's cabinet selections, which was light, on dark people. In the end, however, Biden stayed the course and put his administration's shoulder into the declaration that sexism, anti-Semitism, white supremacy, and the injustice faced by Black, brown, and LBGTQ+ people, must be defeated. Clyburn, much of marginalized America, and I were elated by his inner circle, which was by far the most diverse in U.S. history.

An unprecedented 4,600 women rose up and ran for office after Donald Trump was elected president. Youth, particularly urban and suburban, were energized by the GOP's tone-deaf approach to school violence, disparate treatment of Black and brown men in police encounters, and Trump's unwillingness and inability to work across the aisle with both Democrats and Republicans. Hundreds were elected, and all could revel in the historic swearing-in of the first woman in U.S. history, Kamala Harris, of Jamaican and Indian descent, to be sworn in as vice president.[741]

"While I may be the first to serve in this position," said Harris, "I will not be the last."[742]

Trump exited the stage right as the first U.S. president in 152 years not to celebrate and participate in his successor's inauguration. Thus, he was also absent when his predecessors, Obama, Bush, and Clinton, gathered at the inauguration, as is traditional, to offer their congratulations and support for the incoming leader of the free world. He also left millions of QAnon scratching their heads, feeling misled and confused after being assured that Trump, though he lost the election legitimately, would indeed have a second term.[743] Conversely, Trump's successor asked all Americans to wear masks, something Trump never did.

Biden, in his inaugural address, spoke of "growing inequities, a raging virus and the sting of systemic racism, a climate in crisis," all words the majority of Americans – and the free world – longed to hear again from an American president.

"We must meet this moment as the UNITED States of America," implored the new president. "If we do that, I guarantee you we will not fail. We have never, ever, ever failed in America, when we acted together. We will get through this together."[744]

Biden's Oval Office includes a bust of Martin Luther King, Jr., Rosa Parks, and Cesar Chavez, along with seminal presidents. His office, like his cabinet and leadership team, is a refreshing look into a new America. Biden has substance, unlike our previous White House occupant, who didn't realize that Frederick Douglass is long since gone while showcasing a bust of President Andrew Jackson, who was responsible for the Indian Removal Act of 1830, and was a brutal owner to 161 enslaved Black folk.[745]

Biden chose to retain Christopher Wray, a Trump appointee, as head of the FBI, after he avoided being fired by Trump for asserting "white domestic terrorism" the biggest U.S. terrorism threat.

"I have lived in the South, and I don't want to live there again," the great Hank Aaron said before moving to the city he came to love, Milwaukee. "We can go anywhere in Milwaukee. I don't know what would happen in Atlanta."[746]

I remember that when I was coaching and teaching baseball to my own sons, one of them, as a pee wee, always said "Pank" Aaron. The sort of quiet excellence Aaron exhibited was virtually unprecedented, especially growing up in the Deep South in Mobile, Alabama, and then playing for the Atlanta Braves in 1966 in the segregated South. As a kid growing up playing baseball, Hammerin' Hank was a real-life hero to most young Black boys like me, especially because of his grace under pressure as he daily endured hundreds of racist threats as he challenged, then moved past, the great Babe Ruth on the all-time home run record of 714 in 1974. Sadly, though likely to the jubilation of conspiracy theorists, Aaron died shortly after receiving his COVID vaccination in January of 2021. Robert Kennedy Jr., running for president in 2024 as an anti-vaxxer, implied in a tweet that Aaron died from the vaccine. The Fulton County medical examiner, however, refuted that claim, pointing out that Aaron was 86 and died of natural causes.[747]

Regulations repealed by Biden in his first three days, including the Muslim ban, leaned into inclusion and progressive values.

"The brutal truth is, it's going to take months before we get the majority of Americans vaccinated," Biden said. As terrifying as that was to hear, his hard truth was refreshing.

Epilogue

On July 2, 2024, I joined hundreds of others from across the country in St. Augustine, Florida, to celebrate the city's and its brave souls' vital contributions to the passage of the Civil Rights Act of 1964. Twenty-two years earlier, I made several trips to the coastal burg, the oldest European-settled city in the nation, to interview several of its key leaders of the battles that led to the passage of the act, including Dr. Robert Hayling, whom local activists call the "Father of the Civil Rights Act of 1964." Other key attendees included Al Lingo, a white activist who helped Black activists integrate the Munson Motel, where acid was thrown into the pool to force Blacks out; J.T. Johnson, who jumped into the pool, and several local activists.

One of the highlights of the two-day event was the presence of former King's aide and U.S. Ambassador Andrew Young. Now 92, and on a scooter, Young was badly beaten during one of the numerous night marches in the city that several of his SCLC colleagues called the most racist city they'd ever encountered. Other key SCLC activists who took blows and served jail time in St. Augustine included Rev. Willie Bolden, Rev. C.T. Vivian, Rev. Fred Shuttlesworth, and Dorothy Cotton. In previously unseen footage, Young was cold-cocked by a white anarchist, then repeatedly kicked and punched while on the ground by several men. Young told the audience that the "ass whipping I got that night resulted in the most important night of my life."[748] Young went on to thank all of the local activists, from the cooks to the drivers, those who marched both in the torturous sun and at night, those who were beaten while marching, or wading into the water to integrate the beaches, while baseball bats, brass knuckles, and club-wielding intransigents awaited the non-violent equality-seekers. A great pride and sense of resiliency suffused the room, a knowledge that against incredible odds in a city where the country sheriff and the city's police chief were both Klansmen, their courage and commitment to truth and justice won out. In addition to Young, the program featured presentations by four powerful Black women, including Dr. Cynthia Mitchell Clarke, who, at the tender age of 12, had her nose broken by a blow from a grown man while she was protesting non-violently, as well as Crystal Hayling, the daughter of the St. Augustine movement's leader, Dr. Hayling.

One day earlier, however, the U.S. Supreme Court finally ruled that former President Trump, as well as those who would follow him, would, for the first time ever, have presidential immunity for official acts, even if they were criminal. Bolstered by the three conservative judges Trump had appointed – Amy Coney Barrett, Neil Gorsuch, and Brett Kavanaugh – the Supreme Court upended 234 years of precedent that burst open the doors for American presidents to become czars or dictators, something the founding fathers were resolute should not happen. George Washington, in fact, at Valley Forge, joined up to 600 of his men in signing an oath of allegiance in 1778 to the emerging republic, while vowing no "allegiance or obedience to George the Third, King of Great Britain."[749]

"If you're going to burn the house down, don't be mad that people call it arson," said Sherrilyn Ifill, the Vernon E. Jordan distinguished chair at Howard University, responding to the Supreme Court's gut-wrenching decision.[750]

*

Indeed, if Trump wins the White House in 2024, there is a great chance that he will again have an opportunity to appoint one, or even two more, conservative Supreme Court justices. Conversely, in 1964 and 1965, President Lyndon Baines Johnson, himself a good ole boy from Texas who ascended to the presidency following John F. Kennedy's 1963 assassination, did the right thing by passing the long overdue Civil Rights Act of 1964, and the Voting Rights Act of 1965. Though boasting a checkered past on race, Johnson, when push came to shove, forever stands on the right side of history. Trump, however, has not, and once again will not, if given another term.

Trump's blatant warning of what a second term will portend – not only for the U.S., but the world – must be a clarion call to a justice-seeking nation, especially women, Black people, immigrants, those concerned about gun violence, the environment, gender equity, Muslims, and young people.

Women, especially the Democrats' most loyal voting bloc – Black women – will rise up and vote in protest of Trump's assault on a woman's right to choose, which was largely stripped bare when Roe v. Wade was overturned in 2022, again by a Trump-dominated Supreme Court. Ironically, my boss, Antrell Tyson, and I rode by the Pink House, the only place in Mississippi where women could get an abortion before the Dobbs decision, during my last official trip for HHS.[751] During the visit, we also ran into January 6th Commission Chair Congressman Bennie Thompson at Medgar Evers Airport in Jackson, before later meeting with Mississippi Health Director Dr. Thomas Dobbs, now infamously remembered in the Dobbs v. Jackson Women's Health Organization suit that overturned Wade. On the second half of that same trip, Tyson and I traveled to Tallahassee, Florida, where we met with Florida State Surgeon General Dr. Joseph Ladapo, a DeSantis-empowered, notorious anti-vaxxer.[752]

However, as disheartening and painful as many American women, as well as many men, found the Dobbs decision, it is clear that this election will not be won by women alone. It will require an awakening of the young, the vulnerable, Black men, the ambivalent, the ill-informed, the middle, the independents, and others concerned about sustaining democracy. U.S. Commander George Washington categorically rejected any attempts to designate him king, a sentiment widely shared by the founding fathers.[753] A second Trump presidency, as he has declared, would mean that federal employees pledge loyalty to him, not the flag or the Constitution.

*

This is, in the end, a fight to do as Dr. King, Rev. C.K. Steele, Rev. Fred Shuttlesworth, Rev. Ralph D. Abernathy, and the other 55 or so ministers who formed the Southern Christian Leadership Conference did in 1957, to *Redeem the Soul of America*, the SCLC's motto. This is a Kairos moment for this nation and perhaps the world. When the history books are written about this age in which we lived, what will it say when your children ask you, "Grandma, papa, what did you do to preserve democracy?" Or do we submit, roll over and bow down, and, as former Democrat House Speaker Nancy Pelosi said the GOP has done, "become a cult to a thug?"[754]

Much has changed since Donald J. Trump reluctantly left office in January of 2017. As usual, some of it has been positive, some negative. For me, and I dare say for most democracy-committed Americans, as well as our allies around the world, Biden's 2020 election meant we once again had an ally in the White House, a tried-and-true veteran, experienced politician who would not surprise us, not be accused of being a pawn or friend of dictators like Russia's Putin, or North Korea's Kim Jong Un. Inside our borders, it was comforting not to have to wake up each morning to hear or read the latest preposterous or inflammatory thing the president had said or tweeted.

Also, on the plus side, the Biden administration restored the confidence to the world that the United States is a trusted ally to the NATO (North Atlantic Treaty Organization) nations, Taiwan, Japan, Israel, India, Turkey, Saudi Arabia, Jordan, Morocco, and Kuwait. Two-thirds of Americans who pay attention to such things know that under the Biden administration, we will support our allies (Ukraine, Israel, and Kuwait) while seeking, albeit very late, a real humanitarian solution for innocent Palestinians in Gaza, and for the people of Haiti.

Joblessness in the U.S., as of 2024, is at an all-time low, though inflation is still high, and too many Americans are struggling with paying for food, childcare, and housing.

For women, in particular, the first over-the-counter contraceptive pills are now available without a prescription, something that has become hugely important since the overturning of Roe v. Wade in 2022 by the Trump-driven Supreme Court, even as some states seek to prosecute women who travel to get abortions.

Biden provided $286 million in 2023 to the schools to prevent school violence, and to provide for student wellness and mental health professionals, following a series of school shootings, including in Uvalde, Texas.

Biden introduced and authorized an anti-redlining rule for banks, mandating that they provide loans in low-income communities where they have provided small business loans and mortgages. The Federal Reserve initiative is slated to begin in 2026, though it surely would be repealed under a second Trump administration. The hoped-for result is that banks lend more money in new areas to address the racial homeownership gap, now as wide as in 1968.

A new rule designed to stop airlines from charging numerous junk fees and banks charging $30-$45 for overdrafts is predicted to save consumers 3.5 billion per year.

Under Biden, 4.75 million students have received what amounts to $68 billion dollars in loan forgiveness, though Congress has prevented him from forgiving even more.

The Biden administration has also super-charged funding for cancer research, with a goal of cutting cancer deaths in half by 2049.

Biden has also stepped up the use of telemedicine, making it much easier for vulnerable and transportation-challenged citizens to meet with their doctors on a regular, or emergency basis. The reluctance of HHS to embrace telemedicine under the Trump administration had drastically decreased the numbers of vulnerable patients getting routine checkups and wellness visits during the height of COVID.

Biden also moved to implement new overtime pay, as well as to fight predatory lending practices through the Consumer Financial Protection Bureau, which could save vulnerable Americans $3.5 billion a year.

Biden's Infrastructure Bill has pumped $600 million into building bridges and roads across the nation to bolster a crippled infrastructure, while he has made prioritizing "going green" a major mission.

Though the bill was rejected by the GOP, at Trump's request, Biden proposed the most extensive border reform in decades, which would have drastically reduced illegal immigration.[755]

Trump worked feverishly to kill the ACA, or ObamaCare, during his four years in office. He cut advertising by 90%, reduced the open enrollment period from 12 to six weeks, and forbade federal regional directors and their staff from supporting the assisters in the field. He also stopped federal payments that helped reduce out-of-pocket costs for low-income families, causing insurers to raise rates. Entering office, Biden reversed course, dramatically pumping new blood into Obama's signature legislation, something more critical than ever, in the midst of COVID. As a result, the U.S. uninsured rate is 7.3%, a record low, with 21 million people enrolled in the ACA.[756]

Biden also vigorously attacked and addressed the COVID pandemic, utilizing all federal resources to bolster testing, vaccinations, supply chain issues, and messaging, while appointing a COVID Task Force led by a Black woman, thereby easing the concerns about issues of cultural competency and equity. Perhaps most importantly, Biden and his administration were frank and earnest about the crippling dangers of the disease, instead of saying it would "simply disappear."

Equally important, Biden displayed empathy and an understanding of the pain, hardship, and loss that had been missing during the Trump administration. People believed he cared about their struggles.

I deeply love this country ... and I always will, despite its glaring inconsistencies. I do agree with the ardently pro-American conservatives that this is the greatest nation in the world, where virtually anybody can, in the right circumstances, with the right attitude and the grace of God, become anything they want to be. At the same time, I am deeply disturbed by the regression of freedoms this nation has embraced, led by the far right and often, the Evangelical church, in particular. Project 2025 also looms like a Category 5 hurricane over the political horizon.

In all honesty, I'm deeply concerned that America has not yet matured to the point of electing its first female president in Kamala Harris, much less one of African and Indian descent. My fervent hope and prayer is that the radical actions of the Supreme Court, the fact that election deniers are in strategic places all across the nation and another "January 6th" type assault on democracy could once again be in play, will serve as a clarion call to democracy-seeking Americans to elect the accomplished woman who exemplifies the American dream, not the 34-time convicted felon and would-be dictator, who calls insurrectionists "patriots" and only has love for himself.

May God protect and bless the USA. May God also hold the United States accountable for living up to the ideals upon which the country was founded: to provide "liberty and justice for all."

Acknowledgments

I want to thank my family, who supported this initiative even in the midst of the madness of America, which faces uncertainty that has not been seen in my lifetime. I also want to thank my colleagues, April Washington, Karen Jordan, Theresa Zayas, Karen Ashton, Judy Weaver, Natalia Cales, Judy Trawick, and Beatriz Romero-Escobar, who provided support during the most trying times. I also thank many others, especially those who worked out in the regions, who believed it necessary to illuminate some of the inner workings of government in the Trump administration. Michele Schiavone was exactly what I needed in an editor. She pushed me to be thorough and plainspoken while still respecting my perspectives and taking the time to hear and understand what was most important to me in chronicling my journey.

Tracey Smith, my second editor, helped me bring the project home after Michele, who had taken me most of the way, had to move on to other projects. Tracey was also a God-send. An author herself, she also meticulously, line-by-line, worked with me to ferret out any discrepancies and bring the project to completion, after a host of external issues we had little or no control over. Both Michele and Tracey's willingness to go through the battles between me and hybrid publishers, in the midst of a myriad of challenges, have endeared me for a lifetime to both ladies, whom I consider not only trusted advisors, but dear friends.

I write this with those in mind who believe that guardrails are necessary in a free society. My hope and prayer is that this work adds to the insights of everyday Americans from the perspective of one of your own, someone who struggles to buy groceries and pay for car insurance, not someone who lives in the D.C. bubble and doesn't know the price of a carton of eggs, and has limited relationship with those who do. I thank all those who shared their stories of angst, triumph, despair, and exasperation while insisting on working to undergird and empower the *least of these* against incredible odds and pressure during the Trump administration.

Notes

[1] Charles Dickens, *A Tale of Two Cities*, 1859.

[2] Barack Obama, POTUS, Remarks by the President on Trayvon Martin, The White House, Office of the Press Secretary, July 19, 2013, https://obamawhitehouse.archives.gov/the-press-office/2013/07/19/remarks-president-trayvon-martin

[3] Kobes Du Mez, ***Jesus and John Wayne: How White Evangelicals Corrupted a Faith and Fractured a Nation***, Liveright Publishing, 2020.

[4] **5 Ways the Trump Administration's Policies Have Harmed Children,** *American Progress.org*, October 20, 2020 {Accessed: February 14, 2023}, https://www.americanprogress.org/article/5-ways-trump-administrations-policies-harmed-children/

[5] *Supreme Court of the United States, 19-1392 Dobbs v. Jackson Women's Health Organization*, June 24, 2022 {Accessed: December 7, 2022}, https://www.supremecourt.gov/opinions/21pdf/19-1392_6j37.pdf

[6] Whitehouse.gov, **Confronting the opioid crisis in the United States** {Accessed: September 9, 2019}, https://www.opioids.gov/

[7] O'Neill Institute for National and Global Health Law Georgetown University Law Center, **A Thoughtful Comparison of the Government's Response to Crack Epidemic of the 1980s vs. the Current Opioid Epidemic: A Look at Criminalization, Race, and Treatment,** October 17, 2017 {Accessed: September 9, 2019}, https://oneill.law.georgetown.edu/a-thoughtful-comparison-of-the-governments-response-to-crack-epidemic-of-the-1980s-vs-the-current-opioid-epidemic-a-look-at-criminalization-race-and-treatment/

[8] Tim Dickinson, **How Trump Took the Middle Class to the Cleaners,** *Rolling Stone*, October 26, 2020 {Accessed: February 18, 2023}, https://www.rollingstone.com/politics/politics-features/trump-covid-response-economy-jobs-taxes-inequality-1080345/

[9] Terence P. Jeffrey, **29.2% of U.S. Households Had Incomes of $100,000+ in 2017,** *CNSNews.com*, September 12, 2018 {Accessed: September 9, 2019}, https://www.cnsnews.com/news/article/terence-p-jeffrey/292-us-households-made-more-100000-2017

[10] Isabel Sawhill and Christopher Pulliam, **The middle class needs a tax cut: Trump didn't give it to them,** *The Economist*, October 16, 2018 {Accessed: February 18, 2023}, https://www.brookings.edu/blog/up-front/2018/10/16/the-middle-class-needs-a-tax-cut-trump-didnt-give-it-to-them/

[11] Christine Ammer, **Make bricks without straw,** The American Heritage Dictionary of Idioms, 2003 {Accessed: February 15, 2023}, https://idioms.thefreedictionary.com/make+bricks+without+straw

[12] Camilo Maldonado, **Trump Tax Cuts Helped Billionaires Pay Less Taxes Than The Working Class In 2018,** *Forbes,* October 19, 2019 {Accessed: September 16, 2022}, https://www.forbes.com/sites/camilomaldonado/2019/10/10/trump-tax-cuts-helped-billionaires-pay-less-taxes-than-the-working-class-in-2018/?sh=6715b8c53128

[13] Harvard Kennedy School's Ash Center for Democratic Governance and Innovation, **Can the US Regain the Lead in the Microchip Race?,** July 29, 2022 {Accessed: December 7, 2022}, https://ash.harvard.edu/global-microchip-production-can-we-catch

[14] **This Day in History: March 30th, 1981, Ronald Reagan Shot,** A&E Television Networks, November 24, 2009 {Accessed: December 7, 2022}, https://www.history.com/this-day-in-history/president-reagan-shot

[15] **Moments in U.S. Diplomatic History,** Association for Diplomatic Studies and Training, 1998 {Accessed: July 20, 2019}, https://adst.org/2014/03/al-haig-and-the-reagan-assassination-attempt-im-in-charge-here/

[16] Kate Sullivan, **Record 14,000 immigrant refugee children in U.S. custody, HHS officials confirm,** CNN, November 23, 2018 {Accessed December 4, 2022}, https://www.cnn.com/2018/11/23/politics/hhs-record-14000-immigrant-children-us-custody/index.html

[17] Nicole Hannah-Jones, **The 1619 Project,** *New York Times Magazine,* August 14, 2019 {Accessed: December 7, 2022}, https://www.nytimes.com/interactive/2019/08/14/magazine/1619-america-slavery.thtml

[18] Again, as at many 45 rallies before and after election, 45's fever-pitched zealots yelled, "Build that wall!"

[19] Josh Dawsey, **45 derides protections for immigrants from 'shithole' countries,** *Washington Post,* January 12, 2018 {Accessed: September 12, 2019}, https://beta.washingtonpost.com/politics/45-attacks-protections-for-immigrants-from-shithole-countries-in-oval-office-meeting/2018/01/11/bfc0725c-f711-11e7-91af-31ac729add94_story.html

[20] Jan Zilinski, **Why didn't more congressional Republicans condemn 45's racist tweets about 'The Squad'? This graph explains,** *Washington Post,* July 20, 2019 {Accessed: July 21, 2019}, https://www.washingtonpost.com/politics/2019/07/20/why-didnt-more-congressional-republicans-condemn-45s-racist-tweets-about-squad-this-graph-explains/?utm_term=.53ebac9e5f0b

[21] Dan Merica, **Trump: Frederick Douglass is being recognized 'more and more,'** CNN, February 2, 2017 {Accessed: June 16, 2021},

https://www.cnn.com/2017/02/02/politics/donald-trump-frederick-douglass/index.html

[22] Tommy Beer, **Prominent NBA Players And Even Some Owners Protested This Weekend,** *Forbes*, June 8, 2020 {Accessed: February 18, 2023}, https://www.forbes.com/sites/tommybeer/2020/06/08/prominent-nba-players-and-even-some-owners-protested-this-weekend/?sh=1addd400b05c

[23] Sean Illing, **Race and football: why NFL owners are so scared of Colin Kaepernick,** *Vox*, September 6, 2018 {Accessed: June 26, 2021}, https://www.vox.com/2018/4/25/17257978/kaepernick-nfl-nike-protest-race-football

[24] Tamara Gilkes Borr, **What is Critical Race Theory? Checks and Balances,** part 1, *The Economist*, July 15, 2022 {Accessed: September 16, 2022}, https://www.economist.com/podcasts/2022/07/15/what-is-critical-race-theory?utm_medium=cpc.adword.pd&utm_source=google&utm_campaign=a.22brand_pmax&utm_content=conversion.direct-response.anonymous&gclid=Cj0KCQjwvZCZBhCiARIsAPXbajsUcTkTzdhqLxAX5Ktg-Agegedt-ullnrybtbQADcSVC-_2lMCYyu0aArdfEALw_wcB&gclsrc=aw.ds

[25] Trump speech at West Columbia, South Carolina, June 26, 2018.

[26] Justin Elliot, Derek Kravitz, and Al Shaw, **Meet the hundreds of officials Trump has quietly installed across the government,** *Salon*, March 10, 2017 {Accessed: September 10,2022}, https://www.salon.com/2017/03/10/meet-the-hundreds-of-officials-trump-has-quietly-installed-across-the-government/

[27] Tracy Jan and Jose A. Del Real, **Carson compares slaves to immigrants coming to 'a land of dreams and opportunity,'** *Washington Post*, March 6, 2017 {Accessed: September 16, 2022}, https://www.washingtonpost.com/news/wonk/wp/2017/03/06/carson-compares-slaves-to-immigrants-coming-to-a-land-of-dreams-and-opportunity/

[28] *Equity Forward,* **Darcie Johnston** {Accessed: September 10, 2022}, https://equityfwd.org/te-johnston

[29] Equity Forward, **Shot and Chaser, Shannon Royce admits Christian bias at HHS,** May 7, 2018 {Accessed September 10, 2022}, https://equityfwd.org/shot-and-chaser-shannon-royce-admits-christian-bias-hhs

[30] Ibid.

[31] German Lopez, **Study: President Obama's election scared Americans into buying more guns,** *Vox*, January 21, 2016 {Accessed: January 22, 2023}, https://www.vox.com/2016/1/21/10801664/obama-gun-sales

[32] History on the Net, **Obama Death Threats: From Empty to Serious,** *Salem Media*, January 19, 2023.

[33] Jeff Zeleny and Jim Rutenberg, **Threats Against Obama Spiked Early,** *New York Times,* December 6, 2009 {Accessed: January 22, 2023}, https://www.nytimes.com/2009/12/06/us/06threat.html

[34] Baltimore Sun Editorial Board, **Trump said he wanted more immigrants from places like Norway. Now he's using policy to try to make it happen,** *Baltimore Sun*, August 13, 2019 {Accessed: June 21, 2021}, https://www.baltimoresun.com/opinion/editorial/bs-ed-trump-green-cards-20190813-mp2pfpdtevc25j24qft7enasoi-story.html

[35] Christina Caron, **A black student was napping and a white student called the police,** *New York Times*, May 9, 2018 {Accessed: October 2, 2019}, https://www.nytimes.com/2018/05/09/nyregion/yale-black-student-nap.html

[36] Niraj Chokshi, **White Woman Nicknamed 'Permit Patty' Regrets Confrontation Over Black Girl Selling Water,** *New York Times*, June 25, 2019 {Accessed: April 10, 2021}, https://www.nytimes.com/2018/06/25/us/permit-patty-black-girl-water.html?auth=login-google1tap&login=google1tap

[37] Adam Horton and Keith McMillan, **#IDAdam, the white man who called police on a woman at their neighborhood pool, loses his job,** *Washington Post,* July 8th, 2018 {Accessed: November 20, 2021},

https://www.washingtonpost.com/news/post-nation/wp/2018/07/06/idadam-the-white-man-who-called-police-on-a-woman-at-their-neighborhood-pool-loses-his-job/

[38] Sinead Baker, **A black lawmaker says someone called the police on her when she was canvassing in her district,** *Business Insider*, July 5, 2018 {Accessed: February 9, 2021}, https://www.businessinsider.com/janelle-bynum-police-called-canvassed-in-oregon-2018-7

[39] MSNBC, Ali Velshi Show, July 6, 2018.

[40] Josh Magness, **'Suspicious' 11-year-old was delivering newspapers — so a neighbor called the police,** *Miami Herald*, July 11, 2018 {Accessed: February 9, 2021}, https://www.miamiherald.com/news/nation-world/national/article214684265.html

[41] Lemon, Don, CNN host, July 12, 2018.

[42] Ann Smajstrla, Cox Media Group National Content Desk, **Referee with previous allegations of racism forces wrestler to cut off dreadlocks,** *Atlanta Journal-Constitution*, December 21, 2018 {Accessed: December 21, 2018}, https://www.ajc.com/news/national/referee-with-previous-allegations-racism-forces-wrestler-cut-off-dreadlocks/uNGiacbIfzWkIvEW3UcVNL/

[43] Associated Press, **Appeals court upholds conviction of ex-Dallas officer Amber Guyger,** *New York Post*, August 21, 2021 {Accessed: May 30, 2022}, Amber Guyger's murder conviction upheld in Texas appeals court (nypost.com)

[44] Alobar Bandaloop, Facebook post, August 21, 2018.

[45] Aaron Randle, **Westport guard who asked Black bartender for a 'Trayvon Martini' is fired,** *Kansas City Star*, August 22, 2018 {Accessed: September 25, 2019}, https://www.kansascity.com/news/local/article217136730.html

⁴⁶ Karu F. Daniels, **Florida judge sentences 21-year-old to ten days for missing jury duty,** *The Root*, September 25, 2019 {Accessed: October 6, 2019}, https://www.courts.ca.gov/partners/documents/felony_sentencing.pdf

⁴⁷ Criminal Justice Realignment, https://www.courts.ca.gov/partners/realignment.htm#:~:text=Criminal%20justice%20realignment%20changes%20the,their%20time%20in%20county%20jail.

⁴⁸ Janine Phakdeetham, **PREDATOR: How long was Brock Turner in jail for?**, *The U.S. Sun*, August 4, 2020 {Accessed: April 10, 2021}, https://www.the-sun.com/news/1253032/brock-turner-stanford-university-swimmer-rape-sex-offender/

⁴⁹ Khaleda Rahman, **Twitter Users Point Out Dylann Roof Was Fed Burger King by Officers in Wake of Rayshard Brooks Shooting,** *Newsweek*, June 15, 2020 {Accessed: February 18, 2023}, https://www.newsweek.com/comparisons-between-police-treatment-rayshard-brooks-dylann-roof-1510896

⁵⁰ Yair Rosenberg, **'Jews will not replace us': Why white supremacists go after Jews,** *Washington Post*, August 14, 2017 {Accessed: July 25, 2022}, https://www.washingtonpost.com/news/acts-of-faith/wp/2017/08/14/jews-will-not-replace-us-why-white-supremacists-go-after-jews/

⁵¹ Nurith Aizenman, **Trump Wishes We Had More Immigrants From Norway. Turns Out We Once Did,** NPR, January 12, 2018 {Accessed: January 18, 2019}, https://www.npr.org/sections/goatsandsoda/2018/01/12/577673191/trump-wishes-we-had-more-immigrants-from-norway-turns-out-we-once-did

⁵² John Haltiwanger, **Trump doesn't deny calling African countries 'shitholes' while meeting with Nigeria's president,** *Business Insider*, April 30, 2018 {Accessed: November 20, 2021}, https://www.businessinsider.com/trump-doesnt-deny-calling-african-countries-shitholes-2018-4

[53] Jesse J. Holland and Gerald Herbert, **New Orleans takes down white supremacist monument,** *AJC,* April 25, 2017, p. A10.

[54] Nation, PBS, **Obama team left pandemic playbook for Trump administration, officials confirm,** May 15, 2020 {Accessed: September 30, 2022}, https://www.pbs.org/newshour/nation/obama-team-left-pandemic-playbook-for-trump-administration-officials-confirm

[55] Matthew Lee, **Tillerson condemns hate speech, 'un-American' bigotry,** *PBS.org,* August 18, 2017 {Accessed: October 10, 2022}, https://www.pbs.org/newshour/politics/watch-tillerson-condemns-hate-speech-says-bigotry-un-american

[56] Maggie Aston, **Trump's Call for 'Termination' of Constitution Draws Rebukes,** *New York Times,* December 3, 2022 {Accessed: December 15, 2022}, https://www.nytimes.com/2022/12/04/us/politics/trump-constitution-republicans.html

[57] Jesse J. Holland, **Stephen Miller is on a crusade to help white men. And it's working,** MSNBC, December 17, 2022 {Accessed: December 15, 2022}, https://www.msnbc.com/opinion/msnbc-opinion/stephen-miller-crusade-help-white-men-working-rcna61538

[58] Adam Fairclough, *To Redeem the Soul of America: The Southern Christian Leadership Conference and Martin Luther King, Jr.,* University of Georgia Press, 1987.

[59] Southern Poverty Law Center, **Civil Rights Martyrs** {Accessed: December 12, 2021}, https://www.splcenter.org/what-we-do/civil-rights-memorial/civil-rights-martyrs

[60] Arri Grewal, **'THEY WANT OUR RHYTHM BUT NOT OUR BLUES',** *Artefact* {Accessed: December 27, 2021}, https://www.artefactmagazine.com/2019/01/07/modern-day-blackface/

[61] News One, **Rev. Traci Blackmon chronicles terrifying events in Charlottesville,** Interviewer Roland Martin, August 15, 2017 {Accessed: December 5, 2023},

https://www.bing.com/videos/riverview/relatedvideo?q=Traci+Blacmon%2c+Charlottesville+tragedy&mid=2F5EDDD1B06E4E1992DB2F5EDDD1B06E4E1992DB&FORM=VIRE

[62] Anthony Zurcher, **A White House meltdown in the making**, BBC, August 16, 2017 {Accessed: January 15, 2018}, https://www.bbc.com/news/world-us-canada-40952797

[63] Matt Pearce, Robert Armengol, and David S. Cloud, **Three dead, dozens hurt after Virginia white nationalist rally is dispersed; Trump blames 'many sides'**, *Los Angeles Times*, August 12, 2017 {Accessed: December 22, 2021}, https://www.latimes.com/nation/nationnow/la-na-charlottesville-white-nationalists-rally-20170812-story.html

[64] Politico/Morning Consult Poll, **Looking Back, Clashes in Charlottesville**, MSNBC, Morning Joy, August 12, 2018 {Accessed: October 15, 2023}, https://www.msnbc.com/am-joy/watch/looking-back-clashes-in-charlottesville-1297460803764

[65] Statement of President Joe Biden on the Fourth Anniversary of the Events at Charlottesville, Virginia, White House Briefing Room, August 12, 2021.

[66] Omarosa Manigault Newman, CNN, the Fredricka Whitfield Show, August 12, 2018.

[67] Erin Blakemore, **How the GI Bill's Promise Was Denied to a Million Black WWII Veterans**, History.com, June 21, 2019 {Accessed: December 27, 2021}, https://www.history.com/news/gi-bill-black-wwii-veterans-benefits

[68] Scott Horsley, **FACT CHECK: White House Apologizes For False Claim About African American Jobs**, NPR, August 15, 2018 {Accessed: December 12, 2021}, https://www.npr.org/2018/08/15/638851896/fact-check-white-house-apologizes-for-false-claim-about-African American-jobs

[69] Dominique DuBois Gilliard, *Subversive Witness*, Zondervan Reflective, 2021.

⁷⁰ Jacob Pamuk, **Trump revokes former CIA Director John Brennan's security clearance,** CNBC, August 15, 2018 {Accessed: January 22, 2023}, https://www.cnbc.com/2018/08/15/trump-revokes-former-cia-director-john-brennans-security-clearance.html

⁷¹ Frank Figliuzzi, former assistant director for counter-intelligence at the FBI, interviewed on MSNBC, August 19, 2018.

⁷² Norma Josephine Norwood and Carol J. Williams, **No Grandchildren Left Behind: Educational Issues Faced By Grandparents,** *Human Services Today*, Fall 2007 {Accessed: January 7, 2023}, https://uwosh.edu/hst/no-grandchildren-left-behind-educational-issues-faced-by-grandparents/

⁷³ Anna North, **The Trump administration's war on birth control,** The Center for Public Integrity, September 24, 2020 {Accessed: January 2, 2023}, https://publicintegrity.org/politics/system-failure/the-trump-administrations-war-on-birth-control/

⁷⁴ Gregory Korte, **Here's the truth about Meals on Wheels in Trump's budget,** *USA Today*, March 19, 2017 {Accessed: January 2, 2023, https://www.usatoday.com/story/news/politics/2017/03/18/meal-on-wheels-trump-budget-proposal-cuts/99308928/

⁷⁵ Washington Post staff, **President Obama's October 1 remarks on the government shutdown and ObamaCare,** October 1, 2013 {Accessed: February 3, 2024}, https://www.washingtonpost.com/politics/transcript-president-obamas-oct-1-remarks-on-obamacare-and-the-government-shutdown/2013/10/01/2f7d071c-2ab7-11e3-97a3-ff2758228523_story.html

⁷⁶ Visualutions, The History of Federally Qualified Health Centers {Accessed: January 31, 2023}, https://www.visualutions.com/blog/the-history-of-federally-qualified-health-centers/

⁷⁷ Aaron Cooley, **War on Poverty,** United States History, *Britannica* {Accessed: January 31, 2023}, https://www.britannica.com/topic/Economic-Opportunity-Act

[78] **Countdown to Open Enrollment,** DHHS, Healthcare.gov, October 24, 2016.

[79] Ibid.

[80] **Rollout GO**: Mississippi, www.healthcare.gov, 2016.

[81] U.S. Dept. of Health & Human Services, **New data show improvements in health care access, affordability and quality in Florida under the Affordable Care Act**, press release, September 14, 2016.

[82] Ibid.

[83] Office of the Secretary, **Access to Quality, Affordable Health Care: Progress and Promise of the Affordable Care Act and Other Administration Efforts,** The White House, October 20, 2016.

[84] Editorial board, *Raleigh News & Observer*, **Time for Ellmers to end the Obamacare bashing,** August 24, 2015 {Accessed: January 31, 2023}, https://www.newsobserver.com/opinion/editorials/article32257041.html

[85] Colin Kaepernick, **Nike's ad and believing in something,** *ADL*, October 11, 2018 {Accessed: January 31, 2023}, https://www.adl.org/resources/tools-and-strategies/nikes-ad-and-believing-something

[86] Lisa De Moraes, **Donald Trump Whips Up Base Blasting Nike Ad Featuring Colin Kaepernick,** *Deadline*, September 15, 2018 {Accessed: January 31, 2023}, https://deadline.com/2018/09/donald-trump-nike-colin-kaepernick-ad-nfl-knee-national-anthem-1202457485/

[87] Matthew Choi, **Trump's most outrageous storm descriptions — a series,** *Politico,* September 12, 2018 {Accessed: July 23, 2021}, https://www.politico.com/story/2018/09/12/trump-storms-statements-817202

⁸⁸ Nicole Chavez, **Hurricane Maria killed 2,975 people in Puerto Rico. It's the second deadliest U.S. storm in over a century,** CNN, August 29, 2018 {Accessed: September 22, 2018, https://www.cnn.com/2018/08/29/us/puerto-rico-deaths-new-york-9-11-trnd/index.html

⁸⁹ Phone call from *Atlanta Inquirer* editor David Stokes, September 24, 2018.

⁹⁰ Fannin County (GA) *Sentinel* Editor Elaine Owen's response to electronic message to editors to print op/ed by HHS Secretary Alex Azar touting Trump's success fighting the opioid epidemic in Georgia, October 7, 2019.

⁹¹ Email from HHS Region IV Public Affairs Specialist Deric Gilliard to MHAP, the Mississippi Primary Care Association, Oak Hill Ministries and other Mississippi enrollment leaders, dated September 26, 2017.

⁹² W.E.B. DuBois, **Strivings of the Negro People,** *The Atlantic*, August 1897 {Accessed: July 4, 2023}, https://www.theatlantic.com/magazine/archive/1897/08/strivings-of-the-negro-people/305446/

⁹³ Email from Dylan Scott, policy reporter, VOX, to Deric Gilliard, about HHS participation in OE4, September 18, 2017.

⁹⁴ **Social Determinants of Health,** CDC, December 8, 2022, {Accessed: July 4, 2023}, https://www.cdc.gov/about/sdoh/index.html

⁹⁵ Kate Nocera and Paul McLeod, **The Trump administration is pulling out of Obamacare enrollment events,** *BuzzFeed News*, September 27, 2017 {Accessed: May 20, 2022}, https://www.buzzfeednews.com/article/katenocera/the-trump-administration-wont-support-state-obamacare

⁹⁶ Ibid.

[97] Ari Melber, **The Beat,** MSNBC, September 28, 2017, Transcript 9/28/17, Guests: Barbara McQuade, William Steinem, Roy Mitchell and Mya Wiley {Accessed: October 31, 2020}, https://www.msnbc.com/transcripts/msnbc-live-with-ari-melber/2017-09-28-msna1026731

[98] Ibid.

[99] Ibid.

[100] Ari Melber, **Exclusive: Health care insider reveals Trump Planned to Sabotage ACA,** MSNBC, September 28, 2017, https://www.msnbc.com/msnbc-news/watch/exclusive-health-care-insider-reveals-trump-planned-to-sabotage-aca-1057442371683

[101] Conversation between MHAP Director Roy Mitchell and author Deric Gilliard, February 8, 2023.

[102] Erica Hensley, **Amid Obamacare uncertainty, Mississippi among states with health care enrollment gains,** *Mississippi Today*, December 28, 2018 {Accessed: September 20, 2022}, https://mississippitoday.org/2018/12/28/despite-obamacare-uncertainty-mississippi-among-states-with-health-care-enrollment-gains/

[103] Mississippi remains near the bottom of national health rankings, beating only Louisiana, December 26, 2018.

[104] Heidi Przybyla, **Trump's undermining of Obamacare violates the Constitution, new lawsuit charges,** NBC News, August 2, 2018.

[105] Trump tweet from June 4, 2018.

[106] Glenn C. Altschuler, Opinion: **'I alone can fix it,' Trump said, but has he?,** *The Hill*, June 30, 2019 {Accessed November 15, 2022}, https://thehill.com/opinion/white-house/451050-president-trump-said-i-alone-can-fix-it-has-he/

[107] Keira Phillips, ABC Evening News with David Muir, August 21, 2019.

[108] Jonathan Greenblatt, Director of the Anti-Defamation League, responding to President Trump, August 21, 2019.

[109] **45, Donald**, ABC Evening News with David Muir, August 21, 2019.

[110] John McWhorter, **Why the right thinks Obama's a narcissist, and why they're wrong,** *The Daily Beast*, April 14, 2017 {Accessed September 3, 2022}, https://www.thedailybeast.com/why-the-right-thinks-obamas-a-narcissistand-why-theyre-wrong

[111] Email from Dr. Conners to RD Renee Ellmers, January 3, 2019.

[112] https://www.britannica.com/topic/Republican-Party

[113] University of North Carolina, **183 Rural Hospital Closures since January 2005,** The Cecil G. Sheps Center for Health Services Research {Accessed: January 8, 2022}, https://www.shepscenter.unc.edu/programs-projects/rural-health/rural-hospital-closures/

[114] Ernie Suggs, **What Kavanaugh drama says about due process and the Central Park 5,** *AJC*, October 4, 2018 {Accessed: December 18, 2021}

[115] Ibid.

[116] Jan Ransom, **Trump Will Not Apologize for Calling for Death Penalty Over Central Park Five,** *New York Times*, June 18, 2019 {Accessed: December 18, 2021}, https://www.nytimes.com/2019/06/18/nyregion/central-park-five-trump.html

[117] Cheryl Thomson, **Fatal Police Shootings Of Unarmed Black People Reveal Troubling Pattern,** NPR, January 25, 2021 {Accessed: January 17, 2022}, https://www.npr.org/2021/01/25/956177021/fatal-police-shootings-of-unarmed-black-people-reveal-troubling-patterns

[118] Bill Torpy, *AJC*, **Torpy at Large: Black man, white kids, and our arrested development,** October 12, 2018 {Accessed: July 12, 2023},

https://www.ajc.com/news/local/torpy-large-black-man-white-kids-and-our-arrested-development/GR0Tb7KE9aIS7qbrjba4jP/

[119] Ibid.

[120] Ibid.

[121] NBC Evening News, **Retired firefighter found guilty for shooting at lost black teen on doorstep,** October 12, 2018 {Accessed: June 8, 2019}, https://www.nbcnews.com/news/us-news/retired-firefighter-found-guilty-shooting-lost-black-teen-doorstep-n919656; ABC Evening News, reported by Alex Perez, October 12, 2018.

[122] Alex Horton and Eli Rosenberg, **A teen missed a school bus; when he knocked on the door for directions, a man shot at him,** *Washington Post*, October 11, 2018 {Accessed: October 11, 2018}, https://www.washingtonpost.com/nation/2018/10/11/teen-missed-school-bus-when-he-knocked-door-directions-man-shot-him/?noredirect=on&utm_term=.ad8a6ce6c9b5

[123] Melissa Gomez, **White woman who blocked black neighbor from building is fired,** *New York Times*, October 15, 2018 {Accessed: October 15, 2018}, https://www.nytimes.com/2018/10/15/us/hilary-brooke-apartment-patty-st-louis.html

[124] John Bowden, **Woman called 'Golfcart Gail' called police on black father at soccer game,** *The Hill*, October 17, 2018 {Accessed: October 17, 2018}, https://thehill.com/blogs/blog-briefing-room/news/411877-woman-dubbed-golfcart-gail-called-police-on-black-father-at

[125] **Dixiecrat**, Britannica, https://www.britannica.com/topic/Dixiecrat

[126] The Leadership Conference on Civil and Human Rights, **Trump Administration Civil and Human Rights Rollbacks** {Accessed: July 20, 2023}, https://civilrights.org/trump-rollbacks/

127 Tom Kludt, CNN Business, **Megyn Kelly apologizes for defending blackface Halloween costumes,** October 25, 2018 {Accessed: July 12, 2019}, https://www.cnn.com/2018/10/23/media/megyn-kelly-blackface/index.html

128 Brad Knickerbocker, **Flash! Fox's Megyn Kelly now admits Jesus may not be 'white,'** *Christian Science Monitor,* December 4, 2013 {Accessed: July 18, 2017}, https://www.csmonitor.com/USA/Politics/Decoder/2013/1214/Flash!-Fox-s-Megyn-Kelly-now-admits-Jesus-may-not-be-white

129 Lindsey Davis, *ABC Evening News,* October 25, 2018.

130 Ibid.

131 Rachel Kaadzi Ghansah, **A Most American Terrorist: The making of Dylann Roof,** *GQ,* August 21, 2017, https://www.gq.com/story/dylann-roof-making-of-an-american-terrorist

132 Mahita Gajanan, Helen Regan, Tara John, and Joseph Hincks, **These are the victims of the Texas church shooting,** *Time,* November 7, 2018 {Accessed: October 28, 2018}, https://time.com/5010967/texas-church-shooting-victims/

133 **Historical racial and ethnic demographics** *of the United States.* Wikipedia, June 21, 2024. https://w.wiki/Ajvw

134 Theodore R. Johnson, **We need to count black people as 3/5 of a person: For Reparations, give them 5/3 of a vote,** *Washington Post,* August 21, 2015 {Accessed: November 1, 2018}, https://www.washingtonpost.com/posteverything/wp/2015/08/21/we-used-to-count-black-americans-as-35-of-a-person-instead-of-reparations-give-them-53-of-a-vote/?utm_term=.530b5565aef6

135 **The Mississippi Black Codes** (1866), https://blackpast.org/African American-history-primary-documents. These are among the first post-Civil War statutes designed to establish the rights and regulate the behavior of ex-slaves at the state level.

¹³⁶ The Conversation, **Andrew Johnson's failed presidency echoes in 45 White House,** February 13, 2018 {Accessed: November 2, 2018}, http://theconversation.com/andrew-johnsons-failed-presidency-echoes-in-45s-white-house-91139

¹³⁷ Impeachment of Andrew Johnson, https://en.wikipedia.org/wiki/Impeachment_of_Andrew_Johnson#Presidential_Reconstruction {Accessed: November 2, 2018}

¹³⁸ Rosalind Early, **The Sweat and Blood of Fannie Lou Hamer,** *HUMANITIES*, Volume 42, Number 1 (Winter 2021) {Accessed: July 12, 2023}, https://www.neh.gov/article/sweat-and-blood-fannie-lou-hamer#:~:text=In%201961%2C%20a%20white%20doctor,nicknamed%20a%20%E2%80%9CMississippi%20appendectomy.%E2%80%9D

¹³⁹ J. Morgan Kousser, *The Shaping of Southern Politics: Suffrage Restriction and the Establishment of the One-Party South, 1880-1910,* Yale University Press, 1974; Keisha N. Blain, **Fannie Lou Hamer's Dauntless Fight for Black Americans' Right to Vote,** *Smithsonian Magazine*, August 20, 2020 {Accessed: June 3, 2021}, https://www.smithsonianmag.com/history/100-years-women-ballot-box-180975366/

¹⁴⁰ John Blake, **These two photos show who Georgia's new elections law benefits – and hurts,** CNN, March 26, 2021 {Accessed: April 3 2023}, https://www.cnn.com/2021/03/26/politics/georgia-voting-law-two-photos/index.html

¹⁴¹ Jake Tapper, State of the Union, CNN, November 3, 2018.

¹⁴² Mark Niesse, **Georgia ranks high in voter cancellations and new registrations,** *Atlanta Journal-Constitution*, September 12, 2019 {Accessed May 2, 2022}, https://www.ajc.com/news/state--regional-govt--politics/voter-purges-and-registrations-detailed-report-georgia-elections/n3tgnePbnGQbpGL1JaplEP/

¹⁴³ Jake Tapper, State of the Union, CNN, November 3, 2018.

¹⁴⁴ Lance Simmens, **We Cannot Make America Great Again Before We Make America Good Again!,** *Huffington Post,* November 19,

2017 {Accessed: January 17, 2022}, https://www.huffpost.com/entry/we-cannot-make-america-great-again-before-we-make-america_b_5a112360e4b0e6450602ebd2

[145] Jason Hart, **Ohio Gov. John Kasich's Medicaid expansion is a faith-based mistake,** *Washington Examiner*, October 10, 2013 {Accessed June 1, 2023}, https://www.washingtonexaminer.com/op-eds/1400732/ohio-gov-john-kasichs-medicaid-expansion-is-a-faith-based-mistake/

[146] Tim Sweeney, Georgia Budget and Policy Institute, **Adding Up the Net Cost of Medicaid Expansion - $353 Million for 10 Years,** Fact Sheet, February 2014 {Accessed: July 2, 2023], https://gbpi.org/wp-content/uploads/2014/02/Adding-UP-the-Net-Cost-of-Medicaid-Expansion1.pdf

[147] Ben Leonard, **'QAnon shaman' granted organic food in jail after report of deteriorating health,** *Politico,* February 3, 2021 {Accessed: May 8, 2023}, https://www.politico.com/news/2021/02/03/qanon-shaman-organic-food-465563

[148] Scott Neuman, **First Lady's Parents Become U.S. Citizens Thanks To 'Chain Migration,'** *NPR*, August 10, 2018 {Accessed: October 21, 2022}, https://www.npr.org/2018/08/10/637371714/first-ladys-parents-become-u-s-citizens-thanks-to-chain-migration

[149] Nicole Chavez, Emanuella Grinberg, and Elliott McLaughlin, **Pittsburgh synagogue gunman said he wanted all Jews to die, criminal complaint says,** CNN, October 31, 2018 {Accessed: January 17, 2022}, https://www.cnn.com/2018/10/28/us/pittsburgh-synagogue-shooting/index.html

[150] John Beeler, **A City too Busy to Hate**, Medium.com {Accessed: January 17, 2022}, https://medium.com/@johnthebeeler/a-city-too-busy-to-hate-29533b219477

[151] Tia Mitchell, **Judge Sides with Democrats, Dougherty must accept late-arriving absentee ballots,** *Atlanta Journal-Constitution,* November 9, 2018.

[152] Maria Papadopoulos, Boston25News.com, **Boston historical society apologizes for 'dreaming of a white Dorchester' holiday card,** November 26, 2018 {Accessed: November 28, 2018}, https://www.ajc.com/news/national/boston-historical-society-apologizes-for-dreaming-white-dorchester-holiday-card/On85tesgsCZkbnsUaqfCBL/

[153] Cindy Skrzycki, **ATT Apologizes for 'Racist' Illustration,** *Washington Post,* September 17, 1993 {Accessed: January 18, 2022}, https://www.washingtonpost.com/archive/politics/1993/09/17/att-apologizes-for-racist-illustration/22b85908-8c5b-47dd-ad10-0a293c9a8623/

[154] Ibid.

[155] The Last Word with Lawrence O'Donnell, MSNBC, December 14, 2018.

[156] Gil Scott-Heron, *The Revolution will not be Televised, The Revolution Begins,* Ace Records, 1971 {Accessed: July 1, 2023}, https://www.youtube.com/watch?v=vwSRqaZGsPw

[157] Mary Bruce, covering President 45, ABC Evening News, March 27, 2019.

[158] Delories Williams, on countless occasions.

[159] Healthcare 'mandate' invalid, federal court rules, AJC, December 19, 2017, p. A3.

[160] Ricardo Alonso-Zaldivar, **Plan to import cheaper Canadian drugs advances under Trump,** *Associated Press,* December 18, 2019 {Accessed: March 3, 2019}, https://apnews.com/article/e9d09fe0ad100efe44992e0b9d9d0cbe

[161] Kara Phillips, ABC Evening News, March 27th, 2019.

[162] Minyvonne Burke, **James Alex Fields found guilty of killing Heather Heyer during violent Charlottesville white nationalist rally,** NBC News, December 7, 2018 {Accessed: March 26, 2019},

https://www.nbcnews.com/news/crime-courts/james-alex-fields-found-guilty-killings-heather-heyer-druing-violent-n945186

[163] Ibid.

[164] ACF, Fact Sheet: Unaccompanied Children Program, August 1, 2023 {Accessed: August 1, 2023}, https://www.hhs.gov/sites/default/files/uac-program-fact-sheet.pdf

[165] Alfredo Corchado, **Central American migrants face grueling journey north,** *Dallas Morning News,* Mexico Bureau {Accessed: July 16, 2020}, http://res.dallasnews.com/interactives/migrantroute/

[166] Walt Hunter, **The story behind the poem on the Statue of Liberty,** *The Atlantic,* January 16, 2018 {Accessed: March 20, 2020}, https://www.theatlantic.com/entertainment/archive/2018/01/the-story-behind-the-poem-on-the-statue-of-liberty/550553/

[167] Paul Heintz, **The Undertaker's Daughter: Darcie Johnston Wants to Kill Vermont Health Care Reform,** Seven DaysVT.com, October 2, 2013 {Accessed: July 1, 2015}, https://www.sevendaysvt.com/vermont/the-undertakers-daughter-darcie-johnston-wants-to-kill-vermont-health-care-reform/Content?oid=2266249

[168] Arin Youn, **How a Military Base's New Name Honors a Military Spouse and Mother,** *New York Times,* May 14th, 2023 {Accessed: July 18, 2023}, https://www.nytimes.com/2023/05/14/us/politics/fort-benning-renamed-fortmoore.html#:~:text=%E2%80%9CBy%20honoring%20them%2C%20Fort%20Moore,the%20success%20of%20our%20military.%E2%80%9D

[169] Tara Copp, **Thousands of undocumented children could be housed at Fort Benning. What's next?,** *Columbus Ledger-Enquirer,* June 5, 2019 [Accessed: July 30, 2020}, https://www.ledger-enquirer.com/article231201518.html#storylink=cpy

[170] Sabrina Maggiore, **Mayor Coppinger 'embarrassed' by scant information on migrant children housing situation,** New Channel

9/ABC, April 9, 2021 {Accessed: April 11, 2021}, https://newschannel9.com/news/local/report-immigrant-children-relocated-to-old-tennessee-temple-dorms-in-chattanooga

[171] Owen Quinn, **10-month-old baby found dead after migrants' raft capsizes on Rio Grande,** ABC News, May 2, 2019 {Accessed: February 15, 2023}, https://abcnews.go.com/Politics/10-month-baby-found-dead-migrants-raft-capsizes/story?id=62789806

[172] Natalie Gallón, Ana Melgar, and Steve Almasy, **A shocking image of a drowned man and his daughter underscores the crisis at the US-Mexico border,** CNN, June 26, 2019 {Accessed: June 28, 2019}, https://www.cnn.com/2019/06/25/americas/mexico-photo-of-father-and-daughter-dead-in-rio-grande/index.html

[173] Ibid.

[174] Farrell Evans, **When Abraham Lincoln Tried to Resettle Free Black Americans in the Caribbean,** *History.com,* February 10, 2022 {Accessed: February 4, 2023}, https://www.history.com/news/abraham-lincoln-black-resettlement-haiti

[175] Kate Masur, **The African American Delegation to Abraham Lincoln: A Reappraisal,** *Civil War History,* Volume 56, Number 2, June 2010, pp. 117-144 {Accessed: July 17, 2019}, http://housedivided.dickinson.edu/sites/emancipation/files/2012/07/Masur-article.pdf

[176] **Ten Quick Facts: The Emancipation Proclamation, The American Battlefield Trust** {Accessed: July 18, 2019}, https://www.battlefields.org/learn/articles/10-facts-emancipation-proclamation

[177] Library of Congress, **COLLECTION: Abraham Lincoln Papers at the Library of Congress** {Accessed: July 12, 2020}, https://www.loc.gov/collections/abraham-lincoln-papers/articles-and-essays/abraham-lincoln-and-emancipation/#:~:text=If%20I%20could%20save%20the,this%20represented%20his%20official%20position.

[178] Devan Cole, **45 tweets racist attacks at progressive Democratic congresswomen,** *CNN*, July 14, 2019.

[179] Michael Schaub, **'Lion Of Liberty': Patrick Henry's Fiery Life,** NPR, November 22, 2010 {Accessed: October 12, 2023}, https://www.npr.org/2011/07/15/131444425/-lion-of-liberty-patrick-henry-s-fiery-life

[180] POTUS, tweet from the White House, retweeted by HHS Secretary Alex Azar, January 20, 2020.

[181] CMS Administrator Seema Verma tweet on King holiday, January 20, 2020.

[182] CMS Administrator Seema Verma tweet on King's birthday, January 15, 2020.

[183] CMS Administrator Seema Verma tweet on January 8, 2020.

[184] HHS Deputy Secretary Eric Hargan retweeted this from the Office of Minority Health, January 20, 2020.

[185] U.S. Surgeon General Jerome Adams, tweeting on the King holiday, January 20, 2020.

[186] Martin Luther King, Jr., at a March, 25, 1966, Chicago press conference, **Dr. Martin Luther King on health care injustice,** *PNHP.org* {Accessed: June 12, 2021}, https://pnhp.org/news/dr-martin-luther-king-on-health-care-injustice/

[187] Jesse Holland, **D.C. plaques honor slaves' contributions,** AP, *Atlanta Journal-Constitution*, June 17, 2010.

[188] PBS, **Emancipation Proclamation,** WABE {Accessed: August 1, 2023}, https://www.pbs.org/wgbh/aia/part4/4h1549.html

[189] Douglas A. Blackmon, *Slavery by Another Name: The Re-Enslavement of Black Americans from the Civil War to World War II,* Random House, 2009.

[190] Tali Hadavi, **Support for a program to pay reparations to descendants of slaves is gaining momentum, but could come with a**

$12 trillion price tag, CNBC, August 12, 2020 {Accessed: June 5, 2021}, https://www.cnbc.com/2020/08/12/slavery-reparations-cost-us-government-10-to-12-trillion.html

[191] Grace Dean, "All of the 91 US cruises currently at sea have confirmed or suspected COVID-19 on board, the CDC says," *Business Insider,* updated January 7, 2022 {Accessed: March 20, 2022}, https://www.businessinsider.com/cruise-ships-covid-outbreaks-cdc-norwegian-carnival-caribbean-disney-2022-1

[192] Kevin Breuninger, **Media's coronavirus stories trying to hurt Trump, Mick Mulvaney says as he urges public to turn off TV,** CNBC, February 28, 2020 {Accessed: January 12, 2021}, https://www.cnbc.com/2020/02/28/trump-chief-of-staff-mulvaney-suggests-people-ignore-coronavirus-news-to-calm-markets.html

[193] Holly Yan, Dan Simon, and Faith Karimi, **A cruise ship that carried a man who died from coronavirus is held off the California coast with 3,500 people on board,** CNN, March 6, 2020 {Accessed: November 13, 2022}, https://www.cnn.com/2020/03/05/health/california-coronavirus-cruise-ship-thursday/index.html

[194] Ryan Kruger, 11-Alive, NBC News, **'We're here to help our fellow citizens:' Irma, Maria injured arrive Sunday night at Dobbins,** October 2, 2017 {Accessed: November 13, 2022}, https://www.11alive.com/article/news/local/were-here-to-help-our-fellow-citizens-irma-maria-injured-arrive-sunday-night-at-dobbins/85-479968862

[195] Asia Simone Burns, **Dobbins takes in cruise passengers,** *AJC*, March 9, 2020, p. 1A.

[196] Conversation overheard by anonymous source at HHS Humphrey building.

[197] John McDonough, **Republicans Have Stopped Trying to Kill Obamacare. Here's What They're Planning Instead,** *Politico*, April 26, 2022 {Accessed: December 30, 2022}, https://www.politico.com/news/magazine/2022/04/26/gop-obamacare-aca-health-care-00027585

[198] McKenna King and Sarah Hollenbeck, **Mayor Castor joins with doctors from 3 local hospitals, says Tampa is in midst of a COVID-19 crisis,** ABC News-WFTS Tampa Bay, August 13, 2021 {Accessed: November 13, 2022}, https://www.abcactionnews.com/news/region-tampa/mayor-jane-castor-says-tampa-is-in-the-midst-of-a-covid-19-crisis

[199] Graham Readfearn, **Veteran Climate Science Denialist Bob Carter Dies of Heart Attack,** *Desmog* {Accessed: January 22, 2016}, https://www.desmogblog.com/2016/01/22/veteran-climate-science-denialist-bob-carter-dies-heart-attack

[200] Paul Heintz, **The Undertaker's Daughter: Darcie Johnston Wants to Kill Vermont Health Care Reform,** *Seven Days,* October 2, 2013 {Accessed: July 2, 2023}, https://www.sevendaysvt.com/vermont/the-undertakers-daughter-darcie-johnston-wants-to-kill-vermont-health-care-reform/Content?oid=2266249

[201] **Tears of a Clown,** *Vermont Political Observer,* January 22, 2021 {Accessed: December 20, 2022}, https://thevpo.org/2021/01/22/tears-of-a-clown/#more-6953

[202] Ibid.

[203] Justin Elliott, **Trump Then: 'I Would Have No Problem' Banning Lobbyists. Trump Now: You're Hired!,** *ProPublica,* February 14, 2017 {Accessed: February 28, 2018}, https://www.propublica.org/article/trump-before-would-have-no-problem-banning-lobbyists-trump-now-youre-hired

[204] Suzanne Dixon, **Maternity care crisis in rural areas,** NBC News, October 24, 2022.

[205] Laurie Garrett, **45 Has Sabotaged America's Coronavirus Response,** *Foreign Policy,* January 31, 2020 {Accessed: March 14, 2020}, https://foreignpolicy.com/2020/01/31/coronavirus-china-45-united-states-public-health-emergency-response/

²⁰⁶ 45, being questioned by WH reporter Yamiche Alcindor, MSNBC's The Last Word, March 13, 2020.

²⁰⁷ 45, being questioned by WH NBC reporter Kristen Welker, MSNBC's The Last Word, March 13, 2020.

²⁰⁸ Brianna Keilar, CNN News with Brook Baldwin, **Birx denies being 'trump apologist' in reputation rehab tour,** January 21, 2021 {Accessed: February 3, 2021}, https://www.bing.com/videos/riverview/relatedvideo?q=Brianna+Keilar%2c+CNN+News+with+Brook+Baldwin%2c+Birx+denies+being+%e2%80%9ctrump+apologist%22&mid=8000541BFBC53E9548458000541BFBC53E954845&FORM=VIRE

²⁰⁹ **Congressman Ro Khanna, A Bernie Sanders surrogate**, *The Last Word*, March 13, 2020.

²¹⁰ 94th Airlift Wing Public Affairs, **UPDATE: Second wave of cruise ship passengers arrive,** Dobbins Air Reserve Base, March 12, 2020 {Accessed: April 2, 2021}, https://www.dobbins.afrc.af.mil/News/Article-Display/Article/2109663/update-second-wave-of-cruise-ship-passengers-arrive/

²¹¹ A millennial responds to Biden's position that Americans don't want a revolution, March 15, 2020.

²¹² Deb Riechmann, **45 disbanded NSC pandemic unit that experts had praised,** Associated Press, March 14, 2020 {Accessed: March 16, 2020}, https://apnews.com/ce014d94b64e98b7203b873e56f80e9a

²¹³ Ibid.

²¹⁴ Nick Watt interview of Michigan Governor Gretchen Whitmer, CNN, AC, March 23, 2020.

²¹⁵ C-Span, **Kellyanne Conway Comments to Reporters at the White House,** March 6, 2020 {Accessed: June 4, 2020}, https://www.c-span.org/video/?470121-1/kellyanne-conway-comments-reporters-white-house

[216] Russell Honoree, interviewed by Ali Melber, MSNBC News, March 28, 2020.

[217] Stephen Fowler, **BREAKING: Kemp Will Issue Stay-At-Home Order, Close K-12 Schools Through End Of Semester,** *GPBnews.org*; April 1, 2020 {Accessed: April 1, 2020}, https://www.gpbnews.org/post/breaking-kemp-will-issue-stay-home-order-close-k-12-schools-through-end-semester

[218] Greg Bluestein, **Politicians, celebrities seize on Kemp's 'game-changing' coronavirus remarks,** *Atlanta Journal-Constitution*, April 2, 2020 {Accessed: April 10, 2020}, https://www.ajc.com/blog/politics/politicians-celebrities-seize-kemp-game-changing-coronavirus-remarks/litedB5Vf9oJreeWiHb1KN/

[219] Ibid.

[220] Tara Subramaniam and Veronica Stracqualursi, **Fact check: Georgia governor says we only just learned people without symptoms could spread coronavirus. Experts have been saying that for months,** CNN, April 3, 2020 {Accessed: April 28, 2020}, https://www.cnn.com/2020/04/02/politics/fact-check-georgia-gov-brian-kemp-coronavirus-no-symptoms-stay-at-home/index.html

[221] Peter Baker, **45 Confronts a New Reality on Expected Wave of Disease and Death,** *New York Times,* April 1, 2020 {Accessed: May 29, 2022}, https://www.nytimes.com/2020/04/01/us/politics/coronavirus-trump.html

[222] Michael Steele, interviewed on The Last Word with Brian Williams, April 1, 2020.

[223] Zeke Miller, Jill Colvin, Darlene Superville, Deb Riechmann, and Mary Clark Jalonick, **Surgeon general says U.S. cases are at the point where Italy was 2 weeks ago,** AP, March 16, 2020 {Accessed: April 5, 2020}, https://www.pbs.org/newshour/health/surgeon-general-says-u-s-cases-are-at-the-point-where-italy-was-2-weeks-ago

[224] Editorial Board, **A president unfit for a pandemic,** *Boston Globe,* March 30, 2020 {Accessed: April 5, 2020},

https://www.bostonglobe.com/2020/03/30/opinion/president-unfit-pandemic/

[225] Dr. Ami Bera, interviewed by Joy Reid on MSNBC's Decision 2020, April 8, 2020.

[226] Andy Slavitt, former administrator for the Centers for Medicare and Medicaid under the Obama Administration, on Rachel Maddow Show, MSNBC, April 10, 2020.

[227] Jonathan Shorman and Dion Leffler, **Kelly's order limiting Kansas church services stands, justices rule hours before Easter,** *Kansas City Star*, April 11, 2020 {Accessed: April 11, 2020}, https://www.kansascity.com/news/politics-government/article241942766.html

[228] Congressman Lloyd Doggett, **Trump's Coronavirus Timeline,** March 2, 2023 {Accessed: June 4, 2023}, https://doggett.house.gov/media/blog-post/timeline-trumps-coronavirus-responses

[229] Alan Judd, **Georgia to expand COVID-19 testing, key to reaching 'new norm',** *Atlanta Journal-Constitution,* April 15, 2020 {Accessed: April 23, 2020}, https://www.ajc.com/news/georgia-expand-covid-testing-key-reaching-new-norm/4jtiJdhPgSN3FMUz9aRBQL

[230] Conversation by one HHS Regional Director to an HHS public affairs specialist, April 18, 2020.

[231] Alan Judd, **No rest for Kemp as critics as Georgia launches reopening amid COVID-19,** *Atlanta Journal-Constitution*, April 24, 2020 {Accessed: April 26, 2020}, https://www.ajc.com/news/rest-for-kemp-from-critics-launches-reopening-amid-covid/iFRXx4Ws0sAqqIdMJpnKSN/

[232] Marcel Terry, a text, April 22, 2020.

[233] Jim Galloway, Greg Bluestein, and Tia Mitchell, **The Jolt: Conspiracy theories thrive in an information vacuum,** *Atlanta Journal-Constitution*, April 27, 2020 {Accessed: April 27, 2020},

https://www.ajc.com/blog/politics/the-jolt-conspiracy-theories-thrive-information-vacuum/dP5sge7RhkaRDRO87AB9HJ/

[234] Elizabeth Nix, **Tuskegee Experiment: The Infamous Syphilis Study,** *History.com*, July 29, 2029 {Accessed: April 27, 2020}, https://www.history.com/news/the-infamous-40-year-tuskegee-study

[235] Harriet A. Washington, *Medical Apartheid: The Dark History of Medical Experimentation on Black Americans from Colonial Times to the Present,* Doubleday, 2007.

[236] Meredith Wadman, **What does the historic settlement won by Henrietta Lacks's family mean for others?** *Science.org*, August 7, 2023 {Accessed: August 9, 2023}, https://www.science.org/content/article/what-does-historic-settlement-won-henrietta-lacks-s-family-mean-others

[237] Patrick Kiger, **Did Colonists Give Infected Blankets to Native Americans as Biological Warfare?**, *History.com*, November 25, 2019 {Accessed: April 27, 2020}, https://www.history.com/news/colonists-native-americans-smallpox-blankets

[238] Aaron Carroll, **Doctors and Racial Bias: Still a Long Way to Go,** *New York Times,* February 25, 2019 {Accessed: April 27, 2020}, https://www.nytimes.com/2019/02/25/upshot/doctors-and-racial-bias-still-a-long-way-to-go.html

[239] Philip Bump, **The rise and fall of 45's obsession with hydroxychloroquine,** *Washington Post*, April 24, 2020 {Accessed: April 26, 2020}, https://www.washingtonpost.com/politics/2020/04/24/rise-fall-45s-obsession-with-hydroxychloroquine/

[240] Brittany Schmidt, **Doctors warn against use of 'horse dewormer' to treat COVID-19,** WBAY-2, September 7, 2021 {Accessed: October 3, 2021}, https://www.wbay.com/2021/09/07/doctors-warn-against-use-horse-dewormer-treat-covid-19/

[241] Zachary Snowdon Smith, **The Strange Return Of Ivermectin and Hydroxychloroquine: Republicans Push Drug In State Bills,** *Forbes,* May 3, 2020 {Accessed: August 2, 2021},

https://www.forbes.com/sites/zacharysmith/2022/05/03/the-strange-return-of-ivermectin-and-hydroxychloroquine-republicans-push-drug-in-state-bills/?sh=5f91fa893ea2

[242] Joelle Goldstein, **First NY Coronavirus Patient Released from the Hospital After 53 Days: 'We Needed This Win'**, *People*, May 1, 2020 {Accessed: January 15, 2023}, https://people.com/human-interest/first-ny-coronavirus-patient-released-hospital-sendoff/

[243] W.J. Hennigan, **45 Says U.S. Will Run 5 Million Daily Virus Tests 'Very Soon.' His Testing Chief Says That's Impossible**, *Time*, April 28, 2020 {Accessed: May 9, 2020}, https://time.com/5828843/45-coronavirus-testing-giroir/

[244] Florida Representative Val Demings, MSNBC, May 7, 2020, hosted by Ayman Mohyeldin.

[245] Chandi Bozeman, interviewed on CNN Newsroom with Poppy Harlow and Jim Sciutto, May 7, 2020.

[246] Gabe Gutierrez, reporting, **Meat plants linked to hundreds of cases, reopening**, NBC Evening News with Lester Holt, May 7, 2020.

[247] Ibid.

[248] **Heroes on the Front Lines: The Country Won't Work Without Them. 12 Stories of People Putting Their Lives on the Line to Help Others During Coronavirus,** *Time*, April 9, 2020 {Accessed: May 9, 2020}, https://time.com/collection/coronavirus-heroes/

[249] Michael Ellison Hayden, **Stephen Miller's Affinity for White Nationalism,** Southern Poverty Law Center, November 12, 2019 {Accessed: May 9, 2020}, https://www.splcenter.org/hatewatch/2019/11/12/stephen-millers-affinity-white-nationalism-revealed-leaked-emails

[250] Sarah Sidner and Rachel Clark, **Former Breitbart Editor: Stephen Miller is a white supremacist. I know, I was one too,** CNN, December 16, 2019 {Accessed: May 9, 2020}, https://www.cnn.com/2019/12/13/politics/katie-mchugh-stephen-miller/index.html

[251] Ashley Southall, **Scrutiny of Social-Distance Policing as 35 of 40 Arrested Are Black,** *New York Times*, May 7, 2020 {Accessed: May 9, 2020}, https://www.nytimes.com/2020/05/07/nyregion/nypd-social-distancing-race-coronavirus.html

[252] Leah Asmelash, **Woman body-slammed by off-duty cop in Alabama Walmart grew disorderly after associate asked she wear a mask, police say,** CNN, May 9, 2020 {Accessed: May 9, 2020}, https://www.cnn.com/2020/05/09/us/walmart-woman-takedown-mask-trnd/index.html

[253] Michael Collins and Tom Vanden Brook, **White House adopts new safety precautions as coronavirus moves closer to 45's inner circle,** *USA Today*, May 10, 2010 {Accessed: May 11, 2020}, https://www.usatoday.com/story/news/politics/2020/05/10/coronavirus-white-house-takes-new-precautions-protect-45-staff/3105283001/

[254] Corey Kilgannon, **'Flying Wallendas' Cross Times Square on High Wire in Death-Defying Stunt,** *New York Times*, June 23, 2019 {Accessed: May 13, 2020}, https://www.nytimes.com/2019/06/23/nyregion/flying-wallendas-times-square.html

[255] Lizzie Presser, **The Black American Amputation Epidemic,** *ProPublica*, May 19, 2020 (Accessed: May 20, 2020}, https://features.propublica.org/diabetes-amputations/black-american-amputation-epidemic/

[256] Tim Nelson, Cody Nelson, and Andy Kreuger, **Hundreds protest Minneapolis police shooting of 31-year-old man,** MPRNews, June 24, 2018 {Accessed: May 26, 2020}, https://www.mprnews.org/story/2018/06/24/hundreds-protest-minneapolis-police-shooting-of-31yearold-man

[257] German Lopez, **Philando Castile Minnesota police shooting: officer cleared of manslaughter charge,** *Vox*, June 16, 2017 {Accessed: May 27, 2020}, https://www.vox.com/2016/7/7/12116288/minnesota-police-shooting-philando-castile-falcon-heights-video

258 Tim Darnell, **Breaking News: Minneapolis mayor calls for criminal charges in suspect's death,** AJC, May 27, 2020 {Accessed: May 27, 2020}, https://www.ajc.com/news/protesters-clash-with-minneapolis-police-after-death-man-custody/RxVSSHEfJFshApPTLegNtK/

259 Eric Levenson, **Former officer knelt on George Floyd for 9 minutes and 29 seconds – not the infamous 8:46,** *CNN.com*, March 30, 2021 {Accessed: June 29, 2024}, https://www.cnn.com/2021/03/29/us/george-floyd-timing-929-846/index.html

260 Lily Rothman, **What Martin Luther King Jr. Really Thought About Riots,** *Time*, April 28, 2015 {Accessed: May 28, 2020},https://time.com/3838515/baltimore-riots-language-unheard-quote/

261 Martin Luther King, Jr., ***Why We Can't Wait,*** Harper & Row, 1964.

262 Liz Hardaway, **Peter Manfredonia's 2020 deadly CT crime spree case faces another delay,** *CT Insider*, September 15, 2022 {Accessed: January 15, 2023}, https://www.ctinsider.com/news/article/Peter-Manfredonia-murder-Newtown-Ansonia-17443392.php

263 USA Today Network, **NATION, UConn student Peter Manfredonia, wanted for 2 killings, caught in Maryland after six-day manhunt,** May 28, 2020 {Accessed: May 30, 2020}, https://www.usatoday.com/story/news/nation/2020/05/27/peter-manfredonia-uconn-student-wanted-murder-maryland/5272129002/

264 Sarah Maslin Nir, **How 2 Lives Collided in Central Park, Rattling the Nation,** *New York Times*, June 14, 2020 {Accessed: January 5, 2021}, https://www.nytimes.com/2020/06/14/nyregion/central-park-amy-cooper-christian-racism.html

265 Mola Lenghi, **Central Park Encounter,** CBS Evening News, May 26, 2020.

266 Douglas Jones, **Man exonerated after 36 years in prison delivers unforgettable 'America's Got Talent' audition,** WKYC Studios, May 26, 2020 {Accessed: May 26, 2020},

https://www.wkyc.com/article/news/nation-world/man-exonerated-after-37-years-in-prison-stuns-agt-audience/507-37553e38-e939-402f-81ad-db9651bf578a

[267] SAMHSA, **2018 National Survey of Drug Use and Health (NSDUH) Releases, Substance Abuse & Mental Health Administration,** {Accessed: January 12, 2020}, https://www.samhsa.gov/data/release/2018-national-survey-drug-use-and-health-nsduh-releases

[268] Jordan Culver, **Trump says violent Minneapolis protests dishonor George Floyd's memory, Twitter labels 'shooting' tweet as 'glorifying' violence,** *USA Today*, May 29, 2020 {Accessed: June 3, 2020}, https://www.usatoday.com/story/news/politics/2020/05/28/george-floyd-donald-trump-twitter-jacob-frey-thugs/5281374002/

[269] CNN live coverage of the Atlanta protests of George Floyd murder, May 29, 2020.

[270] Cornell Brooks, former NAACP president, interviewed by Alex Whitt, MSNBC, May 31, 2020.

[271] The Police, 2010, "Every Move You Make" {Accessed: May 31, 2020}, https://www.youtube.com/watch?v=OMOGaugKpzs

[272] Samuel Francis Smith, "My country, 'tis of Thee," Lyrics on Demand, https://www.lyricsondemand.com/miscellaneouslyrics/patrioticsongslyrics/mycountrytisoftheelyrics.html

[273] Mandy McLauren and Darcy Castello, **Breonna Taylor's mother asks for Louisville cops to be fired and an end to violence,** *Louisville Courier-Journal*, June 1, 2020 {Accessed: June 1, 2020}, https://www.courier-journal.com/story/news/2020/06/01/breonna-taylors-mom-calls-cops-fired-louisville-police/5308506002/

[274] Sadiqa Reynolds, president of Louisville Urban League, interviewed by Don Lemon, CNN News, June 1, 2020.

275 History.com editors, **Boston Tea Party,** Updated: June 2, 2020 {Accessed: June 4, 2020}, https://www.history.com/topics/american-revolution/boston-tea-party

276 Fox News, Washington D.C.: **End 'taxation without representation,'** *Washington Post,* April 20, 2016 {Accessed: June 4, 2020}, https://www.foxnews.com/entertainment/washington-dc-end-taxation-without-representation

277 Mitch Kachun, *First Martyr of Liberty: Crispus Attucks in American Memory,* Oxford University Press, 2017.

278 The National World War II Museum, **African Americans Fought for Freedom at Home and Abroad during World War II,** February 1, 2020 {Accessed: June 4, 2020}, https://www.nationalww2museum.org/war/articles/African Americans-fought-freedom-home-and-abroad-during-world-war-ii

279 Chelsea Brasted, **America's oldest living WWII veteran faced hostility abroad – and at home,** *National Geographic,* May 12, 2020 {Accessed: June 6, 2020}, https://www.nationalgeographic.com/history/2020/05/americas-oldest-living-wwii-veteran-faced-hostility-abroad-home/

280 Rodney Welch, **How the blinding of a SC soldier kicked off the civil rights movement,** *Charleston Post & Courier,* January 22, 2019 {Accessed: June 6, 2020}, https://www.postandcourier.com/free-times/news/local_and_state_news/how-the-blinding-of-an-sc-soldier-kicked-off-the-civil-rights-era/article_7adc4567-54ee-5667-bb68-7f7878834058.html

281 NBC Washington staff, **Man Gets Probation for Assault on Maryland Bike Trail Over George Floyd Flyers,** February 2, 2021 {Accessed: January 13, 2022}, https://www.nbcwashington.com/news/local/cyclist-gets-probation-for-maryland-assault-over-george-floyd-flyers/2559267/

282 Neal Augenstein, **EXCLUSIVE: Lawyer of suspect in viral bike trail assault says client was on his way to priest when stopped by police,** WTOP News, June 6, 2020 {Accessed: June 7, 2020}, https://wtop.com/montgomery-county/2020/06/exclusive-lawyer-of-

suspect-in-viral-bike-trail-assault-says-client-was-on-his-way-to-priest-when-stopped-by-police/

[283] Diocesan Bishop Mariann Edgar Budde, **America in Pain: Where do we go Next,** *ABC News* Special, June 2, 2020.

[284] Ben Feuerherd, **Video: Elderly man pushed to ground by Buffalo police starts bleeding from head,** *New York Post,* June 4, 2020 {Accessed: June 4, 2020}, https://nypost.com/2020/06/04/buffalo-police-shove-man-to-the-ground-causing-him-to-bleed-from-head/

[285] Meagan Flynn, Hanna Knowles, and Marisa Lati, **57 Buffalo officers resign from special squad over suspension of two who shoved 75-year-old,** *Washington Post,* June 5, 2020 {Accessed: June 6, 2020}, https://www.washingtonpost.com/nation/2020/06/05/buffalo-officers-suspended-shoving-man/

[286] Barack Obama, *The Shop: Uninterrupted*, HBO, Season 3, Episode 3.

[287] **Frederick Douglass: Without A Struggle There Can Be No Progress,** Bartleby Research, Essays, https://www.bartleby.com/essay/Frederick-Douglass-Without-A-Struggle-There-Can-95072C923BEF9046#:~:text=%20Frederick%20Douglass%20once%20said%20%E2%80%9CWithout%20a%20struggle%2C%20himself%20and%20other%20African%20Americans%20oppressed%20from%20slavery

[288] Justin Rohrlich, **Riverboat Captain: Wild Dockside Attack on My Deckhand WAS Racially Motivated,** *The Daily Beast,* August 8, 2023 {Accessed: August 11, 2023}, https://www.thedailybeast.com/montgomery-brawl-riverboat-captain-says-attack-was-racially-motivated

[289] Lizzette Alvarez and Clara Buckley, **Zimmerman Is Acquitted in Trayvon Martin Killing,** *New York Times,* July 13, 2013 {Accessed: July 25, 2023}, https://www.nytimes.com/2013/07/14/us/george-zimmerman-verdict-trayvon-martin.html

²⁹⁰ Jule Boseman and Joseph Goldstein, **Timeline for a Body: 4 Hours in the Middle of a Ferguson Street,** *New York Times,* August 23, 2014 {Accessed: November 30, 2014}, https://www.nytimes.com/2014/08/24/us/michael-brown-a-bodys-timeline-4-hours-on-a-ferguson-street.html

²⁹¹ **Gun Purchases Under Obama's Presidency Four Times the Number Of Babies Born,** *Huffington Post,* February 12, 2013 {Accessed: November 30, 2023}, https://www.huffpost.com/entry/gun-sales-obama_n_2671167

²⁹² Maureen Dowd, Opinion: **Boy, Oh, Boy,** *New York Times,* September 12, 2009 {Accessed: September 15, 2021}, https://www.nytimes.com/2009/09/13/opinion/13dowd.html

²⁹³ Fox News, **Charlottesville white nationalist rally blamed for 3 deaths, dozens of injuries,** August 12, 2017 {Accessed: November 15, 2023}, https://www.foxnews.com/us/charlottesville-white-nationalist-rally-blamed-for-3-deaths-dozens-of-injuries

²⁹⁴ Maggie Haberman and Neil Vigdor, **Trump Assesses John Lewis's Legacy: 'He Didn't Come to My Inauguration,'** *New York Times,* August 4, 2020 {Accessed: September 22, 2020}, https://www.nytimes.com/2020/08/04/us/politics/trump-john-lewis-axios.html

²⁹⁵ BBC, **The Legacy of the Murder of James Byrd, Jr.**, YouTube, June 2, 2021 {Accessed: August 2, 2022}, https://www.youtube.com/watch?v=HmetUwqtD8g

²⁹⁶ History.com editors, **Jim Crow Laws,** August 11, 2023 {Accessed: August 11, 2023}, https://www.history.com/topics/early-20th-century-us/jim-crow-laws

²⁹⁷ Governor Abbott, interviewed by Marcus Moore, ABC World News Tonight, June 8, 2020.

²⁹⁸ Priscilla Alvarez and Hannah Rabinowitz, **Justice Department Sues to Force Texas to Remove Floating Barriers in the Rio**

Grande, CNN, July 24, 2023 {Accessed: August 11, 2023}, https://www.cnn.com/2023/07/24/politics/doj-texas-border-water-barriers/index.html#:~:text=The%20US%20Department%20of%20Justice,into%20the%20state%20from%20Mexico

[299] Madalyn Mendoza, **Texas trooper details 'inhumane' border policies in on Rio Grande,** *Axios San Antonio,* July 18, 2023 {Accessed: July 24, 2023}, https://www.axios.com/local/san-antonio/2023/07/18/abott-texas-border-initiative-rio-grande-trooper-email

[300] The Martin Luther King, Jr. Research and Education Institute, Chapter 21: Death of Illusions, Stanford University {Accessed: July 12, 2023}, https://kinginstitute.stanford.edu/chapter-21-death-illusions#:~:text=Man's%20inhumanity%20to%20man%20is,of%20those%20who%20are%20good.

[301] ESPN News Services, **NASCAR bans Confederate flags from all racetracks,** ESPN, June 10, 2020 {Accessed: June 18, 2020}, https://www.espn.com/racing/nascar/story/_/id/29293767/nascar-bans-confederate-flags-racetracks

[302] David Close, **This is the noose that was found in Bubba Wallace's garage stall at the Talladega Superspeedway**, CNN, June 26, 2020 {Accessed: October 12, 2020}, https://www.cnn.com/2020/06/25/us/nascar-noose-investigation-complete-trnd/index.html

[303] Reddit Hudson, former St. Louis policeman being interviewed on CNN by Jake Tapper, June 9, 2020.

[304] Benjamin Seigel and Libby Cathey, **'Stop the pain': George Floyd's brother testifies on policing reform,**
ABC News, June 10, 2020 {Accessed: June 10,2020}, https://abcnews.go.com/Politics/george-floyds-brother-testify-house-police-brutality-hearing/story?id=71161017

[305] Melissa Quinn, **Trump suggests without evidence 75-year-old man shoved to the ground by Buffalo police was a "set up,"** CBS News, June 10, 2020 {Accessed: October 17, 2021},

https://www.cbsnews.com/news/trump-comments-on-buffalo-protester-martin-gugino-antifa-police/

[306] Fleming Smith, **'Remarkable' Judy Scott, mother of Walter Scott, dies at 76,** *Charleston Post & Courier,* January 30, 2020 {Accessed: January 31, 2020}, https://www.postandcourier.com/news/remarkable-judy-scott-mother-of-walter-scott-dies-at-76/article_ede47cee-4365-11ea-a487-ab876ede6039.html

[307] Walter White, **The Eruption of Tulsa: An NAACP Official Investigates the Tulsa Race Riot of 1921,** *Nation,* June 29, 1929, pp. 909-910 {Accessed: June 12, 2020}, http://historymatters.gmu.edu/d/5119/

[308] Aimee Ortiz and Katharine Seelye, **Herman Cain, Former C.E.O. and Presidential Candidate, Dies at 74,** *New York Times,* July 30, 2020 {Accessed: October 23, 2020}, https://www.nytimes.com/2020/07/30/us/politics/herman-cain-dead.html

[309] *Newsweek,* **Tulsa Major Says Police Are Shooting African Americans 'Less Than We Probably Ought to Be',** June 10, 2020 {Accessed: June 12, 2020}, https://www.newsweek.com/tulsa-police-comments-shooting-1509967

[310] Lucia Walinchus and Richard Perez-Pena, **White Tulsa Officer Is Acquitted in Fatal Shooting of Black Driver,** *New York Times,* May 17, 2018 {Accessed: June 12, 2020}, https://www.nytimes.com/2017/05/17/us/white-tulsa-officer-is-acquitted-in-fatal-shooting-of-black-driver.html

[311] Ibid.

[312] Andy Rose and Omar Jiminez, **Oklahoma Supreme Court dismisses lawsuit brought by survivors of Tulsa Race Massacre,** CNN, June 12, 2024 {Accessed: July 2, 2024}, https://www.cnn.com/2024/06/12/us/tulsa-race-massacre-lawsuit-dismissed-reaj/index.html

[313] Eric Ortiz, **Amber Guyger was on phone with partner before shooting neighbor, prosecutor reveals,** NBC News, September 23, 2019 {Accessed: October 20, 2023}, https://www.nbcnews.com/news/us-news/prosecutors-reveal-amber-guyger-was-phone-partner-shooting-neighbor-n1057706

[314] Annette Nevins, Brittany Shammas, Hannah Knowles, and Reis Thebault, **Amber Guyger's 10-year murder sentence spark both protests and an act of forgiveness,** October 2, 2019 {Accessed: June 12, 2020}, https://www.washingtonpost.com/nation/2019/10/02/botham-jeans-family-friends-testify-during-amber-guyger-sentencing/

[315] Southern Poverty Law Center, **Civil Rights Martyrs,** {Accessed: June 12, 2012}, https://www.splcenter.org/what-we-do/civil-rights-memorial/civil-rights-martyrs

[316] Todd Beer, **POLICE KILLING OF BLACKS: Do Black Lives Matter?,** *The Society Pages,* Sociology Toolbox, May 26, 2020 {Accessed: June 12, 2020}, https://thesocietypages.org/toolbox/police-killing-of-blacks/

[317] Brakkton Booker and Mark Katkov, **Illinois Teen Arrested After Fatal Shootings Of 2 Kenosha, Wis., Protesters,** NPR, August 26, 2020 {Accessed: August 30, 2020}, https://www.npr.org/sections/live-updates-protests-for-racial-justice/2020/08/26/906145086/3-shot-1-fatally-in-kenosha-wis-as-protests-continue-over-police-shooting

[318] Jim Vertuno, **Man guilty in Texas protest killing posted 'I am a racist,'** AP, May 9, 2023 {Accessed: October 23, 2023}, https://apnews.com/article/black-lives-matter-protest-shooting-texas-sentence-04abb51c52d41fa259b2f2ed8ee72f37

[319] Donald Trump, at first return rally, June 20, 2020, in Tulsa, Oklahoma.

[320] Kenneth Gamble, Leon Huff, and Anthony Jackson, O'Jays, "For the Love of Money," 1973, https://en.wikipedia.org/wiki/For_the_Love_of_Money

[321] Donald Trump, interviewed by Harris Faulkner, Fox News, June 12, 2020.

[322] Joseph Flipper, **Breonna Taylor lived and died in a part of the U.S. where rights do not matter,** *Americamagazine.org,* June 4, 2020 {Accessed: October 18, 2020}, https://www.americamagazine.org/politics-society/2020/06/04/breonna-taylor-lived-and-died-part-us-where-rights-do-not-matter?gad=1&gclid=CjwKCAjwxOymBhAFEiwAnodBLAUh3OFUGmjeqH0zRkRrcbvtlXSGypNv6a_Fnk3RN6BJ8Z-QPqSc2hoCEr0QAvD_BwE

[323] CBS News, London, June 13, 2020.

[324] Center for the Study of Social Policy, **Key Equity Terms & Concepts,** https://cssp.org/wp-content/uploads/2019/09/Key-Equity-Terms-and-Concepts-vol1.pdf

[325] Chris Kitching and Talia Shadwell, **Black hero Patrick Hutchinson, who rescued white protester, speaks out for first time,** *Mirror,* June 14, 2020 {Accessed: May 3, 2021} , https://www.mirror.co.uk/news/uk-news/black-hero-patrick-hutchinson-who-22190796

[326] Tera Hunter, **Slaves weren't immigrants. They were property,** *Washington Post,* March 9, 2017 {Accessed: June 14, 2020}, https://www.washingtonpost.com/posteverything/wp/2017/03/09/slaves-werent-immigrants-they-were-property/

[327] A.O. Scott, **Review: 'I Am Not Your Negro' Will Make You Rethink Race,** *New York Times,* February 2, 2017 {Accessed: October 12, 2023}, https://www.nytimes.com/2017/02/02/movies/review-i-am-not-your-negro-review-james-baldwin.html

[328] Kalee Hartung, ABC World News Tonight, June 13, 2020.

[329] **U.S. History Primary Source Timeline, Civil War and Reconstruction, 1861-1877,** Library of Congress {Accessed: June 1, 2023}, https://www.loc.gov/classroom-materials/united-states-history-primary-source-timeline/civil-war-and-reconstruction-1861-1877/

[330] History.com editors, **Ku Klux Klan**, History, April 20, 2023.

[331] Governor George Wallace, NPR Radio diaries, 'Segregation Forever': A Fiery Pledge Forgiven, But Not Forgotten, January 10, 2013 {Accessed: October 3, 2021}, https://www.npr.org/2013/01/14/169080969/segregation-forever-a-fiery-pledge-forgiven-but-not-forgotten#:~:text=It%20was%20just%20a%20single,The%20year%20was%201963

[332] Ken Bredemeier, **Trump Assails Prosecutor, Judge in Election Interference Cases,** *VOA News*, August 14, 2023 {Accessed: August 15, 2023}, https://www.voanews.com/a/trump-assails-prosecutor-judge-in-election-interference-cases-/7224551.html

[333] Thomas Frieden, on MSNBC Live with Stephanie Ruhle, MSNBC, June 18, 2020.

[334] Ellison Barber, *Inequity in America*, NBC Evening News, June 19, 2020.

[335] Graham Rapier, **How a small Georgia city far from New York became one of the worst coronavirus hotspots in the country,** *Business Insider*, April 7, 2020 {Accessed: November 8, 2023}, https://www.businessinsider.com/coronavirus-hotspot-albany-georgia-funderals-covid-19-cases-per-capita-2020-4

[336] Harry Smith, NBC Nightly News, June 9, 2020.

[337] Mark Moore, **Trump says he made Juneteenth 'famous,' sees some systemic racism in US,** *New York Post*, June 18, 2020 {Accessed: June 22, 2023}, https://nypost.com/2020/06/18/trump-says-he-made-juneteenth-famous-sees-some-racism-in-us/

[338] Seung Min Kim, **Top State Department official resigns in protest of 45's response to racial tensions in the country,** *Washington Post*, June 18, 2020 {Accessed: June 19, 2020} https://www.washingtonpost.com/politics/top-state-department-official-resigns-in-protest-of-45s-response-to-racial-tensions-in-the-

country/2020/06/18/e142e342-b181-11ea-a567-6172530208bd_story.html

[339] Lauren Theisen, **State Dept. official Mary Elizabeth Taylor resigns in protest,** *New York Daily News*, June 18, 2020 {Accessed: January 3, 3031}, https://www.nydailynews.com/2020/06/18/state-department-official-whod-been-with-trump-administration-since-day-one-resigns-in-protest/

[340] 45 at first campaign rally following the outbreak of COVID-19, June 20, 2020.

[341] Trump tweet, June 19, 2020.

[342] Dominic-Madori Davis, **PHOTOS: Trump's Tulsa rally saw low turnout, groups of protesters, not much social distancing, and the return of the Baby Trump balloon,** *Insider*, June 21, 2020 {Accessed: August 1, 2023}, https://www.businessinsider.com/photos-trumps-rally-in-tulsa-saw-low-audience-turnout-2020-6

[343] Eddie Glaude, MSNBC contributor, Princeton University African American Studies chairman, June 20, 2020.

[344] Jemar Tisby, **Moving Beyond Graham's Legacy: Raising the Bar on Evangelical Participation in Civil Rights,** June 27, 2018 {Accessed: June 20, 2020}, https://jemartisby.com/2018/06/27/moving-beyond-grahams-legacy-raising-the-bar-on-evangelical-participation-in-civil-rights/

[345] Caitlin Dickson, **Capitol riot was false-flag operation by leftists, Trump backers claim, with no basis,** *Yahoo News,* January 7, 2021 {Accessed: January 21, 2021}, https://news.yahoo.com/capitol-riot-was-falseflag-operation-by-leftists-trump-backers-claim-with-no-basis-051703320.html

[346] Andrea Shalal, **After George Floyd's death, a groundswell of religious activism,** *U.S. News*, Reuters, June 9, 2020 {Accessed: October 2, 2020}, https://www.reuters.com/article/us-minneapolis-police-usa-religion-idUSKBN23G1FS

[347] Bill Murphy, Jr., **17 Inspirational Quotes From Martin Luther King Jr. About Speaking Up When It Matters,** {Accessed: August

12, 2023}, https://www.inc.com/bill-murphy-jr/17-inspirational-quotes-by-martin-luther-king-jr-about-speaking-up-when-it-matters.html

[348] Eric Harrison, **Joseph Lowery,** *Los Angeles Times*, July 7, 1996 {Accessed: July 20, 2023}, https://www.latimes.com/archives/la-xpm-1996-07-07-op-21904-story.html

[349] Thomas Frieden, former CDC director, reported by Janet Shamlian, CBS Weekend News, June 27, 2020.

[350] Email from Debra Rotollo on behalf of John Bennett, chief of staff for Tampa mayor Jane Castor, March 12, 2020, to Deric Gilliard.

[351] Anastasia Dawson, **Tampa mayor readies for stay-at-home order, slams federal response to coronavirus pandemic,** *Tampa Bay Times*, March 21, 2020 {Accessed: July 15,2020}, https://www.tampabay.com/news/health/2020/03/21/tampa-mayor-readies-for-stay-at-home-order-slams-federal-response-to-coronavirus-pandemic/

[352] NPR, **Florida Joins Other States Issuing Stay-At-Home Orders,** WBUR, April 2, 2020 {Accessed: July 15, 2020}, https://www.wbur.org/npr/825800542/florida-joins-other-states-issuing-stay-at-home-orders

[353] Scott Neuman, **Pence Urges Americans To Wear Masks To Stop Spread Of COVID-19,** NPR, June 30, 2020 {Accessed: October 22, 2020}, https://www.npr.org/sections/coronavirus-live-updates/2020/06/30/885834633/pence-urges-americans-to-wear-masks-to-stop-spread-of-covid-19#:~:text=Vice%20President%20Pence%20wore%20a,the%20spread%20of%20COVID%2D19

[354] BBC, Princeton to remove Woodrow Wilson's name from policy school, June 27, 2020 {Accessed: March 20, 2021}, https://www.bbc.com/news/world-us-canada-53207649

[355] U.S. Surgeon General Jerome Adams, March 18, 2020.

[356] Scott Neuman, **Pence Urges Americans To Wear Masks To Stop Spread Of COVID-19,** NPR, June 30, 2020 {Accessed: January 2, 2021}, https://www.npr.org/sections/coronavirus-live-

updates/2020/06/30/885834633/pence-urges-americans-to-wear-masks-to-stop-spread-of-covid-19#:~:text=Vice%20President%20Pence%20wore%20a,the%20spread%20of%20COVID%2D19.

357 Kayleigh McEnany, WH Press Secretary, June 25, 2020, at first WH Coronavirus press conference in two months.

358 Brooke Wolford, **'A humanitarian catastrophe.' Texas COVID-19 spike could be 'apocalyptic,' expert says,** *Star-Telegram,* June 25, 2020 {Accessed: June 29, 2020}, https://www.star-telegram.com/news/coronavirus/article243807202.html

359 Teo Armus and Kim Bellware, **St. Louis couple point guns at crowd of protesters calling for mayor to resign,** *Washington Post,* June 29, 2020 {Accessed: June 29, 2020}, https://www.washingtonpost.com/nation/2020/06/29/st-louis-protest-gun-mayor/

360 Veronica Stracqualursi and Sarah Westwood, **Trump thanked 'great people' shown in Twitter video in which a man chants 'white power',** CNN Politics, June 29, 202 {Accessed: July 3, 2022}, https://www.cnn.com/2020/06/28/politics/trump-tweet-supporters-man-chants-white-power/index.html

361 Max Cohen, **45: Black Lives Matter is a 'symbol of hate',** *Politico,* July 1, 2020 {Accessed: July 8, 2020}, https://www.politico.com/news/2020/07/01/trump-black-lives-matter-347051

362 Colin Dwyer, **Donald Trump: 'I Could ... Shoot Somebody, And I Wouldn't Lose Any Voters,'** NPR, January 23, 2016 {Accessed: February 6, 2021}, https://www.npr.org/sections/thetwo-way/2016/01/23/464129029/donald-trump-i-could-shoot-somebody-and-i-wouldnt-lose-any-voters

363 President Donald Trump, during interview with FOX News, July 1, 2020.

364 Michael Hiltzik, **Column: My apology to Florida Gov. DeSantis: Sorry, you're even worse than I imagined,** *Los Angeles Times,* June 26, 2020 {Accessed: July 11, 2022},

https://www.latimes.com/business/story/2020-06-26/my-apology-to-gov-desantis-youre-even-worse

[365] Dr. Vin Gupta, "There is No School Reopening Strategy," The Last Word with Lawrence O'Donnell, MSNBC, July 23, 2020 {Accessed: July 30, 2020}

[366] Lisa Shumaker and Doina Chiacu, **U.S. tops 130,000 deaths from COVID-19 after record surge in cases,** Reuters, July 6, 2020 {Accessed: August 2, 2020}, https://www.reuters.com/article/health-coronavirus-usa/u-s-tops-130000-deaths-from-covid-19-after-record-surge-in-cases-idINL1N2ED0QA

[367] **Five Black & Brown Men Have Been Recently Found Hanged in Public. Were Some of Them Lynched?,** *Democracy Now!,* Independent Global News, June 22, 2020 {Accessed: July 1, 2020}, https://www.democracynow.org/2020/6/22/us_public_hangings_lynching_history

[368] ArLuther Lee, **Black man says he was victim of 'attempted lynching' on July 4,** *Atlanta Journal-Constitution*, July 7, 2020 {Accessed: July 7, 2020}, https://www.ajc.com/news/black-man-says-was-victim-attempted-lynching-july/ypQaBOm6vN8glC2OqogqxK/

[369] Frederick Douglass, **A Nation's Story: "What to the Slave is the Fourth of July?",** National Museum of African American History and Culture, Smithsonian, July 5th, 1852 {Accessed: July 7, 2020}, https://nmaahc.si.edu/blog-post/nations-story-what-slave-fourth-july

[370] National Institutes of Health (NIH), *Implicit Bias* I *SWD at NIH*, U.S. Department of Health & Human Services, July 3, 2022 {Accessed: June 18, 2022}, https://diversity.nih.gov/sociocultural-factors/implicit-bias

[371] America's Founding Documents, Declaration of Independence: A Transcription, National Archives, January 31, 2023 {Accessed: August 3, 2023}, https://www.archives.gov/founding-docs/declaration-transcript

[372] UVA Miller Center, **McCarthyism and the Red Scare,** 2003 {Accessed: July 12, 2023}, https://millercenter.org/the-presidency/educational-resources/age-of-eisenhower/mcarthyism-red-scare

373 Clyde Haberman, **George Wallace Tapped Into Racial Fear. Decades Later, Its Force Remains Potent,** *Retroreport.org*, April 1, 2018 {Accessed: October 19, 2022}, https://www.retroreport.org/articles/george-wallace-tapped-into-racial-fear.decades-later-its-force-remains-potent/?gad=1&gclid=CjwKCAjwloynBhBbEiwAGY25dA2MOp5RDNb4ZaSghMCpDfqneemSa0Ofgg3nlK4qBhy9HEtUvDowhxoCP1oQAvD_BwE

374 Ta-Nehisi Coates, *Between the World and Me,* Spiegel & Grau, 2015.

375 AG William Barr, interviewed by Pierre Russell on ABC News with David Muir, July 8, 2020.

376 Miguel Almaguer, interviewing Oakland Public Defender Brian Woods, **New Study finds systematic bias in jury selection,** Inequality in America, NBC Evening News with Lester Holt, July 8, 2020.

377 History, **First confirmed case of COVID-19 found in U.S.,** January 21, 2020 {Accessed: June 12, 2020}, https://www.history.com/this-day-in-history/first-confirmed-case-of-coronavirus-found-in-us-washington-state

378 Alana Wise, **Trump Wears Mask In Public For First Time During Walter Reed Visit,** NPR, July 21, 2020 {Accessed: August 15, 2020}, https://www.npr.org/sections/coronavirus-live-updates/2020/07/11/889810926/trump-wears-mask-in-public-for-first-time-during-walter-reed-visit

379 Ibid.

380 Christina Carrega, **5 years after Eric Garner's death, a look back at the case and the movement it sparked,** ABC News, July 16, 2019 {Accessed: July 16, 2020}

381 Reported July 16, 2020.

382 Kay Jones and Veronica Stracqualursi, **Oklahoma Gov. Kevin Stitt announces he has tested positive for coronavirus,** CNN, July 15, 2020 {Accessed: July 22, 2020},

https://www.cnn.com/2020/07/15/politics/kevin-stitt-oklahoma-governor-coronavirus/index.html

[383] Rachel Riley, **'We still have no answers:' Why a congresswoman named a bill after slain Bragg soldier,** *Fayetteville Observer*, November 22, 2022 {Accessed: January 12, 2022}, https://www.fayobserver.com/story/news/military/2022/11/22/bill-named-after-beheaded-fort-bragg-soldier/69642033007/

[384] The Martin Luther King, Jr., Research and Education Institute, **Cordy Tindell Vivian,** July 30, 1924 to July 17, 2020, Stanford University {Accessed: July 1, 2021}, https://kinginstitute.stanford.edu/vivian-cordy-tindell

[385] David Remnick, **John Lewis's Legacy and America's Redemption,** *New Yorker,* July 18, 2020 {Accessed: September 1, 2020}, https://www.newyorker.com/magazine/2020/07/27/how-to-redeem-america

[386] Deric Gilliard, **Rev. Joseph Lowery: One of the most influential leaders of the latter 20th Century,** *Philadelphia Tribune*, April 14, 2020 {Accessed: May 19, 2020}, https://www.phillytrib.com/rev-joseph-lowery-one-of-the-most-influential-leaders-of-the-latter-20th-century/article_5343f093-49d7-5221-8b4b-ac7861d87eb3.html

[387] Rachel Janfaza, **Atlanta Mayor Keisha Lance Bottoms sees 'personal retaliation' behind Georgia governor's mask lawsuit,** CNN, July 17, 2020 {Accessed: June 15, 2023}, https://www.cnn.com/2020/07/17/politics/keisha-lance-bottoms-brian-kemp-mask-lawsuit-cnntv/index.html

[388] Governor Larry Hogan, **Fighting Alone: I'm a GOP Governor, why didn't Trump help my state with coronavirus testing,** *The Washington Post*, July 16, 2020 {Accessed: March 20, 2022}, https://www.washingtonpost.com/outlook/2020/07/16/larry-hogan-trump-coronavirus/

[389] President Donald Trump, White House Rose Garden speech, July 16, 2020.

[390] Ben Lone, **45 administration rolling back controversial Obama fair housing rule,** January 7, 2020,

https://www.housingwire.com/articles/45-administration-rolling-back-controversial-obama-fair-housing-rule/

[391] John Heilemann, Morning Joe, MSNBC, July 17, 2020.

[392] *History.com* editors, **Congress of Racial Equality (CORE)**, updated January 28, 2021 {Accessed: July 30, 2023}, https://www.history.com/topics/black-history/congress-of-racial-equality

[393] Kimberly P. Johnson, *No Fear for Freedom: The Story of the Friendship 9*, Frown-Free Publications, 2014.

[394] Mitch Weiss, **'Never felt guilty', civil rights 1961 convictions tossed out,** *APnews.com*, January 28, 2015 {Accessed: July 30, 2023}, https://apnews.com/general-news-b1d0fdfb5ed54f88bd627dadcec103d3

[395] Dave Aronberg, state attorney, Palm Beach, FL, interviewed by Willie Geist, MSNBC, July 17, 2020.

[396] Ben Sisario, **The Dixie Chicks change their name, dropping the "Dixie,"** *New York Times*, June 25, 2000 {Accessed: July 17, 2020}, https://www.nytimes.com/2020/06/25/arts/music/dixie-chicks-change-name.html

[397] Martin Luther King, Jr., *Strength to Love*, Harper & Row, 1963.

[398] Rashida Tlaib: **Congresswoman's 45 profanity sparks furor**, BBC News, January 4, 2019 {Accessed: July 18, 2020}, https://www.bbc.com/news/world-us-canada-46764052

[399] Veronica Stracqualursi, **New House Democrat Rashida Tlaib: 'We're gonna impeach the motherf****r'**, CNN, January 4, 2019, {Accessed: June 12, 2019}, https://edition.cnn.com/2019/01/04/politics/rashida-tlaib-trump-impeachment-comments/index.html

[400] Jonah Engel Bromwich, **Congressman Who Shouted 'You Lie' at Obama Hears the Same From Constituents,** *New York Times*, April 11, 2017 {Accessed: July 17, 2020},

https://www.nytimes.com/2017/04/11/us/politics/joe-wilson-you-lie-obama-town-hall.html

[401] Howard Koplowitz, **Troy University renames Bibb Graves Hall after John Lewis,** *AL.com*, November 13, 2020 {Accessed: January 12, 2021}, https://www.al.com/news/montgomery/2020/11/troy-university-renames-bibb-graves-hall-after-john-lewis.html

[402] Sarah Whites-Koditschek, **Martin Luther King III calls for voting rights reform in honor of John Lewis,** *Al.com*, July 26, 2020 {Accessed: August 2, 2023}, https://www.al.com/news/2020/07/martin-luther-king-iii-calls-for-voting-rights-reform-in-honor-of-john-lewis.html

[403] Michael Weiss, editor at large, *The Daily Beast*, interviewed on Morning Joe, July 17, 2020.

[404] Amit Paley, **The Trevor Project,** Interviewed on Morning Joe, July 17, 2020.

[405] Zeke Miller and Lolita C. Baldor, **White House receives Mattis memo on transgender troops,** AP, February 23, 2018 {Accessed: August 8, 2021}, https://apnews.com/general-news-67e08c050d0e4045844f799f327d8a08

[406] CBS Evening News, July 21, 2020.

[407] Meaghan Ellis, **NAACP Hits Betsy DeVos With Lawsuit Over CARES Act Rule Giving More Money to Private Schools,** IJR.org, July 22, 2020 {Accessed: July 22, 2020}, https://ijr.org/naacp-hits-betsy-devos-lawsuit-cares-act-clause/

[408] VP Mike Pence, NBC Evening News, Kelly O'Donnell, July 25, 2020.

[409] Amelia Ceja, interviewed by Gadi Schwartz, **Inequality in America,** NBC Evening News, July 25, 2020.

[410] Ibid.

[411] Anthony Salvanto, Jennifer De Pinto, Fred Backus, Kabir Khanna, and Elena Cox, **Battleground Tracker poll: Trump up one point in Ohio as Biden leads Michigan,** POLITICS, CBS News, July 26, 2020 {Accessed: July 30, 2020}, https://www.cbsnews.com/news/trump-biden-opinion-poll-economy-race-covid-26-07-2020/

[412] Lee Roop, **A small Alabama church had a revival and now 40 people have coronavirus,** *AL.com*, July 27, 2020 Accessed: July 30, 2020}, https://www.al.com/coronavirus/2020/07/a-small-alabama-church-had-a-revival-and-now-40-people-have-coronavirus.html

[413] Eugene Robinson, NBC evening News, July 26, 2020.

[414] CBS Evening News with Norah O'Donnell, July 27, 2020.

[415] Mac Smiff, interviewed during Portland protest, **Violent Protests,** NBC Evening News, July 27, 2020.

[416] Jacqueline Howard and Elizabeth Cohen, CNN, **Georgia news anchor receives first shot in US Phase 3 trial of a Covid vaccine: 'I never thought that I'd do something like this',** *Gwinnett Daily News*, July 27, 2020 {Accessed: July 27, 2020}, https://www.gwinnettdailypost.com/features/health/georgia-news-anchor-receives-first-shot-in-us-phase-3-trial-of-a-covid-vaccine/article_2b2bdcd0-1a03-5f9b-ba3d-fc149044b6ce.html

[417] Jenny Durkan, Seattle mayor, on Rachel Maddow Show, MSNBC, July 27, 2020.

[418] Fox Five-Digital team, CNN Wire, **Doctor in virus video shared by Trump has preached on alien DNA, sex with spirits,** Fox Five San Diego, July 29, 2020 {Accessed: August 3, 2023}

[419] Teo Armus, **Social distancing a week earlier could have saved 36,000 American lives, study,** *Washington Post*, May 21, 2020 {Accessed: August 18, 2020}, https://www.washingtonpost.com/nation/2020/05/21/columbia-study-coronavirus-deaths/

[420] Tim Darnell, **READ: Barack Obama's eulogy of Rep. John Lewis,** *Atlanta Journal-Constitution,* July 30, 2020 {Accessed: August

12, 2023}, https://www.ajc.com/john-lewis/read-barack-obamas-eulogy-of-rep-john-lewis/HLQCS4HLSBHEFAHXRTV6YDNQNA/

[421] Laurel Wamsley, **NYC Begins Painting Black Lives Matter Mural In Front Of Trump Tower,** NPR, July 9, 2020, {Accessed: October 19, 2020}, https://www.npr.org/sections/live-updates-protests-for-racial-justice/2020/07/09/889380500/nyc-begins-painting-black-lives-matter-mural-in-front-of-trump-tower

[422] Peter Baker, **Bush Made Willie Horton an Issue in 1988, and the Racial Scars Are Still Fresh,** *New York Times,* December 3, 2018 {Accessed: December 1, 2023}, https://www.nytimes.com/2018/12/03/us/politics/bush-willie-horton.html

[423] Tessa Berenson Rogers, **Trump Suggests Delaying 2020 Election, Claiming It Will Be Fraudulent Without Evidence,** *Time,* June 30, 2020 {Accessed: May 12, 2021}, https://time.com/5873615/donald-trump-delaying-election/

[424] Kelcie Willis, **Oprah gives cover to Breonna Taylor for O magazine,** *AJC,* July 30, 2020 {Accessed: December 1, 2023}, https://www.ajc.com/news/nation-world/oprah-gives-cover-to-breonna-taylor-for-o-magazine/YJ6CH4TCDZGPDEFYKBZLCKFICE/

[425] Pilar Melendez, **Fire and Fury: Angry Crowd attacks CNN Center in Atlanta,** *Daily Beast,* May 30, 2020 {Accessed: December 1, 2023}, https://www.thedailybeast.com/furious-demonstrators-swarm-cnn-center-in-atlanta-during-protest-of-george-floyds-death

[426] Young man interviewed in Boston, NBC Evening News, July 31, 2020.

[427] Victor Oquendo, **Relentless Rise in Deaths,** ABC Evening News, July 31, 2020.

[428] Terry Moran, Election Delay Backlash, ABC Evening News, July 31, 2020.

[429] Tia Mitchell and Chris Joyner, **Kelly Loeffler takes BLM criticism to host with white supremacist ties,** *AJC,* August 1, 2020 {Accessed:

August 1, 2020}, https://www.ajc.com/politics/politics-blog/kelly-loeffler-takes-blm-criticism-to-host-with-white-supremacist-ties/YFGCMWR3DJD3RCLGFSAK3BXVGE/

[430] Bernard Ashby, interviewed by Joy Reid, *The ReidOut*, MSNBC, August 3, 2020.

[431] Claire McCaskill, former Missouri senator, interviewed by Joy Reid on *The ReidOut*, August 3, 2020.

[432] https://spia.princeton.edu/news/native-american-deaths-covid-19-highest-among-racial-groups

[433] https://www.nytimes.com/2020/10/08/us/choctaw-indians-coronavirus.html

[434] ArLuther Lee, **Police apologize after officers draw guns on innocent Black family,** *AJC*, August 4, 2020 {Accessed: August 4, 2020}, https://www.ajc.com/news/police-apologize-after-officers-draw-guns-on-innocent-black-family/MRDGYJ73FRBQLAHRSZHQKSAKBY/

[435] Ben Kesslen, **Black women and girls ordered to ground, handcuffed in mistaken stolen-car stop,** NBC News, August 4, 2020 {Accessed: November 12, 2023}, https://www.nbcnews.com/news/us-news/black-women-girls-ordered-ground-handcuffed-mistaken-stolen-car-stop-n1235737

[436] Lucy Thompkins, **Here's What You Need to Know About Elijah McClain's Death,** *New York Times*, January 18, 2022 {Accessed: January 15, 2023}, https://www.nytimes.com/article/who-was-elijah-mcclain.html

[437] Tweet by Caroline Gohmert, Rep. Rudy Gohmert's daughter, after her COVID-denying father contracted the disease August 3, 2020.

[438] Rebecca Shabad, **'It is what it is': Trump in interview on COVID-19 death toll in U.S.,** CBS News, August 4, 2020 {Accessed: September 3, 2020}, https://www.nbcnews.com/politics/donald-trump/it-what-it-trump-interview-covid-19-death-toll-u-n1235734

⁴³⁹ Brad Spellberg, chief medical office of the LAC-USC Medical Center, interviewed by Miguel Almaguer, NBC Evening News, August 4, 2020.

⁴⁴⁰Harry Litman, interviewing Ron Klain, **A Tale of Two Cities: Paris, Texas and Paris, France,** Talking Feds Podcast August 10, 2020 {Accessed: August 12, 2023}, https://www.talkingfeds.com/transcripts/2020/8/10/a-tale-of-two-cities-paris-texas-and-paris-france

⁴⁴¹ Dr. Anthony Fauci, speaking to Harvard School of Public Health, August 5, 2020.

⁴⁴² Jeff Amy, AP, **Images of Student Crowds Raise Questions in Georgia Schools,** U.S. News and World Report, August 4, 2020 {Accessed: August 6, 2020}, https://www.usnews.com/news/best-states/georgia/articles/2020-08-04/images-of-student-crowds-raise-questions-in-georgia-schools

⁴⁴³ Madeline Holcombe, **Georgia student who posted photo of a crowded school hallway and called it 'good and necessary trouble' is no longer suspended, her mom says,** CNN, August 7, 2020 {Accessed: December 8, 2020}, https://www.cnn.com/2020/08/07/us/georgia-teen-photo-crowded-school-hallway-trnd/index.html

⁴⁴⁴ Fedrick Ingram, president of the Florida Education Association, NBC Evening News, August 5, 2020.

⁴⁴⁵ University of Oxford News and Events, **Human challenge trial launches to study immune response to COVID-19,** April 19, 2021 {Accessed: August 3, 2023}, https://www.ox.ac.uk/news/2021-04-19-human-challenge-trial-launches-study-immune-response-covid-19

⁴⁴⁶ Adrian Hill, **Race for a Vaccine: Challenge Trials,** reported by Richard Engel, NBC Evening News, August 6, 2020.

⁴⁴⁷ Marlene Lenthang, **Black Alabama high school cheerleader quits squad after white members pose with 'racist' Confederate flag T-shirt that says 'I love Redneck Boys,'** *Dailymail.com,*

https://www.usnews.com/news/best-states/georgia/articles/2020-08-04/images-of-student-crowds-raise-questions-in-georgia-schools

[448] Stephen Hahn, FDA Commissioner, OP/ED: **FDA commissioner: No matter what, only a safe, effective vaccine will get our approval,** *Washington Post,* August 5, 2020 {Accessed: August 6, 2020}, https://www.washingtonpost.com/opinions/fda-commissioner-no-matter-what-only-a-safe-effective-vaccine-will-get-our-approval/2020/08/05/e897d920-d74e-11ea-aff6-220dd3a14741_story.html

[449] Nicole Lyn Pesce, **'Will the public be ready for a vaccine?' Many Americans say they won't get the coronavirus vaccine if one is developed,** *MarketWatch,* August 6, 2020 {Accessed: August 6, 2020}, https://www.marketwatch.com/story/will-the-public-be-ready-for-a-vaccine-many-americans-say-they-wont-get-the-coronavirus-vaccine-if-one-is-developed-2020-08-06

[450] Juliegrace Brufke, **Watchdog calls for probe into Gohmert 'disregarding public health guidance' on COVID-19,** *The Hill,* August 11, 2020 {Accessed: August 23, 2020}, https://thehill.com/homenews/house/511538-watchdog-calls-for-probe-into-gohmert-disregarding-public-health-guidance-on/

[451] Dr. Desmond Carson, interviewed on Frontline Doctors on COVID-19, CNN with Sanjay Gupta, August 6, 2020.

[452] MSNBC, **The Pandemic's Racial Disparity**, *Forbes Statista*, The Covid Trafficking Project, July 30, 2020.

[453] Courtney Kueppers, **Even with PPE, front-line workers face three times the risk of COVID, AJC,** August 6, 2020 {Accessed: August 12, 2020}, https://www.ajc.com/life/even-with-ppe-front-line-workers-face-three-times-the-risk-of-covid/PBNWGJ5QDRBXZF24CICGM5XO6E/

[454] Hollie Silverman and Kay Jones, **Two police officers in Georgia put on leave after shooting at minors,** CNN, August 9, 2020 {Accessed: August 4, 2023}, https://www.cnn.com/2020/08/09/us/georgia-police-officers-shot-at-minors/index.html

455 Stuart Stevens, author of *It Was All a Lie: How the Republican Party Became Donald 45,* interviewed on The Last Word with Lawrence O'Donnell, MSNBC, August 12, 2020.

456 Donald Trump, **'What you're seeing and what you're reading is not what's happening,'** BBC News, July 18, 2018 {Accessed: July 20, 2020}, https://www.bbc.com/news/av/world-us-canada-44959340

457 **Kellyanne Conway**, Biography.com, February 22, 2017 {Accessed: August 20, 2023}, https://www.biography.com/political-figures/kellyanne-conway

458 Dennis Brady and Jacqueline Dupree, **U.S. reports highest number of covid-19 deaths in one day since mid-May,** *Washington Post,* August 12, 2020.

459 David Bowie and John Lennon, "Fame," released July 15, 1975 {Accessed: August 12, 2020}, https://genius.com/David-bowie-fame-lyrics

460 President Trump, daily Coronavirus Task Force briefing, August 12, 2020.

461 Marie Tichenor, interviewed by Meg Oliver, CBS Evening News with Nora O'Donnell, August 12, 2020.

462 **Breonna Taylor is killed by police in botched raid, This Day in History,** History.com, March 13, 2020 {Accessed: May 15, 2020}, https://www.history.com/this-day-in-history/breonna-taylor-is-killed-by-police

463 Human Rights Campaign, **Fatal Violence Against the Transgender and Gender Non-Conforming Community in 2020** {Accessed: August 3, 2023}, https://www.hrc.org/resources/violence-against-the-trans-and-gender-non-conforming-community-in-2020

464 Miles Parks, **Trump, While Attacking Mail Voting, Casts Mail Ballot Again,** NPR, August 19, 2020 {Accessed: October 4, 2023}, https://www.npr.org/2020/08/19/903886567/trump-while-attacking-mail-voting-casts-mail-ballot-again

465 Greg Bluestein and J. Scott Trubey, **Kemp lashes out at coverage of White House COVID report critical of Georgia,** *AJC,* August 19, 2020 {Accessed: August 22, 2020}, https://www.ajc.com/politics/politics-blog/kemp-lashes-out-after-white-house-coronavirus-report-criticizes-georgias-response/JZLGAGA57BEKTEZJNKFOJIALR4/

466 Anthony Fauci, Manuel Bojorquez, CBS Evening News with Norah O'Donnell, August 14, 2020.

467 Greg Bluestein, **Kemp's latest order allows local mask mandates for the first time,** *AJC,* August 15, 2020 {Accessed: August 15, 2020}, https://www.ajc.com/politics/politics-blog/kemps-latest-order-allows-local-mask-mandates-for-the-first-time/GJRZ2AXEB5GEPN2TX6BPJGEC24/

468 J. Scott Trubey, **How White House virus recommendations square with Georgia's policies,** *AJC,* August 14, 2020 {Accessed: August 15, 2020}, https://www.ajc.com/politics/politics-blog/kemp-lashes-out-after-white-house-coronavirus-report-criticizes-georgias-response/JZLGAGA57BEKTEZJNKFOJIALR4/ https://www.ajc.com/news/how-white-house-virus-recommendations-square-with-georgias-policies/LE6YJR4UZBBWBM3O5NKMI4AH6U/

469 Andrew Prokop, **Trump once said Obama wasn't authentically American. Last night, Obama returned the favor,** *Vox*, updated July 28, 2016 {Accessed: January 4, 2018}, https://www.vox.com/2016/7/28/12306830/obama-dnc-speech-trump-demagogue

470 Warren Kulo, **Tuberville 'mad' that Trump's immigrants 'poisoning the blood' comments were not 'tougher,'** *AL.com,* December 19, 2023 {Accessed: December 19, 2023}, https://www.msn.com/en-us/news/other/tuberville-mad-that-trump-s-immigrants-poisoning-the-blood-comments-were-not-tougher/ar-AA1lKYiN

471 Jonece Starr Dunigan, **Black in white coats: how Alabama's black healthcare workers are battling pandemic, racism,** *AL.com*, August 14, 2020 {Accessed: August 15, 2020},

https://www.al.com/news/2020/06/black-in-white-coats-how-alabamas-black-healthcare-workers-are-battling-pandemic-racism.html

[472] Jesse Mitchell, **Doctors wear black scrubs in support of Black Lives,** CBS Weekend News, August 15, 2020.

[473] Trevor Ault, Make or break Moment, ABC Evening News, August 15, 2020.

[474] Kia Caldwell, **Inequality Amplifies African Americans' COVID-19 Risk,** May 14, 2020, University of North Carolina Research, https://www.lgbtqnation.com/2020/08/man-died-covid-extremely-angry-widow-wrote-blistering-obituary/;
Alex Bollinger, **A man died of COVID & his "extremely angry" widow wrote this blistering obituary,** *LGBTQ Nation* August 8, 2020 {Accessed: August 13, 2020},
https://apnews.com/ae2b6d71bdc3a9391ae02910d8f0491f

[475] By Path, **New COVID-19 study points to systemic racism in US,** *PATH,* June 10, 2020 {Accessed: April 3, 2021}, https://www.path.org/our-impact/articles/new-covid-19-study-points-systemic-racism-us/

[476] Editorial Board, *The Observer*, University of Notre Dame, St. Mary's and Holy Cross, **Don't make us write obituaries,** August 21, 2020.

[477] *Diamondback* Editorial Board, **When there's a COVID-19 outbreak at UMD, blame the administration,**
The Diamondback, August 20, 2020 {Accessed: August 23, 2020}, https://dbknews.com/2020/08/20/umd-darryll-pines-coronavirus-reopening-administration/

[478] Kenneth Coffey, **45, Donald, School COVID-19 Crisis,** interviewed by Victor Oquendo, World News Tonight with David Muir, August 22, 2020.

[479] Katie Wedell, Josh Salman*, and Dak Le,* **USPS removes thousands of mailboxes each year; in 2020, mail-in ballots make it political,** *USA Today,* August 31, 2020 {Accessed: September 2, 2020},

https://www.usatoday.com/in-depth/news/2020/08/31/usps-mailbox-removals-drew-ire-trump-attacked-mail-ballots/3442736001/

[480] David Williams, interviewed by Nancy Cordes, CBS Evening News with Norah O'Donnell, August 21, 2020.

[481] BET staff, **Former Black Security Guard Becomes Medical Student At Hospital Where He Once Worked**, BET, August 19, 2020 {Accessed: August 23, 2020}, https://www.bet.com/news/national/2020/08/19/russell-ledet-security-guard-becomes-medical-student-at-louisiana-hospital-.html

[482] Russell Ledet, **There's good news,** NBC Nightly News, August 22, 2020.

[483] Andrew Greif, **Doc Rivers: 'It's amazing why we keep loving this country, and this country does not love us back'**, *Los Angeles Times*, August 25, 2020 {Accessed: August 30, 2020}, https://www.latimes.com/sports/clippers/story/2020-08-25/doc-rivers-loving-this-country-and-does-not-love-us-back

[484] Jon Meacham, historian, *Andrea Mitchell Reports*, CNN, August 28, 2020.

[485] DeNeen Brown, **Martin Luther King Jr.'s scorn for 'white moderates' in his Birmingham jail letter,** *Washington Post*, January 15, 2018 {Accessed: January 23, 2018}, https://www.washingtonpost.com/news/retropolis/wp/2018/01/15/martin-luther-king-jr-s-scathing-critique-of-white-moderates-from-the-birmingham-jail/

[486] Susie Linfield, **Trading Truth for Justice?**, *Boston Review*, June 1, 2000 {Accessed: July 8, 2023], https://www.bostonreview.net/articles/susie-linfield-trading-truth-justice/

[487] Analysis by Ayal Feinberg, Regina Branton, and Valerie Martinez-Ebers, **Counties that hosted a 2016 Trump rally saw a 226 percent increase in hate crimes,** *Washington Post*, March 22, 2019 {Accessed: August 30, 2023}, https://www.washingtonpost.com/politics/2019/03/22/trumps-rhetoric-does-inspire-more-hate-crimes/

⁴⁸⁸ Eileen Street, **Women's History: Remembering the Legacy of Civil and Human Rights Activist Anne Braden,** *Spectrum News* 1, March 8, 2021 {Accessed: August 30, 2023}, https://spectrumnews1.com/ky/louisville/news/2021/03/07/women-s-history-month--the-legacy-of-civil-and-human-rights-activist-anne-braden-

⁴⁸⁹ Deric Gilliard, interview with Anne Braden, *Living in the Shadows of a Legend: Unsung Heroes and 'Sheroes who Marched with Dr. Martin Luther King, Jr.*, 2002, p. 46.

⁴⁹⁰ Chris Cuomo, CNN, describing a video of alleged shooter walking past police, hands up, with assault weapon over his shoulder, being told to get on the sidewalk.

⁴⁹¹ Jacob Blake, Sr., repeating words of Jacob Blake, **America in Crisis,** CNN, August 28, 2020.

⁴⁹² Steve Inskeep, Simone Popperl, and Lilly Quiroz, **Former DHS Official: Trump Pouring 'Fuel On The Fire' Of Domestic Extremism,** NPR, September 2, 2020 {Accessed: July 12, 2023}, https://www.npr.org/2020/09/02/908347989/former-dhs-official-white-house-failed-to-take-far-right-extremism-seriously

⁴⁹³ Dr. Anthony Fauci, National Director of Allergy and Infectious Diseases, **Fighting the Virus,** World News Tonight with David Muir, August 25, 2020.

⁴⁹⁴ Chloe Hurckes, **Kenosha County Sheriff David Beth apologizes for heated comments made about theft, chase suspects,** WTMJ-TV (NBC), Milwaukee, January 28, 2018 {Accessed: August 1, 2023}, https://www.tmj4.com/news/local-news/kenosha-county-sheriff-david-beth-apologizes-for-heated-comments-made-about-theft-chase-suspects

⁴⁹⁵ Katie Beck, **2020 Vote Watch,** NBC Evening News with Lester Holt, September 12, 2020 {Accessed: October 28, 2020}

⁴⁹⁶ Kevin Morris, **Digging into the Georgia Primary,** *Brennan Center for Justice,* last updated September 10, 2020 {Accessed: October 12,

2021}, https://www.brennancenter.org/our-work/research-reports/digging-georgia-primary

[497] Bruce Y. Lee, **Trump's Top Health Spokesman Michael Caputo Goes On Social Media Rant,** *Forbes,* September 14, 2020 {Accessed: October 1, 2020}, https://www.forbes.com/sites/brucelee/2020/09/14/trumps-top-health-spokesman-michael-caputo-goes-on-social-media-rant/?sh=62231fd73dc2

[498] Sharon LaFraniere, **Trump Health Aide Pushes Bizarre Conspiracies and Warns of Armed Revolt,** *New York Times,* September 14, 2020 {Accessed: October 30, 2021}, https://www.nytimes.com/2020/09/14/us/politics/caputo-virus.html

[499] PBS News Hour, **CDC's politicization 'extremely dangerous' for Americans, says its former head,** July 14, 2020 {Accessed: November 1, 2021}, https://www.pbs.org/newshour/show/cdcs-politicization-extremely-dangerous-for-americans-says-its-former-head

[500] Helen Branswell, **As controversies swirl, CDC director is seen as allowing agency to buckle to political influence,** *Stat,* September 16, 2020 {Accessed: September 19, 2020}, https://www.statnews.com/2020/09/16/as-controversies-swirl-cdc-director-is-seen-as-allowing-agency-to-buckle-to-political-influence/

[501] Alan Feuer and Zach Montague, **Four Proud Boys Convicted of Sedition in Key Jan. 6 Case,** *New York Times,* May 4, 2023 {Accessed: August 12, 2023}, https://www.nytimes.com/2023/05/04/us/politics/jan-6-proud-boys-sedition.html

[502] Tom Frieden, former CDC director, interviewed by Paula Reid, CBS News wit Norah O'Donnell, September 18, 2020.

[503] Ibid.

[504] Julia Marnin, **Fact Check: Did Christopher Wray Say White Supremacy is Biggest Domestic Terror Threat?,** *Newsweek,* March 2, 2021 {Accessed: December 5, 2023},

https://www.newsweek.com/fact-check-white-supremacy-biggest-domestic-threat-us-wray-says-1573320

[505] Ibid.

[506] Olivia Troye, interviewed for The Lead with Jake Tapper, CNN, September 17, 2020.

[507] Antonia Noori Farzan, Rick Noack, Lateshia Beachum, Adam Taylor, Marisa Lati, Kim Bellware, Hannah Denham, Reis Thebault and Meryl Kornfield, **Live updates: CDC reverses statement on airborne transmission of coronavirus, says draft accidentally published,** *Washington Post*, September 21, 2020 {Accessed: September 21, 2020}, https://www.washingtonpost.com/nation/2020/09/21/coronavirus-covid-live-updates-us/

[508] Richard Besser, former CDC director, interviewed by Chris Cuomo on Anderson Cooper 360, September 21, 2020.

[509] Kim Bellware, **He slashed their tires and shot into their home over their BLM sign. His Black neighbors forgave him,** *Washington Post*, August 19, 2021 {Accessed: December 12, 2023}, https://www.washingtonpost.com/nation/2021/08/19/michael-frederick-sentencing/

[510] Oralandar Brand-Williams, **Man charged in attacks on Black family in Warren asks for forgiveness,** *Detroit News*, October 1, 2020 {Accessed: October 4, 2020}, https://www.detroitnews.com/story/news/local/macomb-county/2020/10/01/man-charged-attacks-black-family-warren/5878390002/

[511] Josh Margolin and Lucien Bruggeman, **34 people connected to White House, more than previously known, infected by coronavirus: Internal FEMA memo,** ABC News, October 7, 2020 {Accessed: October 18, 2020}, https://abcnews.go.com/Politics/34-people-connected-white-house-previously-infected-coronavirus/story?id=73487381

⁵¹² CBS Evening News with Norah O'Donnell, October 7, 2020 {Accessed: October 7, 2020}, https://www.facebook.com/CBSEveningNews/videos/718674465395555/

⁵¹³ Dr. Anthony Fauci, commenting on 45's comparison between the flu and COVID 19, NBC Evening News, October 7, 2020.

⁵¹⁴ Gina Kolata, **In a First, New England Journal of Medicine Joins Never-Trumpers,** *New York Times,* October 7, 2020 {Accessed: October 7, 2020}, https://www.nytimes.com/2020/10/07/health/new-england-journal-trump.html

⁵¹⁵ Geoffrey Skelley and Amelia Thomson-DeVeaux, **How Americans are reacting to Trump's COVID-19 diagnosis,** *FiveThirtyEight,* October 5, 2020 {Accessed: October 7, 2020}, https://fivethirtyeight.com/features/will-trumps-diagnosis-change-the-way-republicans-think-about-covid-19/

⁵¹⁶ Sheila Kaplan, **White House Blocked C.D.C. From Requiring Masks on Public Transportation,** *New York Times,* October 9, 2020 {Accessed: October 18, 2020}, https://www.nytimes.com/2020/10/09/health/coronavirus-covid-masks-cdc.html

⁵¹⁷ Gov. Gretchen Whitmer, **Kidnap plot charges, Michigan Gov. Whitmer rips Trump for comments,** *ABC World News Tonight,* October 9, 2020.

⁵¹⁸ Brian X. McCrone, and Brian Sheehan, **Ex-Philly Cop Found Guilty of Manslaughter in 2017 Shooting of Unarmed Man,** NBC10 Philadelphia, September 21, 2021 (Accessed: January 15, 2023), https://www.nbcphiladelphia.com/news/local/verdict-reached-in-murder-trial-of-ex-philly-cop-charged-with-shooting-unarmed-man/3368734/

⁵¹⁹ David Choi, **Hate crimes increased 226% in places Trump held a campaign rally in 2016, study claims,** *Business Insider,* March 23, 2019 {Accessed: October 1, 2019}, https://www.businessinsider.com/trump-campaign-rally-hate-crimes-study-maga-2019-3

520 Elise Schmelzer, **Former security guard pleads not guilty to murder in Denver protest shooting,** *Denver Post,* May 28, 2021 {Accessed: June 1, 2021}, https://www.denverpost.com/2021/05/28/matthew-dolloff-shooting-lee-keltner-denver/

521 **One year after leaving border detention facility, immigrant mother says she's grateful to be in America,** CBS Evening News with Norah O'Donnell, October 12, 2020 {Accessed: June 1, 2021}, https://www.cbsnews.com/news/detention-center-mcallen-texas-immigrant-mother-says-shes-grateful-america/

522 Richard Barron, interviewed by Blaine Alexander, NBC Evening News with Lester Holt, October 12, 2020.

523 Senator Amy Klobuchar, during Senate questioning of Supreme Court nominee Amy Coney Barrett, October 13, 2020 {Accessed: October 28, 2020}

524 Associated Press, **California GOP says it won't remove unofficial ballot boxes,** PBS News Hour, October 14, 2020 {Accessed: October 18, 2020}, https://www.pbs.org/newshour/politics/california-gop-says-it-wont-remove-unofficial-ballot-boxes

525 Stephanie Goss, **On the front lines in battle against alarming virus,** NBC Evening News with Lester Holt, October 14, 2020.

526 Caroline Rose Giuliani, **Rudy Giuliani Is My Father. Please, Everyone, Vote for Joe Biden and Kamala Harris,** *Vanity Fair,* October 15, 2020 {Accessed: October 18, 2020}, https://www.vanityfair.com/style/2020/10/rudy-giulianis-daughter-on-voting-for-biden

527 Anna North, **In 2017, women marched against Trump. Now they're marching to get rid of him,** *Vox,* October 17, 2020 {Accessed: October 28, 2023}, https://www.vox.com/2020/10/17/21520709/womens-march-dc-2020-rbg-ginsburg-barrett

528 Scott Gottlieb, **New crackdowns in U.S. to curb possible second wave,** NBC Evening News with Lester Holt, October 16, 2020.

[529] Dan Mangan, **Trump calls Dr. Anthony Fauci a 'disaster,' says Americans 'are tired of Covid' as nation faces spiking cases,** CNBC, October 19, 2020 {Accessed: September 4, 2020}, https://www.cnbc.com/2020/10/19/coronavirus-trump-calls-fauci-a-disaster-says-people-are-tired-of-covid.html

[530] CBS Evening News with Norah O'Donnell, October 19, 2020.

[531] Celine Castronuovo, **Feds say far-right group coordinated attack on Minneapolis police precinct during protest,** *The Hill,* October 23, 2020 {Accessed: October 23, 2020}, https://thehill.com/homenews/news/522509-feds-say-far-right-group-coordinated-attack-on-minneapolis-police-precinct

[532] Kate Snow, **Inequality in America,** NBC Evening News with Lester Holt, October 17, 2020; **2017 NAACP & Clean Air Task Force.**

[533] Kate Snow, **Inequality in America,** NBC Evening News with Lester Holt, October 17, 2020.

[534] Caitlin Dickerson, **Inquiry Ordered Into Claims Immigrants Had Unwanted Gynecology Procedures,** *New York Times,* September 16, 2020 {Accessed: October 13, 2021}, https://www.nytimes.com/2020/09/16/us/ICE-hysterectomies-whistleblower-georgia.html

[535] Suzanne Gamboa, **Coronavirus is causing the 'historic decimation' of Latinos, medical expert says,** NBC News, September 30, 2020 {Accessed: September 2, 2023}, https://www.nbcnews.com/news/latino/coronavirus-causing-historic-decimation-latinos-medical-expert-says-n1241576

[536] **Ending the COVID-19 Pandemic: The White House Office of Science and Technology Policy,** press release on Trump's first term accomplishments, October 28, 2020.

[537] Stephanie Ruhle, The 11th Hour with Brian Williams, MSNBC, October 28, 2020.

[538] Michelle Griffith, **If North Dakota was a country, it would have the world's worst confirmed COVID outbreak, one analysis shows,** *Grand Forks Herald*, October 21, 2020 {Accessed: October 28, 2020}, https://www.twincities.com/2020/10/21/if-north-dakota-was-a-country-it-would-have-the-worlds-worst-confirmed-covid-19-outbreak-one-analysis-shows/

[539] Anderson Cooper, **"There has been a coup": Bernstein reacts to new evidence on Trump's role in riot,** CNN, October 8, 2021 {Accessed: December 12, 2023}, https://www.cnn.com/videos/politics/2021/10/08/bernstein-trump-executive-privilege-january-6-ac360-vpx.cnn

[540] Melissa Quinn, **Birx says Americans who gathered for Thanksgiving should assume they're infected and get tested,** CBS News-Face the Nation, November 30, 2020 {Accessed: June 22, 2023}, https://www.cbsnews.com/news/thanksgiving-covid-deborah-birx-testing-face-the-nation/

[541] Lawrence Williams, **U.S. hits all-time high of nearly 100,000 new COVID cases,** NBC News, October 31, 2020.

[542] Stephanie Fuerte, **Latinos see new meaning in Dia de Los Muertos after losing loved ones to COVID-19,** ABC News, October 28, 2020 {Accessed: September 1, 2023}, https://abcnews.go.com/Health/latinos-meaning-da-de-los-muertos-losing-loved/story?id=73890114

[543] Suzanne Gamboa, **Coronavirus is causing the 'historic decimation' of Latinos, medical expert says,** Dr. Peter Hotez, NBC News, September 30, 2020 {Accessed: September 2, 2023}, https://www.nbcnews.com/news/latino/coronavirus-causing-historic-decimation-latinos-medical-expert-says-n1241576

[544] Fidel Martinez, **Latinx Files: United Farm Workers marches to Sacramento,** *Los Angeles Times*, August 18, 2022 {Accessed: August 28, 2023}, https://www.latimes.com/world-nation/newsletter/2022-08-18/latinx-files-ufw-march-sacramento-latinx-files

⁵⁴⁵ AP, **Trump pleas [sic] with suburban women, "please like me,"** October 14, 2020 {Accessed: December 24, 2023}, https://www.bing.com/videos/riverview/relatedvideo?q=%22suburban+women%2c+please+love+me%2c%22+said+Trump&mid=D837ABF613BCF8514CFBD837ABF613BCF8514CFB&FORM=VIRE

⁵⁴⁶ Larry King, **Looking Back: Civil rights protestors take back Forsyth County (January 25, 1987),** *Tampa Bay Times*, January 25, 1987, reprinted May 11, 2017 {Accessed: October 5, 2022}, https://www.tampabay.com/news/nation/looking-back-protestors-take-back-forsyth-county-january-25-1987/2323535/

⁵⁴⁷ Becky Little, **In 1912, This Georgia County Drove Out Every Black Resident,** *History.com*, May 23, 2018 {Accessed: June 2, 2021}; https://www.history.com/news/georgia-racial-expulsion-stacey-abrams

⁵⁴⁸ The White House, **Remarks by President Trump on the Election,** November 5, 2020 {Accessed: December 23, 2023}, https://trumpwhitehouse.archives.gov/briefings-statements/remarks-president-trump-election/

⁵⁴⁹ Mark Scolforo and Colleen Long, **In Blistering Ruling, Judge Throws out Trump Suit in PA.,** AP, November 21, 2020 {Accessed: January 10, 2021}, https://apnews.com/article/judge-throws-out-trump-suit-pennsylvania-87eaf4df86d5f6ccc343c3385c9ba86c

⁵⁵⁰ Matthew Daly, **GOP senator: no evidence to support Trump vote-fraud claims,** WPRO 630AM/99.7FM, Associated Press, November 6, 2020 {Accessed: August 3, 2023}, https://www.997wpro.com/2020/11/06/gop-senator-no-evidence-to-support-trump-vote-fraud-claims/

⁵⁵¹ **Philadelphia Mayor Tells Trump to "Put Big Boy Pants On,"** November 6, 2020 {Accessed: November 23, 2021}, https://www.youtube.com/watch?v=BtOKaGCR1Xc

⁵⁵² Quincy Drone, story by Kathy Park, **U.S. hits COVID record third day in a row,** NBC Evening News with Lester Holt, November 7, 2020.

553 Christina Wilkie, **GOP Sens. Loeffler and Perdue demand that Georgia's Republican secretary of state resign,** CNBC, November 9, 2020 {Accessed: March 2, 2021}, https://www.cnbc.com/2020/11/09/loeffler-perdue-demand-resignation-of-georgia-gop-secretary-of-state-.html#:~:text=WASHINGTON%20%E2%80%94%20Republican%20Sens.-,Kelly%20Loeffler%20and%20David%20Perdue%20of%20Georgia%20demanded%20the%20resignation,did%20not%20offer%20specific%20examples.

554 Caitlin O'Kane, **POLITICS Jon Ossoff becomes the youngest Democrat elected to the Senate since Joe Biden in 1973,** CBS News, January 6, 2021 {Accessed: September 1, 2023}, https://www.cbsnews.com/news/jon-ossoff-youngest-democrat-senator-since-joe-biden/

555 Veronica Stracqualursi, **Warnock will make history as Georgia's first Black senator,** CNN, January 6, 2021 {Accessed: January 22, 2022}, https://www.cnn.com/2021/01/06/politics/warnock-georgia-first-black-senator/index.html

556 Emma Hurt, **GOP Senator On Defense As WNBA Team She Co-Owns Embraces Black Lives Matter,** NPR, July 15, 2020 {Accessed: October 22, 2021}, https://www.wkyufm.org/2020-07-15/gop-senator-on-defense-as-wnba-team-she-co-owns-embraces-black-lives-matter

557 Julie Watson, chief medical officer, ABC Evening News with Norah O'Donnell, November 11, 2020.

558 Scott Gottlieb, NBC News with Lester Holt, November 11, 2020.

559 Alex Marquardt, Geneva Sands, and Zachary Cohen, **Top DHS official ratchets up rebukes of Trump's false election claims,** CNN, November 13, 2020 {Accessed: November 13, 2020}, https://www.cnn.com/2020/11/13/politics/dhs-krebs-rebukes-trump-election-claims/index.html

560 Martin Pengelly, **Kayleigh McEnany a 'liar and opportunist', says former Trump aide,** The Guardian, December 30, 2022 {Accessed: December 3, 2023}, https://www.theguardian.com/us-

news/2022/dec/30/kayleigh-mcenany-liar-opportunist-trump-alyssa-farah-griffin

[561] Derrick Johnson, NAACP president, interviewed on MSNBC, November 15, 2020.

[562] Stuart Stevens, advisor to the Lincoln Project, interviewed on *The ReidOut*, MSNBC, November 10, 2020.

[563] Bruce C.T. Wright, **Man Who Killed Ahmaud Arbery texted with friend about 'crackhead gold-teeth wearing' Black People: Bond Hearing,** NewsTalk 1490, November 13, 2020 {Accessed: November 13, 2020}, https://newstalkcleveland.com/3051913/man-who-killed-ahmaud-arbery-texted-with-friend-about-crackhead-gold-teeth-wearing-black-people-bond-hearing/

[564] Jaclyn Peiser and Lateshia Beachum, **Men charged with murder in death of Ahmaud Arbery are denied bond,** *Washington Post*, November 13, 2020 {Accessed: November 13, 2020}, https://www.washingtonpost.com/nation/2020/11/13/ahmaud-arbery-mcmichael-racist-messages/

[565] Nightline, Turning Point, October 17, 2020.

[566] Deric Gilliard, *Living in the Shadows of a Legend: Unsung Heroes and 'Sheroes' who Marched with Dr. Martin Luther King, Jr.*, Gilliard Communications, 2002, pp. 97-102.

[567] **Hate Crimes and the Rise of White Nationalism, Hearing before the Sub-Committee on Crime, Terrorism and Homeland Security, of the Committee of the Judiciary, House of Representatives, 116th Congress First Session,** April 9, 2019 {Accessed: December 3, 2023}, https://www.govinfo.gov/content/pkg/CHRG-116hhrg36563/html/CHRG-116hhrg36563.htm

[568] Libby Cathey, **Dr. Scott Atlas under fire for telling Michigan to 'rise up' against COVID-19 restrictions,** ABC News, November 16, 2020 {Accessed: December 3, 2020}, https://abcnews.go.com/Politics/dr-scott-atlas-fire-telling-michigan-rise-covid/story?id=74234276

⁵⁶⁹ David Axelrod, interviewed on Cuomo Prime Time, CNN, November 16, 2020.

⁵⁷⁰ Terry Moran, **Legal challenges failing,** ABC World News Tonight, November 16, 2020.

⁵⁷¹ Wilson Wong, **Iowa Gov. Kim Reynolds issues mask mandate after disparaging it as 'feel good' measure,** NBC News, November 17, 2020 {Accessed: December 13, 2023}, https://www.nbcnews.com/news/us-news/iowa-gov-kim-reynolds-issues-mask-mandate-after-disparaging-it-n1247972

⁵⁷² Alana Wise, **Trump Fires Election Security Director Who Corrected Voter Fraud Disinformation,** NPR, November 17, 2020 {Accessed: January 16, 2023}, https://www.npr.org/2020/11/17/936003057/cisa-director-chris-krebs-fired-after-trying-to-correct-voter-fraud-disinformati

⁵⁷³ Ashley Bartholomew, **Cases rising in every state,** ABC World News Tonight, November 17, 2020 {Accessed: January 16, 2023}, https://www.npr.org/2020/11/17/936003057/cisa-director-chris-krebs-fired-after-trying-to-correct-voter-fraud-disinformati

⁵⁷⁴ Brad Raffensperger, GA Secretary of State, interviewed by Mary Bruce, **Transition in Turmoil,** ABC World News Tonight, November 17, 2020.

⁵⁷⁵ Thomas Donohue, CEO of U.S. Chamber of Commerce, CBS News with Norah O'Donnell, November 19, 2020.

⁵⁷⁶ Kevin Davenport, **New Medicare Designation Could Prevent Closure of Struggling Rural Hospitals,** NCLS, May 11, 2023 {Accessed: November 12, 2023}, https://www.ncsl.org/state-legislatures-news/details/new-medicare-designation-could-prevent-closure-of-struggling-rural-hospitals#:~:text=Since%202010%2C%20at%20least%20149,no%20longer%20provide%20inpatient%20care

⁵⁷⁷ WGST-Radio, The Dana Barrett Show, **Dana Debunks the 'you call everything racist defense" from conservatives** (clip), July 29,

2019 {Accessed: July 18, 2023},
https://www.iheart.com/podcast/1248-the-dana-barrett-show-30965679/

[578] Josh Stack, **Racism is alive and well in Loudoun County. It always has been,** *Loudoun Times-Mirror*, June 14, 2020 {Accessed: May 12, 2021}, https://www.loudountimes.com/opinion/stack-racism-is-alive-and-well-in-loudoun-county-it-always-has-been/article_8ae43658-ae99-11ea-9b20-93d9d34f2803.html

[579] Trevor Baratko, **MORE: Trump team making major push in Loudoun, state in final days of campaign,** *Loudoun Times-Mirror*, November 5, 2016 {Accessed: February 2, 2017}, https://www.loudountimes.com/news/more-trump-team-making-major-push-in-loudoun-state-in-final-days-of-campaign/article_b68e08b2-a40e-58a1-a657-17993705a6e8.html

[580] Jacob Blake, **Trump visits Kenosha to back police after shooting,** BBC, September 2, 2020 {Accessed: October 3, 2020}, https://www.bbc.com/news/world-us-canada-53989076

[581] Adam Brewster, **Wisconsin court rejects Trump campaign's recount challenge,** CBS News, December 11, 2020 {Accessed: January 4, 2021}, https://www.cbsnews.com/news/wisconsin-court-rejects-trump-campaign-election-recount-challenge/

[582] Eric Katz, **If Trump Is Reelected, His Aides Are Planning to Purge the Civil Service,** *Government Executive*, July 22, 2022 {Accessed: December 20, 2023}, https://www.govexec.com/workforce/2022/07/va-touts-improvements-warns-challenges-digital-gi-bill-platform/374866/

[583] Richard Brody, **"C.S.A.: The Confederate States of America," a Faux Documentary That Skewers Real White Supremacy,** February 15, 2017 {Accessed: August 1, 2023}, https://www.newyorker.com/culture/richard-brody/c-s-a-the-confederate-states-of-america-a-faux-documentary-that-skewers-real-white-supremacy

[584] **No Kid Hungry,** ABC World News Tonight, November 20, 2020.

585 Vanessa Romo, **Kyle Rittenhouse Released On $2 Million Bail, Awaiting Trial In Kenosha, Wis., Deaths,** NPR.org, November 20, 2020 {Accessed: November 21, 2020}, https://www.npr.org/2020/11/20/937323873/kyle-rittenhouse-released-on-2-million-bail-awaiting-trial-in-kenosha-wis-deaths

586 Leana Wen, **Coronavirus Pandemic,** CNN, November 21, 2020.

587 Deborah Birx, **Coronavirus Pandemic,** CNN, November 21, 2020.

588 NBC Evening News, November 22, 2020.

589 Adrianne Murchison, **Black dad organizes police, teen event in Roswell to discourage violence,** *Atlanta Journal-Constitution*, November 21, 2020 {Accessed: November 22, 2020}, https://www.ajc.com/news/atlanta-news/black-dad-organizes-police-teen-event-in-roswell-to-discourageviolence/PQYOSSPXW5AJTNAIJRNC4W3USY/

590 Katy Waldman, **"Fragility" that prevents white Americans from confronting racism,** *New Yorker*, July 23, 2018 {Accessed: November 30, 2021}, https://www.newyorker.com/books/page-turner/a-sociologist-examines-the-white-fragility-that-prevents-white-americans-from-confronting-racism

591 NBC Evening News with Lester Holt, **Massive Effort underway to shore up vaccine trust,** November 23, 2020.

592 Berkeley Lovelace, Jr., **Doctors say CDC should warn people the side effects from Covid vaccine shots won't be 'a walk in the park',** CNBC, November 23, 2020 {Accessed: November 25, 2020}, https://www.cnbc.com/2020/11/23/covid-vaccine-cdc-should-warn-people-the-side-effects-from-shots-wont-be-walk-in-the-park-.html

593 Caitlin Dickerson, Seth Freed Wessler, and Miriam Jordan, **Immigrants Say They Were Pressured Into Unneeded Surgeries,** *New York Times*, September 29, 2020 {Accessed: November 16, 2022}, https://www.nytimes.com/2020/09/29/us/ice-hysterectomies-surgeries-georgia.html

594 John Brownstein, ABC World News Tonight, November 25, 2020.

[595] Kate Sullivan, **Here are the historic firsts in Biden's administration,** CNN Politics, December 30, 2020 {Accessed: January 3, 2021}, https://www.cnn.com/2020/11/30/politics/historic-firsts-biden-administration/index.html

[596] Eric Tucker, AP, **Rewriting history? Trump pardons Michael Flynn,** *Christian Science Monitor,* November 25, 2020 {Accessed: September 1, 2023}, https://www.csmonitor.com/USA/Justice/2020/1125/Rewriting-history-Trump-pardons-Michael-Flynn?cmpid=mkt:ggl:dsa-np&gclid=CjwKCAjwu4WoBhBkEiwAojNdXr0s08lUrUtGUETZZky y3-lPsXFSdjvsvTE0yeDPbfXSlmm6N5StSRoC9bMQAvD_BwE

[597] **Feeding America,** Sam Brock, NBC Evening News, November 25, 2020.

[598] President Donald Trump, first public comments after losing election, NBC Evening News, November 26, 2020.

[599] Trump tweet from November 27, 2020.

[600] **Trump's losses mount,** ABC World News Tonight, November 29, 2020.

[601] Audio from Fox Business Sunday Morning Futures with Maria Bartiromo, ABC World News Tonight, November 29, 2920.

[602] **National Nurses United,** NBC Nightly News, November 27, 2020.

[603] President Trump tweet, November 30, 2020.

[604] Don Eberhart, **Trump pushes false election claims as key states certify results,** CBS News with Norah O'Donnell, November 30, 2020.

[605] Georgia Secretary Brad Raffensperger, **Opinion: Georgia secretary of state: My family voted for Trump. He threw us under the bus anyway,** *USA Today,* November 25, 2020 {Accessed: May 8, 2021},

https://eu.usatoday.com/story/opinion/voices/2020/11/25/georgia-secretary-of-state-election-integrity-2020-column/6407586002/

[606] Annie Karni, **In a Fox News interview, Parscale blames Trump's lack of coronavirus empathy for his election loss,** *New York Times*, December 1, 2020 {Accessed: October 30, 2021}, https://www.nytimes.com/2020/12/01/us/politics/in-a-fox-news-interview-parscale-blames-trumps-lack-of-coronavirus-empathy-for-his-election-loss.html

[607] Jordan Williams, **Gingrich: 'Lin Wood and Sidney Powell are totally destructive,'** *The Hill*, December 3, 2020 {Accessed: October 3, 2021}, https://thehill.com/homenews/campaign/528547-gingrich-lin-wood-and-sidney-powell-are-totally-destructive/

[608] Charlie Daniels, "The Devil Went Down to Georgia," https://www.google.com/search?q=the+devil+went+down+to+georgia&rlz=1C1GCEA_enUS864US911&oq=the+devil+went+&aqs=chrome.0.0i457j0j69i57j0l2j46l3.11226j0j7&sourceid=chrome&ie=UTF-8

[609] Alexandra Jaffe, **McConnell recounts handwritten thank-you note from Obama,** CNN, May 11, 2015 {Accessed: December 8, 2023}, https://www.cnn.com/2015/05/11/politics/mcconnell-obama-lynch-thank-you-note/index.html

[610] Ron Allen, **Many in communities of color distrustful of vaccine,** NBC Nightly News, December 3, 2020.

[611] **Black Coalition Against COVID-19,** NBC Nightly News, December 3, 2020.

[612] Dr. Valerie Smith, **Delivering the Vaccine,** Gio Benitez, ABC World News Tonight, December 3, 2020.

[613] Harriet Washington, *Medical Apartheid: The Dark History of Medical Experimentation on Black Americans from Colonial Times to the Present,* Doubleday Books, 2007.

[614] Valeria Pelet, **Puerto Rico's Invisible Health Crisis,** *The Atlantic*, September 3, 2016 {Accessed: January 16, 2023}, https://www.theatlantic.com/politics/archive/2016/09/vieques-invisible-health-crisis/498428/

615 The White House, **President Biden Announces Members of the Biden-Harris Administration COVID-19 Health Equity Task Force,** February 10, 2021 {Accessed: December 28, 2023}, https://www.whitehouse.gov/briefing-room/press-briefings/2021/02/10/president-biden-announces-members-of-the-biden-harris-administration-covid-19-health-equity-task-force/

616 Dr. Robert Redfield, CDC Director, U.S. Chamber of Commerce Foundation, December 3, 2020.

617 Letter from Governor Tony Evers to HHS Secretary Alex Azar, CBS Evening News with Norah O'Donnell, December 4, 2020.

618 Michael Daly, **COVID Hypocrites Like Denver Mayor Preach Safety, Then Gamble With Lives,** *Daily Beast,* November 27, 2020 {Accessed: April 4, 2021}, https://www.thedailybeast.com/covid-hypocrites-like-denver-mayor-michael-hancock-preach-safety-then-gamble-with-lives

619 Jim Zarroli, **The Dow Surpasses 30,000 For 1st Time Ever,** NPR, November 24, 2020 {Accessed: January 12, 2020}, https://www.npr.org/2020/11/24/938593059/the-dow-surpasses-30-000-for-1st-time-ever,

620 Aaron Weaver, **What Is Qanon? Here Are 5 Core Beliefs of the Shocking Conspiracy Theory,** CNN, September 26, 2020 {Accessed: October 18, 2021}, https://www.ccn.com/what-is-qanon-conspiracy-theory/

621 Peter Dreier, **The Red Scare Took Aim at Black Radicals Like Langston Hughes,** *Jacobin*, March 31, 2023 {Accessed: September 10, 2023}, https://jacobin.com/2023/03/langston-hughes-red-scare-black-radicals-leftists-huac-red-baiting

622 Austin Sarat and Dennis Aftergut, **Is America on the brink of tyranny? Trump's plan if elected in 2024 should frighten us all,** *USA Today*, July 20, 2023 {Accessed: September 1, 2023}, https://www.usatoday.com/story/opinion/2023/07/20/trump-campaign-presidential-power-grab-2024-election/70430661007/

623 Bob Dylan.

⁶²⁴ Dr. Albert Bourla, Pfizer CEO, FDA finds Pfizer vaccine safe and effective, NBC Evening News, December 8, 2020.

⁶²⁵ Wilson Wong, **'We let our guard down': Former Alabama senator dies of COVID-19 at age 78,** *Today,* December 7, 2020 {Accessed: January 4, 2021}, https://www.today.com/health/former-alabama-senator-larry-dixon-dies-covid-19-age-78-t202946

⁶²⁶ Natalie O'Neill, **National Guard soldier killed herself after being gang-raped by colleagues: mom,** *New York Post*, November 18, 2020 {Accessed: December 8, 2020}, https://nypost.com/2020/11/18/soldier-killed-herself-after-being-gang-raped-by-colleagues-mom/

⁶²⁷ Jeffrey Goldberg, **Trump: Americans Who Died in War Are 'Losers' and 'Suckers',** *The Atlantic*, September 3, 2020 {Accessed: September 8, 2023}, https://www.theatlantic.com/politics/archive/2020/09/trump-americans-who-died-at-war-are-losers-and-suckers/615997/

⁶²⁸ Luke Baker, **Trump cancels WW1 memorial at U.S. cemetery in France due to rain,** Reuters, November 10, 2018 {Accessed: July 2, 2021}, https://www.reuters.com/article/us-usa-trump-france-memorial-idUSKCN1NF0NU

⁶²⁹ Letter from Atty. Ron Filipkowski to Florida Governor DeSantis in resignation and protest.

⁶³⁰ Stephanie Bauer, **Here Are The Names Of 126 Members Of The House Who Refuse To Accept That Biden Won,** *Buzzfeed News*, December 10, 2020 {Accessed: December 18, 2020}, https://www.buzzfeednews.com/article/skbaer/list-republican-house-members-overturn-election

⁶³¹ Rehema Ellis, **Inspiring America,** NBC Evening News, December 10, 2020.

⁶³² Emma Platoff, **U.S. Supreme Court throws out Texas lawsuit contesting 2020 election results in four battleground states,** *Texas Tribune*, December 11, 2020 {Accessed: December 14, 2020},

https://www.texastribune.org/2020/12/11/texas-lawsuit-supreme-court-election-results/

[633] Pew Research Center, NBC World News, December 14, 2020.

[634] Dr. Richard Feifer, NBC Evening News, December 14, 2020.

[635] Anh Do and Luke Money, **Some restaurants are defying California lockdown rules: 'We have to make a living'**, *Los Angeles Times*, December 8, 2020 {Accessed: September 2, 2023}, https://www.latimes.com/california/story/2020-12-08/restaurants-defy-california-coronavirus-lockdown-rules

[636] Congressman Jim Clyburn, AC 360, CNN interview, December 15, 2020.

[637] Lisa Macon Harrison, **Vaccinating America**, CBS Evening News with Norah O'Donnell, December 15, 2020.

[638] Matt Gutman, **California "mass fatality plan" activated**, ABC World News Tonight, December 15, 2020.

[639] Stephanie Baker and Cynthia Koons, **Inside Operation Warp Speed's $18 Billion Sprint for a Vaccine**, *Businessweek,* October 29, 2020 {Accessed: June 15, 2021}, https://www.bloomberg.com/news/features/2020-10-29/inside-operation-warp-speed-s-18-billion-sprint-for-a-vaccine

[640] Emmanuel Camarillo, **In botched Anjanette Young raid, Chicago Police Board votes to fire sergeant in charge**, *Chicago Sun-Times*, June 15, 2023 {Accessed: September 8, 2023}, https://chicago.suntimes.com/crime/2023/6/15/23763033/anjanette-young-chicago-police-board-alex-wolinski-botched-raid

[641] Li Zhou, **The MLB's long-overdue decision to add Negro Leagues' stats, briefly explained**, *VOX*, May 31, 2024 {Accessed: June 29, 2024}, https://www.vox.com/culture/353108/mlb-negro-leagues-stats

[642]Roxana Hegeman, **New voters get notices listing wrong Dodge City polling site**, AP, October 25, 2018 {Accessed May 15, 2022}, https://apnews.com/general-news-e1b4e441d4a448b98f129fcde0556a98

⁶⁴³ Ariana Eunjung Cha and Laurie McGinley, **Antimalarial drug touted by President Trump is linked to increased risk of death in coronavirus patients, study says,** *Washington Post,* May 22, 2020 {Accessed: June 10, 2020}, https://www.washingtonpost.com/health/2020/05/22/hydroxychloroquine-coronavirus-study/

⁶⁴⁴ Brad Spellberg, **Hospitals at the brink as state brace for surge in COVID deaths,** CBS Evening News with Norah O'Donnell, December 18, 2020.

⁶⁴⁵ Rebecca Shabad, **'It is what it is': Trump in interview on COVID-19 death toll in U.S.,** NBC News, August 4, 2020 {Accessed: June 3, 2020}, https://www.nbcnews.com/politics/donald-trump/it-what-it-trump-interview-covid-19-death-toll-u-n1235734

⁶⁴⁶ Ed White and Jill Colvin, Associated Press, **General Perna says sorry for 'miscommunication' over vaccine shipments,** Boston.com, December 19, 2020 {Accessed: January 16, 2023}, https://www.boston.com/news/politics/2020/12/19/general-perna-says-sorry-for-miscommunication-over-vaccine-shipments/

⁶⁴⁷ Leslie Herod and Mari Newman, **Colorado took a revolutionary step to reform policing. Here's how we did it,** *USA Today,* October 28, 2021 {Accessed: August 12, 2023}, https://www.usatoday.com/story/opinion/2021/10/28/colorado-hold-cops-accountable-qualified-immunity/6101915001/

⁶⁴⁸ **14M U.S. Households face eviction as protections set to end,** CNN Newsroom with Fredricka Whitfield, December 19, 2020.

⁶⁴⁹ Austin Landis, **House Lawmakers Subpoena CDC Director Redfield, HHS Secretary Azar,** *Spectrum News* 1, December 21, 2020 {Accessed: December 23, 2021}, https://spectrumlocalnews.com/nys/central-ny/news/2020/12/21/house-panel-coronavirus-subpoena-health-officials-investigation-cdc-hhs

⁶⁵⁰ Armand Dorian, USC Verdugo Hills Hospital, CBS Evening News with Norah O'Donnell, December 21, 2020.

⁶⁵¹ Christy Gatos, **Congress reaches deal on $900 Billion pandemic relief package,** Nancy Cordis, CBS Evening News, December 21, 2020.

⁶⁵² Kate Snow, **Coping with pandemic stress through tough winter,** NBC News, December 22, 2020.

⁶⁵³ John Eligon, **Black Doctor dies of COVID-19 after complaining of racist treatment,** *New York Times*, December 23, 2020 {Accessed: September 1, 2023}, https://www.nytimes.com/2020/12/23/us/susan-moore-black-doctor-indiana.html

⁶⁵⁴ **Black doctor dies of COVID after alleging racist treatment,** CNN, December 26, 2020.

⁶⁵⁵ James Brierton, **Rock Hill man, who accused police in 2019 of wrongfully ordering him out of his home in the middle of the night, has died,** WCNC Charlotte, June 6, 2022 {Accessed: January 17, 2023}, https://www.wcnc.com/article/news/local/rock-hill/rock-hill-man-accused-police-2019-wrongfully-ordering-home-night-dies/275-2d833b4c-7caa-46d4-9639-b7e92ea090a#:~:text=Rock%20Hill%20man%2C%20who%20accused,police%20officers%20with%20guns%20drawn.

⁶⁵⁶ Rebecca Falconer, **GOP Sen. Ben Sasse on Trump pardons: "Rotten to the core,"** *Axios*, December 23, 2020 {Accessed: July 3, 2021}, https://www.axios.com/2020/12/24/gop-sen-ben-sasse-trump-pardons-rotten

⁶⁵⁷ Stacey Abrams, *The Shop: Uninterrupted*, Season 3, Episode 2, HBO.

⁶⁵⁸ Victor Oquendo, **Vaccine speed bump,** ABC Evening News with David Muir, December 29, 2020.

⁶⁵⁹ Brenna Ehrlich, **Woman Who Accosted Jazz Musician's Son, Falsely Accusing Him of Theft, Has Been Arrested,** *Rolling Stone*, January 8, 2020 {Accessed: December 8, 2021}, https://www.rollingstone.com/music/music-news/keyon-harrold-racial-profiling-iphone-son-1107908/

[660] John Florio and Ouisie Shapiro, **How New York City vaccinated six million people in a month,** *New York Times,* December 18, 2020 {Accessed: January 30, 2021}, https://www.nytimes.com/2020/12/18/nyregion/nyc-smallpox-vaccine.html

[661] Maggie Haberman and Zolan Kanno-Youngs, **Trump weighed naming election conspiracy theorist as special counsel,** *New York Times*, December 19, 2020 {Accessed: December 23, 2021}, https://www.nytimes.com/2020/12/19/us/politics/trump-sidney-powell-voter-fraud.html

[662] Aila Slisco, **Mike Pence's Smackdown of Trump's 'Crackpot Lawyers' Goes Viral,** *Newsweek*, August 2, 2023 {Accessed: August 5, 2023}, https://www.newsweek.com/mike-pences-smackdown-trumps-crackpot-lawyers-goes-viral-1817098

[663] **William Barr: no evidence of voter fraud that would change election outcome,** *The Guardian*, December 1, 2020 {Accessed: December 12, 2020}, https://www.theguardian.com/us-news/2020/dec/01/william-barr-no-evidence-voter-fraud

[664] Jason Johnson, Last Word with Lawrence O'Donnell, MSNBC, December 28-9, 2020.

[665] Associated Press, **Changes sought in Cleveland,** *Atlanta Journal-Constitution*, December 4, 2014, p. A4.

[666] Eliott C. McLaughlin, Sonia Moghe, and Hannah Rabinowitz, **Four current, former Louisville police officers federally charged in Breonna Taylor's death,** CNN, August 4, 2022.

[667] PBS, **Former police officer who shot Breonna Taylor has new job in law enforcement,** April 24, 2023, https://www.pbs.org/newshour/nation/former-police-officer-who-shot-breonna-taylor-has-new-job-in-law-enforcement

[668] Will Wright, **Former Columbus Police Officer Is Charged With Murder,** *New York Times,* February 3, 2021, Updated Oct. 11, 2021 {Accessed: November 3, 2021},

https://www.nytimes.com/2021/02/03/us/adam-coy-columbus-murder-andre-hill.html

[669] Matthew Impelli, **Native American Man Tased by Park Ranger Says He Was Off Trail to Maintain Social Distance,** *Newsweek,* December 29, 2020 {Accessed: October 18, 2021}, https://www.newsweek.com/native-american-man-tased-park-ranger-says-he-was-off-trail-maintain-social-distance-1557815

[670] CBS4/AP, **First U.S. Case Of New COVID-19 Variant Is Colorado Guardsmen Deployed To Nursing Home In Simla,** CBS News, December 30, 2020 {Accessed: September 1, 2023}, https://www.cbsnews.com/colorado/news/first-case-covid-19-variant-national-guard-member-deployed-nursing-home-simla/

[671] Meghan Fitzgerald, **California Extends stay-at-home orders as COVID surges**, NBC Evening News, December 29th, 2020.

[672] The Morbidity and Mortality Weekly Report (MMWR) is a weekly scientific publication from the Centers for Disease Control and Prevention (CDC).

[673] NBC vaccine tracker.

[674] Miguel Almaguer, **New Covid strain now detected in three states**, NBC Nightly News with Lester Holt, January 1, 2020.

[675] Azi Paybarah, **Wisconsin Pharmacist Who Tampered With Vaccine Gets 3-Year Sentence,** *New York Times,* June 8, 2021 {Accessed: October 3, 2021}, https://www.nytimes.com/2021/06/08/us/spoiled-covid-vaccines.html

[676] Steve Hartman, **On the Road**, CBS Evening News, January 1, 2021.

[677] Kristine Phillips, **Trump pardons former officer convicted in police brutality, dog bite case,** *USA Today,* December 23, 2020 {Accessed: October 21, 2021}, https://www.usatoday.com/story/news/politics/2020/12/23/stephanie-mohr-officer-police-brutality-case-gets-trump-pardon/3904405001/

⁶⁷⁸ AP, **Trump Defends Comments About Immigrants 'Poisoning the Blood' of America,** *Voice of America,* December 19, 2023 {Accessed: December 23, 2023}, https://www.voanews.com/a/trump-defends-comments-about-immigrants-poisoning-the-blood-of-america/7405198.html

⁶⁷⁹ Elisa Xu, **I'm the first Latino DACA recipient to win a Rhodes Scholarship. Here's how I want to give back to the elementary school teacher and the city that helped me excel,** *Business,* October 4, 2022
{Accessed: September 3, 2023}, https://www.insider.com/daca-recipient-first-latino-rhodes-scholar-santiago-potes-2022-10#:~:text=Santiago%20Potes%20is%20the%20first,excel%20in%20his%20educational%20journey

⁶⁸⁰ CNN, **Read the full transcript and listen to Trump's audio call with Georgia secretary of state,** January 3, 2021 {Accessed: December 13, 2023}

⁶⁸¹ Ibid.

⁶⁸² Ibid.

⁶⁸³ Chelsea Ritschel, **Former anti-masker says he was wrong in video filmed from hospital bed: 'Just wear a mask,'** *The Independent,* January 5, 2021 {Accessed: October 3, 2021}, https://www.independent.co.uk/news/world/americas/anti-mask-hospital-video-chuck-stacey-coronavirus-b1782822.html

⁶⁸⁴ Rick Wilson, interviewed by Ali Velshi, MSNBC, January 6, 2020.

⁶⁸⁵ Sara Totonchi, interviewed on WSB-TV, January 7, 2020.

⁶⁸⁶ Nse' Ufot, interviewed on WSB-TV, January 7, 2020.

⁶⁸⁷ Joy Reid, MSNBC, following Trump protesters' assault on the U.S. Capitol, January 6, 2020.

⁶⁸⁸ Nandita Bose and Mankini Brice, **If rioters were Black, 'hundreds' would have been killed: Washington reflects on Capitol rampage,** Reuters, January 8, 2021 {Accessed: June 3, 2021}, https://www.reuters.com/article/idUSKBN29D1HL/

[689] Ibid.

[690] President-elect Joseph Biden, January 6, 2020.

[691] Michelle Obama, statement issued following the radical right takeover of U.S. Capitol, January 6th, 2020.

[692] Ryan J. Reilly, **'Antiestablishment' activist sought to incite Trump supporters on Jan. 6, DOJ argues,** NBC News, November 15, 2023 {Accessed: November 23, 2023}, https://www.nbcnews.com/politics/justice-department/anti-establishment-activist-sought-incite-trump-supporters-jan-6-doj-a-rcna125397

[693] Congressman Jason Crowe, Interviewed by Savannah Guthrie, **Inside the Trump-Inspired siege on U.S. Capitol,** NBC Evening News, January 7, 2020.

[694] Brandy Zadrozny, **Capitol rioters fueled by Online Extremism,** NBC News, January 7, 2021.

[695] Frank Figliuzzi, author of *The FBI Way*, NBC Evening News interview by Stephanie Gosk, January 7, 2021.

[696] Qiuyue Ma, PhD, Jue Liu, PhD; Qiao Liu, BD; et al., **Global Percentage of Asymptomatic SARS-CoV-2 Infections Among the Tested Population and Individuals with Confirmed COVID-19 Diagnosis: A Systematic Review and Meta-analysis,** December 14, 2021, *JAMA Netw Open.* 2021; 4 (12): e2137257. doi:10.1001/jamanetworkopen.2021.37257 {Accessed: June 3, 2022}, https://jamanetwork.com/journals/jamanetworkopen/fullarticle/2787098

[697] Senator Mitch Romney, from the floor of the U.S. Senate, January 7, 2021.

[698] **Extremists and mainstream Trump supporters plan to protest congressional certification of Biden's victory,** *ADL*, January 4, 2020.

[699] Department of Labor statistics, NBC Nightly News, January 8th, 2020.

700 Ken Dilanian, Tom Winter, Jonathan Dienst and Andrew Blankstein, **FBI, NYPD told Capitol Police about possibility of violence before riot, senior officials say, NBC News,** January 10, 2021.

701 Scott Gottlieb, Face the Nation, January 10, 2020.

702 Harry Dunn, **When Truth isn't Truth, The Rudy Giuliani Story,** MSNBC, Season I, Episode 4.

703 Masood Farivar, **Researchers: More Than a Dozen Extremist Groups Took Part in Capitol Riots,** VOA, January 16, 2021 {Accessed: October 3, 2021}, https://www.voanews.com/a/2020-usa-votes_researchers-more-dozen-extremist-groups-took-part-capitol-riots/6200832.html

704 VOA News, **Three US Lawmakers Are COVID-19 Positive After Capitol Riot Confinement,** January 13, 2021 {Accessed: February 22, 2022}, https://www.voanews.com/a/covid-19-pandemic_three-us-lawmakers-are-covid-19-positive-after-capitol-riot-confinement/6200641.html

705 Jeff Pegues, **FBI report warned of "war" at Capitol day before fatal siege**, CBS Evening News with Norah O'Donnell, January 12, 2020.

706 Ibid.

707 Lauren Miller and Martha Kinsella, **Fact Check: Trump's Georgia Call to Raffensperger,** Brennan Center for Justice, July 27, 2023 {Accessed: September 1, 2023}, https://www.brennancenter.org/our-work/research-reports/fact-check-trumps-georgia-call-raffensperger

708 Sam Brock, **Quelling explosion in children Hospitalized, University of Minnesota,** NBC News, January 12, 2021.

709 Jonathan Chait, **Trump Made the Stupidest Possible Argument on Mike Pence**, Intelligencer, *New York Magazine,* THE NATIONAL INTEREST, January 12, 2021 {Accessed: December 14, 2023}, https://nymag.com/intelligencer/2021/01/trump-told-pence-you-can-go-down-in-history-as-a-pussy.html

710 Amelia Nierenberg, **A Traitor, Burned in Effigy, Again and Again,** *New York Times,* September 19, 2023 {Accessed: September 20, 2023}, https://www.nytimes.com/2023/09/19/nyregion/benedict-arnold-connecticut.html

711 Scott Stump, **Colin Powell says Trump should resign: 'Do what Nixon did,'** *Today,* January 8, 2021 {Accessed: October 18, 2021}, https://www.today.com/news/trump-should-resign-nixon-colin-powell-says-today-t205335

712 X, Lindsey Graham tweet, May 3, 2016.

713 X, Lindsey Graham tweet, November 13, 2015.

714 Mychael Schnell, **Cheney: Trump 'summoned the mob, assembled the mob and lit the flame of this attack,'** *The Hill,* June 9, 2022 {Accessed: July 12, 2022}, https://thehill.com/policy/national-security/3518354-cheney-trump-summoned-the-mob-assembled-the-mob-and-lit-the-flame-of-this-attack/

715 MSNBC, **Transcript: The 11th Hour with Brian Williams,** January 15, 2021 (filmmaker Michael Moore), January 21, 2021 {Accessed: December 3, 2023}, https://www.msnbc.com/transcripts/transcript-11th-hour-brian-williams-january-15-2021-n1259397

716 Dave Roos, **The 1969 Raid That Killed Black Panther Leader Fred Hampton,** *History,* updated August 11, 2023, {Accessed: June 5, 20204}, https://www.history.com/news/black-panther-fred-hampton-killing

717 Christopher Magan, **'Abject failure,' MN Gov. Walz slams federal vaccine rollout,** *Pioneer Press,* January 15, 2021 {Accessed: September 3, 2023}, https://www.twincities.com/2021/01/15/coronavirus-friday-update-minnesota-promised-68625-more-vaccine-doses-few-have-shipped/

718 J. Scott Trubey and Helena Oliviero, **A look at major COVID-19 developments over the past week,** January 16, 2021 {Accessed: February 12, 2023}, https://www.ajc.com/news/atlanta-news/a-look-at-

major-covid-19-developments-over-the-past-week/HWV6VIIKSVAPPA3HM4J5TXSQMA/

[719] Julie Gerberding, **COVID vaccination rules vary state by state,** Miguel Almaguer, NBC Evening News, January 14, 2021.

[720] Cynthia McFadden, **Feeding America, America's seniors facing hunger crisis in pandemic,** NBC News, January 14, 2021.

[721] J. Scott Trubey and Helena Oliviero, **A look at major COVID-19 developments over the past week,** AJC, January 16, 2021 {Accessed: October 3, 2021}, https://www.ajc.com/news/atlanta-news/a-look-at-major-covid-19-developments-over-the-past-week/HWV6VIIKSVAPPA3HM4J5TXSQMA/

[722] WAMU 88.5, **'We're The Ones Who Saved Congress': Meet Three D.C. Police Officers Who Fought For The U.S. Capitol,** January 15, 2020 {Accessed: January 15, 2021, https://wamu.org/story/21/01/15/were-the-ones-who-saved-congress-meet-three-d-c-police-officers-who-fought-for-the-u-s-capitol/

[723] Ryan's Facebook post, since deleted, reported by Jeff Pegues, January 15, 2021, CBS Evening News with Norah O'Donnell.

[724] Lauren Mascarenhas and Amanda Sealey, **There is no "reserve stockpile" of Covid-19 vaccine doses left to release, HHS secretary says,** CNN, January 15, 2021 {Accessed: December 14, 2023}, https://www.cnn.com/world/live-news/coronavirus-pandemic-vaccine-updates-01-15-21/h_e4b5a49a394ff63398d53108c40dbeeb

[725] Alex Azar, **'There's not a reserve stockpile' of vaccine,** NBC Evening News with Lester Holt, January 15, 2021.

[726] COVID Tracking, January 17, 2020.

[727] Tom Perez, DNC chairman, interviewed on This Week with Joshua Johnson, January 17, 2021.

[728] Anti-Defamation League, **NESARA/GESARA** {Accessed: July 3, 2023}, https://www.adl.org/glossary/nesaragesara

⁷²⁹ Holly Honderich, **In Trump's final days, a rush of federal executions,** BBC News, Washington, January 16, 2020 {Accessed: January 18, 2020, https://www.reuters.com/article/us-usa-executions/u-s-to-carry-out-13th-and-final-execution-under-trump-administration-idUSKBN29K2K7

⁷³⁰ Thomas Friedman, AC 360, CNN, January 18, 2020.

⁷³¹ Ryan Bort, **Here's What Has Happened in Syria in the Week Since Trump Abandoned the Kurds,** *Rolling Stone,* October 14, 2019 {Accessed: December 18, 2019}, https://www.rollingstone.com/politics/politics-news/why-trump-decision-abandon-kurds-syria-disaster-898493/

⁷³² Jennifer Hansler, Kylie Atwood, and Nicole Gaouette, **Pompeo attacks multiculturalism, saying it is 'not who America is',** CNN, January 19, 2021 {Accessed: October 20, 2021}, https://www.cnn.com/2021/01/19/politics/pompeo-multiculturalism-tweet/index.html

⁷³³ Debbie Elliott, **'More Conservative Than Attila The Hun': Kelly Loeffler's Push To Keep Senate Seat,** NPR, November 2, 2020 {Accessed: September 3, 2023}, https://www.npr.org/2020/11/02/930389754/more-conservative-than-attila-the-hun-kelly-loeffler-s-push-to-keep-senate-seat

⁷³⁴ Elizabeth Yuko, **Who are the Oath Keepers?,** *Rolling Stone,* January 20, 2021 {Accessed: February 8, 2021}, https://www.rollingstone.com/culture/culture-features/oathkeepers-far-right-militia-january-6th-insurrection-arrest-1116673/

⁷³⁵ Lisa Mascaro and Mary Clare Jalonick, **McConnell: Trump 'provoked' Capitol siege, mob was fed lies,** AP, January 19, 2021 {Accessed: May 5, 2021}, https://apnews.com/article/mcconnell-trump-fed-lies-to-mob-36871d68df56a10be1c46ed364ad6de6

⁷³⁶ Martin Luther King Jr., speech, Washington Cathedral, March 31, 1968. https://www.seemeonline.com/history/mlk-jr-awake.htm

⁷³⁷ Statement of Christopher A. Wray, Director Federal Bureau of Investigation Before the Committee on the Judiciary United States Senate, August 4, 2022 {Accessed: October 12, 2022},

https://www.judiciary.senate.gov/imo/media/doc/Testimony%20-%20Wray%20-%202022-08-04.pdf

738 Amanda Gorman, "The Hill We Climb," January 20, 2021.

739 John Haltiwanger, **Secretary of State Mike Pompeo's departing message to the US is that multiculturalism is 'not who America is'**, *Business Insider*, January 19, 2021 {Accessed: January 20, 2021}, https://www.businessinsider.com/mike-pompeo-says-multiculturalism-is-not-who-america-is-2021-1

740 Matthew Brown, **Trump's '1776 Commission' report excuses slavery, condemns legacy of civil rights movement,** *USA Today*, January 19, 2020 {Accessed: January 20, 2021}, https://www.usatoday.com/story/news/politics/2021/01/19/trumps-1776-report-condemns-legacy-civil-rights-movement/4209531001/

741 Charlotte Alter, **A Year Ago, They Marched. Now a Record Number of Women Are Running for Office,** *Time*, January 18, 2018 {Accessed: January 19, 2023}, https://time.com/5107499/record-number-of-women-are-running-for-office/

742 Kamala Harris, presidential inauguration, January 20, 2021.

743 Joseph Menn, Elizabeth Culliford, Katie Paul, and Carrie Monihan, **'No plan, no Q, nothing': QAnon followers reel as Biden inaugurated,** Reuters, January 20, 2021 {Accessed: July 3, 2023}, https://www.reuters.com/article/us-usa-biden-qanon/no-plan-no-q-nothing-qanon-followers-reel-as-biden-inaugurated-idUSKBN29P2VO

744 Joseph Biden, presidential inauguration, January 20, 2021.

745 Erin Blakemore, **Why Andrew Jackson's Legacy Is So Controversial,** History.com, August 29, 2018 {Accessed: October 5, 2022}, https://www.history.com/news/andrew-jackson-presidency-controversial-legacy

746 Ernie Suggs, **How Henry Aaron made baseball a form of civil rights activism,** *AJC*, January 22, 2021 {Accessed: January 24, 2021}, https://www.ajc.com/news/hank-aarons-civil-rights-work-recognized/H55RYZB3ABAQDPR27JZSBFUQ6U/

[747] Brian Linder, **Did Hank Aaron die from the COVID-19 vaccine? RFK Jr.'s controversial tweet review,** *Penn Live*, July 21, 2023 {Accessed: September 2, 2023}, https://www.pennlive.com/news/2023/07/did-hank-aaron-die-from-the-covid-19-vaccine-reviewing-rfk-jrs-controversial-tweet.html

[748] Former King aide and Ambassador Andrew Young, 9th Annual Freedom ACCORD Luncheon, St. Augustine, Florida, July 2, 2024.

[749] Trevor Plante, National Archives, interviewed on CBS Evening News with Nora O'Donnell, July 3, 2024.

[750] Sherrilyn Ifill, The Rachel Maddow Show, July 2, 2024.

[751] By Maisie Crow, produced by Miki Meek and Lilly Sullivan, *The Pink House at the Center of the World*, This American Life, July 1, 2022 {Accessed: September 18, 2022}, https://www.thisamericanlife.org/774/the-pink-house-at-the-center-of-the-world

[752] Madison Czopek, **Fact-checking Florida's surgeon general on COVID-19 vaccine requirements for kids, masking,** *Politifact*, March 18, 2022 {Accessed: November 12, 2022}, https://www.politifact.com/article/2022/mar/18/fact-checking-floridas-surgeon-general-covid-19-va/

[753] Matthew Spaulding, **The Man Who Would Not Be King,** The Heritage Foundation, February 5, 2007 {Accessed: June 18, 2021}, https://www.heritage.org/commentary/the-man-who-would-not-be-king

[754] The Last Word with Lawrence O'Donnell, June 13, 2024 {Accessed: June 15, 2024}, https://www.msnbc.com/the-last-word/watch/-a-cult-to-a-thug-nancy-pelosi-torches-gop-s-trump-revisionist-history-212964421696

[755] Mary Clare Jalonick and Stephen Groves, **Abandoned by his colleagues after negotiating a border compromise, GOP senator faces backlash alone,** AP, February 8, 2024 {Accessed: May 3, 2024}, https://apnews.com/article/congress-border-deal-rejected-lankford-immigration-045fdf42d42b26270ee1f5f73e8bc1b0

[756] Tami Luhby, **Trump had 4 years to remake Obamacare. Here's what he did,** CNN, April 12, 2024 {Accessed: May 3, 2024}, https://www.cnn.com/2024/04/12/politics/obamacare-trump-administration/index.html

Index

A

Aaron, Hank, 393, 394
Abbott, Greg, 84, 108, 186, 196, 215, 223, 283
ABC, 155, 313, 327, 373
Abernathy, Keri, 54
Abernathy, Lt. Alan, 121
Abernathy, Rev. Ralph, 174, 363, 399
Abhulimen, Jasmine, 17
Abrams, Stacey, 91, 92, 140, 305, 352, 358, 361
ACF, 39, 106
Adams, Dr. Jerome, 4, 8, 114, 115, 142, 145, 212, 244, 256, 292
AFDC, 4
Affordable Care Act, 4, 24, 33, 36, 37, 40, 43, 45, 52, 60, 62, 101, 102, 104, 114, 124, 138, 153, 319, 332, 381, 512
African Methodist Episcopal, 42
Alcindor, Yamiche, 134
ALNG, 160
Amin, Dr. Mahendra, 327
Anderson, Dr. William, 77
Antifa, 188, 206, 282, 369, 373, 374
anti-LGBTQ+, 10
Arbery, Ahmaud, 80, 165, 176, 177, 200, 204, 243, 273, 312, 313
Aronberg, Dave, 229, 230
Aryan, 173

Ashby, Dr. Bernard, 246
ASPA, 55, 57, 276
ASPR, 119, 125, 135
Atlanta, 8, 11, 15, 41, 42, 58, 75, 79, 98, 108, 109, 112, 114, 119, 120, 123, 127, 137, 149, 151, 152, 160, 167, 168, 169, 182, 184, 185, 199, 219, 225, 226, 237, 243, 245, 250, 263, 270, 276, 304, 320, 326, 329, 347, 363, 372, 393, 512
Atlanta Journal-Constitution, 79
Atlas, Dr. Scott, 314
Axelrod, David, 314
Azar, Alex, 4, 10, 101, 103, 114, 151, 155, 208, 210, 288, 314, 348, 349, 374, 381, 384

B

Bailey, De'Von, 347
Baker, Charlie, 233
Baker, Dawn, 236
Baker, Josephine, 334
Baldwin, James, 199, 334
Baltimore, 7, 15, 63, 138, 250, 267, 320, 325, 366
Bandaloop, Alobar, 19
Bannon, Steve, 29
Barr, Bill, 175, 188, 198, 219, 343, 354, 369
Barrett, Amy Coney, 286, 292, 397
Barrett, Dana, 79, 320
Barron, Richard, 292
Bartholomew, Ashley, 316, 318

Beauregard, P.G.T., 23
Bennett, Fred, 251
Bennett, John, 125, 208, 209
Benson, Jocelyn, 335
Benson, Shaftel, 43
Bera, Ami, 144
Berg Family, 287
Bernstein, Carl, 300, 304
Beshear, Andy, 141
Besser, Richard, 139, 278, 281
Beth, David, 274
Biden Administration, 24, 62, 122, 132, 307, 332, 400, 401, 512
Biden, President Joe, 2, 7, 24, 30, 33, 51, 100, 136, 138, 229, 231, 235, 249, 255, 272, 279, 281, 286, 293, 295, 304, 305, 306, 307, 309, 310, 311, 317, 325, 326, 328, 329, 330, 334, 342, 344, 349, 351, 352, 353, 354, 362, 363, 365, 367, 368, 373, 374, 375, 380, 382, 383, 386, 387, 388, 389, 390, 392, 393, 394, 399, 400, 401, 402
Bipartisan Policy Center, 292
BIPOC, 4, 70, 98
Birx, Dr. Deborah, 134, 135, 196, 210, 247, 279, 299, 301, 325
Blackmon, Rev. Traci, 29-30
Blackwell, Unita, 90
Blake, Jacob, 268, 271, 273, 275, 321
Bland, Sandra, 80, 185, 192, 193, 240
Blevins, Thurman J., 163
BLM, 197, 198, 235, 240, 245, 367, 369, 374, 386
Bloom, Adam, 17
Bolden, Rev. Willie, 396
Booker, Vauhxx, 216

Boortz, Neal, 99
Borders, James, 86
Bossie, David, 309
Bottoms, Keisha Lance, 151, 226, 243
Bouchard, Mike, 82
Bourla, Dr. Albert, 336
Bowden, Cathy, 42
Bowie, David, 257
Bowman, Tom, 119, 253
Bowser, Muriel, 240
Boyce, Mike, 125
Boynton, Amelia, 36
Bozeman, Chadwick, 356
Bozeman, Chandi, 157
Braden, Anne, 270
Braden, Carl, 270
Brandenberg, Stephen, 359
Brann, Matthew, 305
Bratcher-Bowman, Nikki, 54, 55, 56
Brechin, Sarah, 42
Breitbart, 158
Brennan, Anthony, III, 174, 175
Brennan, John, 33, 34
Brittingham, Kody, 15
Bro, Susan, 103
Brock, James, 368
Brock, Lou, 356
Brooke, Edward, 231
Brooks, Caroline, 248
Brooks, Cornell William, 168
Brooks, Lawrence, 173
Brooks, Rayshard, 199, 204, 240, 243
Brown, Chelsey, 20
Brown, John, 391
Brown, Kate, 385
Brown, Michael, 162, 183
Brownstein, Dr. John, 328
Bryan, William "Roddie", 313
Bryant, Kobe, 356

Burr, Richard, 324
Burwell, Sylvia, 45
Bush, George Herbert Walker, 37
Bush, George W., 12, 24, 33, 36, 37, 38, 39, 51, 129, 176, 230, 240, 314, 332, 392
Bynum, Janelle, 17
Byrd, James, 185

C

CACs, 61, 91
Cain, Herman, 191, 253
Caldwell, Thomas, 387
Cales, Natalia, 73, 107, 109, 122, 123, 132, 136, 253, 389, 404
Cameron, Beth, 136
Cameron, David, 67
Cannon, Park, 91
Cantrell, LaToya, 138
Caputo, Michael, 276, 277, 278
Carlson, Tucker, 78
Carmichael, Stokely, 334
Carnes, Jim, 43
Carrillo, Julio, 74
Carson, Dr. Ben, 9, 10, 28, 199, 309
Carson, Dr. Desmond, 253
Carter, Bob, 126
Caserta, Brandon, 289, 290
Cassel, Glen, 74
Castile, Philando, 80, 163, 164, 185, 368
Castor, Jane, 125, 208, 209
CBS, 85, 248
CDC, 37, 56, 100, 120, 125, 135, 139, 140, 147, 152, 155, 159, 178, 196, 200, 202, 208, 210, 221, 224, 233, 243, 273, 277, 278, 279, 281, 282, 288, 327, 333, 341, 348, 349, 380
Ceja, Amelia, 234
Ceja Vineyards, 234
Center for Pan Asian Communities (CPAC), 42
CERC, 133
Chansley, Jacob, 96, 97, 381
Chansley, Martha, 96
Chao, Elaine, 367
Charleston, SC, 21
Charlotte, 137, 178
Charlottesville, VA, 22, 29, 30, 103, 184, 245, 378
Chauvin, Derek, 163, 189, 368
Chavez, Cesar, 393
Cheney, Liz, 310, 373, 376
Chicago, 15, 16, 18, 36, 63, 100, 144, 147, 163, 186, 193, 219, 236, 237, 247, 250, 265, 299, 311, 313, 320, 345, 377
China, 6, 22, 67, 96, 101, 133
Chisolm, Shirley, 231
Christensen, Heidi, 126
Christie, Chris, 272, 319
Chung, Marianne, 42
Cincinnati, 63
Cipollone, Pat, 353
Clark, Joe, 356
Clark, Mark, 377
Clarke, Dr. Cynthia Mitchell, 397
Cleaver, Wally, 278
Clinton, Bill, 2, 12, 24, 33, 51, 176, 306, 313, 332, 392
Clinton Administration, 36, 37, 38
Clinton, Hillary, 11, 66, 90, 382
Clyburn, James "Jim", 43, 231, 344, 348, 349, 392
CMS, 39, 61, 69, 76, 114, 115, 159

Cobb, Ty, 345
Cochran, John, 351
Coffey, Kenneth, 266
COFO, 90
Cohen, Michael, 100
Colbert, Stephen, 230
Coleman, Reagan, 252
Collins, Doug, 245
Collins, Susan, 324
Colorado, 22, 87, 158, 223, 247, 248, 347, 356
Columbus, GA, 91, 108, 109
Columbus, OH, 18, 63, 355
Conners, Dr. Kathleen, 69
Conners, Kathleen, 76
Consumer Financial Protection Bureau, 401
Conway, Kellyanne, 139, 256, 305, 384
COOP, 133
Cooper Jones, Wanda, 313
Cooper, Amy, 166, 175, 220
Cooper, Carl, 193
Cooper, Christian, 166, 220
Cooper, Roy, 178
Coppinger, Jim, 109
CORE, 229
Cortez, Richard, 232
Cosgrove, Myles, 354
Costello, John, 367
Cotton, Dorothy, 396
Coy, Adam, 355
Critical Race Theory, 8, 23
Crow, Jason, 369
Crowfoot, Wade, 279
Crutcher, Terence, 80, 185, 191
Cruz, Ted, 230, 314, 340
Cummings, Elijah, 7, 16, 112, 114, 320
Cuomo, Andrew, 141, 142, 148, 330, 349
Cuomo, Chris, 271, 277

D

Dandridge, Dorothy, 334
Daniels, Rev. Jonathan, 29, 193
Dargy, Michael, Jr., 19
Davis Direction Foundation, 127
Davis, Dr. Matifadza Hlatshwayo, 351
Davis, Jefferson, 23
Davis, Jennifer, 118
De Havilland, Olivia, 356
Decatur, Georgia, 91, 223
DEI, 23
DeJoy, Louis, 244, 267
Dekalb County, 144, 149, 364, 365
Demings, Val, 157
DeSantis, Ron, 84, 108, 125, 140, 141, 214, 215, 224, 233, 256, 294, 398
Detroit, 15, 250, 320, 329
Devane, Jethro, 351
DeVos, Betsy, 233, 367
DeWine, Mike, 294
Diamond, Jeremy, 57
Dickens, Charles, 2
Diggs, Charles, 231
Dinkins, David, 356
Dixiecrat, 84, 300, 304
Dixon, Dr. Suzanne, 132
Dixon, Gaynell, 336
Dixon, Larry, 336, 337
Dobbs v. Jackson, 398
Donohue, Thomas, 319
Dorian, Armand, 349
Dougherty County, 98
Douglas, Kirk, 356
Douglass, Frederick, 7, 180, 216, 271, 393
Dove, Wendy, 327
Downs, Hugh, 356
Draheim, Kelly, 225

Draper, Jack, 128
Dreiband, Eric, 368
Drone, Quincy, 307
DuBois, Janet, 356
DuBois, W.E.B., 48, 57, 334
Duckworth Jr., Corporal Roman, 193
Duke, David, 97
Dunlap, Johnny, 346
Dunn, Harry, 372
Durkan, Jenny, 236, 320
Dylan, Bob, 335

E

East Carolina University, 264
Eastman, Jim, 84
Eastman, John, 353
Ebenezer Baptist, 114, 239
Eberhart, Dan, 330
Ebola Virus, 4, 119, 249
Eisenberg, John, 266
Eisenhower, Dwight D., 141
El Salvador, 6, 106
Eleanor, 172
Ellmers, Renee, 9, 45, 53, 54, 56, 57, 68, 69, 70, 72, 73, 75, 76, 126, 127, 129, 386
Epstein, Jeffrey, 252
ESL, 258
Estrada, Angelina, 291
Ettel, Alison, 17
EUA, 273
Evangelicals, white, 19
Evans, Crystal, 42
Evers, Medgar, 251, 398
Evers, Tony, 334

F

Fakorede, Dr. Foluso, 161
Fanone, Michael, 380, 381

Fauci, Dr. Anthony, 4, 134, 136, 145, 148, 160, 210, 238, 249, 255, 262, 273, 279, 287, 295, 309, 358
Feifer, Dr. Richard, 343
Fields, James Alex, 103
Figliuzzi, Frank, 33, 370
Figueroa, Marvin, 123
Filipkowski, Ron, 339
Fisher, Yolanda, 158
Flagg, Lisa, 42
Fletcher, Arthur, 391
Fletcher, Viola, 192
Florida, 38, 41, 43, 44, 45, 59, 61, 74, 75, 84, 90, 92, 93, 106, 107, 109, 122, 125, 128, 129, 139, 140, 151, 157, 202, 208, 209, 212, 214, 215, 223, 229, 233, 234, 235, 238, 244, 246, 251, 255, 256, 257, 261, 265, 266, 290, 294, 313, 321, 339, 340, 360, 365, 368, 396, 398
Floyd, George, 80, 162, 163, 164, 165, 167, 168, 170, 174, 176, 177, 180, 185, 186, 188, 189, 190, 199, 201, 204, 216, 240, 243, 273, 295, 369, 370
Flynn, Michael, 29, 328
Flynt, Wayne, 232
Ford, Dr. Christine Blasey, 79
Ford, Whitey, 356
Fort Benning, 108, 109
Fort Moore, 108
FQHC, 41, 42, 61
Franklin, John Hope, 31
Frederick, Michael, 283
Frederiksen, Mette, 66
Frey, Jacob, 162, 163
Frieden, Tom, 202, 208, 278, 279
Friedman, Thomas, 384

G

Gaetz, Matt, 334
Gaither, Thomas, 229
Gandhi, 29
Garfunkel, Art, 202
Garland, Merrick, 354
Garner, Eric, 164, 183, 223
Garnet, Henry Highland, 162
Gatos, Christy, 350
Gavin, Gary, 301
Georgia, 16, 22, 41, 42, 43, 50, 52, 56, 59, 61, 69, 74, 77, 84, 90, 91, 92, 93, 108, 118, 120, 135, 140, 145, 146, 149, 150, 151, 152, 156, 199, 223, 225, 226, 229, 236, 239, 243, 245, 250, 254, 256, 257, 258, 262, 263, 276, 292, 297, 299, 304, 305, 306, 307, 308, 310, 312, 314, 319, 330, 331, 340, 342, 349, 358, 359, 361, 364, 365, 366, 372, 375, 380, 386, 390
Gerberding, Dr. Julie, 380
Gibson, Bob, 356
Gibson, Josh, 345
Gilliam, Andrew, 214
Gilliam, Brittany, 247
Gilliard, Deric, 69, 215, 512
Gillum, Andrew, 91
Gingrich, Newt, 331
Giroir, Dr. Admiral Brett (Assistant Secretary of Health), 114, 156, 244, 300
Giuliani, Caroline Rose, 293
Giuliani, Rudy, 293, 334, 336
Glaude, Dr. Eddie, 205, 276
Gohmert, Louie, 248, 253
Golfcart Gail, 83
Golsteyn, Maj. Matthew, 101
Goodman, Andrew, 29, 193
Goodman, Dominique, 254
Goodman, Eugene, 372
Goodspeed, Tyler, 367
Goodwin, Roz, 42
GOP, 29, 30, 102, 110, 124, 154, 178, 190, 191, 244, 253, 271, 273, 282, 292, 293, 294, 310, 330, 331, 332, 336, 352, 354, 361, 373, 374, 392, 399, 401
Gorman, Amanda, 390
Gorsuch, Neil, 397
Gottlieb, Dr. Scott, 4, 294, 310, 372
Graham, Billy, 205, 206
Graham, Lindsey, 375, 377, 388
Graham, Rev. Franklin, 206
Gray, Freddie, 366
Greenblatt, Jonathan, 66
Greene, Ronald, 80
Greiffenstein, Dr. Patrick, 267
Griffin, Alyssa Farah, 311
Grijalva, Raul, 248
Grisham, Stephanie, 367
Guatemala, 6, 106
Gugino, Martin, 177, 188
Gunn, Anton, 37
Gupta, Dr. Sanjay, 134, 138
Gupta, Dr. Vin, 213, 215
Guyger, Amber, 19, 192, 193
Guyot, Lawrence, 89

H

Haaland, Deb, 328
Hahn, Dr. Stephen, 252
Haig, Al, 6
Hall, Candace, 283
Hall, Eddie, 283
Hamer, Fannie Lou, 88, 89, 90, 251, 333
Hammond Jr., Samuel Ephesians, 193
Hampton, Fred, 377

Hancock, Michael, 334
Hanna, Dwight, 43
Hannity, Sean, 67, 78
Hargan, Eric, 114, 115, 129
Harriott II, 181
Harris, Kamala, 66, 255, 390, 392, 402
Harrison, Lisa Macon, 344
Hawley, Josh, 354
Hayes, Mark, 229
Hayling, Crystal, 397
Hayling, Dr. Robert, 396, 397
Heilemann, John, 229
Helton, Joey, 75
Henderson, Skip, 109
Henry, Aaron, 89
Henry, Patrick, 113
Heyer, Heather, 29, 103, 245
HHS, 4, 6, 8, 10, 12, 33, 37, 41, 43, 45, 50, 52, 53, 54, 55, 56, 57, 58, 59, 60, 61, 72, 73, 74, 75, 76, 106, 107, 114, 115, 119, 120, 121, 124, 125, 127, 129, 132, 133, 148, 155, 184, 221, 243, 253, 276, 288, 314, 333, 349, 367, 374, 381, 384, 401, 512
Highlander Folk School, 270
Hill, Adrian, 251
Hill, Andre, 355
Hiltachk, Tom, 293
HIM (Health Insurance Marketplace), 40, 41, 43, 54, 56, 64, 68, 69, 91, 104, 145, 332
Hines, Dr. Jeff, 263
Hitler, Adolph, 102, 158, 173, 360
HIV, 3, 4, 75, 167, 307
Hogan, Larry, 154, 228, 326
Holt, Lester, 85
Honduras, 6, 106
Honoré, Russell, 139
Horne, Lena, 334

Horton, Abina, 313
Horton, Alex, 313
Horton, Willie, 240
Hotez, Dr. Peter, 213, 298, 302
Houser, John, 118
Houston, 15, 49, 196, 206, 283, 360
HPP, 118
HUAC, 335
Hudson, Redditt, 187
Huerta, Dolores, 106, 302
Hunt, Greg, 54
Hurd, Will, 272
Hurricane Florence, 49
Hurricane Hanna, 234
Hurricane Irma, 119, 244
Hurricane Katrina, 38
Hurricane Laura, 270
Hurricane Maria, 49, 119
Hurricane Michael, 68, 69, 70
Hussein, Saddam, 38
Hutchinson, Asa, 272
Hutchinson, Patrick, 197, 198

I

Ifill, Sherrilyn, 397
Illinois, 25, 135, 169, 274, 334
Immanuel, Stella, 237
Ingraham, Laura, 78
Ingram, Fredrick, 251
Inslee, Jay, 142, 385
Isakson, Johnny, 245, 308
Ivey, Kay, 230, 235

J

Jackson, Andrew, 393
Jackson, Jimmie Lee, 193
Jackson, Maynard, 226
Jackson, Rev. Jesse, 198
Jackson, Ronnie, 288
Jackson, Stonewall, 335

James, Lebron, 290
Jane Crow, 185
Janes, Joshua, 354
Jean, Botham, 18, 19, 80, 164, 192, 193
Jean, Brandt, 19, 193
Jefferson, Thomas, 72, 243
Jeremiah, Dr. David, 19
Jesus, 29, 84, 85, 146, 193, 335, 349, 369
Jewish, 22, 25, 66, 86, 98, 102, 158, 198, 390
Jim Crow, 31, 77, 84, 89, 93, 252, 312, 364, 378
John, Elton, 100
Johns Hopkins, 68
Johnson, Andrew (President), 89
Johnson, Andrew (Wrestler), 18
Johnson, Derrick, 233, 312
Johnson, Dr. Veda, 74
Johnson, J.T., 193, 396
Johnson, Jason, 354
Johnson, Jeh, 369
Johnson, Katherine, 356
Johnson, Kendrick, 185
Johnson, Lyndon, 41, 141, 397
Johnson, Robert Wood, 139
Johnston, Darcie, 10, 108, 109, 118, 128
Johnston, Kathryn, 185, 192
Jones, Rebecca, 339
Jordan, Barbara, 231
Jordan, Karen, 73, 107, 109, 123, 126, 253, 404
Jordan, Vernon E., 397

K

Kaepernick, Colin, 48, 282
Kalavritinos, Jack, 129
Kansas City, 19, 219, 236, 244, 250, 294
Kanye, 29
Karl, John, 155
Kasich, John, 93
Kastrenakes, John S., 20
Katz, Elinore McCance, 367
Kavanaugh, Brett, 78, 79, 367, 397
Kavka, Duane, 42
Keilar, Brianna, 135
Kelley, Devin, 86
Kelly, Laura, 146
Kelly, Megyn, 84, 85
Kelly, Walt, 1
Keltner, Lee, 291
Kemp, Brian, 84, 90, 91, 92, 93, 108, 140, 145, 150, 151, 152, 223, 224, 226, 229, 230, 243, 245, 256, 261, 262, 305, 308, 330
Kemp, Tammy, 193
Kennedy, Chris, 341
Kennedy, John F., 141, 340, 398
Kennedy, Robert, Jr., 394
Kenney, Jim, 306
Kessler, Jason, 28, 29
Khanna, Ro, 135
Khashoggi, Jamal, 7, 99
Kim-Farley, Robert, 359
King, C.B., 77
King, Dr. Martin Luther, Jr., 2, 28, 29, 36, 70, 98, 99, 114, 115, 116, 164, 165, 173, 174, 187, 193, 205, 206, 230, 239, 264, 269, 270, 273, 304, 308, 362, 363, 384, 385, 387, 391, 393, 396, 399, 512
King, John William, 185
King, Martin Luther, III, 232, 273
King, Rev. Bernice, 168
King, Rodney, 162
King, Steve, 85

King, Yolanda Renee, 273
Kinney, John, 359
Kittrell, Jim, 181
Klain, Ron, 249
Klobuchar, Amy, 140, 142, 274, 292, 385
Klunder, Rev. Bruce, 29
Knighton, Barry, 42
Kobach, Chris, 90, 91
Krauthammer, Charles, 67
Krebs, Chris, 311, 318
Krishnamoorthi, Raja, 274
Kudlow, Larry, 188, 198
Kushner, Jared, 97
Kyrie, 29

L

Lacks, Henrietta, 153
Ladapo, Dr. Joseph, 398
Lady Antebellum, 230
Landrieu, Mitch, 23
Lavigne, Sharon, 296
Lazarus, Emma, 108
Ledet, Russell, 267, 268
Lee, Bill, 84
Lee, Joshua, 186
Lee, Robert E., 23
Legend, John, 140
Lehman, Larry, 75
Lenin, 92
LePage, Paul, 72
Leventhal, Willy, 251
Lewis, Corey, 81
Lewis, John, 16, 114, 184, 212, 225, 231, 232, 239, 240, 243, 245, 250, 320, 356
Lewis, Reginald, 7
LGBTQ+, 9, 10, 22, 42, 218, 232, 313
Lightfoot, Lori, 16, 144, 311, 320

Limbaugh, Rush, 67, 78
Lincoln, Abraham, 83, 112, 113, 190, 203, 382
Lincoln Project, 255, 312, 365
Lincoln, Zachary, 312
Lindell, Mike, 325
Little Richard, 356
Liuzzo, Viola, 29, 193
Loeffler, Kelly, 245, 246, 307, 308, 319, 349, 361, 386
Loehmann, Tim, 354
Lofthouse, Michael, 220
Logan, Rayford, 31
Lopez, Alejandro, 42
Lott, Trent, 84
Lovejoy, Rev. Elijah, 29
Lowery, Dr. Joseph Echols, 2, 21, 149, 206, 225, 239, 243, 340, 363, 512
Lu, Chris, 136
Lynch, Willie, 236

M

Maddow, Rachel, 149, 160
Maher, Bill, 3
Mahoney, Alan, 18
Malcolm X, 228
Manafort, John, 352
Mando, Beatrice, 367
Manfredonia, Peter, 165
Mardi Gras, 138
Marietta, GA, 80, 91, 118, 135
Markle, Meghan, 66
Marsalis, Ellis, 356
Marshall, Royal, 99
Martin, Trayvon, 3, 19, 81, 162, 182, 183, 290, 321
Martinez, Enrique, 224
Martinez, Lucero, 301
Matthews, Sarah, 368
Mattis, Jim, 232

Maxwell, Ghislaine, 252
Mayorkas, Alejandro, 328
McCain, John, 30, 63
McCarthy, Joe, 97
McCarthy, Joseph, 219, 334
McCarthy, Kevin, 388
McCaskill, Claire, 367
McClain, Elijah, 80, 185, 200, 248, 347
McClellan, Mark, 39
McCloskey, Mark, 213
McConnell, Mitch, 40, 332, 344, 363, 387, 388
McCrory's, 229
McDonald, Laquan, 18, 193
McEnany, Kayleigh, 213, 311, 384
McGough, John, 72, 73, 76, 122, 124, 125, 209, 307
McGowan, Kyle, 56
McKay, Dante, 91
McMaster, Henry, 84
McMichael, Travis, 176, 177, 312, 313
McPike, Craig, 118
Meacham, Jon, 268
Meadows, Mark, 305
Melber, Ari, 59, 60
Memark, Dr. Janet, 118
Mentesana, Vincent, 351
MHAP, 53, 54, 59
Michigan, 66, 81, 138, 139, 283, 289, 290, 335, 342, 343, 375, 376, 377, 378, 380
Michiganders, 314
Middleton, Delano Herman, 193
Miller, Katie, 158
Miller, Stephen, 28, 158
Milley, Mark, 176
Minaj, Hasan, 352
Mingo Warriors, 153
Minor, Dr. Michael, 43, 53
Minor, Lottie, 43
Miskis, Constantinos, 38
Missouri, 19, 162, 183, 340, 342, 367
Mitchell, Roy, 52, 59, 60, 61, 62
MMWR, 277, 356
Mnuchin, Steven, 267
Mohr, Stephanie, 360
Moody, Paula, 74
Moore, Amzie, 89, 251
Moore, Dr. Susan, 351
Moore, Michael, 376
Moore, William Lewis, 29
Morgenstern, Brian, 287
Morris, Maria, 42, 53
Moseley, Chris, 43
Moses, Bob, 90
Mother Emanuel Church, 21, 86, 158
Mountain Area Health Education Center (MAHEC), 132
MSNBC, 59, 93, 100, 149, 160, 187, 190, 229, 276, 299, 366, 367, 377
Mueller, Hilary Brooke, 82
Mueller, Robert, 99, 101
Mulvaney, Mick, 118, 367
Murkowski, Lisa, 324
Murphy, Phil, 142, 260

N

NAACP, 7, 42, 77, 168, 174, 233, 292, 312
Nadeau, Kelly, 118
NASCAR, 187, 210
Nash, Johnny, 356
National Baptist Convention, 42
Native Americans, 9, 15, 25, 96, 102, 153, 172, 247, 253, 298
NATO, 400
Navarro, Peter, 133

NBC, 85, 134, 156, 203, 306, 370
NCAA, 255
Neal, Curley, 356
Neumann, Elizabeth, 272
New Orleans, 23, 38, 138, 144
Newman, Omarosa Manigault, 28, 30, 31
Newsom, Gavin, 142, 148, 334
Niceta, Rickie, 367, 368
NIH, 37, 135, 249
Nix, Jeff, 264
Nixon, E. D., 174
Nixon, Richard M., 141, 229, 300
North Carolina, 9, 17, 39, 41, 45, 49, 56, 61, 72, 73, 74, 93, 132, 263, 264, 299, 324, 344, 366
North Korea, 3, 7, 399
Nunez-Smith, Dr. Marcella, 333

O

O'Connor, Reed, 101, 103
O'Donnell, Lawrence, 100
O'Jays, 197
Obama Administration, 5, 24, 146, 229, 249, 314
Obama, Barack, 3, 12, 14, 15, 24, 30, 32, 33, 38, 39, 40, 45, 51, 60, 63, 67, 68, 93, 104, 124, 136, 146, 150, 177, 184, 185, 215, 216, 231, 239, 245, 261, 262, 300, 301, 314, 332, 334, 362, 363, 382, 392, 402, 512
Obama, Michelle, 368
ObamaCare, 10, 39, 41, 45, 52, 57, 59, 60, 62, 63, 91, 100, 102, 104, 138, 142, 145, 150, 246, 401
OBGYN Rural Health Care, 5

Ocasio-Cortez, Alexandria, 7, 113, 231, 297
Ohio, 18, 63, 93, 135, 155, 157, 237, 294, 355, 364, 366
Oklahoma, 6, 151, 205, 223, 322, 340
Oklahoma City, 293, 310
Oklahoma State Supreme Court, 192
Oklahoma State University, 264
Omar, Ilhan, 7, 113, 231, 297
Omarosa, 28, 30, 31
Osman, Amna, 75
Ossoff, Jon, 239, 300, 308, 349, 352, 359, 361, 363, 364, 365, 390
Osteen, Joel, 206
Osterholm, Dr. Michael, 309
Owen, Elaine, 50

P

Padilla, Alex, 390
Paige, Satchel, 345
Painter, Dr. Christopher, 154
Palestinian, 22, 198, 350, 400
Paley, Amit, 232
Palmer, Tamika, 169
Panetta, Leon, 313
Parker, Carrie Sinkler, 43
Parker, David, 81
Parks, Rosa, 173, 393, 512
Paul, Willard S., 173
Peck, James, 251
Peffley, Meredith, 74
Pelosi, Nancy, 66, 283, 373, 376, 384, 399
Pence, Mike, 97, 134, 139, 141, 151, 155, 158, 208, 210, 213, 233, 244, 279, 280, 288, 301, 353, 363, 366, 374, 375, 377, 381

Perdue, David, 300, 307, 308, 319, 349, 361, 364, 365
Perdue, Jon B., 10
Perez, Tom, 382
Perna, Gustave F., 347, 361
Perot, Ross, 306, 311
PHE, 132
Pickett, Damien, 181
Pinckney, Pastor Clementa C., 21
Plank, Liz, 254
Plowden, Dennis, Jr., 290
POCs, 9, 366
Pointer, Bonnie, 356
Pompeo, Mike, 29, 85, 386, 391
Posobiec, Jack, 245
Potes, Santiago, 360
Pottinger, Matthew, 367
POTUS, 56, 86, 114, 134, 135, 147, 255, 262, 277, 279, 288, 289, 299, 305, 306, 311, 314, 347, 354
Powell, Adam Clayton, 231
Powell, Colin, 375
Powell, Sidney, 331, 353
PPE, 138, 148, 157, 209
Pressley, Ayanna, 7, 113, 231, 273, 297
Price, Tom, 52, 56, 59, 75
Pride, Charlie, 356
Priester, Stephanie, 43
Princeton, 205, 210, 247, 276
Pritchett, Laurie, 77
Pritzker, J. B., 169, 170

Q

QAnon Shaman, 96, 381
Quenga, Shelli, 43, 59

R

Raffensperger, Brad, 307, 308, 319, 330, 331, 335, 358, 361, 362, 364, 375
Raimondo, Gina, 142
Randle, Lessie Benningfield, 192
Ray, Jodi, 43, 44, 59
Reagan, Ronald, 6, 11, 331
Reagon, Cordell, 77
Reddy, Helen, 356
Redfield, Dr. Robert, 125, 139, 221, 222, 278, 288, 333, 341, 342, 348
Reeb, Rev. James, 28, 29, 193
Reed, Steven, 203
Regan, Michael, 328
Reid, Joy, 93, 366, 367
Renfrow, Tony, 86, 156, 318
Reynolds, Kim, 273, 317
Reynolds, Sadiqa, 170
Rice, Dr. Valerie Montgomery, 332
Rice, Tamir, 183, 354
Richards, Edecia, 119
Richardson, Brian, 264
Rigas, Laura, 118, 124, 215
Rio Grande, 109, 186, 234
Rittenhouse, Kyle, 270, 271, 289, 325
Rivers, Glenn "Doc", 260, 268
RMVEs, 389
Robeson, Paul, 334
Robinson, Corey, 326
Robinson, Debbie, 338
Robinson, Eugene, 235
Robinson, Jo Ann, 174
Robinson, Morgan, 338
Rock, Chris, 82
Rodriguez, George, 178
Roe v. Wade, 398, 400
Rogers, Jordan, 17

Rogers, Kenny, 356
Romer, Paul, 156
Romney, Mitt, 362, 370
Roof, Dylann, 21, 86
Rose, Pete, 345
Royce, Shannon, 10, 126, 127
Ruch, Eric, Jr., 290
Ruhle, Stephanie, 299
Russell, Richard, 84
Ruth, Babe, 345, 394
Ryan, Jennifer Leigh, 381

S

Saint Peter, 93
Salman, Mohammed bin, 7
San Francisco, 15, 48, 119, 334
Sanders, Bernie, 300
Sanders, Sarah, 32, 84, 384
Santa, 84, 85, 341
Santana, Raymond, 79
Sasse, Ben, 352
Saudi Arabia, 7, 99, 170, 400
Saval, Rodrigo, 156
Sawyer, Diane, 313
Scalise, Steve, 11
Scarborough, Joe, 187, 190
Scarbrough, Brigid, 42
Schwerner, Michael "Mickey" 29, 93, 193
SCLC (Southern Christian Leadership Conference), 2, 28, 99, 114, 185, 206, 225, 363, 396, 399
Scott, David, 160
Scott, Dylan, 58
Scott, Gloria, 359
Scott, Judy, 188
Scott, Walter, 185, 188
Scott-Heron, Gil, 100
Sealy-Jefferson, Dr. Shawnita, 253

Seaver, Tom, 356
Sebelius, Kathleen, 37
SEEDCO, 43
Selma, AL, 77, 205, 206, 225, 232
Seneca Family Agencies, 350
Senegal, Cierra, 348
Sharp, Brandie, 18
Shawnee Warriors, 153
Shelton, Betty Jo, 191
Shelton, Dr. Penny, 73
Sherrill, Mikie, 379
Sherrod, Charles, 77
Shields, Erika, 167, 168
Shull, Lynnwood, 173
Shuttlesworth, Rev. Fred, 251, 363, 396, 399
Sienko, Carolyn, 293
Silva, Nelisha, 266
Simanek, Stephen, 324
Simmons, Lindsey, 75
Simon, Paul, 202
Simpson, O.J., 93
Sims, Dr. James, 153
Singleton, John, 278
Siyonbola, Lolade, 16
Slager, Michael, 188
Slaoui, Moncef, 352
Slavitt, Andy, 145, 146
Smiff, Mac, 235
Smith, Dr. Victoria, 332, 333
Smith, Harry, 203
Smith, Henry Ezekial, 193
Smith, Sonja, 43
Smyre, Rep. Calvin, 152
SNCC, 77, 90, 225
Snellville, 91
Snyder, Rick, 380
Somalia, 7, 231, 385
Somerville, Deandre, 20
South Carolina, 21, 37, 39, 41, 42, 43, 59, 61, 75, 84, 91, 93,

122, 123, 151, 173, 184, 223, 229, 231, 340, 342, 344, 348, 351, 352, 388, 392
Spellberg, Dr. Brad, 249, 346, 372
Spencer, Richard, 245
Spicer, Sean, 230, 256
St. John, 175
Stacey, Chuck, 365
Stack, Josh, 321
Stager, Peter, 377
Stanford University, 21
Steele, Michael, 141
Steele, Rev. C.K., 363, 399
Sterling, Alton, 193
Stern, Laurie, 75
Stevens, Stuart, 255, 312
Stewart, Darrius, 185
Stewart, Linda, 128
Stitt, Kevin, 223
Stokes, David, 50
Stone, Roger, 352
Strahan, Greg, 124
Strickland, Pam, 75
SUDs, 124, 137, 307, 512
Sullivan, Dr. Louis, 37
Sullivan, John Earle, 369
swastika, 283

T

Talbot County, 7
Taliban, 2, 101
Tampa, 44, 83, 125, 137, 208, 244
Tarrio, Enrique, 369
Taylor, Breonna, 80, 169, 185, 192, 197, 200, 204, 240, 260, 354
Taylor, Mary Elizabeth, 204
Teflon Don, 99
Teigen, Chrissy, 140

Temple, Fred, 193
Templeton, Franklin, 166
Tennessee, 39, 41, 61, 76, 84, 93, 109, 122, 155, 237, 270, 340, 350, 360
Texas, 6, 22, 59, 86, 101,107, 152, 185, 186, 193, 208, 212, 223, 238, 283, 294, 299, 307
Thermo Fisher Scientific, 153
Thomas, Clarence, 199
Thomas, Genny, 20
Thomas, Pierre, 373
Thomas, Tariana, 248
Thompson, Bennie, 398
Thoreau, Henry David, 208
Thrasher, Dr. David, 336
Thurmond, Strom, 84, 97
Tichenor, Marie, 260
Till, Emmett, 240
Tillerson, Rex, 25
Tinsley, Officer, 191
Tlaib, Rashida, 7, 113, 231
Toles, D'Arreion, 82
Toomey, Pat, 306
Totonchi, Sara, 366
Troy, AL, 239
Troy State University, 231
Troye, Olivia, 280
Trueman, Laura, 11, 54
Truman, Harry S., 141
Trump, Barron, 246
Trump, Donald, 3, 4, 5, 6, 7, 8, 11, 14, 15, 22, 24, 28, 30, 31, 33, 39, 40, 44, 45, 48, 52, 56, 61, 63, 66, 72, 76, 78, 80, 84, 88, 90, 96, 98, 100, 120, 127, 132, 133,141, 154, 158, 178, 184, 190, 196, 201, 204, 208, 218, 228, 240, 262, 286, 287, 292, 295, 304, 310, 311, 316, 324, 359, 379
Trump, Donald, Jr., 80
Trump, Eric, 79

Trump, Lara, 289
Trump, Melania, 80
Tuberville, Tommy, 263
Tubman, Harriet, 180
Tulsa, Oklahoma, 22, 190, 191, 192, 205, 210, 223, 290, 320, 321
Ture, Kwame, 334
Turner, Brock, 21
Turner, Dan, 21
Turner, Emmett, 43
Turner, Sylvester, 196
Tyson, Antrell, 398

U

U.S. Department of Health & Human Services, 6, 24, 36, 185
U.S. Immigration and Customs Enforcement (ICE), 24
U.S. Justice Department, 62
U.S. Supreme Court, 78
UAC, 75, 106, 107, 109, 128, 137
Un, Kim Jong, 3, 7, 399
USC, 249, 346, 349

V

Venezuela, 3, 291
Verma, Seema, 114, 115
Virgin Islands, 119
Virginia, 22, 113, 321, 335
Vivian, C.T., 193, 225, 239, 396

W

Waddy, DePriest, 74
Walker, Brennan, 81
Wallace, Bubba, 187
Wallace, George, 97, 201, 206, 219, 239
Wallace, Kay, 84

Walter Reed Army Hospital, 222, 286
Walz, Tim, 167, 378, 381
Warnock, Rev. Raphael, 239, 308, 349, 350, 352, 361, 363, 364, 365, 386, 390
Warren, Elizabeth, 66
Washington, April, 41
Washington, Dr. Harriet, 153
Waters, Maxine, 295
Watkins, Hollis, 90
Watson, Dr. Julie, 310
Watters, Hannah, 250
Wayne, John, 3, 109, 128
Weaver, RD April, 72, 73, 75, 76, 122
Weissman, Dr. Sharon, 75
Welker, Kristen, 134, 156
Wells, Dawn, 356
Wen, Dr. Leana, 138, 325
West Virginia, 340
White House, 30, 31, 49, 63, 121, 133, 135, 136, 138, 155, 159, 175, 176, 205, 228, 256, 262, 274, 277, 278, 279, 286, 288, 299, 300, 305, 309, 329, 336, 343, 353, 392, 393, 397, 399
Whitmer, Gretchen, 66, 138, 289, 375
Wiki Leaks, 90
Wilkins, Huxie, 43
Will, George, 67
Williams, Archie Charles, 166
Williams, Brian, 377
Williams, David, 267
Williams, Ginger, 83
Williams, Lauren, 301
Williams, Lula, 193
Williams, Rev. Hosea, 42, 225, 304
Williams, Riley June, 384
Williams, Sam, 37

Willmott, Kevin, 324
Wilson, Frank, 69, 76, 77
Wilson, Joe, 184, 231
Wilson, Rick, 365
Wilson, Woodrow, 210
Winfrey, Oprah, 240, 261
Winston-Salem, 17
Withers, Bill, 356
WNBA, 245, 246, 308, 386
Wolinski, Alex, 345
Wood, Lin, 325
Woodard, Dawn, 327
Woodard, Isaac, 173
Woodard, Lathran, 42
Woods, Brandon, 221
Woodward, Bob, 300
Woolery, Chuck, 224
World War I, 31
World War II, 31, 104, 172, 173, 253, 331, 335, 391
Wray, Christopher, 280, 373, 389, 393
Wright, Betty, 356
Wright, Daunte, 80
Wright, Rev. Bryant, 126
WSB, 79, 99
WTOC, 236

Y

Yanez, Jeronimo, 163
Yates, Travis, 191
Yellen, Janet, 328
Yost, Charmaine, 46, 57
Yost, Dave, 355
Young, Andrew "Andy", 114, 193, 251, 396
Young, Anjanette, 345

Z

Zadrozny, Brandy, 370
Ziegler, Jeffrey, 82

Zimmerman, George, 19, 81, 182, 183, 193, 290, 321
Zwerg, James, 251

About the Author

Deric Gilliard retired after 25 years as a federal employee in 2022, after working from political appointees in the Clinton, Bush, Obama, Trump, and Biden administrations. Prior to Gilliard's work as public affairs advisor to the HHS regional directors for the eight southeastern states, Gilliard served as the national communications director for Dr. King's organization, the Southern Christian Leadership Conference. Gilliard also worked in communications for two HBCUs, wrote for USA Today, Time, and the Wichita Eagle-Beacon, and was an editor for the Atlanta Daily World. Gilliard is currently working as a consultant with WSP, a multi-national company that was awarded a grant from the DOI to develop an NPS national monument to honor and memorialize the contributions of the 1961 Freedom Riders. He is a career communications professional who is adept at strategic planning, and the execution of communication strategies that promote organizational messaging and branding. Key policy issues within his portfolio include the Affordable Care Act, maternal health, HIV/AIDS, SUDS, Medicaid expansion, health care access, COVID-19, diversity, and the Cares Act. A public speaker and historian, Gilliard spoke to the troops in Germany shortly before Desert Storm, and served as the first keynote speaker at the Rosa Parks Museum in Montgomery, AL. The son of military parents, Gilliard also served as the principal non-Muslim promoter of the Million Man March, covered the Atlanta Missing and Murdered Children cases, and worked with SCLC President Lowery to raise the issues of economic justice, voter redistricting, and the burning of the Black churches. Gilliard authored his thesis on Joseph Echols Lowery and the Resurrection of the Southern Christian Leadership Conference, and is the author of *Living in the Shadows of a Legend: Unsung Heroes and 'Sheroes' who Marched with Dr. Martin Luther King, Jr.* Gilliard earned his B.A. in Journalism at the University of Kansas, and his M.A. in African-American Studies at Georgia State University. Gilliard is a member of Omega Psi Phi Fraternity, Inc., and the National Association of Black Journalists.

The Longest Four Years of My Life

ISBN (Paperback): 979-8-9906200-8-7

ISBN (Ebook): 979-8-9906200-7-0

Price: $25

www.ingramcontent.com/pod-product-compliance
Lightning Source LLC
Chambersburg PA
CBHW060126190426
43198CB00047B/2384